Undergraduate Topics in Computer Science

Undergraduate Topics in Computer Science (UTiCS) delivers high-quality instructional content for undergraduates studying in all areas of computing and information science. From core foundational and theoretical material to final-year topics and applications, UTiCS books take a fresh, concise, and modern approach and are ideal for self-study or for a one- or two-semester course. The texts are all authored by established experts in their fields, reviewed by an international advisory board, and contain numerous examples and problems. Many include fully worked solutions.

More information about this series at http://www.springer.com/series/7592

Brahma Dathan · Sarnath Ramnath

Object-Oriented Analysis, Design and Implementation

An Integrated Approach

Second Edition

Brahma Dathan
Department of Information and Computer
  Science
Metropolitan State University
St. Paul, MN
USA

Sarnath Ramnath
Department of Computer Science
  and Information Technology
St. Cloud State University
St. Cloud, MN
USA

Series editor
Ian Mackie

A co-publication with the Universities Press (India) Private Ltd., licensed 'for sale in all countries outside of India, Pakistan, Bhutan, Bangladesh, Sri Lanka, Nepal, The Maldives, Middle East, Malaysia, Indonesia and Singapore. Sold and distributed within these territories by the Universities Press (India) Private Ltd.

ISSN 1863-7310   ISSN 2197-1781   (electronic)
Undergraduate Topics in Computer Science
ISBN 978-3-319-24278-1   ISBN 978-3-319-24280-4   (eBook)
DOI 10.1007/978-3-319-24280-4

Library of Congress Control Number: 2015950443

Springer Cham Heidelberg New York Dordrecht London

Printed on acid-free paper

Springer International Publishing AG Switzerland is part of Springer Science+Business Media
(www.springer.com)

Preface to the Second Edition

The second edition of the book includes revisions based on the feedback received from a number of sources on the first edition. The case-study-based approach to the principles of object-oriented design has been mostly well-received. There were two suggestions that we felt needed action on our part:

1. A complete reference for UML.
   The first edition was built on the pedagogical philosophy that the tools of the trade would be presented on an as-needed basis. Accordingly, UML diagrams were introduced in the context of case studies, and we avoided discussing the UML diagrams that were not needed. Some readers felt that the book was incomplete without connecting the content to the remainder of UML.
2. The need for a conclusion.
   Although each chapter ended with a conclusion that connected the material with previous chapters, some readers and critics felt that a concluding chapter would be useful.

Chapter 13 in the new edition addresses both these issues. In this chapter we have attempted to provide a concise introduction to the remainder of UML diagrams. In keeping with our philosophy, we have avoided presenting simply the technicalities of the diagrams with disjointed examples and gone with a holistic approach. We have used the OMG classification of the UML diagrams as the six views of object-oriented system, and explained the role played by each view. We have then discussed the diagrams that represent each view and connected these views to the case studies presented in the book. We hope that this chapter will both provide the user with a concise introduction to all of UML and also round off the text by connecting all aspects of object-oriented design.

The authors wish to thank everyone who used the first edition in their classrooms and those who provided valuable feedback. Special thanks are due to

Sreelatha Menon for editorial support. Brahma Dathan wishes to thank his wife, Asha, and his children, Anupama and Alok, for the many hours that would have otherwise been spent with them. They were incredibly patient and understanding.

Brahma Dathan
Sarnath Ramnath

Preface to the First Edition

At least some people reading the title of this book may wonder why there should be one more book on the topic of Object-Oriented Analysis and Design (OOAD). The short answer to this question is that in our teaching of the subject for over a decade, we have not been able to find a suitable textbook on this topic at our respective universities.

We wrote up a long answer to the above question in a paper published in the 2008 SIGCSE conference. (So, if you are not satisfied with this preface, we hope you will consider reading our paper.) To summarise some of the observations and experiences in that paper, we note that our approach has always been to find ways to give a comprehensive introduction to the field of OOAD. Over the years the field has become quite vast, comprising diverse topics such as design process and principles, documentation tools (Unified Modelling Language), refactoring and design and architectural patterns. In our experience, for most students the experience is incomplete without implementation, so, that is one more addition to the laundry list of topics to be covered in the course.

It was impossible to find a single book that gave a balanced coverage of all these topics in a manner that is understandable to an average college student. There are, of course, a number of books, some of them are profound that cover one or more of the above topics quite well. Besides their specialised nature, these books are primarily not meant to be textbooks. Expecting our students to read parts of these books and assimilate the material was not a realistic option for us.

This text is the result of our efforts over several years and provides the following:

1. A sound footing on object-oriented concepts such as classes, objects, interfaces, inheritance, polymorphism, dynamic linking, etc.
2. A good introduction to the stage of requirements analysis.
3. Use of UML to document user requirements and design.
4. An extensive treatment of the design process. The design step is, arguably, the most demanding activity (from an intellectual perspective) in the OOAD process. It is thus imperative that the student go through the design of complete systems. For pedagogical reasons we have kept the systems simple, yet

sufficiently interesting to offer design choices. Going through these design exercises should help the student gain confidence to undertake reasonably complex designs.
5. Coverage of implementation issues. The reader will find critical excerpts from the implementation in Java. But he/she would be well advised to remember that this is not a book on Java. (More on this later.)
6. Appropriate use of design and architectural patterns.
7. Introduction to the art and craft of refactoring.
8. Pointers to resources that further the reader's knowledge.

It is important to remember what this book is *not* about.

1. It is not a book on Java. While the appendix has a short tutorial on the language and most of the code in the book is in Java, we do not cover constructs for the sake of teaching the language. Coverage is limited to the extent needed for understanding the implementation and for highlighting object-oriented concepts.
2. It does not cover software engineering concepts such as project management, agile technology, etc.
3. It does not treat UML extensively. Although we mention the various types of UML diagrams, many of them are not expanded because an occasion does not arise for such an undertaking.
4. It is not a catalogue of design patterns or refactoring techniques. We cover only those patterns that arise naturally in our case studies. It has been our experience that design pattern discussions without a meaningful context are not well received by students.

Who will find this book useful?

Although the material in this text has primarily evolved out of a course taught for computer science senior undergraduates, others without a formal computer science background may also find this handy. In our program, students taking this are expected to have completed a course in data structures, but the material in this text does not require an intimate knowledge of the intricacies of any of these. A programmer who has used and is familiar with the APIs for some of the data structures could easily handle the material in the text. However, a certain amount of maturity with the programming process is needed, and for a typical undergraduate student this is usually obtained through a data structures course.

All the main case studies used for this book have been implemented by the authors using Java. The text is liberally peppered with snippets of code wherever we felt that a more 'concrete' feel for the design would be helpful. Most of these snippets are short and should be fairly self-explanatory and easy to read. Familiarity with a Java-like syntax and a broad understanding of the structure of Java would certainly be extremely helpful. The reader not familiar with Java but having significant software experience, need not, however, be deterred by this and can get a good feel of the entire OOAD process even without examining the code.

How to use this as computer science text?

There clearly are several ways of structuring a computer science program, and the way in which this text could be used would depend on that structure.

The text is divided into three parts:

- **Part I** provides a thorough coverage of object-oriented ideas.
- **Part II** introduces the concepts of object-oriented analysis, design, implementation and refactoring.
- **Part III** deals with more advanced design issues and approaches.

Part I, which comprises Chapters 1 through 4, gives a broad and solid foundation in concepts that are central to OOAD. The amount of time spent on covering these materials would vary considerably, depending on the program structure.

Part II begins in Chapter 5 with three useful design patterns. This part also includes Chapters 6 through 8, which introduces the first case study involving the analysis, design and implementation of a simple library system. This is a critical choice since the entire process of design is being introduced through this case study. We chose this application because it met the following three major goals we had in selecting the case study: (i) the system should be simple so that it can be covered from analysis to implementation in a reasonable amount of time; (ii) students have an intuitive understanding of the application; (iii) several areas can be 'naturally' touched upon within the scope of the case study.

Several areas are touched upon in this case study and it would be pedagogically useful to emphasise these in the classroom.

- The importance of (and the quirks associated with) precisely specifying requirements and creating use case model.
- The design process. We naturally progress from the use case model to the the process of identifying classes and assigning responsibilities and coming up with sequence diagrams to implement use cases. The case study explores options in the design, which can result in lively discussions and contribute to student learning.
- The data is stored on stable storage so as to give students a sense of completeness. In this process, the student can see how the language quirks are affecting the implementation.
- The case study incorporates several design patterns in the code: Facade, Iterator, Adapter, Singleton and Factory.
- Chapter 8 introduces refactoring and applies it to the completed design. This is done to underscore the fact that an awareness of refactoring is integral to the design process.

Covering this case study and assigning a similar project for students would be, in our opinion, essential. The amount of time spent on discussing these materials would depend on the background of the students.

Part III covers more advanced topics and spans Chapters 9 through 12. Chapter 9 introduces the use of inheritance in design and also extends the case study. The use of inheritance was deliberately avoided in the main case study, not only to keep the case study simple, but also to ensure that the issues associated with the use of inheritance can be dealt with in context. The extension involves some inheritance hierarchies that allow us to illustrate sound object-oriented principles including the *Liskov Substitution Principle* and the *Open–Closed Principle*. A natural extension to the library system case study leads to a discussion of the Visitor pattern.

Chapter 10 deals with the second case study, which is from the domain of electronic devices that are controlled by software. Our example concerns a microwave oven that allows the user to perform the most common functions. To keep the case study manageable we have restricted the microwave functionality, but the model is enough for our purpose. Here we introduce the concept of states, finite state machines and state transition diagrams and compare and contrast it with the use case model. In this context, we introduce the State and Observer patterns.

The third case study, in Chapter 11, is an interactive program that can be used for creating figures. The objective here is to also examine the creation of larger systems that may require decomposition into subsystems. Before presenting the case study, the student is familiarised with the Model–View–Controller architecture. During the course of the case study, the student learns the Bridge, Command and Composite patterns.

Chapter 12 shows how to design an object-oriented system for a distributed environment. As more and more applications become available remotely, we believe it is important for students to learn how to design and implement a distributed, object-oriented system. We have focused on Java Remote Method Invocation and the implementation of web-based systems using Java Servlets. To keep the discussion within reasonable size, we have left out other technologies such as ASP.NET and some important topics such as CORBA and distributed garbage collection.

Normally, while each case study is being discussed, we expect students to work on similar projects. This may be adapted as necessary to suit each situation. Presenting the topics in this integrated manner using case studies has been very helpful in giving students a complete picture of the OOAD process. We hope that by writing this textboot we have, in some small way, contribute to the advancement of the discipline.

Acknowledgments

The following individuals at Universities Press and Springer deserve special thanks: Madhu Reddy, Manoj Karthikeyan and Beverley Ford for help with the negotiations and the contract, and Sreelatha Menon for her efficient editorial work.

Brahma Dathan would like to thank his wife, Asha, and children, Anupama and Alok, for their support during the several years it took to complete this project.

Sarnath would like to thank his family, friends and colleagues for their encouragement and support during the years he worked on the project.

The authors would like to thank Dr. Bina Ramamurthy for her helpful suggestions on an early draft of the book.

As we mentioned earlier, the book was shaped by our experience in teaching the subject over a fairly long period of time. Although the courses have stabilised now, the current form does not resemble much the original version taught a decade, or even four years ago. We experimented with the topics (adding, deleting, emphasising, de-emphasising and rearranging) and changed the pedagogical approach, moving from a theory-first-practice-later approach to a more case-study-based approach. Needless to say, we did all this at the expense of our students, but they took it all in good spirit. Many of our students also provided valuable, creative criticisms on different versions of the manuscript of the book. We cannot thank our students, past and present, enough!

Brahma Dathan
Sarnath Ramnath

Contents

Part I
Basic Object-Oriented Concepts

Chapter 1
Introduction

The object-oriented paradigm is currently the most popular way of analysing, designing, and developing application systems, especially large ones. To obtain an understanding of this paradigm, we could begin by asking: *What exactly does the phrase 'object-oriented' mean?* Looking at it quite literally, labelling something as 'object-oriented' implies that objects play a central role, and we elaborate this further as *a perspective that views the elements of a given situation by decomposing them into objects and object relationships.* In a broad sense, this idea could apply to any setting and examples of its application can in fact be found in business, chemistry, engineering and, even philosophy. Our business is with creating software and therefore this book concentrates on the object-oriented analysis, design, and implementation of software systems. Our situations are therefore problems that are amenable to software solutions, and the software systems that are created in response to these problems.

Designing is a complex activity in any context simply because there are competing interests and we have to make critical choices at each step with incomplete information. As a result, decisions are often made using some combination of rules of thumb derived from past experience. Software design is no exception to this, and in the process of designing a system, there are several points where such decisions have to be made. Making informed choices in any field of activity requires an understanding of the underlying philosophy and the forces that have shaped it. It is therefore appropriate to start our study of object-oriented software analysis and design by outlining its philosophy and the developments in this field up to the present time. Throughout the case studies used in this text, the reader will find examples of how this guiding philosophy is helping us make choices at all stages.

This chapter, therefore, intends to give the reader a broad introduction to the complex topic of object-oriented software development. We start with an overview of the circumstances that motivated its development and why it came to be the desired approach for software development. In the course of this discussion, we present

© Universities Press (India) Private Ltd. 2015
B. Dathan and S. Ramnath, *Object-Oriented Analysis, Design and Implementation*,
Undergraduate Topics in Computer Science, DOI 10.1007/978-3-319-24280-4_1

the central concepts that characterise the methodology, how this development has influenced our view of software, and some of its pros and cons. We conclude by presenting a brief history of the evolution of the object-oriented approach.

1.1 What Is Object-Oriented Development?

The traditional view of a computer program is that of a process that has been encoded in a form that can be executed on a computer. This view originated from the fact that the first computers were developed mainly to automate a well-defined process (i.e., an algorithm) for numerical computation, and dates back to the first stored-program computers. Accordingly, the software creation process was seen as a translation from a description in some 'natural' language to a sequence of operations that could be executed on a computer. As many would argue, this paradigm is still the best way to introduce the notion of programming to a beginner, but as systems became more complex, its effectiveness in developing solutions became suspect. This change of perspective on part of the software developers happened over a period of time and was fuelled by several factors including the high cost of development and the constant efforts to find uses for software in new domains. One could safely argue that the software applications developed in later years had two differentiating characteristics:

- Behaviour that was hard to characterise as a process
- Requirements of reliability, performance, and cost that the original developers did not face

The 'process-centred' approach to software development used what is called *top-down functional decomposition*. The first step in such a design was to recognise what the process had to deliver (in terms of input and output of the program), which was followed by decomposition of the process into *functional modules*. Structures to store data were defined and the computation was carried out by invoking the modules, which performed some computation on the stored data elements. The life of a process-centred design was short because changes to the process specification (something relatively uncommon with numerical algorithms when compared with business applications) required a change in the entire program. This in turn resulted in an inability to reuse existing code without considerable overhead. As a result, software designers began to scrutinise their own approaches and also study design processes and principles that were being employed by engineers in other disciplines. Cross-pollination of ideas from other engineering disciplines started soon after, and the disciplines of 'software design' and 'software engineering' came into existence.

In this connection, it is interesting to note the process used for designing simple electromechanical systems. For several decades now, it has been fairly easy for people with limited knowledge of engineering principles to design and put together simple systems in their backyards and garages. So much so, it has become a hobby that even a 10 years old could pursue. The reasons for this success are easy to see: *easily understandable designs, similar (standard) solutions for a host of problems, an easily accessible and well-defined 'library' of 'building-blocks', interchangeability of components across systems,* and so on. Some of the pioneers in the field of software design began to ask whether they could not also design software using such 'off-the-shelf' components. The object-oriented paradigm, one could argue, has really evolved in response to this outlook. There are, of course, several differences with the hardware design process (inevitable, because the nature of software is fundamentally different from hardware), but parallels can be drawn between many of the defining characteristics of hardware design and what today's advocates of good software design recommend. This methodology, as we shall see in the chapters to follow, provides us with a step-by-step process for software design, a language to specify the output from each step of the process so that we can transition smoothly from one stage to the next, the ability to reuse earlier designs, standard solutions that adhere to well-reasoned design principles and, even the ability to incrementally fix a poor design without breaking the system.

The overall philosophy here is to define a software system as a collection of objects of various types that interact with each other through well-defined interfaces. Unlike a hardware component, a software object can be designed to handle multiple functions and can therefore participate in several processes. A software component is also capable of storing data, which adds another dimension of complexity to the process. The manner in which all of this has departed from the traditional process-oriented view is that instead of implementing an entire process end-to-end and defining the needed data structures along the way, we first analyse the entire set of processes and from this identify the necessary software components. Each component represents a data abstraction and is designed to store information along with procedures to manipulate the same. The execution of the original processes is then broken down into several steps, each of which can be logically assigned to one of the software components. The components can also communicate with each other as needed to complete the process.

1.2   Key Concepts of Object-Oriented Design

During the development of this paradigm, as one would expect, several ideas and approaches were tried and discarded. Over the years the field has stabilised so that we can safely present the key ideas whose soundness has stood the test of time.

The Central Role of Objects

Object-orientation, as the name implies, makes objects the centrepiece of software design. The design of earlier systems was centred around processes, which were susceptible to change, and when this change came about, very little of the old system was 're-usable'. The notion of an object is centred around a piece of data and the operations (or **methods**) that could be used to modify it. This makes possible the creation of an abstraction that is very stable since it is not dependent on the changing requirements of the application. The execution of each process relies heavily on the objects to store the data and provide the necessary operations; with some additional work, the entire system is 'assembled' from the objects.

The Notion of a Class

Classes allow a software designer to look at objects as different types of entities. Viewing objects this way allows us to use the mechanisms of classification to categorise these types, define hierarchies and engage with the ideas of specialisation and generalisation of objects.

Abstract Specification of Functionality

In the course of the design process, the software engineer specifies the properties of objects (and by implication the classes) that are needed by a system. This specification is abstract in that it does not place any restrictions on how the functionality is achieved. This specification, called an **interface** or an **abstract class**, is like a *contract* for the implementer which also facilitates formal verification of the entire system.

A Language to Define the System

The Unified Modelling Language (UML) has been chosen by consensus as the standard tool for describing the end products of the design activities. The documents generated in this language can be universally understood and are thus analogous to the 'blueprints' used in other engineering disciplines.

Standard Solutions

The existence of an object structure facilitates the documenting of standard solutions, called **design patterns.** Standard solutions are found at all stages of software development, but design patterns are perhaps the most common form of reuse of solutions.

An Analysis Process to Model a System

Object-orientation provides us with a systematic way to translate a functional specification to a *conceptual design*. This design describes the system in terms of *conceptual classes* from which the subsequent steps of the development process generate the *implementation classes* that constitute the finished software.

The Notions of Extendability and Adaptability

Software has a flexibility that is not typically found in hardware, and this allows us to modify existing entities in small ways to create new ones. *Inheritance*, which creates a new *descendant class* that modifies the features of an existing (**ancestor**) class, and **composition**, which uses objects belonging to existing classes as elements to constitute a new class, are mechanisms that enable such modifications with classes and objects.

1.3 Other Related Concepts

As the object-oriented methodology developed, the science of software design progressed too, and several desirable software properties were identified. Not central enough to be called object-oriented concepts, these ideas are nonetheless closely linked to them and are perhaps better understood because of these developments.

1.3.1 Modular Design and Encapsulation

Modularity refers to the idea of putting together a large system by developing a number of distinct components independently and then integrating these to provide the required functionality. This approach, when used properly, usually makes the individual modules relatively simple and thus the system easier to understand than one that is designed as a monolithic structure. In other words, such a design must be *modular.* The system's functionality must be provided by a number of well-designed, cooperating modules. Each module must obviously provide certain functionality that is clearly specified by an interface. The interface also defines how other components may interact or communicate with the module.

We would like that a module clearly specify what it does, but not expose its implementation. This separation of concerns gives rise to the notion of **encapsulation**, which means that the module hides details of its implementation from external agents. The **abstract data type (ADT)**, the generalisation of primitive data types such as integers and characters, is an example of applying encapsulation. The programmer specifies the collection of operations on the data type and the data structures that are needed for data storage. Users of the ADT perform the operations without concerning themselves with the implementation.

1.3.2 Cohesion and Coupling

Each module provides certain functionality; **cohesion** of a module tells us how well the entities within a module work together to provide this functionality. Cohesion is a measure of how focused the responsibilities of a module are. If the responsibilities of a module are unrelated or varied and use different sets of data, cohesion is reduced. Highly cohesive modules tend to be more reliable, reusable, and understandable than less cohesive ones. To increase cohesion, we would like that all the constituents contribute to some well-defined responsibility of the module. This may be quite a challenging task. In contrast, the worst approach would be to arbitrarily assign entities to modules, resulting in a module whose constituents have no obvious relationship.

Coupling refers to how dependent modules are on each other. The very fact that we split a program into multiple modules introduces some coupling into the system. Coupling could result because of several factors: a module may refer to variables defined in another module or a module may call methods of another module and use the return values. The amount of coupling between modules can vary. In general, if modules do not depend on each others implementation, i.e., modules depend only on the published interfaces of other modules and not on their internals, we say that the coupling is *low*. In such cases, changes in one module will not necessitate changes in other modules as long as the interfaces themselves do not change. Low coupling allows us to modify a module without worrying about the ramifications of the changes on the rest of the system. By contrast, *high* coupling means that changes in one module would necessitate changes in other modules, which may have a domino effect and also make it harder to understand the code.

1.3.3 Modifiability and Testability

A software component, unlike its hardware counterpart, can be easily modified in small ways. This modification can be done to change both *functionality* and *design*. The ability to change the functionality of a component allows for systems to be more **adaptable**; the advances in object-orientation have set higher standards for adaptability. Improving the design through incremental change is accomplished by *refactoring*, again a concept that owes its origin to the development of the object-oriented approach. There is some risk associated with activities of both kinds; and in both cases, the organisation of the system in terms of objects and classes has helped develop systematic procedures that mitigate the risk.

Testability of a concept, in general, refers to both *falsifiability*, i.e., the ease with which we can find counterexamples, and the *practical feasibility* of reproducing such counterexamples. In the context of software systems, it can simply be stated as the ease with which we can find bugs in a software and the extent to which the structure of the system facilitates the detection of bugs. Several concepts in software testing (e.g., the idea of *unit testing*) owe their prominence to concepts that came out of the development of the object-oriented paradigm.

1.4 Benefits and Drawbacks of the Paradigm

From a practical standpoint, it is useful to examine how object-oriented methodology has modified the landscape of software development. As with any development, we do have pros and cons. The advantages listed below are largely consequences of the ideas presented in the previous sections.

1. Objects often reflect entities in application systems. This makes it easier for a designer to come up with classes in the design. In a process-oriented design, it is much harder to find such a connection that can simplify the initial design.
2. Object-orientation helps increase productivity through reuse of existing software. Inheritance makes it relatively easy to extend and modify functionality provided by a class. Language designers often supply extensive libraries that users can extend.
3. It is easier to accommodate changes. One of the difficulties with application development is changing requirements. With some care taken during design, it is possible to isolate the varying parts of a system into classes.
4. The ability to isolate changes, encapsulate data, and employ modularity reduces the risks involved in system development.

The above advantages do not come without a price tag. Perhaps the number one casualty of the paradigm is efficiency. The object-oriented development process introduces many layers of software, and this certainly increases overheads. In addition, object creation and destruction is expensive. Modern applications tend to feature a large number of objects that interact with each other in complex ways and at the same time support a visual user interface. This is true whether it is a banking application with numerous account objects or a video game that has often a large number of objects. Objects tend to have complex associations, which can result in *non-locality*, leading to poor memory access times.

Programmers and designers schooled in other paradigms, usually in the imperative paradigm, find it difficult to learn and use object-oriented principles. In coming up with classes, inexperienced designers may rely too heavily on the entities in the application system, ending up with systems that are ill-suited for reuse. Programmers also need acclimatisation; some people estimate that it takes as much as a year for a programmer to start feeling comfortable with these concepts. Some researchers are of the opinion that the programming environments also have not kept up with research in language capabilities. They feel that many of the editors and testing and debugging facilities are still fundamentally geared to the imperative paradigm and do not directly support many of the advances such as design patterns.

1.5 History

History of the object-oriented programming approach could be traced to the idea of ADTs and the concept of objects in Simula 67 programming language, which was developed in the 1960s for performing simulations. The first true object-oriented programming language that appeared before the larger software development community was Smalltalk in 1980, developed at Xerox PARC. Smalltalk used objects and messages as the basis for computation. Classes could be created and modified dynamically. Most of the vocabulary in object-oriented paradigm has originated from this language.

Toward the end of the 1970s, Bjarne Stroustrup, who was doing doctoral work in England, needed a language for doing simulation of distributed systems. He developed a language based on the class concept in Simula, but this language was not particularly efficient. However, he pursued his attempt and developed an object-oriented language at Bell Laboratories as a derivative of C, which would blossom into one of the most successful programming languages, C++. The language was standardised in 1997 by the American National Standards Institute (ANSI).

The 1980s saw the development of several other languages such as ObjectLisp, CommonLisp, Common Lisp Object System (CLOS), and Eiffel. The rising popularity of the object-oriented model also propelled changes to the language Ada, originally sponsored by the U.S. Department of Defense in 1983. This resulted in Ada 9x, an extension to Ada 83, with object-oriented concepts including inheritance, polymorphism, and dynamic binding.

The 1990s saw two major events. One was the development of the Java programming language in 1996. Java appeared to be a derivative of C++, but many of the controversial and troublesome concepts in C++ were deleted in it. Although it was a relatively simple language when it was originally proposed, Java has undergone substantial additions in later versions making it a moderately difficult language. Java also comes with an impressive collection of libraries (called packages) to support application development. A second watershed event was the publication of the book *Design Patterns* by Gamma et al. in 1994. The book considered specific design questions (23 of them) and provided general approaches to solving them using object-oriented constructs. The book (as also the approach it advocated) was a huge success as both practitioners and academicians soon recognised its significance.

The last few years saw the acceptance of some dynamic object-oriented languages that were developed in the 1990s. Dynamic languages allow users more flexibility, for example the ability to dynamically add a method to an object at execution time. One such language is Python, which can be used for solving a variety of applications including web programming, databases, scientific and numeric computations and networking. Another dynamic language, Ruby, is even more object-oriented in that everything in the language, including numbers and primitive types, is an object.

1.6 Discussion and Further Reading

In this chapter, we have given an introduction to object-oriented paradigm. The central object-oriented concepts such as classes, objects, and interfaces will be elaborated in the next three chapters. Cohesion and coupling, which are major software design issues, will be recurring themes for most of the text.

The reader would be well-advised to learn or refresh the non-object-oriented concepts of the Java language by reading Appendix before moving onto the next chapter. It is worthwhile and enjoyable to read a short history of programming languages from a standard text on the subject such as Sebesta [1]. The reader might also find it helpful to get the perspectives of the designers of object-oriented languages (such as the one given on C++ by Stroustrup [2]).

1.7 Exercises

1. Identify the players who would have a stake in software development process. What are the concerns of each? How would they benefit from the object-oriented model?
2. Think of some common businesses and the activities software developers are involved in. What are the sets of processes they would like to automate? Are there any that need software just for one process?
3. How does the object-oriented model support the notion of ADTs and encapsulation?
4. Consider an application that you are familiar with, such as a university system. Divide the entities of this application into groups, thus identifying the classes.
5. In Question 4, suppose we put all the code (corresponding to all of the classes) into one single class. What happens to cohesion and coupling?
6. What are the benefits of learning design patterns?

References

1. R.W. Sebesta, *Concepts of Programming Languages* (Addison-Wesley, Boston, 2007)
2. B. Stroustrup, *The Design and Evolution of C++* (Addison-Wesley, Boston, 1994)

Chapter 2
Basics of Object-Oriented Programming

In the last chapter, we saw that the fundamental program structure in an object-oriented program is the object. We also outlined the concept of a class, which is similar to ADTs in that it can be used to create objects of types that are not directly supported by language.

In this chapter, we describe in detail how to construct a class. We will use the programming language Java (as we will do throughout the book). We will introduce the Unified Modelling Language (UML), which is a notation for describing the design of object-oriented systems. We also discuss interfaces, a concept that helps us specify program requirements and demonstrate its uses.

2.1 The Basics

To understand the notion of objects and classes, we start with an analogy. When a car manufacturer decides to build a new car, considerable effort is expended in a variety of activities before the first car is rolled out of the assembly lines. These include:

- Identification of the user community for the car and assessment of the user's needs. For this, the manufacturer may form a team.
- After assessing the requirements, the team may be expanded to include automobile engineers and other specialists who come up with a preliminary design.
- A variety of methods may be used to assess and refine the initial design (the team may have experience in building a similar vehicle): prototypes may be built, simulations and mathematical analysis may be performed.

Perhaps after months of such activity, the design process is completed. Another step that needs to be performed is the building of the plant where the car will be produced. The assembly line has to be set up and people hired.

© Universities Press (India) Private Ltd. 2015
B. Dathan and S. Ramnath, *Object-Oriented Analysis, Design and Implementation*,
Undergraduate Topics in Computer Science, DOI 10.1007/978-3-319-24280-4_2

After such steps, the company is ready to produce cars. The design is now reused many times in manufacture. Of course, the design may have to be fine-tuned during the process based on the company's observations and user feedback.

The development of software systems often follows a similar pattern. User needs have to be assessed, a design has to be made, and then the product has to be built.

From the standpoint of object-oriented systems, a different aspect of the car manufacturing process is important. The design of a certain type of car will call for specific types of engine, transmission, brake system, and so on, and each of these parts in itself has its own design (blue print), production plants, etc. In other words, the company follows the same philosophy in the manufacture of the individual parts as it does in the production of the car. Of course, some parts may be bought from manufacturers, but they in turn follow the same approach. Since the design activity is costly, a manufacturer reuses the design to manufacture the parts or the cars.

The above approach can be compared with the design of object-oriented systems which are composed of many objects that interact with each other. Often, these objects represent real-life players and their interactions represent real-life interactions. Just as design of a car is a collection of the individual designs of its parts and a design of the interaction of these parts, the design of an object-oriented system consists of designs of its constituent parts and their interactions.

For instance, a banking system could have a set of objects that represent customers, another set of objects that stand for accounts, and a third set of objects that correspond to loans. When a customer actually makes a deposit into her account in real life, the system acts on the corresponding account object to mimic the deposit in software. When a customer takes out a loan, a new loan object is created and connected to the customer object; when a payment is made on the loan, the system acts on the corresponding loan object.

Obviously, these objects have to be somehow created. When a new customer enters the system, we should be able to create a new customer object in software. This software entity, the customer object, should have all of the relevant features of the real-life customer. For example, it should be possible to associate the name and address of the customer with this object; however, customer's attributes that are not relevant to the bank will not be represented in software. As an example, it is difficult to imagine a bank being interested in whether a customer is right-handed; therefore, the software system will not have this attribute.

Definition 2.1.1 An attribute is a property that we associate with an object; it serves to describe the object and holds some value that is required for processing.

The class mechanism in object-oriented languages provides a way to create such objects. A class is a design that can be reused any number of times to create objects. For example, consider an object-oriented system for a university. There are student objects, instructor objects, staff member objects, and so on. Before such objects are created, we create classes that serve as blue-prints for students, instructors, staff members, and courses as follows:

```
public class Student {
   // code to implement a single student
}

public class Instructor {
   // code to implement a single instructor
}

public class StaffMember {
   // code to implement a single staff member
}

public class Course {
   // code to implement a single course
}
```

The above definitions show how to create four classes, without giving any details. (We should put in the details where we have given comments.) The token `class` is a keyword that says that we are creating a class and that the following token is the name of the class. We have thus created four classes `Student`, `Instructor`, `StaffMember`, and `Course`. The left-curly bracket (`{`) signifies the beginning of the definition of the class and the corresponding right-curly bracket (`}`) ends the definition. The token `public` is another keyword that makes the corresponding class available throughout the file system.

Before we see how to put in the details of the class, let us see how to create objects using these classes. The process of creating an object is also called **instantiation.** Each class introduces a new type name. Thus `Student`, `Instructor`, `StaffMember` and `Course` are types that we have introduced.

The following code instantiates a new object of type `Student`.

```
new Student();
```

The `new` operator causes the system to allocate an object of type `Student` with enough storage for storing information about one student. The operator returns the address of the location that contains this object. This address is termed a **reference.**

The above statement may be executed when we have a new student admitted to the university. Once we instantiate a new object, we must store its reference somewhere, so that we can use it later in some appropriate way. For this, we create a variable of type `Student`.

```
Student harry;
```

Notice that the above definition simply says that `harry` is a variable that can store references to objects of type `Student`. Thus, we can write

```
harry = new Student();
```

We cannot write

```
harry = new Instructor();
```

because `harry` is of type `Student`, which has no relationship (as far as the class declarations are concerned) to `Instructor`, which is the type of the object created on the right-hand side of the assignment.

Whenever we instantiate a new object, we must remember the reference to that object somewhere. However, it is not necessary that for every object that we instantiate, we declare a different variable to store its reference. If that were the case, programming would be tedious.

Let us illustrate by giving an analogy. When a student drives to school to take a class, she deals with only a relatively small number of objects: the controls of the car, the road, the nearby vehicles (and sometimes their occupants, although not always politely), and traffic signals and signs. (Some may also deal with a cell phone, which is not a good idea!) There are many other objects that the driver (student) knows about, but is not dealing with them at this time.

Similarly, we keep references to a relatively small number of objects in our programs. When a need arises to access other objects, we use the references we already have to discover them. For instance, suppose we have a reference to a `Student` object. That object may have an attribute that remembers the student's adviser, an `Instructor` object. If it is necessary to find out the adviser of a given student, we can query the corresponding `Student` object to get the `Instructor` object. A single `Instructor` object may have attributes that remember all the advisees of the corresponding instructor.

2.2 Implementing Classes

In this section we give some of the basics of creating classes. Let us focus on the `Student` class that we initially coded as

```
public class Student {
  // code to implement a single student
}
```

We certainly would like the ability to give a student a name: given a student object, we should be able to specify that the student's name is `"Tom"` or `"Jane"`, or, in general, some string. This is sometimes referred to as a **behaviour** of the object. We can think of student objects having the behaviour that they respond to assigning a name.

For this purpose, we modify the code as below.

```
public class Student {
  // code for doing other things
  public void setName(String studentName) {
    // code to remember the name
  }
}
```

The code that we added is called a method. The method's name is `setName`. A method is like a procedure or function in imperative programming in that it is a unit of code that is not activated until it is invoked. Again, as in the case of procedures and functions, methods accept parameters (separated by commas in Java). Each parameter states the type of the parameter expected. A method may return nothing (as is the case here) or return an object or a value of a primitive type. Here we have put `void` in front of the method name meaning that the method returns nothing. The left and right curly brackets begin and end the code that defines the method.

Unlike functions and procedures, methods are usually invoked through objects. The `setName` method is defined within the class `Student` and is invoked on objects of type `Student`.

```
Student aStudent = new Student();
aStudent.setName("Ron");
```

The method `setName()` is invoked on that object referred to by `aStudent`. Intuitively, the code within that method must store the name somewhere. Remember that every object is allocated its own storage. This piece of storage must include space for remembering the name of the student.

We embellish the code as below.

```
public class Student {
  private String name;
  public void setName(String studentName) {
    name = studentName;
  }
  public String getName() {
    return name;
  }
}
```

Inside the class we have defined the variable `name` of type `String`. It is called a **field**.

Definition 2.2.1 A field is a variable defined directly within a class and corresponds to an attribute. Every instance of the object will have storage for the field.

Let us examine the code within the method `setName`. It takes in one parameter, `studentName`, and assigns the value in that String object to the field `name`.

It is important to understand how Java uses the `name` field. Every object of type `Student` has a field called `name`. We invoked the method `setName()` on the object referred to by `aStudent`. Since `aStudent` has the field `name` and we invoked the method on `aStudent`, the reference to `name` within the method will act on the `name` field of `aStudent`.

The `getName()` method retrieves the contents of the `name` field and returns it.

To illustrate this further, consider two objects of type `Student`.

```
Student student1 = new Student();
Student student2 = new Student();
student1.setName("John");
student2.setName("Mary");
System.out.println(student1.getName());
System.out.println(student2.getName());
```

Members (fields and methods for now) of a class can be accessed by writing

```
<object-reference>.<member-name>
```

The object referred to by student1 has its name field set to "John," whereas the object referred to by student2 has its name field set to "Mary." The field name in the code

```
name = studentName;
```

refers to different objects in different instantiations and thus different instances of fields.

Let us write a complete program using the above code.

```
public class Student {
  // code
  private String name;
  public void setName(String studentName) {
    name = studentName;
  }
  public String getName() {
    return name;
  }
  public static void main(String[] s) {
    Student student1 = new Student();
    Student student2 = new Student();
    student1.setName("John");
    student2.setName("Mary");
    System.out.println(student1.getName());
    System.out.println(student2.getName());
  }
}
```

The keyword public in front of the method setName() makes the method available wherever the object is available. But what about the keyword private in front of the field name? It signifies that this variable can be accessed only from code within the class Student. Since the line

```
name = studentName;
```

is within the class, the compiler allows it. However, if we write

```
Student someStudent = new Student();
someStudent.name = "Mary";
```

outside the class, the compiler will generate a syntax error.

As a general rule, fields are often defined with the `private` access specifier and methods are usually made public. The general idea is that fields denote the state of the object and that the state can be changed only by interacting through pre-defined methods which denote the behaviour of the object. Usually, this helps preserve data integrity.

In the current example though, it is hard to argue that data integrity consideration plays a role in making `name` private because all that the method `setName` does is change the name field. However, if we wanted to do some checks before actually changing a student's name (which should not happen that often), this gives us a way to do it. If we had kept `name` public and others coded to directly access the field, making the field private later would break their code.

For a more justified use of private, consider the grade point average (GPA) of a student. Clearly, we need to keep track of the GPA and need a field for it. GPA is not something that is changed arbitrarily: it changes when a student gets a grade for a course. So making it public could lead to integrity problems because the field can be inadvertently changed by bad code written outside. Thus, we code as follows.

```
public class Student {
  // fields to store the classes the student has registered for.
  private String name;
  private double gpa;
  public void setName(String studentName) {
    name = studentName;
  }
  public void addCourse(Course newCourse) {
    // code to store a ref to newCourse in the Student object.
  }
  private void computeGPA() {
    // code to access the stored courses, compute and set the gpa
  }
  public double getGPA() {
    return gpa;
  }
  public void assignGrade(Course aCourse, char newGrade) {
    // code to assign newGrade to aCourse
    computeGPA();
  }
}
```

We now write code to utilise the above idea.

```
Student aStudent = new Student();
Course aCourse = new Course();
aStudent.addCourse(aCourse);
aStudent.assignGrade(aCourse, 'B');
System.out.println(aStudent.getGPA());
```

The above code creates a `Student` object and a `Course` object. It calls the `addCourse` method on the student, to add the course to the collection of courses taken by the student, and then calls `assignGrade`. Note the two parameters: `aCourse` and `'B'`. The implied meaning is that the student has completed the course (aCourse) with a grade of 'B'. The code in the method should then compute the new GPA for the student using the information presumably in the course (such as number of credits) and the number of points for a grade of 'B'.

2.2.1 Constructors

The Student class has a method for setting the name of a student. Here we set the name of the student after creating the object. This is somewhat unnatural. Since every student has a name, when we create a student object, we probably know the student's name as well. It would be convenient to store the student's name in the object as we create the student object.

To see where we are headed, consider the following declarations of variables of primitive data types.

```
int counter = 0;
double final PI = 3.14;
```

Both declarations store values into the variables as the variables are created. On the other hand, the Student object, when created, has a zero in every bit of every field.

Java and other object-oriented languages allow the initialisation of fields by using what are called **constructors.**

Definition 2.2.2 A constructor is like a method in that it can have an access specifier (like public or private), a name, parameters, and executable code. However, constructors have the following differences or special features.

1. Constructors cannot have a return type: not even void.
2. Constructors have the same name as the class in which they are defined.
3. Constructors are called when the object is created.

For the class Student we can write the following constructor.

```
public Student(String studentName) {
   name = studentName;
}
```

The syntax is similar to that of methods, but there is no return type. However, it has a parameter, an access specifier of public, and a body with executable code. If needed, one could put local variables as well inside constructors.

Let us rewrite the Student class with this constructor and a few other modifications.

```
public class Student {
   private String name;
   private String address;
   private double gpa;
```

```
    public Student(String studentName) {
       name = studentName;
    }
    public void setName(String studentName) {
      name = studentName;
    }
    public void setAddress(String studentAddress) {
      address = studentAddress;
    }
    public String getName() {
      return name;
    }
    public String getAddress() {
      return address;
    }
    public double getGpa() {
      return gpa;
    }
    public void computeGPA(Course newCourse, char grade) {
      // use the grade and course to update gpa
    }
}
```

We now maintain the address of the student and provide methods to set and get the name and the address.

With the above constructor, an object is created as below.

```
Student aStudent = new Student("John");
```

When the above statement is executed, the constructor is called with the given parameter, "John." This gets stored in the name field of the object.

In previous versions of the Student class, we did not have a constructor. In such cases where we do not have an explicit constructor, the system inserts a constructor with no arguments. Once we insert our own constructor, the system removes this default, no-argument constructor.

As a result, it is important to note that the following is no longer legal because there is no constructor with no arguments.

```
Student aStudent = new Student();
```

A class can have any number of constructors. They should all have different signatures: that is, they should differ in the way they expect parameters. The following adds two more constructors to the Student class.

```
public class Student {
  private String name;
  private String address;
  private double gpa;
  public Student(String studentName) {
     name = studentName;
  }
  public Student(String studentName, String studentAddress) {
```

```
      name = studentName;
      address = studentAddress;
   }
   public Student() {
   }
   public void setName(String studentName) {
     name = studentName;
   }
   public void setAddress(String studentAddress) {
     address = studentAddress;
   }
   public String getName() {
     return name;
   }
   public String getAddress() {
     return address;
   }
   public double getGpa() {
     return gpa;
   }
   public void computeGPA(Course newCourse, char grade) {
      // use the grade and course to update gpa
   }
}
```

Notice that all constructors have the same name, which is the name of the class. One of the new constructors accepts the name and address of the student and stores it in the appropriate fields of the object. The other constructor accepts no arguments and does nothing: as a result, the name and address fields of the object are `null`.

2.2.2 Printing an Object

Suppose we want to print an object. We might try

```
System.out.println(student);
```

where `student` is a reference of type `Student`.

The statement, however, will not produce anything very useful for someone expecting to see the name and address of the student. For objects, unless the programmer has provided specific code, Java always prints the name of the class of which the object is an instance, followed by the @ symbol and a value, which is the unsigned hexadecimal representation of the hash code of the object. It does not make any assumptions on the fields to be printed; it prints none of them!

This problem is solved by putting a method called `toString()` in the class. This method contains code that tells Java how to convert the object to a String.

```
public String toString() {
   // return a string
}
```

Whenever an object is to be converted to a String, Java calls the `toString` method on the object just as any other method. The method call `System.out.println()` attempts to convert its arguments to the string form. So it calls the `toString()` method.

We can complete the `toString` method for the Student class as below.

```
public String toString() {
    return "Name " + name + " Address " + address + " GPA " + gpa;
}
```

It is good practice to put the `toString` method in every class and return an appropriate string. Sometimes, the method may get slightly more involved than the simple method we have above; for instance, we may wish to print the elements of an array that the object maintains, in which case a loop to concatenate the elements is in order.

2.2.3 Static Members

So far, all members of a class were accessed using the syntax

```
<object_reference>.<member_name>
```

This is quite logical because we wanted to act on specific objects. Every `Student` object, for example, has its own `name`, `gpa`, and `address` fields. If we did not specify the object and merely specified the field/method, the specification would be incomplete.

Sometimes, we need fields that are common to all instances of an object. In other words, such fields have exactly one instance and this instance is shared by all instances of the class. Such fields are called **static** fields. In contrast, fields maintained separately for each object are called **instance** fields.

Let us turn to an example. Most universities usually have the rule that students not maintaining a certain minimum GPA will be put on academic probation. Let us assume that this minimum standard is the same for all students. Once in a while, a university may decide that this minimum standard be raised or lowered. (Grade inflation can be a problem!)

We would like to introduce a field for keeping track of this minimum GPA. Since the value has to be the same for all students, it is unnecessary to maintain a separate field for each student object. In fact, it is risky to keep a separate field for each object: since every instance of the field has to be given the same value, special effort will have to be made to update all copies of the field whenever we decide to change its value. This can give rise to integrity problems. It is also quite inefficient.

Suppose we decide to call this new field, `minimumGPA`, and make its type `double`. We define the variable as below.

```
private static double minimumGPA;
```

The specifier static means that there will be just one instance of the field minimumGPA; The field will be created as soon as the class is loaded by the system. Note that there does not have to be any objects for this field to exist. This instance will be shared by all instances of the class.

Suppose we need to modify this field occasionally and that we also want a method that tells us what its value is. We typically write what are called **static methods** for doing the job.

```
public static void setMinimumGPA(double newMinimum) {
  minimumGPA = newMinimum;
}
public static double getMinimumGPA() {
  return minimumGPA;
}
```

The keyword static specifies that the method can be executed without using an object. The method is called as below.

```
<class_Name>.<method_name>
```

For example,

```
Student.setMinimumGPA(2.0);
System.out.println("Minimum GPA requirement is "
+ Student.getMinimumGPA());
```

Methods and fields with the keyword static in front of them are usually called **static methods** and **static fields** respectively.

It is instructive to see, in the above case, why we want the two methods to be static. Suppose they were instance methods. Then they have to be called using an object as in the following example.

```
Student student1 = new Student("John");
student1.setMinimumGPA(2.0);
```

While this is technically correct, it has the following disadvantages:

1. It requires that we create an object and use that object to modify a static field. This goes against the spirit of static members; they should be accessible even if there are no objects.
2. Someone reading the above fragment may be lead to believe that setMinimum GPA() is used to modify an instance field.

On the other hand, a static method cannot access any instance fields or methods. It is easy to see why. A static method may be accessed without using any objects at all. Therefore, what object should the method use to access the member? In fact, there may not be any objects created yet when the static method is in use.

2.3 Programming with Multiple Classes

Even the simplest object-oriented application system will have multiple classes that are related. For the university system we discussed earlier in this chapter, we identified and wrote the skeletons of four classes: `Student`, `Instructor`, `StaffMember`, and `Course`. In this section, we look at how to structure the classes for such cases.

Let us consider the `Course` class. A course exists in the school catalog, with a name, course id, brief description and number of credits.Here is a possible definition.

```
public class Course {
  private String id;
  private String name;
  private int numberofCredits;
  private String description;
  public Course(String courseId, courseName) {
    id = courseId;
    name = courseName;
  }
  public void setNumberOfCredits(int credits) {
    numberOfCredits = credits;
  }
  public void setDescription(String courseDescription) {
    description = courseDescription;
  }
  public String getId() {
    return id;
  }
  public String getName() {
    return name;
  }
  public int getNumberOfCredits() {
    return numberOfCredits;
  }
  public String getDescription() {
    return description;
  }
}
```

A department selects from the catalog a number of courses to offer every semester. A section is a course offered in a certain semester, held in a certain place on certain days at certain times. (We will not worry about the instructor for the class, capacity, etc.) Let us create a class for this.

We will use `String` objects for storing the place, days, time, and semester. Thus, we have three fields named `place`, `daysAndTimes`, and `semester` with the obvious semantics.

Clearly, this is inadequate: the class does not hold the name and other details of the course. But it is redundant to have fields for these because the information is available in the corresponding `Course` object. What is required is a field that remembers the corresponding course. We can do this by having the following field declaration.

```
private Course course;
```

When the Section instance is created, this field can be initialised.

```
public class Section {
  private String semester;
  private String place;
  private String daysAndTimes;
  private Course course;
  public Section(Course theCourse, String theSemester,
                 String thePlace, String theDaysAndTimes) {
    course = theCourse;
    place = thePlace;
    daysAndTimes = theDaysAndTimes;
    semester = theSemester;
  }
  public String getPlace() {
    return place;
  }
  public String getDaysAndTimes() {
    return daysAndTimes;
  }
  public String getSemester() {
    return semester;
  }
  public Course getCourse() {
    return course;
  }
  public void setPlace(String newPlace) {
    place = newPlace;
  }
  public void setDaysAndTimes(String newDaysAndTimes) {
    daysAndTimes = newDaysAndTimes;
  }
}
```

Where do we create an instance of Section? One possibility is to do this in Course. Let us assume that we add a new method named createSection in Course, which accepts the semester, the place, days, and time as parameters and returns an instance of a new Section object for the course. We will then use it as follows.

```
Course cs350 = new Course("CS 350", "Data Structures");
Section cs350Section1 = cs350.createSection("Fall 2004",
                                  "Lecture Hall 12", "T H 1-2:15");
Section cs350Section2 = cs350.createSection("Fall 2004",
                                  "Lecture Hall 25", "'M W F 10-10:50");
```

Let us get to the task of coding the createSection method. It looks like the following:

```
public Section createSection(String semester, String place, String time) {
  return new Section(/* parameters */);
}
```

How do we invoke the constructor of Section from the createSection method? The problem is that although we do have references to the semester, place, and days and times available in the parameters of this method, we need a reference to the Course object itself. This is not an explicit parameter to the method, but the Course object on which the createSection method is invoked is indeed the reference we need! Here the language comes to our aid. In the createSection method, the reference to the object that was used in its invocation is available via a special keyword called this.

In general, assume that we have a class C with a method m in it as shown below. Also shown is another class C2, which has a method named m2 that requires an object of type C as its only parameter.

```
public class C {
  public void m() {
    // this refers to the object on whom m is being invoked
  }
}

public class C2 {
  public void m2(C aC) {
    // code
  }
}
```

Suppose that we create an instance of C from the outside and invoke m as below.

```
C c1 = new C();
c1.m();
```

This is depicted in Fig. 2.1. The reference c1 points to an instance of C. Suppose the method m contained the following code:

```
public void m(){
  C2 c2 = new C2();
  c2.m2(this);
}
```

In the above, this is a reference that points to the same object as c1. In summary, an object can refer to itself by using the keyword this.

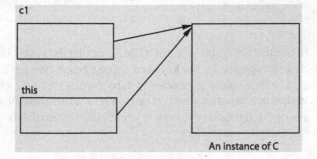

Fig. 2.1 The notion of this

Continuing with the example of courses and their sections, we can code the `createSection` method as below.

```
public Section createSection(String semester, String place, String time) {
    return new Section(this, semester, place, time);
}
```

The keyword `this` obtains the reference to the course object and is passed to the constructor of `Section`.

In addition to passing a reference to itself to methods, we can use `this` to obtain the fields of the object, which come in handy for resolving conflicts. For example,

```
class Section {
    private String place;
    public void setPlace(String place) {
        this.place = place;
    }
}
```

The identifier `place` on right hand side of the assignment refers to the formal parameter; on the left hand side it is prefixed by `this` and is therefore a reference to the private field.

2.4 Interfaces

We design classes based on specifications. These specifications could be written in English and augmented with diagrams, but a compiler cannot read such documents and ensure that the class meets the specifications.

An interface is one way of partially specifying our requirements. Suppose we need to create a list of all students in our university. Let us say that we should be able to add a student, remove a student, and print all students in the list. We can specify the syntax for the methods by creating an interface as given below.

```
public interface StudentList {
    public void add(Student student);
    public void delete(String name);
    public void print();
}
```

Notice that the syntax of the first line resembles the syntax for a class with the keyword `class` replaced by the keyword `interface`. We have *specified* three methods: `add` with a single parameter of type `Student`; `delete` with the name of the student as a parameter, and `print` with no parameters. Notice that we haven't given a body for the methods; there is a semicolon immediately after the right parenthesis that ends the parameters.

Let us see how to utilise the above entity. We can now create a class that implements the above three operations as below.

```
public class StudentLinkedList implements StudentList {
  // fields for maintaining a linked list
  public void add(Student student) {
    // code for adding a student to the list
  }
  public void delete(String name) {
    // code for deleting a student from the list
  }
  public void print() {
    // code for printing the list
  }
  // other methods
}
```

The first line states that we are creating a new class named `StudentLinkedList`. The words `implements StudentList` mean that this class will have all of the methods of the interface `StudentList`. It is a syntax error if the class did not implement the three methods because it has claimed that it implements them.

Just as a class introduces a new type, an interface also creates a new type. In the above example, `StudentList` and `StudentLinkedList` are both types. All instances of the `StudentLinkedList` class are also of type `StudentList`.

We can thus write

```
StudentList students;
students = new StudentLinkedList();
// example of code that uses StudentList;
Student s1 = new Student(/* parameters */);
students.add(s1);
s1 = new Student(/* parameters */);
students.add(s1);
students.print();
```

We created an instance of the `StudentLinkedList` class and stored a reference to it in `students`, which is of type `StudentList`. We can invoke the three methods of the interface (and of the class) via this variable.

Part of these probably seems like wasted effort. Although at this time we cannot discuss all the benefits of using interfaces, let us discuss one: In the above, pay special attention to the following facts:

1. The class `StudentLinkedList` implements the interface `StudentList`. So variables of type `StudentLinkedList` are also of type `StudentList`.
2. We declared `students` as of type `StudentList` and *not* `StudentLinked List`.
3. We restricted ourselves to using the methods of the interface `StudentList`.

Next, assume that we find that the class `StudentLinkedList` is not satisfacatory: perhaps it is not efficient enough. We would like to try and create a new class `StudentArrayList` which uses arrays rather than a linked implementation.

```
public class StudentArrayList implements StudentList {
  // fields for maintaining an array-based list
  public void add(Student student) {
    // code for adding a student to the list
  }
  public void delete(String name) {
    // code for deleting a student from the list
  }
  public void print() {
    // code for printing the list
  }
}
```

Now, we can rewrite the code that manipulates StudentList as below.

```
StudentList students;
students = new StudentArrayList();
// code that uses StudentList;
```

The only change that we need to make in our code for using the list is the one
that creates the StudentList object. Since we restricted ourselves to using the
methods of StudentList in the rest of the code (as opposed to using methods
or fields unique to the class StudentLinkedList), we do not need to change
anything else. This makes maintenance easier.

It is instructive to complete the code for StudentLinkedList and Student
ArrayList.

2.4.1 Implementation of StudentLinkedList

A linked list consists of nodes each of which stores the address of the next. We thus
write the following class.

```
public class StudentNode {
  private Student data;
  private StudentNode next;
  public StudentNode(Student student, StudentNode initialLink) {
    this.data = student;
    next = initialLink;
  }
  public Student getData() {
    return data;
  }
  public void setData(Student student) {
    this.data = student;
  }
  public StudentNode getNext() {
    return next;
  }
  public void setNext(StudentNode node) {
    next = node;
  }
}
```

This class will be needed in `StudentLinkedList` only. Therefore, we can use what are called **inner classes** in Java. An inner class is a class enclosed within another class. Thus, we write

```java
public class StudentLinkedList implements StudentList {
  private StudentNode head;
  private class StudentNode {
    private Student data;
    private StudentNode next;
    public StudentNode(Student student, StudentNode initialLink) {
      this.data = student;
      next = initialLink;
    }
    public Student getData() {
      return data;
    }
    public void setData(Student student) {
      this.data = student;
    }
    public StudentNode getNext() {
      return next;
    }
    public void setNext(StudentNode node) {
      next = node;
    }
  }
  public void add(Student student) {
    // code for adding a student to the list
  }
  public void delete(String name) {
    // code for deleting a student from the list
  }
  public void print() {
    // code for printing the list
  }
}
```

The inner class `StudentNode` is now declared as private, so that it cannot be used from code outside of the class.

Let us code the `add` method.

```java
public void add(Student student) {
  head = new StudentNode(student, head);
}
```

The code creates a new `StudentNode` and puts it at the front of the list.

Next, we code the `print` method.

```java
public void print() {
  System.out.print("List: ");
  for (StudentNode temp = head; temp != null; temp = temp.getNext()) {
    System.out.print(temp.getData() + " ");
  }
  System.out.println();
}
```

The code starts at the front of the list, extracts the data in the corresponding node and prints that data. Printing ends when the node it points to is null; that is, it doesn't exist. Assuming that the Student class has a proper toString() method, we will get the name, address and GPA of each student printed.

Finally, we code the method to delete a student. We will need to look at each Student object and see if the name field matches the given name. How do we do this comparison? Suppose temp is a variable that refers to a Student object. The call temp.getData() retrieves the Student object, and temp.getData(). getName() gets the name of the student. Consider the following comparison:

```
temp.getData().getName() == studentName
```

Both sides of the equality comparison generate a reference. The system simply compares these references and the expression is true if and only if the two are the same. In general, this is not a correct comparison.

When we need to compare two objects, say, object1 and object2, we should write

```
object1.equals(object2)
```

which returns a logical value which is true if the two objects are equal and false otherwise.

The code for the delete method is given below.

```
public void delete(String studentName) {
  if (head == null) {
    return;
  }
  if (head.getData().getName().equals(studentName)) {
    head = head.getNext();
  } else {
    for (StudentNode temp = head.getNext(), previous = head;
                      temp != null; temp = temp.getNext()) {
      if (temp.getData().getName().equals(studentName)) {
        previous.setNext(temp.getNext());
        return;
      }
    }
  }
}
```

The code first checks if the list is empty; if so, there is nothing to do. With an non-empty list, it checks if the name of the student at the front of the list is the same as the name supplied in the parameter. If they match, the Student object at the front of the list is deleted from the list by moving the head to the next object (which may not exist, in which case we have a null). If the element at the front of the list is not what we want, execution proceeds to a loop that examines all elements starting at the second position until the end of the list is reached or the student with the given name is located. The variable previous always refers to the object preceding the object referred to by temp. Once it is located, the object can be deleted using previous.

2.4.2 Array Implementation of Lists

We need to set up an array of Student objects. This is done as follows.

1. Declare a field in the class StudentArrayList, which is an array of type Student.
2. Allocate an array of the required size. We will allocate storage for as many students as the user wishes; if the user does not specify a number, we will allocate space for a small number, say, 10, of objects. In any case, when this array fills up, we will allocate more.

Therefore, we need two constructors: one that accepts the initial capacity and the other that accepts nothing. The code for the array field and the constructor is given below.

```
public class StudentArrayList implements StudentList {
   private Student[] students;
   private int initialCapacity;
   public StudentArrayList() {
     students = new Student[10];
     initialCapacity = 10;
   }
   public StudentArrayList(int capacity) {
     students = new Student[capacity];
     initialCapacity = capacity;
   }
   // other methods
}
```

Note that the code for the first constructor is a special case of the second constructor. This is undesirable. We should try to reuse the code in the second constructor because it is general enough. Thus, when the user does not supply an initial capacity, we should somehow invoke the second constructor with a value of 10. This reuse can be achieved by rewriting the first constructor as follows:

```
public StudentArrayList() {
   this(10);
}
```

In this case, this refers to another constructor of the class. We are specifying a constructor that has a single int parameter and invoking it with a parameter value of 10. The net effect would be the same as that of the user writing new StudentArrayList(10).

The use of `this` in the above context should not be confused with the one that is
used to refer to the object used in instance methods. Also, note the following aspects.

1. There can be no code before the statement `this()`. In other words, this call
   should be the very first statement in the constructor.
2. You can have code in the constructor after the call to another constructor.
3. You can call at most one other constructor from a constructor.

We will use the following approach to manage the list. We will have two variables,
`first` that gives the index of the first occupied cell, and `count`, the number of
objects in the list. When the list is empty, both are 0. When we add an object to
the list, we will insert it at `(first + count) % array size` and increment
count.

```java
public class StudentArrayList implements StudentList {
  private Student[] students;
  private int first;
  private int count;
  private int initialCapacity;
  public StudentArrayList() {
    students = new Student[10];
    initialCapacity = 10;
  }
  public StudentArrayList(int capacity) {
    students = new Student[capacity];
    initialCapacity = capacity;
  }
  public void add(Student student) {
    if (count == students.length) {
      reallocate(count * 2);
    }
    int last = (first + count) % students.length;
    students[last] = student;
    count++;
  }
  public void delete(String name) {
    for (int index = first, counter = 0; counter < count;
             counter++, index = (index + 1) % students.length) {
      if (students[index].getName().equals(name)) {
        students[index] = students[(first + count - 1) % students.length];
        students[(first + count - 1) % students.length] = null;
        count--;
        return;
      }
    }
  }
  public Student get(int index) {
    if (index >= 0 && index < count) {
      return students[index];
    }
    return null;
  }
  public int size() {
    return count;
  }
  public void print() {
    for (int index = first, counter = 0; counter < count;
                    counter++, index = (index + 1)
```

```
                                  % students.length) {
      System.out.println(students[index]);
    }
  }
  public void reallocate(int size) {
    Student[] temp = new Student[size];
    if (first + count >= students.length) {
      int count1 = students.length - first;
      int count2 = count - count1;
      System.arraycopy(students, first, temp, 0, count1);
      System.arraycopy(students, first + count1, temp, count1, count2);
    } else {
      System.arraycopy(students, first, temp, 0, count);
    }
    students = temp;
    first = 0;
  }
}
```

2.5 Abstract Classes

In a way, classes and interfaces represent the extreme ends of a spectrum of possible implementations. When we write a class, we code every field and method; in other words, the code is complete in a sense. Interfaces are merely specifications.

Sometimes, we might know the specifications for a class, but might not have the information needed to implement the class completely. For example, consider the set of possible shapes that can be drawn on a computer screen. While the set is infinite, let us consider only three possibilities: triangles, rectangles, and circles. We know that the set of fields needed to represent each object is different, but there are some commonalities as well. For example, all shapes have an area.

In such cases, we can implement a class partially using what are called **abstract** classes. In the case of a shape, we may code

```
public abstract class Shape {
  private double area;
  public abstract void computeArea();
  public double getArea() {
    return area;
  }
  // more fields and methods
}
```

The class is declared as abstract (using the keyword abstract prior to the keyword class), which means that the class is incomplete. Since we know that every shape has an area, we have defined the double field area and the method getArea() to return the area of the shape. We require that there be a method to compute the area of a shape, so we have written the method getArea(). But since the formula to compute the area is different for the three possible shapes, we have left out the implementation and declared the method itself as abstract.

Any class that contains an abstract method must be declared abstract. We cannot create an instance of an abstract class. The utility of an abstract class comes from the fact that it provides a basic implementation that other classes can "extend". This is done using the technique of inheritance, covered in Chap. 3.

2.6 Comparing Objects for Equality

We have seen the need to use the `equals` method to compare two objects. In this section we explore this issue a little more.

Given any two variables of the same primitive type, it is easy for Java to decide whether they are equal: the variables are equal if they have the same value. However, consider a class such as `Student`. It is a user defined class. When do you say that two `Student` objects are equal? Here are some possibilities.

1. The language specifies that two objects are equal if they occupy the same physical storage.
2. The language provides a facility to check whether the corresponding fields of the objects are equal. This is a recursive definition. For example, in the `Student` class, the fields are `name`, `address` and `gpa`. For the `name` field of two objects to be equal, we have to know when two `String` objects are equal. Since `gpa` is a `double`, that field presents no problems.
3. The language leaves the responsibility to the class itself; that is, it lets the class specify when two of its objects are equal.

Java supports both (1) and (3) above. Since a class can specify when another object is equal to an object of its type, we can implement (2) as a special case.

To specify how objects should be compared for equality, we need to write a special method called `equals` which has the following format:

```
public boolean equals(Object someObject) {
   // implement the policy for comparison in this method.
   // return true if and only if this object is equal to someObject
}
```

We are given two objects: `this`, the one on which we invoke `equals()`, and `someObject`, an arbitrary object, which can be of any type. It is enough at this stage to know that `Object` is a special class in Java and every object can be thought of as an instance of this class. The method is free to decide whether `someObject` is equal to `this` in any way it pleases.

For example, let us say that a `Student` object is equal to another object only if that object is a `Student` object, the names are equal and they have the same address. One could definitely argue that the policy is flawed, but that is not our focus. Here is how to implement the equals method.

```
public boolean equals(Object anObject) {
  Student student = (Student) anObject;
  return student.name.equals(name) && student.address.equals(address);
}
```

As explained earlier, the method is placed inside the Student class and is invoked as below.

```
Student student1 = new Student("Tom");
student1.setAddress("1 Main Street");
// some other code
Student student2 = new Student("Tom");
student2.setAddress("1 Main Street");
// more code
if (student1.equals(student2)) {
  System.out.println("student1 is the same as student2");
} else {
  System.out.println("student1 is not the same as student2");
}
```

After creating the two Student objects with the same name and address, we invoked the equals method on student1 with student2 as the actual parameter. The first thing that the equals method does is cast the incoming object as a Student object. The resulting reference can be used to access all of the members of the corresponding Student object and, in particular, the name and address fields.

After the cast, we check if the name field of the cast object is equal to the name field of this, which in our example is student1. Note that we are doing this by invoking the equals method on the object student.name, which is a String; thus, we are invoking the equals method of the String class. It turns out that the equals method of the String class returns true if and only if every character in one string is equal to the corresponding character of the other string.

The address fields are compared in a similar way. The method returns true if and only if the two fields match.

What happens when you pass an object other than a Student, for instance, a Course object? This is valid because a Course object can also be viewed as of type Object. The cast in the equals method will fail and the program may crash if this problem is not addressed.

2.7 A Notation for Describing Object-Oriented Systems

We all know that it is important to document systems and programs. In this section, we introduce a notation called **Unified Modeling Language** (UML), which is the standard for documenting object-oriented systems. Many different ideas had been suggested to document object-oriented systems in the past and the term "Unified" reflects the fact that UML was an attempt to unify these different approaches. Among the ones who contributed to the development of this notation, the efforts of Grady Booch, James Rumbaugh, and Ivor Jacobson deserve special mention. After the initial notation was developed around 1995, the Object Management Group (OMG) took over the task of developing the notation further in 1997. As the years went by, the language became richer and, naturally, more complex. The current version is UML 2.0.

UML provides a pictorial or graphical notation for documenting the artefacts such as classes, objects and packages that make up an object-oriented system. UML diagrams can be divided into three categories.

1. **Structure diagrams** that show the static architecture of the system irrespective of time. For example, structure diagrams for a university system may include diagrams that depict the design of classes such as Student, Faculty, etc.
2. **Behaviour diagrams** that depict the behaviour of a system or business process.
3. **Interaction diagrams** that show the methods, interactions and activities of the objects. For a university system, a possible behaviour diagram would show how a student registers for a course.

Structure diagrams could be one of the following.

1. **Class diagrams**: They show the classes, their methods and fields.
2. **Composite structure diagrams**: They provide a means for presenting the details of a structural element such as a class. As an example, consider a class that represents a microcomputer system. Each object contains other objects such as CPU, memory, motherboard, etc, which would be shown as parts that make up the microcomputer system itself. The composite structure diagram for such a system would show these parts and exhibit the relationships between them helping the reader understand the details.
3. **Component diagrams**: Components are software entities that satisfy certain functional requirements specified by interfaces. These diagrams show the details of components.
4. **Deployment diagrams**: An object-oriented system consists of a number of executable files sometimes distributed across multiple computing elements. These diagrams show the assignment of executable files on the computing elements and the communication that involves between these entities.
5. **Object diagrams**: They are used to show how objects are related and used at runtime. For instance, in a university system we may show the object corresponding to a specific course and show other objects that represent students who have registered for the course. Since this shows an actual scenario that involves students and a course, it is far less abstract than class diagrams and contributes to a better understanding of the system.
6. **Package diagrams**: Classes may be grouped into packages and packages may reside in other packages. These diagrams show packages and dependencies among them: whether a change in one package may affect other packages.

Each of the six diagrams is a structure diagram. This hierarchy is illustrated in Fig. 2.2 as a tree with nodes representing these six diagrams as children of the Structure diagram node. It turns out that this method of showing a hierarchy is used in UML; so we are using UML notation itself to describe UML!

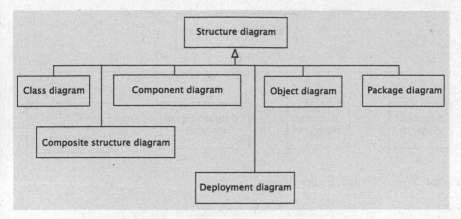

Fig. 2.2 Types of UML structure diagrams

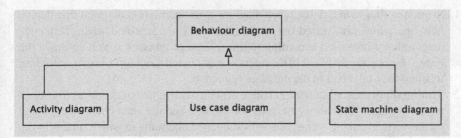

Fig. 2.3 Types of UML behaviour diagrams

Behaviour diagrams can be any of the following (see Fig. 2.3).

1. **Activity diagrams**: This is somewhat like a flowchart in that it shows the sequence of events in an activity. Just as a flowchart, it uses several types of nodes such as actions, decisions, merge points, etc. It accommodates objects with suitable types that depict objects, *object flows*, etc.
2. **Use case diagrams**: A use case is a single unit of some useful work. It involves a user (called an actor) and the system. An example of a use case in a university environment is a student registering for a course. A use case diagram shows the interaction involved in a use case.
3. **State machine diagrams**: It shows the sequence of states that an object goes through during its lifetime, e.g., the software that controls a washer for clothes. Initially, the washer is in the off state. After the soap is put in, the clothes are loaded and the on button pressed, the system goes to a state where it takes in water. In this state the system waits for a signal from the water sensor to indicate that the water has reached the required level. Then the system goes into the wash state where washing takes place. After this the system may go through further states such as rinse and spin and eventually reaches the washed state.

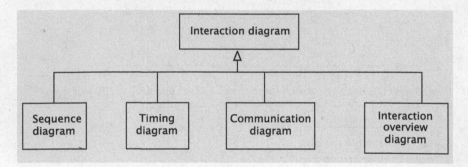

Fig. 2.4 Types of UML interaction diagrams

There are four types of interaction diagrams as shown in Fig. 2.4.

1. **Sequence diagrams**: A sequence diagram is an interaction diagram that details how operations are carried out—what messages are sent and when. Sequence diagrams are organised according to time. Time progresses as you go down the page. The objects involved in the operation are listed from left to right according to when they take part in the message sequence.
2. **Timing diagrams**: It shows the change in state of an object over time as the object reacts to events. The horizontal axis shows time and the state changes are noted on the vertical axis. Contrast this with sequence diagrams in which time is in the vertical axis.
3. **Communication diagrams**: A communication diagram essentially serves the same purpose as a sequence diagram. Just as in a sequence diagram, this diagram also has nodes for objects and uses directed lines between objects to indicate message flow and direction. However, unlike sequence diagrams, vertical direction has no relationship with time and message order is shown by numbering the directed lines that represent messages.
   Interactions that involve a large number of objects can be somewhat inconvenient to show using sequence diagrams because they must be arranged horizontally. Since no such restrictions are placed on communication diagrams, they are easier to draw. However, the order of messages can be harder to see in communication diagrams.
4. **Interaction overview diagrams**: An interaction overview diagram shows the high-level control flow in a system. It shows the interactions between interaction diagrams such as sequence diagrams and communication diagrams. Each node in the diagram can be an interaction diagram.

We will see examples of many of these diagrams as we develop concepts in this book. At this time, we show an example of a class diagram.

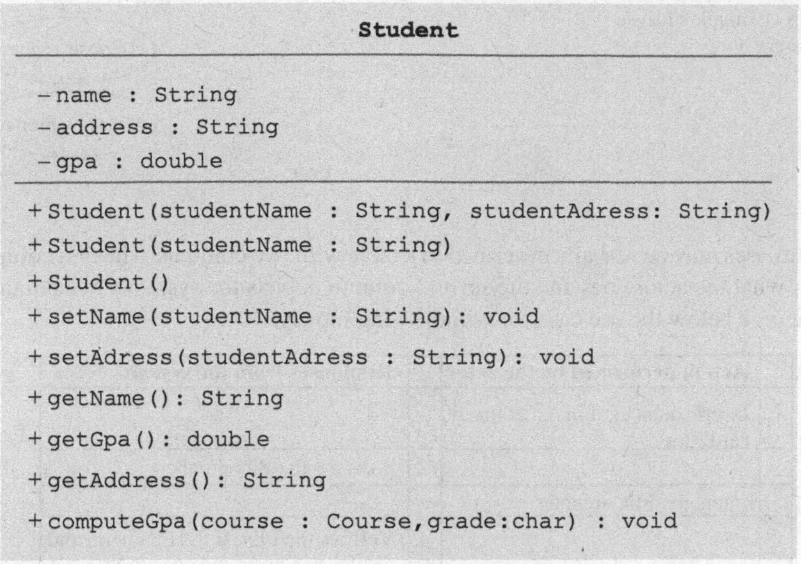

Student
− name : String − address : String − gpa : double
+ Student (studentName : String, studentAdress: String) + Student (studentName : String) + Student () + setName (studentName : String) : void + setAdress (studentAdress : String) : void + getName () : String + getGpa () : double + getAddress () : String + computeGpa (course : Course, grade:char) : void

Fig. 2.5 Example of a class diagram

2.7.1 Class Diagrams

Figure 2.5 is an example of a class diagram. Each class is represented by a box, which is divided into three rectangles. The name of the class is given in the top rectangle. The attributes are shown with their names and their types in the second box. The third box shows the methods with their return types and parameters (names and types). The access specifier for each field and method is given just in front of the field name or method name. A − sign indicates private access, + stands for public access and # (not shown in this example) is used for protected access which we will discuss in Chap. 3.

2.7.2 Use Cases and Use Case Diagrams

A use case describes a certain piece of desired functionality of an application system. It is constructed during the analysis stage. It shows the interaction between an **actor**, which could be a human or a piece of software or hardware and the system. It does *not* specify *how* the system carries out the task.

As an example of a simple use case, let us describe what a simple ATM machine will do. A user may withdraw or deposit money into his bank account using this machine. This functionality is shown in the use case diagram in Fig. 2.6.

Fig. 2.6 Example of a use
case diagram

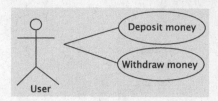

Use cases may be verbally described in a table with two columns: The first column
shows what the actor does and the second column depicts the system's behaviour.
We give below the use case for withdrawing money.

	Action performed by the actor		Responses from the system
1.	Inserts debit card into the 'Insert card' slot		
		2.	Asks for the PIN number
3.	Enters the PIN number		
		4.	Verifies the PIN. If the PIN is invalid, displays an error and goes to Step 8. Otherwise, asks for the amount
5.	Enters the amount		
		6.	Verifies that the amount can be withdrawn If not, display an error and goes to Step 8 Otherwise, dispenses the amount and updates the balance
7.	Takes the cash		
		8.	Ejects the card
9.	Takes the card		

Notice that the use case specifies the responsibilities of the two entities but does not
show *how* the system processes the request. Throughout the book, we express use
cases in a two-column format as above.

The use case as specified above does not say what the system is supposed to do
in all situations. For example, what should the system do if something other than
a valid ATM card is inserted? Such considerations may result in a more involved
specification. What is specified above is sometimes called the **main flow.**

2.7.3 Sequence Diagrams

One of the major goals of design is to determine the classes and their responsibilities
and one way of progressing toward the above goal is to create sequence diagrams
for each use case we identify in the analysis stage. In such a diagram we break down
the system into a number of objects and decide what each object should accomplish
in the corresponding use case. That is, we delegate responsibilities.

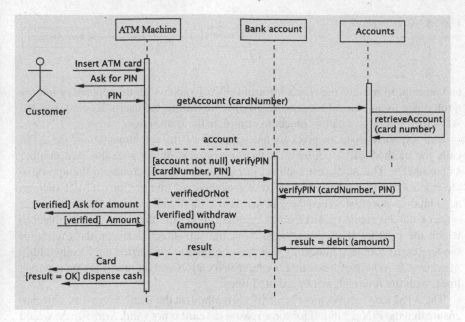

Fig. 2.7 Example of a simple sequence diagram

We have one column for each entity that plays a role in the use case. The vertical direction represents the flow of time. Horizontal arrows represent functionalities being invoked; the entity at the tail of the arrow invokes the named method on the entity at the head of the arrow.

For example, Fig. 2.7 shows the sequence diagram corresponding to the use case we gave above for withdrawing from an ATM. The rectangles at the top of the diagram represent the customer, the ATM, and two objects that reside in the bank database: `Accounts`, which stores all the account objects and `BankAccount`, which stores account-related information for a single account. For each object, we draw a dashed vertical line, called a **lifeline**, for showing the actions of the object. The long and thin rectangular boxes within these lifelines show when that object is active.

In many use cases, the actor interacts only with the left most entity, which usually represents some kind of interface. These interactions mirror the functionality described in the use case. The first arrow denotes the customer (actor) inserting the debit card into the ATM, which, in turn, asks for the PIN, as shown by the arrow from the ATM to the customer. Notice that the latter line is lower than the line that stands for the card insertion. This is because time increases as we go down in the diagram. The events in the sequence diagram that happen after the customer enters the PIN depend on how the system has been implemented. In our hypothetical example, we assume that the ATM has to access a central repository (viz., `Accounts`)

Fig. 2.8 An example of
association

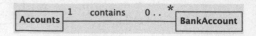

and attempt to retrieve the user's information.[1] If successful, the repository returns a reference to an object (BankAccount) representing the user's account, and the ATM then interacts with this object to complete the transaction.

The sequence diagram gives us the specifics of the implementation: the ATM calls the method getAccount on the Accounts object with the card number as parameter. The Accounts object either returns the reference to the appropriate BankAccount object corresponding to the card number, or null if such an account does not exist. When the getAccount method is invoked, the Accounts object calls the method retrieveAccount to get the BankAccount object to which the card number corresponds. Note the self-directed arc on the lifeline of the Accounts object, indicating that this computation is carried out locally within Accounts. The getAccount method invocation and its return are on separate lines, with the return shown by a dotted line.

The ATM then invokes the verifyPIN method on the BankAccount object to ensure that the PIN is valid. If for some reason the card is not valid, Accounts would have returned a null reference, in which case further processing is impossible. Therefore, the call to verify the PIN is conditional on reference being non-null. This is indicated in the sequence diagram by writing [account not null] along with the method call verifyPIN. Such a conditional is called a **guard**.

Just as Accounts called a method on itself, BankAccount calls the method verifyPIN to see if the PIN entered by the user is valid. The result, a boolean, is returned and shown on a separate dotted line in the diagram. If the PIN is valid, the ATM asks the user for the amount to be withdrawn. Once again, note the guard associated with this action. After receiving the value (the amount to be withdrawn), the machine sends the message withdraw with the amount as parameter to the BankAccount object, which verifies whether the amount can be withdrawn by calling the method debit on itself. The result is then returned to the ATM, which dispenses cash provided the result is acceptable.

Association

In our example that involved the ATM, Accounts and BankAccount, the Accounts instance contained all of the BankAcount objects, each of which could be retrieved by supplying a card number. This relationship can be shown using an association as in Fig. 2.8. Notice the number 1 above the line near the rectangle that represents Accounts and 0...* at the right end of the line near BankAccount. They mean that one Accounts object may hold references to zero or more BankAccount objects.

---

[1]This may not reflect a real ATM's behaviour, but bear in mind that this is a pedagogical exercise in UML, not banking.

Fig. 2.9 Depicting interfaces and their implementation

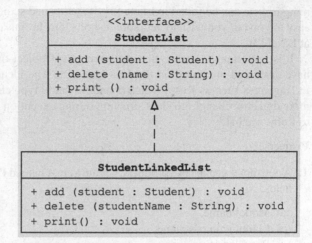

Interfaces and Their Implementation

Interfaces and their implementation can be depicted in UML as in Fig. 2.9. With the `StudentList` interface and the class `StudentLinkedList` class that implements it, we draw one box to represent the interface and another to stand for the class. The methods are shown in both. The dotted line from the class to the interface shows that the class implements the interface.

2.8 Discussion and Further Reading

The concept of a class is fundamental to the object-oriented paradigm. As we have discussed, it is based on the notion of an abstract data type and one can trace its origins to the Simula programming language. This chapter also discussed some of the UML notation used for describing classes. In the next chapter we look at how classes interconnect to form a system, and the use of UML to denote these relationships.

The Java syntax and concepts that we have described in this chapter are quite similar to the ones in C++; so the reader should have little difficulty getting introduced to that language. A fundamental difference between Java and C++ is in the availability of pointers in C++, which can be manipulated using pointer arithmetic in ways that add considerable flexibility and power to the language. However, pointer arithmetic and other features in the language also make C++ more challenging to someone new to this concept.

Since our intention is to cover just enough language features to complete the implementations, some readers may wish to explore other features of the language. For those who want an exposure to the numerous features of Java, we suggest *Core Java* by Cornell and Horstmann [1]. A more gentle and slow exposure to programming in Java can be found in Liang [2]. If syntax and semantics of Java come fairly easy to you but you wish to get more insights into Java usage, you could take a look at Eckel [3].

It is important to realise that the concepts of object-oriented programming we have discussed are based on the Java language. The ideas are somewhat different in languages such as Ruby, which abandons static type checking and allows much more dynamic changes to class structure during execution time. For an introduction to Ruby, see [4].

Projects

1. A consumer group tests products. Create a class named Product with the following fields:

   (a) Model name,
   (b) Manufacturer's name,
   (c) Retail price,
   (d) An overall rating ('A', 'B', 'C', 'D', 'F'),
   (e) A reliability rating (based on consumer survey) that is a double number between 0 and 5,
   (f) The number of customers who contributed to the survey on reliability rating.

   Remember that names must hold a sequence of characters and the retail price may have a fractional part.

   The class must have two constructors:

   (a) The first constructor accepts the model name, the manufacturer name, and the retail price in that order.
   (b) The second constructor accepts the model name and the manufacturer name in that order, and this constructor must effectively use the first constructor.

   Have methods to get every field. Have methods to set the retail price and the overall rating.

   Reliability rating is the average of the reliability ratings by all customers who rated this product. A method called `rateReliability` should be written to input the reliability rating of a customer. This method has a single parameter that takes in the reliability of the product as viewed by a customer. The method must then increment the number of customers who rated the product and update the reliability rating using the following formula.

   New value of reliability rating = (Old value of reliability rating * Old value of number of customers + Reliability rating by this customer) / New value of number of customers.

   For example, suppose that the old value of reliability was 4.5 based on the input from 100 customers. If a new customer gives a reliability rating of 1.0, then the new value of reliability would be

```
(4.5 * 100 + 1.0) / 101
```

which is 4.465347.

Override the `toString` method appropriately.

2. Write a Java class called `LongInteger` as per the following specifications. Objects of this class store integers that can be as long as 50 digits. The class must have the following constructors and methods.

(a) `public LongInteger()`: Sets the integer to 0.
(b) `public LongInteger(int[] otherDigits)`: Sets the integer to the given integer represented by the parameter. A copy of `otherDigits` must be made to prevent accidental changes.
(c) `public LongInteger(int number)` Sets the integer to the value given in the parameter.
(d) `public void readIn()`: reads in the integer from the keyboard. You can assume that only digits will be entered.
(e) `public LongInteger add(int number)` Adds number to the integer represented by this object and returns the result.
(f) `public LongInteger add(LongInteger number)` Adds number to the integer represented by this object and returns the result.
(g) `public String toString()` returns a `String` representation of the integer.

Use an array of 50 `int`s to store the digits of the number.

3. Study the interface `Extendable` given below.

```
public interface Extendable {
  public boolean append(char c);
  public boolean append(char[] sequence);
}
```

The method `append(char c)` appends a character to the object (or, more precisely the object's class) that implements this interface. The second version of the method appends all characters in the array to this object. If there is no space in the object to append, the methods return `false`; otherwise they return `true`. Write code for the class `SimpleBuffer` that implements the above interface which has a constructor of the following signature.

```
public SimpleBuffer(int size)
```

The initial size of the array is passed as a parameter.

The class must have two fields: one which stores the `char` array and the other which stores the number of elements actually filled in the array.

This class must also implement the `toString` method to bring back correctly a `String` representation of the `char` array. It should also implement the `equals` method such that two buffers are equal if and only if they contain the same set of characters.

2.9 Exercises

1. Given the following class, write a constructor that has no parameters but uses the given constructor so that x and y are initialised at construction time to 1 and 2 respectively.

```
public class SomeClass {
  private int x;
  private int y;
  public SomeClass(int a, int b) {
    x = a;
    y = b;
  }
  // write a no-argument (no parameters)
  // constructor here, so that x and y are
  // initialised to 1 and 2 respectively.
  // You MUST Utilise the given constructor.
}
```

2. In Sect. 2.3, we had a class called `Course`, which had a method that creates `Section` objects. Modify the two classes so that

   (a) `Course` class maintains the list of all sections.
   (b) `Section` stores the capacity and the number of students enrolled in the class.
   (c) `Course` has a search facility that returns a list of sections that are not full.

3. In Sect. 2.7, we had a discussion on two possible use cases for using an ATM. Develop the use case for depositing money using an ATM machine.
4. Draw the sequence diagram for the use case you developed for Exercise 3.
5. Take a look at the use case and sequence diagram we developed for withdrawing money through an ATM. Design the method `getAccount()` in the class `Accounts`. Does this need interaction between the two classes, `Accounts` and `BankAccount`? If so, what additional methods do you need in `BankAccount`?

References

1. C.S. Horstmann, G. Cornell, *Core Java(TM)*, vol. 1, Fundamentals 8th edn. (Sun Microsystems, California, 2007)
2. Y.D. Liang, *Introduction to Java Programming Comprehensive Version* (Pearson Prentice Hall, New Jersey, 2007)
3. B. Eckel, *Thinking in Java*, 4th edn. (Prentice Hall, New Jersey, 2006)
4. P. Cooper, *Beginning Ruby: From Novice to Professional (Beginning from Novice to Professional)*. (Apress, New York, 2007)

Chapter 3
Relationships Between Classes

In the previous chapter we studied classes and objects as the two building blocks of object-oriented systems. The structure of a software system is defined by the way in which these building blocks relate with one another and the behaviour of the system is defined by the manner in which the objects interact with one another. Therefore, in order to construct a software system, we need mechanisms that create connections between these building blocks. In this chapter we introduce the basic types of relationships between classes (and objects) that make the connections.

The simplest and most general kind of relationships is **association**, which simply indicates that the objects of the two classes are related in some non-hierarchical way. There are almost no other restrictions on how an association can be formed, although we shall see throughout this text the good design practices that ought to be followed when creating associations.

When two or more classes have a hierarchical relationship based on generalisation, it is referred to as **inheritance**. Classes connected by inheritance share some commonalities and therefore, this kind of relationship is more restrictive than association.

The third kind of relationship we see is **genericity**. This is more restrictive than inheritance due to the fact that the only variations permitted across related classes are those that can be captured by **type parametrisation**, i.e., providing parameters of differing types when creating an instance of the generic entity.

In the rest of this chapter we elaborate on each of these, discussing the basic principles and examining situations where they can be applied. Since these mechanisms are basic to OOAD, they will all be revisited in later chapters when dealing with real examples of more complex systems.

© Universities Press (India) Private Ltd. 2015
B. Dathan and S. Ramnath, *Object-Oriented Analysis, Design and Implementation*,
Undergraduate Topics in Computer Science, DOI 10.1007/978-3-319-24280-4_3

3.1 Association

An association is formally defined as a relation among two or more classes describing a group of links with common structure and semantics. An association implies that an object of one class is making use of an object of another class and is indicated simply by a solid line connecting the two class icons. In the previous chapter we defined a class `Student` that keeps track of information about the courses that the student has registered for. This information is represented as shown in Fig. 3.1. In our example, `Student` objects may make use of `Course` objects when transcripts are generated, when tuition is computed or when a course is dropped. The link to the course provides the student object with the necessary information.

An association does not imply that there is always a link between all objects of one class and all objects of the other. As one would expect, in our example, a link is formed between a `Student` object and a `Course` object only when the operation that links them is completed, i.e., the student represented by the `Student` object registers for that particular course. However, an association does imply that there is a persistent, identifiable connection between two classes. If class A is associated with class B, it means that given an object of class A, you can always find an object of class B, or you can find that no B object has been assigned to the association yet. But in either case there is always an identifiable path from A to B. Associations thus represent conceptual relationships between classes as well as physical relationships between the objects of these classes.

In terms of implementation, what the above implies is that class A must provide a mechanism using the constructs of the chosen programming language to form a link. This could take several forms, for example,

- Class A stores a key (or several keys) that uniquely identifies an object of class B.
- Class A stores a reference(s) to object(s) of class B.
- Class A has a reference to an object of class C, which, in turn is associated with a unique instance of class B.

The first two of these create a direct association, whereas the third one is an indirect association. The mechanism chosen may depend on the requirements that the system has to satisfy (for instance, the kinds of queries that need to be answered) and also on how the rest of system is designed. In our example, when a student registers for a course, he/she actually enrolls in a specific section of the course. The mechanism to make this connection may simply be that the `Student` object stores a reference to the `section` object. Each section is associated with a unique course, completing the picture (see Fig. 3.2).

Fig. 3.1 Association between classes

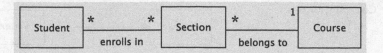

Fig. 3.2 Association involving three classes

An association is assumed to be **bi-directional** unless we place a directional arrow on the connecting line to indicate otherwise. The association usually has a descriptive **name**. The name often implies a direction, but in most cases this can be inverted. Our figure says student *enrolls in* a section, which *belongs to* a course, but this could be stated as a course *has* sections that *enroll* students. The diagram is usually drawn to read the link or association from left to right or top to bottom.

The entities at the ends of the association usually have assigned **roles**, which may have names. We could have an association named 'employs' that connects a class representing a Business to a class representing a Person employed by the business. Here Business plays the role of of the *employer* and Person has the role of *employee*.

3.1.1 Characteristics of Associations

Since associations represent very general relationships, they allow for variation in the nature of the connection. The common variation is the arity of the connection, i.e., how many objects of class A can be linked to one object of class B and vice-versa. Another variation involves whether there is some form of containment involved in the relationship. In other cases there is some specific kind of information that is added to the system whenever a link is made between objects. These characteristics are usually represented in UML by annotating the connection between classes. Some of these are discussed below.

Arity of Relationships

The **arity** of a relationship could be **one–one**, **one–many**, or **many–many**. An example of a one–one relationship could be between a User-Interface class accepting user input and a Display-Window class displaying information. A multi-user system, however, can interact with several users in parallel. Each interaction has a dedicated Display-Window object and all these objects are deployed through the common User-Interface. This is an example of a one–many relationship. From our example, a course may have several sections but each section is associated with only one course, thus creating a one(course)–many(section) connection. A student can enroll in several sections and each section can have several students enrolled. This would be an example of a many–many relationship.

Fig. 3.3 Composition across
classes

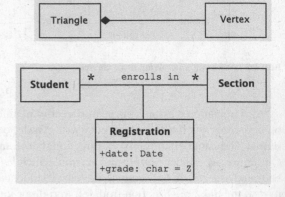

Fig. 3.4 Using an
association class

Containment Relationships

Aggregation is a kind of association where the object of class A is 'made up of' objects of class B. This suggests some kind of a whole–part relationship between A and B. Most experts have downplayed the importance of this kind of association as not something that deserves to be embellished in any way. However, **composite aggregation**, also known as **composition**, has been recognised as being significant. Composition implies that each instance of the part belongs to only one instance of the whole, and that the part cannot exist except as part of the whole. Composition is indicated with a filled-in diamond and is usually not named since some form of whole–part relationship is assumed. In Fig. 3.3, a vertex cannot exist unless it is a part of a triangle. If the triangle object is destroyed, so are the individual vertices.

Association Classes

An association usually results in some information being added to the system since it adds a path connecting two objects. In some situations we add some information that qualifies the nature and describes the properties of the relationship. Outside the context of the association, this information does not have any relevance to either of the objects involved. In such cases we treat the association itself as a class. An example of this is shown in Fig. 3.4. When a student enrolls in a section, a registration record is created to store the date of registration and a grade. Such a record does not make sense if a particular student does not enroll in a given section.

FAQs About Forming Associations

What does an association represent?
An association normally represents something that will be stored as part of the data and reflects all links between objects of two classes that may ever exist. It describes a relationship that will exist between instances at run time and has an example.

When can we call a relationship an association?
In UML class diagrams, associations should be shown if a class possesses, controls, is connected to, is related to, is a part of, has as parts, is a member of, or has as

members some other class in the system. As association should *not* be used to denote relationships that: (i) can be drawn as a hierarchy, (ii) stems from a dependency alone, (iii) or relationships whose links will not survive beyond the execution of any particular operation.

How is an association represented?
An association shows how two classes are related to each other and this relationship should be made clear. It is denoted by a line connecting the two classes, with sufficient annotation to make the relationship clear and unambiguous. This annotation includes a name, the arity, roles and any association classes. In particular, if the annotation includes neither an association name nor a role name, the default name 'has' is applied.

3.2 Inheritance

There are situations when two classes have not only a great deal of similarity, but also significant differences. The classes may be similar enough that association does not capture the similarity, and differ too much so that the idea of genericity cannot be profitably employed. Suppose that C_1 and C_2 are two such classes. We then extract the common aspects of C_1 and C_2 and create a class, say, B, to implement that functionality. The classes C_1 and C_2 could then be smaller, containing only properties and methods that are unique to them. This idea is called **inheritance**—C_1 and C_2 are said to **inherit** from B. B is said to be the **baseclass** or **superclass**, and C_1 and C_2 are termed *derived classes* or **subclasses**. The superclasses are generalisations or **abstractions**: we move toward a more general type, an 'upward' movement, and subclasses denote *specialisation* toward a more specific class—a 'downward' movement. The class structure then provides a *hierarchy*.

Inheritance can be defined as the mechanism provided in programming languages to achieve the idea of vertical generalisation outlined above. Formally, an inheritance is a relationship characterised by an **ancestor** and a **descendant** represented using UML notation as in Fig. 3.5. Here, the baseclass is the ancestor and the derived classes are the descendants. We draw one box per class and draw an arrow from the derived classes to the baseclass.

3.2.1 An Example of a Hierarchy

Consider a company that sells various products such as television sets and books. Obvious differences between the products imply that they have different attributes to be tracked and that we need two classes, Television and Book. One way to accomplish this task is to create a class for television sets, say, Television, and a second class, for books, say, Book. However, in many situations the company would

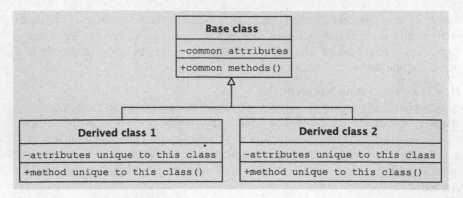

Fig. 3.5 Basic idea of inheritance

like to think of books and televisions as simply products. For instance, the company needs to keep track of sales, profits (or losses), etc., for all products. Now, add to the above situation more products, say, CDs, DVDs, cassette players, pens, etc. Each may warrant a separate class, but, as just discussed, they all have common properties and behaviours and to the company, they are all products.

What we see is an example of a situation where two classes have a great deal of similarities, but also substantial differences. The need to view different entities such as televisions and books as products suggests that we may benefit by having a new type, `Product`, introduced into the system. Since there is a fair amount of common functionality between the two products, we would like `Product` to be a class that implements the commonality found in `Television` and `Book`.

In Java, we do this as follows. We start off with a class that captures the essential properties and methods common to all products.

```
public class Product {
    // functionality for a product
}
```

The above class may have attributes such as number of units sold and unit price. It also will have constructors and methods for recording sales, computing profits, and so on.

We are now ready to create a class that represents a single TV set. For this, we note that a television is a product and that we would like to utilise the functionality that we just implemented for products. In Java, we do this as below:

```
public class Television extends Product {
    // functionality that is unique for televisions
    // modifications
}
```

Informally speaking, the `Television` class inherits all of the properties and methods from the class `Product`. All we have done is add properties and methods unique to televisions, which will not, for obvious reasons, be implemented in `Product`.

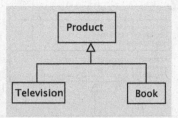

Fig. 3.6 Inheriting from product

In a similar manner, we implement the class Book.

```
public class Book extends Product {
    // functionality that is unique for books
    // modifications
}
```

The relationships between the three classes is depicted in Fig. 3.6.

Class Structure

Our purpose in this section is to describe how inheritance works. We do not worry about the details of the functionality, and so we do not describe the use cases. Moreover, due to necessity, we give a simplistic view of the application.

First, let us consider the two entities, television and book, in isolation without worrying about the relationships between them. The functionalities required of the two classes, Television and Book, are given in Fig. 3.7.

Now, notice the similarities and differences between the two classes: both classes, since they represent products, carry the fields quantitySold and price with their obvious meanings. The method sale() in both classes is invoked whenever one unit (a book or a TV set) is sold. The meaning of the setPrice() method should be obvious.

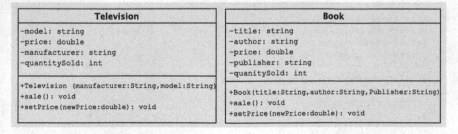

Fig. 3.7 An example of similar classes

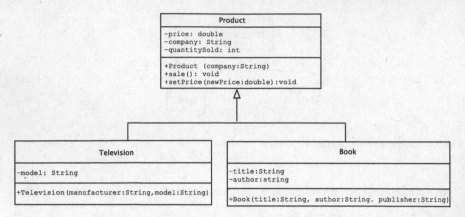

Fig. 3.8 Inheriting from product

The two classes are somewhat different in other respects: `Book` has attributes `title` and `author` whereas `Television` class has the attribute `brand`. The `manufacturer` attribute is named differently from, but not dissimilar to, `publisher`.

Here is where the power of the object-oriented paradigm comes into play. It allows the development of a baseclass or superclass that reflects the commonalities of the two classes and then *extends* or sub classes this base class to arrive at the functionalities we discussed before. A UML diagram that shows the arrangement is shown in Fig. 3.8. The class `Product` keeps track of the common attributes of `Book` and `Television` and implements the methods necessary to act on these attributes. `Television` and `Book` are now constructed as subclasses of `Product`; they will both inherit the functionalities of `Product` so that they are now capable of keeping track of sales of these two products.

The code for `Product`, given below, is fairly simple. The variable `company` stores the manufacturer of the product. Otherwise, there are no special features to be discussed.

```
public class Product {
    private String company;
    private double price;
    private int quantitySold;

    public Product(String company, double price) {
        this.company = company;
        this.price = price;
    }
    public void sell() {
        quantitySold++;
    }
    public void setPrice(double newPrice) {
        price = newPrice;
    }
```

```
    public String toString() {
      return "Company:" + company +  "price:" +
        price + "quantity sold" + quantitySold;
    }
  }
```

Let us now construct `Television`, which extends `Product`. Any object of type `Television`, the subclass, can be thought of as having two parts: one that is formed from `Television` itself and the other from `Product`, the superclass. Thus, this object has four fields in it, `model`, `quantitySold`, `price`, and `company`. Often, the code within the subclass is responsible for managing the fields within it and the code in the superclass deals with the fields in the superclass.

Recall that objects are initialised via code in the constructor. When inheritance is involved, the part of the object represented by the superclass must be initialised *before* the fields of the subclass are given values; this is so because the subclass is built from the superclass and thus the former may have fields that depend on the fact that the superclass's attributes are initialised. An analogy may help: when a house is built, the roof is put in only after the walls have been erected, which happens only after the foundation has been laid.

To create a `Television` object, we to invoke a constructor of that class as below, where we pass the brand name, manufacturer name, and price.

```
Television set = new Television("RX3032", "Modern Electronics", 230.0);
```

Thus the constructor of `Television` must be defined as below.

```
public Television(String model, String manufacturer, double price) {
    // code to initialise the Product part of a television
    // code to initialise the television part of the object
}
```

We already have a piece of code that initialises fields of a `Product` object: the constructor of `Product`. So all we need to do is call that constructor! This is accomplished by the statement

```
super(/* appropriate parameters go here*/)
```

The call `super` with proper parameters always invokes the superclass's constructor. The superclass' constructor call can be invoked only as the very first statement from the code within a constructor of a subclass; it cannot be placed after some code or placed in methods.

In this example, the parameters to be passed would be the manufacturer's name and price. The code for the constructor is then

```
public Television(String model, String manufacturer, double price) {
    super(manufacturer, price);
    // store the model name
}
```

`super` is a keyword in Java which denotes superclass. Invocation of the super-class's constructor is done using this keyword followed by the required parameters in parentheses.

The fields of the superclass are initialised before fields in the subclass. What this means in the context of object creation is that the constructor of `Television` can begin its work only after the constructor of the superclass, `Product`, has completed execution. Of course, when you wish to create a `Television` object you need to invoke that class's constructor, but the first thing the constructor `Television` does (and must do) is invoke the constructor of `Product` with the appropriate parameters: the name of the company that manufactured the set and the price.

The result of `super(manufacturer, price)` is, therefore, to invoke `Product`'s constructor, which initialises `company` and `price` and then returns. The `Television` class then gives a value to the `model` field and returns to the invoker.

As is to be expected, the class `Television` needs a field for storing the model name. We thus have a more complete piece of code for this class as given below.

```
public class Television extends Product {
  private String model;
  public Television(String model, String manufacturer, double price) {
    super(manufacturer, price);
    this.model = model;
  }
  public String toString() {
    return super.toString() + "model:" + model;
  }
}
```

The `toString()` method of `Television` works by first calling the `toString()` method of `Product`, which returns a string representation of `Product` and concatenates to it the model name.

3.2.2 Inheriting from an Interface

A specialised kind of inheritance is one where a class inherits from an interface. Recollect that in Chap. 2 we had defined an interface as a collection of methods that can be implemented by a class. An interface has been likened to a contract signed by the class implementing the interface. In the context of this chapter, it should be pointed out that implementing the interface can also be viewed as a form of inheritance, where the implementing class inherits an abstract set of properties from the interface.

Java recognises an interface as a type (as do several other object-oriented languages), which means that objects that belong to classes that implement a given interface also belong to the type represented by the interface. Likewise, we can declare an identifier as belonging to the type of the interface and we can then use it to access the objects of any class that implements the interface.

```
public interface I {
  // details of I
}

public class  A implements I {
  //code for A
}

public class  B implements I {
  //code for B
}

I i1 = new A(); // i1 holds an A

I i2 =  new B(); // i2 holds a B
```

In the UML notation, this kind of a relationship between the interface and the implementing class is termed **realisation** and is represented by a dotted line with a large open arrowhead that points to the interface as shown in Fig. 3.8.

3.2.3 Polymorphism and Dynamic Binding

Consider a university application that contains, among others, three classes that form a hierarchy as shown in Fig. 3.9. A student can be either an undergraduate student or a graduate student. Just as in real life where we would think of an undergraduate or a graduate student as a student, in the object-oriented paradigm also, we consider an UndergraduateStudent object or a GraduateStudent object to be of the type Student. Therefore, we can write

```
Student student1 = new UndergraduateStudent();
Student student2 = new GraduateStudent();
```

This is a powerful idea. We can now write methods that accept a Student and pass either an UndergraduateStudent or a GraduateStudent object to it as below.

Fig. 3.9 Student hierarchy

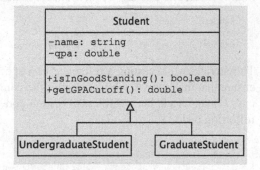

```
public void storeStudent(Student student) {
  // code to store the Student object
}
```

We can then create UndergraduateStudent and GraduateStudent objects
and pass them to the above method.

```
storeStudent(new UndergraduateStudent());
storeStudent(new GraduateStudent());
```

Once again, in real life, we usually do not think of a graduate student as an undergraduate student or vice-versa. In the same way, we cannot write the following code
in Java.

```
UndergraduateStudent student1 = new GraduateStudent(); // wrong
GraduateStudent student2 = new UndergraduateStudent(); // wrong
```

Since we allow Student references to point to both Undergraduate
Student and GraduateStudent objects, we can see that some, but not all
Student references may point to objects of type UndergraduateStudent;
similarly, some Student references may refer to objects of type Graduate
Student. Thus, we cannot write,

```
Student student1;
student1 = new UndergraduateStudent();
GraduateStudent student2 = student1; // wrong!
```

The compiler will flag that the code is incorrect.
   But, the following code, intuitively correct, is flagged by the compiler as incorrect.

```
Student student1;
student1 = new GraduateStudent();
GraduateStudent student2 = student1; // compiler generates a syntax error.
```

The reason for this error is that the compiler *does not execute the code* to realise
that student1 is actually referring to an object of type GraduateStudent.
It is trying to protect the programmer from the absurd situation that could occur
if student1 held a reference to an UndergraduateStudent object. It is the
responsibility of the programmer to tell the compiler that student1 actually points
to a GraduateStudent object. This is done through a cast as shown below.

```
Student student1;
student1 = new GraduateStudent();
GraduateStudent student2 = (GraduateStudent) student1; //  O.K. Code works.
```

To reiterate, while casting a reference to a specialised type, the programmer must
ensure that the cast will work correctly; the compiler will happily allow the code to
pass syntax check, but a carelessly-written code will crash when executed. See the
following code.

```
Student student1;
student1 = new UndergraduateStudent();
GraduateStudent student2 = (GraduateStudent) student1; // crashes
```

Fig. 3.10 Illustrating
polymorphic assignment

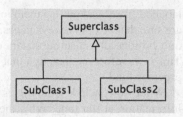

Student1 does not point to a GraduateStudent object in the last line, so the system's attempt to cast the instance of UndergraduateStudent to an instance of GraduateStudent will fail and the code will crash.[1]

The general rules are as follows. Refer to Fig. 3.10.

1. Any object of type SubClass1 or SubClass2 can be stored in a reference of type SuperClass.
2. No object of type SubClass1 (SubClass2) can be stored in a reference of type SubClass2 (SubClass1).
3. A reference of type SuperClass can be cast as a reference of type SubClass1 or SubClass2.

Assignments of the above kind are termed *polymorphic*. A reference is able to point to objects of different types as long as the actual types of these objects *conform* to the type of reference. The above rules informally give the notion of **conformance**.

It is instructive to compare assignments and casts given above with the rules for assignments and casts of variables of primitive types. Some type conversions, for example, from int to float, do not need any casting; float variables have a wider range than int variables. Some others, double to int being an instance, are fine with casting; however, the programmer must be prepared for loss of precision. And the rest—any casts from (to) boolean to (from) any other type—are always disallowed.

We have so far seen examples of polymorphic assignments. In one of these, we store a reference to an object of the class GraduateStudent in an entity whose declared type is Student. This is equivalent to taking a bunch of bananas and storing them in a box labelled 'fruit'. The declared contents of the box (as given by the label) is fruit, just as the declared type of entity student1 in the LHS of the assignment is Student. By doing this, we have lost some information since we can no longer find out what kind of fruit we have in the box without examining its contents. Likewise, when we operate on the entity student1, all we can assume is that it contains a reference to a Student object. Thus there is a loss of information in this kind of assignment.

The second kind of polymorphic assignment is one where we moved a reference from an entity whose declared type is Student to an entity whose declared type is GraduateStudent. (This would amount to taking the bananas out of the box

---

[1]Technically, the system throws an exception, a topic that will be covered in detail in Chap. 4. In this case, an instance of the class ClassCastException is thrown open.

labelled 'fruit' and putting them in the box labelled 'bananas'; we do this only if we are sure that box did have bananas.) As we saw with our cast and exception, this can only be done after ensuring that the entity being used is of type GraduateStudent. This is therefore an operation that 'recovers' information lost in assignments of the previous kind.

What we conclude from this is that using polymorphism does result in a loss of information at run time. Why, then, do we use this? The answer lies in **dynamic binding**. This ability allows us to invoke methods on members of a class hierarchy without knowing what kind of specific object we are dealing with. To make a rough analogy with the real world, this would be like a manager in a supermarket asking an assistant to put the fruits on display (this is analogous to applying the 'display' method to the 'fruit' object). The assistant looks at the fruit and applies the correct display technique (assuming he wants to keep his job). Here the manager is like a client class invoking the 'display' method and the assistant plays the role of the system and applies dynamic binding.

To get a concrete understanding of how dynamic binding works, let us revisit the example of the Student hierarchy. The code for Student may be written as follows.

```
public abstract class Student {
  private String name;
  private double gpa;
  // more fields
  public Student(String name) {
    this.name = name;
  }
  public String getName() {
    return name;
  }
  public boolean isInGoodStanding() {
    return (gpa >= getGPACutoff());
  }
  public abstract double getGPACutoff();
  // more methods
}
```

In practice, a Student class will be far more complicated; we have omitted a large body of code that would otherwise be present there. The String field name is, as may be guessed, for remembering the name of the student. As you can see, the name of the Student gets initialised in the constructor. The grade point average (GPA) is stored in the double field gpa. As students take classes and complete them, they will get grades, which will be used in computing the GPA. None of that code is shown in this class.

We assume that periodically, perhaps at the end of each semester or quarter, the university will check students to see if they are in 'good standing'. Typically, it would mean ensuring that the student is progressing in a satisfactory manner. We assume that for a student good standing means that the student's GPA meets a certain minimum requirement. The minimum GPA expected of students may change depending on whether the student is an undergraduate or a graduate student. The method getGPACutoff() returns the minimum GPA a student must have to be in good standing. We will assume that this value is 2.0 and 3.0 for undergraduate and graduate students respectively. Note that the method is declared abstract in the `Student` class.

Let us now focus on the code for `UndergraduateStudent`, which is given below.

```
public class UndergraduateStudent extends Student {
  public UndergraduateStudent(String name) {
    super(name);
  }
  public double getGPACutoff() {
    return 2.0;
  }
}
```

The constructor gets the name of the student as its only parameter and calls the superclass's constructor to store it. Since this is a non-abstract class, the `getGPACutoff` method which returns the minimum GPA is implemented.

All of the public and protected[2] methods of a superclass are inherited in the two subclasses. So, the method `isInGoodStanding` can be instantiated on an instance of `UndergraduateStudent` as well. Thus the following code is valid.

```
UndergraduateStudent student = new UndergraduateStudent("Tom");
// code to manipulate student
if (student.isInGoodStanding()) {
  // code
} else {
  // code
}
```

When the method is called, the `isInGoodStanding` method in the superclass `Student` will be invoked.

Finally, we have the code for the class graduate students. The constructor for the class is quite similar to the one for the `UndergraduateStudent` class. To make the class non-abstract, this class, too, should have an implementation of `getGPACutoff`. In addition, we assume that to be in good standing graduate students must meet the requirements imposed on all students and, in addition, they cannot have more than a certain number of courses in which they get a grade below, say, B.

What we would like is a redefinition or **overriding** of the method `isInGood Standing`. Overriding is done by defining a method in a subclass with the same name, return type, and parameters as a method in the superclass so that the subclass's definition takes precedence over the superclass's method. Thus the code for the `isInGoodStanding` method is now different. See below.

```
public class GraduateStudent extends Student {
  public GraduateStudent(String name) {
    super(name);
  }
  public double getGPACutoff() {
```

---

[2]Protected access will be explained shortly.

```
    return 3.0;
  }
  public boolean isInGoodStanding() {
    return super.isInGoodStanding() && checkOutCourses();
  }
  public boolean checkOutCourses() {
    // implementation not shown
  }
}
```

Now, suppose we have the following code.

```
GraduateStudent student = new GraduateStudent("Dick");
// code to manipulate student
if (student.isInGoodStanding()) {
   // code
} else {
   // code
}
```

In this case, the call to isInGoodStanding results in a call to the code defined in the GraduateStudent class. This in turn invokes the code in the Student class and makes further checks using the locally declared method checkOutCourses to arrive at a decision.

Recall the StudentArrayList class we defined in Sect. 2.4 which stores Student objects. The method to add a Student in this class looked as follows:

```
public void add(Student student) {
  // code
}
```

Since a Student reference may point to a UndergraduateStudent or a GraduateStudent object, we can pass objects of either type to the add method and have them stored in the list. For example, the code

```
StudentArrayList students = new StudentArrayList();
UndergraduateStudent student1 = new UndergraduateStudent("Tom");
GraduateStudent student2 = new GraduateStudent("Dick");
students.add(student1);
students.add(student2);
```

stores both objects in the list students.

Suppose the class also had a method to get a Student object stored at a certain index as below.

```
public Student getStudentAt(int index) {
  // Return the Student object at position index.
  // If index is invalid, return null.
}
```

Let us focus on the following code that traverses the list and checks whether the students are in good standing.

```
for (int index = 0; index < students.size(); index++) {
  if (students.getStudentAt(index).isInGoodStanding()) {
    System.out.println(students.get(index).getName()
                          + "is in good standing");
  } else {
    System.out.println(students.getStudentAt(index).getName()
                          + "is not in good standing");
  }
}
```

We assume that students Tom, an undergraduate student, and Dick, a graduate student, are in the list as per the code given a little earlier. The loop will iterate twice, first accessing the object corresponding to Tom and then getting the object for Dick. In both cases, the isInGoodStanding method will be called.

What is interesting about the execution is that the system will determine at run time the method to call, and this decision is based on the actual type of the object. In the case of the first object, we have an instance of UndergraduateStudent, and since there is no definition of the isInGoodStanding method in that class, the system will search for the method in the superclass, Student, and execute that. But when the loop iterates next, the system gets an instance of GraduateStudent, and since there is a definition of the isInGoodStanding method in that class, the overriding definition will be called.

This is a general rule: whenever a method call is encountered, the system will find out the actual type of object referred to by the reference and see if there is a definition for the method in the corresponding class. If so, it will call that method. Otherwise, the search proceeds to the superclass and the process gets repeated. The actual code to be executed is bound dynamically; hence this process is called dynamic binding.

The above code shows the power of dynamic binding. In our calls to isInGood Standing, we were unaware of the type of objects. Simply by examining the code that calls the method, we cannot tell which definition of the isInGoodStanding method will be invoked, i.e., *dynamic binding gives us the ability to hide this detail in the inheritance hierarchy.*

3.2.4 Protected Fields and Methods

Consider the hierarchy as shown in Fig. 3.11. ClosedFigure has an attribute area which stores the area of a ClosedFigure object. Since the classes Polygon and ClosedCurve are kinds of ClosedFigure, we would like to make this attribute available to them. This implies that the attribute cannot be private; on the other hand making it public could lead to inappropriate usage by other clients. The solution to this is found in the protected access specifier. Loosely speaking, what this means is that this field can be accessed by ClosedFigure and its descendants as shown below.

```
public class ClosedFigure extends Figure {
  protected  double area;
  //other fields and methods
```

Fig. 3.11 Figure hierarchy

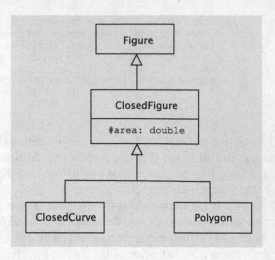

```
  }
public class Polygon extends ClosedFigure {
  public void InsertVertex(Point p, int i) {
    // code to insert vertex at position i
    area = computeArea();
  }
  private double computeArea() {
    //code to compute the area
  }
}
```

Declaring it protected ensures that the field is available to the descendants but cannot be accessed by code that resides outside the hierarchy rooted at ClosedFigure.

The above example is a simple one since the class Polygon is modifying the field of a Polygon object. Consider the following situation.

```
public class ClosedCurve {
  // other fields and methods
  public void areaManipulator(Polygon p) {
    p.area = 0.0;
  }
}
```

Here the class ClosedCurve is modifying the area of a polygon. Our loose definition says that area is visible to ClosedCurve which would make this valid. However, ClosedCurve, is a sibling of Polygon and is therefore not a party to the design constraints of Polygon, and providing such access could compromise the integrity of our code. In fact, an unscrupulous client could easily do the following:

```
class BackDoor extends ClosedFigure {
  public void setArea(double area, ClosedFigure someClosedFigure) {
    someClosedFigure.area = area;
  }
}
```

We therefore need the following stricter definition of protected access.

The code residing in a class A may access a protected attribute of an object of class B only if B is at least of type A, i.e., B belongs to the hierarchy rooted at A.

With this definition, methods such as `setArea` in `BackDoor` would violate the protected access (since `ClosedFigure` is not a subclass of `BackDoor`) and can be caught at compile time. The compiler will not raise an objection if `someClosedFigure` is cast as `BackDoor` as shown below.

```
((BackDoor) someClosedFigure).area = area;
```

If `someClosedFigure` contained a reference to a `Polygon` object, the cast would fail at runtime preventing the access to the protected field.

3.2.5 The Object Class

Java has a special class called `Object` from which every class inherits. In other words, `Object` is a superclass of every class in Java and is at the root of class hierarchy. From our knowledge of polymorphic assignments, we can see that a variable of type `Object` can store the reference to an object of any other type. The following code is thus legal.

```
Object anyObject;
anyObject = new Student();
anyObject = new Integer(4);
anyObject = "Some string";
```

In the above, the variable `anyObject` first stores a `Student` object, then an `Integer` object, and finally a `String` object.

3.3 Genericity

Genericity is a mechanism for creating entities that vary only in the types of their parameters, and this notion can be associated with any entity (class or method) that requires parameters of some specific types. As we have seen before, in the definition of any entity, the types of involved parameters are specified. In case of a method, we specify the types of arguments and the return type. In case of a class, the types of arguments to the constructor(s), the return types and argument types of the methods are all specified. In any instance of the entity, the actual types of all these parameters must conform to the corresponding types specified in the definition. When we specify a generic entity, the types of the parameters are replaced by placeholders, which are called *generic parameters*. The entity is therefore *not fully specified* and cannot be used as such to instantiate any concrete objects. At the time of creating artifacts (objects, if our generic entity was a class), these placeholders must be replaced by actual types.

To understand the usefulness of genericity, consider the following implementation of a stack:

```
public class Stack {
  private class StackNode {
    Object data;
    StackNode next;
    // rest of the class not shown
  }
  public void push(Object data) {
    // implementation not shown
  }
  public Object pop() {
    // implementation not shown
  }
  // rest of the class not shown
}
```

Elements of the stack are stored in the data field of StackNode. Notice that data is of type Object, which means that any type of data can be stored in it.

We create a stack and store an Integer object in it.

```
Stack myIntStack = new Stack(); // line 1
myIntStack.push(new Integer(5)); // line 2
Integer x = (Integer) myIntStack.pop(); //line 3
```

This implementation has some drawbacks. In line 2, there is nothing that prevents us from pushing arbitrary objects into the stack. The following code, for instance, is perfectly valid.

```
Stack myIntStack = new Stack();
myIntStack.push("A string");
```

The reason for this is that the Stack class creates a stack of Object and will, therefore, accept any object as an argument for push. The second drawback follows from the same cause; the following code will generate an error.

```
Stack myIntStack = new Stack();
myIntStack.push("A string");
Integer x = (Integer) myIntStack.pop(); // erroneous cast
```

We could write extra code that handles the errors due to the erroneous cast, but it does not make for readable code. On the other hand, we could write a separate Stack class for every kind of stack that we need, but then we are unable to reuse our code.

Generics provides us with a way out of this dilemma. A generic Stack class would be defined something like this:

```
public class Stack<E> {
  //code for fields and constructors
  public void push(E item) {
    // code to push item into stack
  }
  public E pop() {
```

```
        // code to push item into stack
    }
}
```

A `Stack` that stores only `Integer` objects can now be defined as

```
Stack<Integer>myIntStack = new Stack<Integer>();
```

The statement

```
myIntStack.push("A string");
```

will trigger an error message from the compiler, which expects that the parameter to the `push` method of `myIntStack` will be a subtype of `Integer`.

3.4 Discussion and Further Reading

In this chapter we have discussed how classes in an object-oriented system relate to one another. Association is the simplest and most general of these. Although this chapter touches on several aspects of associations, a more detailed study of UML notation and some of the finer points of using associations would be needed before embarking on a serious project. UML notation provides a mechanism for another kind of relationship between classes, called a **dependency**. A dependency occurs when a client class has knowledge of some aspect of a supplier class and a change in the supplier class could affect the client. A detailed treatment of class relationships and other related issues can be found in [1].

A thorough knowledge of inheritance is vital to anyone engaging in OOAD. While the notion of a class helps us implement abstract data types, it is inheritance that makes the object-oriented paradigm so powerful. Inheriting from a superclass makes it possible not only to reuse existing code in the superclass, but also to view instances of all subclasses as members of the superclass type. Polymorphic assignments combined with dynamic binding of methods makes it possible to allow uniform processing of objects without having to worry about their exact types.

Dynamic binding is implemented using a table of method pointers that give the address of the methods in the class. When a method is overridden, the table in the extending class points to the new definition of the method. For an easily understandable treatment of this approach, the reader may consult Eckel [2].

There is some overhead associated with dynamic binding. In C++, the programmer can specify that a method is *virtual*, which means that dynamic binding will be used during method invocation. Methods not defined as virtual will be called using the declared type of the reference used in the call. This helps the programmer avoid the overhead associated with dynamic binding in method calls that do not really need the power of dynamic binding. In C++ parlance, all Java methods are virtual.

In Java, it is important to note that dynamic binding is not tied to subclassing. It is also applicable in the context of interfaces. For instance, consider the situation where `Student` is not a class, but an interface.

```
public interface Student {
  public boolean isInGoodStanding();
  public abstract double getGPACutoff();
  public String getName();
  // more methods
}
```

Let us assume that the above interface is implemented by the classes
`UndergraduateStudent` and `GraduateStudent`. The implementation is
simple enough, so we do not show the code for it; the only major difference now
is that since there is no subclassing, the `isInGoodStanding()` of `Graduate`
`Student` cannot issue the call `super.isInGoodStanding()` but must compute it locally.

Now, the code given earlier and reproduced below, works via dynamic binding.

```
for (int index = 0; index < students.size(); index++) {
  if (students.getStudentAt(index).isInGoodStanding()) {
    System.out.println(students.get(index).getName()
                          + "is in good standing");
  } else {
    System.out.println(students.get(index).getName()
                          + "is not in good standing");
  }
}
```

Genericity is a very restrictive relationship that can exist between classes and is not
particularly associated with OOAD. However, it is available in most object-oriented
languages and must be used judiciously to facilitate reuse.

3.4.1 A Generalised Notion of Conformance

Most high-level languages perform some kind of type-checking when an assignment
is done. This checking is used to ascertain that the type of entity returned by the
expression on the left-hand side (LHS) of the assignment can indeed be stored in the
type of entity referenced on the RHS. In other words, we say that the type of entity
returned by the expression on the left-hand side (LHS) of the assignment conforms
to the type of entity referenced on the RHS. If conformance is not there, some kind
of casting is required, but the results of the casts cannot be guaranteed by a compiler
since they depend on run-time behaviour.

In the context of inheritance, we have seen that a subclass conforms to the type of
the superclass. When we add genericity to the mix, and the expression on the LHS
evaluates to an instance of a generically defined entity; the corresponding generic
parameters of the LHS and RHS must also be in conformance. This check would have
to be performed recursively since the parameters could themselves be generically
derived [3]. Given the following definitions,

```
public class Polygon {
  // code for Polygon
}
```

```
public class Triangle extends Polygon {
  // code for Triangle
}

public class Square extends Polygon {
  // code for Square
}
```

the generic types `Stack<Square>` and `Stack<Triangle>` conform to `Stack <Polygon>`. However, an assignment of the kind shown below is flagged by a Java compiler.

```
Stack<Square> ssq = new Stack<Square>();
Stack<Polygon> sp = ssq; // Compiler Error!
```

The reason for this appears to be that generics being a later introduction to Java, interoperability with legacy code was required. This was achieved by a mechanism called *erasure*, which resulted in all generic type information being erased at compile time. This implies that if the above statement was not flagged as an error, there is no way that the system could prevent the pushing of a triangle on a stack of squares.

```
Stack<Square> ssq = new Stack<Square>();
Stack<Polygon> sp = ssq;
sp.push(new Triangle()); // no way to detect this
```

Some languages allow for *dynamic casts* which is one way that this situation can be handled. In C++, for instance, the following code would compile, but generate a run-time error [4].

```
Stack<Triangle> * TStack = new  Stack<Triangle>();
Stack <Polygon> * PStack;
PStack = dynamic_cast<Stack <Polygon> *> (TStack); // valid, types conform
Square * s1 = new Square();
Polygon * p1 = dynamic_cast<Polygon*>(s1);
PStack->push(*p1); // run-time error
```

The system keeps track of the fact that `PStack` is a pointer to a `Stack<Triangle>` and that `*p1` is in fact a `Square`.

Projects

1. Implement the interface `Extendable` in Programming Project 3 in Chap. 3 with a class named `AbstractBuffer`. This class stores an array of `chars` whose initial capacity is passed via a constructor.

   The class must have two fields, both `protected`; one stores the `char` array and the other stores the number of elements actually filled in the array.

   Do not implement either of the interface methods. So the class is declared `abstract`.

   This class must also implement the `toString()` method to correctly bring back a `String` representation of the `char` array.

   Next, implement `SimpleBuffer` so that it extends `AbstractBuffer` and actually implements the interface methods correctly. As before, it has a constructor that accepts the size of the array.

2. Consider the interface Shape given below.

```
public interface Shape {
  public double getArea();
  public double getPerimeter();
  public void draw();
}
```

Design and code two classes, Rectangle and Circle, that implement Shape. Put as many common attributes and methods as possible in an abstract class from which Rectangle and Circle inherit. Ensure that your code is modular. For drawing a shape, simply print the shape type and other information associated with the object.

Next, implement the following interface using any strategy you like. The interface maintains a collection of shapes. The draw method draws every shape in the collection.

```
public interface Shapes {
  public void add(Shape shape);
  public void draw();
}
```

Then, test your implementation by writing a driver that creates some Shape objects, puts them in the collection and draws them.

Finally, draw the UML diagram for the classes and interfaces you developed for this exercise.

3. The following interface specifies a data source which consists of a number of x-values and the corresponding set of y-values. The method getNumberOf Points returns the number of x-values for which there is a corresponding y-value. getX (getY) returns the x-value (y-value) for a specific index ($0 \le$ index $<$ getNumberOfPoints).

```
public interface DataSource {
  public int getNumberOfPoints();
  public int getX(int index);
  public int getY(int index);
}
```

The next interface is for a chart that can be used to display a specific data source.

```
public interface Chart {
  public void setDataSource(DataSource sourse);
  public void display();
}
```

A user will create a DataSource object, put some values in it, create a Chart object, use the former as the data source for the latter and then call display to display the data.

Here is a possible use. Note that MyDataSource and LineChart are implementations of DataSource and Chart respectively.

```
DataSource source = new MyDataSource();
Char chart = new LineChart();
chart.setDataSource(source);
chart.display();
```

Implement the interface `DataSource` in a class `MyDataSource`. Have methods in it to store x and y values.

Provide two implementations of `Chart`: `LineChart` and `BarChart`. For displaying the chart, simply print out the x and y values and the type of chart being printed. If needed, put the common functionality in an abstract superclass.

Draw the UML diagram for your design.

4. Implement three classes:

   `BinaryTreeNode`, `BinaryTree` and `BinarySearchTree`.

   The first class implements the functionality of a node in a binary tree, the second is an abstract class that has methods for visiting the tree, computing its height, etc., and the third class extends the second to implement the functionality of a binary search tree.

3.5 Exercises

1. Trace the following code and write that the program prints

```
public class A {
  protected int i;
  public void modify(int x) {
    i = x + 8;
    System.out.println("A: i is" + i);
  }
  public int getI() {
    System.out.println("A: i is" + i);
    return i;
  }
}
public class B extends A {
  protected int j;
  public void modify(int x) {
    System.out.println("B: x is" + x);
    super.modify(x);
    j = x + 2;
    System.out.println("B: j is" + j);
  }
  public int getI() {
    System.out.println("B: j is" + j);
    return super.getI() + j;
  }
}
public class UseB {
  public static void main(String[] s) {
    A a1 = new A();
    a1.modify(4);
    System.out.println(a1.getI());
    B b1 = new B();
    b1.modify(5);
    System.out.println(b1.getI());
    a1 = b1;
    a1.modify(6);
    System.out.println(a1.getI());
  }
}
```

2. Consider the class `Rectangle` in Programming Exercise 2. Extend it to implement a square.
3. A manager at a small zoo instructs the zoo-keeper to 'feed the animals'. Explain how a proper completion of this task by the zoo-keeper implies that the zoo operations are implicitly employing the concepts of inheritance, polymorphism and dynamic binding. (Hint: defining a class `Animal` with method `feed` could prove helpful.)

References

1. C. Larman, *Applying UML and Patterns* (Prentice Hall PTR, New Jersey, 1998)
2. B. Eckel, *Thinking in C++ Volume 1 (2nd Edition)* (Prentice Hall, New Jersey, 2000)
3. B. Meyer, *Object-Oriented Software Construction* (Prentice Hall, New Jersey, 1997)
4. P. Anderson, G. Anderson, *Navigating C++ and Object-Oriented Design* (Prentice Hall, New Jersey, 1998)

Chapter 4
Language Features for Object-Oriented Implementation

Many modern programming language features can be divided into two parts: basic features that are essential to use the programming paradigm and supporting concepts that are needed to facilitate the construction of more complex systems. So far, we have covered core language issues for the object-oriented paradigm, such as classes, inheritance, interfaces, and so on.

In this chapter we will study several concepts that fall in the supporting category. We begin in Sect. 4.1 with a study of how to organise source files (and class files) in a Java application. Following this, in Sect. 4.2, we look at an important type of class called collection class.

In Sect. 4.3 we study exceptions, which are situations in which the system reports an error and abandons the current operation. Dynamic binding in object-oriented languages leads to situations where a type of an object has to be determined explicitly by the program at runtime; this necessitates the need for run time type identification (RTTI), which is introduced in Sect. 4.4. In Sect. 4.5 we study how to build graphical user interface (GUI) programs. The problem of providing long-term storage of objects is discussed in Sect. 4.6.

While these concepts are not directly related to each other, they are all widely regarded as being essential for software system design today, and the reader must gain a reasonable grasp of these topics before undertaking the analysis and design of object-oriented systems (which we start in Chap. 6).

4.1 Organising the Classes

In any complex system, it is essential that the components be located in a manner that facilitates easy access. Classes and interfaces are modules that make up our software system and our first order of business is to have a system for organising these.

© Universities Press (India) Private Ltd. 2015
B. Dathan and S. Ramnath, *Object-Oriented Analysis, Design and Implementation*,
Undergraduate Topics in Computer Science, DOI 10.1007/978-3-319-24280-4_4

4.1.1 Creating the Files

There are some general rules and conventions related to file organisation. Typical practice is to put at most one class or interface in a single file. The file must be named <class/interface name>.java. Java requires that with more than one class or interface in a file, only one of the outer classes/interfaces can be public; if there is a public class/interface in a file, the name of that class/interface must be used for naming the file.

4.1.2 Packages

One major theme in object-oriented paradigm is reuse. This decreases development time, reduces code size, and increases reliability. The Java language comes with a large number of classes (numbering in the thousands) that can be used for a variety of uses: networking, GUI, database management, and so on.

We will use some classes from Java quite extensively so that we can focus more on the design issues. This is also consistent with the theme of reuse.

The Java classes are spread over what are called **packages**, which we briefly discuss here.

A package is a collection of classes. It is usually named as a sequence of lower-case letters and periods. Some of the major packages are java.lang, java.util, java.awt, javax.swing, java.io, and java.lang.reflect.

The package java.lang contains classes and interfaces that are fundamental to the language. These include String, Thread, Runnable, Integer, Double, etc. The package java.util contains interfaces and classes for storing lists and sets, among others. Graphical programs can make use of members in java.awt and/or javax.swing. To perform input and output, one may use the package java.io. Classes and interfaces can be interrogated using java.lang.reflect, which is said to be a sub-package of java.lang.

Java automatically makes the classes and interfaces in the java.lang package available. Programs that use classes from other packages must, however, **import** them from the appropriate package. For instance, to use the class Vector which resides in java.util, the code must resort to one of the several approaches.

One way is to prefix the class name with the name of the package.

```
java.util.Vector myVector = new java.util.Vector();
```

The above can be cumbersome and few programmers resort to it.

A second approach is to import that class. Write

```
import java.util.Vector;
```

This is fine if the code is using only a few classes from a package. To import all of the members of a package, code as below.

```
import java.util.*;
```

There is no serious drawback to doing the above. In some cases, class/interface names from two packages may conflict, which then has to be resolved by prefixing the class name with the package name in the code itself.

Also, note that importing all members of a package does not import sub-packages. For example, although there are packages java.awt and java.awt.image, the statement

```
import java.awt.*;
```

does not import the class java.awt.image.ColorModel. We need to write

```
import java.awt.image.*;
```

as a separate statement.

Users can put classes they create in their own package by writing

```
package <package-name>;
```

This must appear as the first statement in the file.

After compilation, the class file must be copied into a sub-directory with the same name as the package name. This sub-directory must appear within a directory that is listed in the environment variable CLASSPATH, the setting of which is dependent on the operating system.

4.1.3 Protected Access and Package Access

We have seen the use of protected access specifier in Chap. 3. Suppose we have a field x defined as protected in a class C. Then, the field can also be accessed in classes that reside in the same package as C. For example, the following code is legal.

```
package mypackage;
public class C {
   protected int x;
}
package mypackage;
import mypackage.C;
```

```
public class D {
  public void f(C c) {
    c.x = 1;
  }
}
```

If we omit any explicit access specifier in the definition of a method or field, the access is said to be a package access, which means that only the code residing in a class within the same package can access the method or field.

4.2 Collection Classes

The java.util package contains a number of useful interfaces and classes that we will use in our examples. The interface java.util.Collection, for instance, contains methods for manipulating a collection. Some of the methods in this interface are:

1. boolean add(Object object): adds the supplied object to the collection.
2. boolean addAll(Collection collection): adds all objects in the supplied collection to this collection.
3. void clear(): removes all of the elements from this collection.
4. boolean contains(Object object): returns true if and only if this collection contains the supplied object.
5. int size(): returns the number of elements in this collection.
6. Methods for removing objects, checking if the collection is empty, etc.

The List interface extends Collection. A list is a collection of objects where the objects are put in a sequence. Thus, it has all the methods that pertain to a collection and the ones that are specific to lists such as void add(int index, Object object) which inserts the given object at the position specified by the index in this list.

There are two major implementations of List: LinkedList and ArrayList. The names of the classes indicate how they are implemented.

Using the above classes, it is easy to create and use lists. The following simple class creates a sequence of String objects, stores them in a list, and prints the list.

```
import java.util.*;
public class ListUseExample {
  public static void main(String[] s) {
    List list = new ArrayList();
    for (int count = 1; count <= 10; count++) {
      list.add(new String("String " + count));
    }
```

```
        for (int count = 0; count <= 9; count++) {
          System.out.println(list.get(count));
        }
      }
    }
```

Since `ArrayList` implements the `List` interface, the following code is legal:

```
    List list = new ArrayList();
```

Into this list we are adding 10 Strings, '`"String1"` through `"String10"`. The add method adds at the end of the list. Lists are indexed from 0, so `"String1"` is at index 0 and `"String10"` is at index 9. The `get` method returns the element at the specified index. The second `for` loop prints the `String` objects at positions 0 through 9.

4.3 Exceptions

We saw in Chap. 3 that casting an objectto a type to which it does not conform causes an error. More specifically, the system throws an **exception**, which results in a crash. This is a rather loose description of what happens, and the following discussion is more accurate and complete.

Recall the Chap. 3 example of the three classes, `Student`, `Undergraduate Student`, and `GraduateStudent`, where the last two classes inherit from the first. The following code has a problem because we are casting an `Undergraduate Student` object as a `GraduateStudent` object. We are asking the system to do something that it cannot.

```
    Student student = new UndergraduateStudent();
    GraduateStudent graduateStudent = (GraduateStudent) student;
```

To be more precise, when the code reaches the second line and the cast is attempted, the system abandons the operation, generates an object that represents this abnormal operation, and **throws** the object. This and similar problematic situations always cause a `Throwable` object to be generated and thrown and the offending operation to be abandoned. The specific type of the object depends on the type of operation. Here are some examples.

1. An attempt is made to access an array with an invalid index. The object generated is of type `ArrayIndexOutOfBoundsException`.
2. A null reference is used to access a field or method of an object. In this case, the object generated is of type `NullPointerException`.

3. An error occurs while an input or output operation occurs. The object in this case is of type `IOException`.
4. An attempt to cast an object fails as in the student example. The exception type is called `ClassCastException`.

If we want to avoid a crash because of a bad cast or any other erroneous piece of code, we have to put the offending code within a try block and catch the exception object.

```
try {
    Student student = new UndergraduateStudent();
    GraduateStudent graduateStudent = (GraduateStudent) student;
    // process the object
} catch (ClassCastException cce) {
    // Object is not of type graduate student.
    // do some operation to recover from the error
}
```

An application may choose to catch exceptions that its code may throw; for this, these statements have to be enclosed in a `try` block. The block begins with the keyword `try` followed by the left-curly bracket {, a sequence of statements (that may have any statements including more try blocks) ending with a }. This should be followed by at least one `catch` block.

A catch block begins with the keyword `catch` followed by a pair of parentheses with an exception name (which is a class name) and a reference to refer to the exception object. The catch block typically contains code to rectify the problem.

When a statement in a `try` block throws an exception, the system throws an object of a certain exception type and the try block is abandoned. The system then checks to see if there is a `catch` block for that exception type associated with this `try` block. If so, that `catch` block is entered and the code in it is executed. Once the `catch` block is entered, the exception is caught and this instance of the exception cannot crash the program.

Let us trace the above code for the case. When the class cast is performed, Java throws an object of type `ClassCastException`. The rest of the code, including the assignment in the `try` block is abandoned. Java searches to see if there is a `catch` block for the type of the exception raised, which is `ClassCastException`. Since there is one, the corresponding `catch` block is entered and the code in it is executed. The parameter `cce` refers to the object thrown.

We can put multiple `catch` blocks for a single `try` block. Here is a piece of code that handles three different types of exceptions:

```
try {
    if (myObject.getField1().equals(someObject)) {
        int index = myObject.getIndex();
        int value = Integer.parseInt(JOptionPane.showInputDialog(null,
                                     "Enter a number"));
```

```
    myArray[index] = value;
  } catch (NullPointerException npe) {
    System.out.println("Null pointer " + npe);
    System.exit(0);
  } catch (ArrayIndexOutOfBoundsException aiofbe) {
    System.out.println("Array index out of range " + aiofbe);
    return;
  } catch (NumberFormatException nfe) {
    System.out.println("Invalid entry; exception " + nfe);
    return;
  }
}
```

NumberFormatException occurs when we try to convert a string that does not have a numeric value in it to a number.

Although the above pieces of code are technically correct, we should not, in general, use try and catch blocks to handle exceptions such as ArrayIndexOut OfBoundsException and NullPointerException because they can be avoided by properly debugging the program. On the other hand, there is a class of exceptions called **checked exceptions** that can occur even in correct programs. The try and catch blocks are appropriate for processing such checked exceptions. *One of the characteristics of a well-designed software system is that it appropriately uses exceptions to handle unexpected situations.*

4.4 Run-Time Type Identification

Although polymorphism and dynamic binding are powerful tools, they are not sufficient to take care of all the issues that arise when dealing with an inheritance hierarchy. Consider, for example, a Shape class with two subclasses, Square and Circle. Let ShapeList be a collection of Shape. If we access an item from this collection, we know that it will be of type Shape, but we do not know whether it will be a Square or a Circle.

Say, we have an application that needs to know the number of Circle objects in a ShapeList collection. This could be implemented as a public method in ShapeList.

    public int circleCount()
or as a client method that takes a reference to a ShapeList.

    int circleCount(Shapelist shapeList)
In either case, the method will iterate through all the items in the collection, check which ones are of type Circle, etc. We therefore need some mechanism to detect whether a given Shape object is a Circle. Applying polymorphism and dynamic binding would suggest that we have a method in the Shape class (named isCircle, say,) that returns true when a Shape object is a Circle, but having

such a method defeats the purpose of having dynamic binding in the first place! Also, such a solution would be inelegant if we had a large hierarchy.

A more subtle problem arises with client methods. Consider a class `Investment` with two subclasses `Deposit` and `Stock`. A deposit would accrue interest, whereas stocks pay dividend. A client method that computes taxes would look something like this:

```
double computeTax(Investment investment) {
    // find the total amount of income from the investment
    // and take appropriate action
}
```

In case of `Stock` objects, `computeTax` would invoke a method `getDividend` whereas for `Deposit` objects, the method `getInterest` would be invoked. In this case, we have a situation where methods needed for one subclass do not make sense for sibling classes.

Although such scenarios are not very common, we need a mechanism that can handle these. All object-oriented languages provide some form of **run-time type identification (RTTI)** that can take care of these situations cleanly. In the first example, we need a mechanism to test whether a given `Shape` object is a `Circle`, whereas in the second, we want to be sure that we downcast the `Investment` object correctly and apply the right method.

RTTI in Java can be done in one of three ways. In the rest of this section, we elaborate the approaches.

4.4.1 Reflection: Using the `Class` Object

Java supports the notion of **reflection** which is based on the notion of a special class known as `Class`. Associated with each class is a `Class` object, a reference to which can be obtained using the `getClass` method. The `Class` object, which is automatically created at run time, belongs to the class `Class`. This class has several methods that can be invoked to find out various properties of the class, such as the name, the list of fields and methods, etc. In particular, the method `getName` returns a `String` object holding the name of the class. To check if a given `Shape` object is a `Circle` using these methods, we do the following:

```
Shape shape;
// code to create a Shape object
// and store its reference in shape
if (shape.getClass().getName().equals("Circle")) {
    // take appropriate action
}
```

The method getClass() is defined by Java for the Object class, and is therefore automatically available for any user-defined class. In our example, getClass returns an object that stores information about the Circle class, and the method getName on that object returns the string "Circle". While this serves our purpose, it suffers from one drawback: *the compiler cannot check for typographical errors in the string against which we are checking the name.* The following code, for instance, would compile correctly.

```
Shape shape;
// code to create s Shape object
// and store its reference in shape
if (shape.getClass().getName().equals("circle")) {
  // take appropriate action
}
```

Typing "circle" instead of "Circle" gives us an incorrect answer because the error in code cannot be caught by the compiler.

4.4.2 Using the `instanceof` Operator

This problem that we talked about above can be resolved if we use the instanceof operator to query the type of an object. Our code would the look like this:

```
Shape shape;
// code to create s Shape object
// and store its reference in shape
if (shape instanceof Circle) {
  // take appropriate action
}
```

The operator returns true if the object shape is an instance of the class Circle. In this case, the compiler ensures that Circle is a known class and flags an error otherwise. In case of the computeTax method, we create a similar solution.

```
double computeTax(Investment investment) {
  double amount;
  if (investment instanceof Deposit) {
    amount = (Deposit) investment.getInterest();
    // code for computing tax on amount
  } else if (investment instanceof Stock) {
    amount = (Stock) investment.getDividend();
    // code for computing tax amount
  }
  // return tax
}
```

The example above seems to suggest that using the `instanceof` operator is always a better alternative to using `getClass().getName()`, but that is not the case. In some situations `instanceof` does not give us sufficient information since it would return `true` for all ancestors. An example of a situation where `instanceof` cannot be used is given in Chap. 5.

4.4.3 Downcasting

As we know from Chap. 3, we can cast a superclass reference to a subclass. For example, we could code

```
double computeTax(Investment investment) {
  double amount;
  Deposit deposit = (Deposit) investment;
  amount = deposit.getInterest();
  // code for computing tax on amount
  // rest of the method not shown
}
```

The downcast could, of course, fail, in which case the system throws an instance of `ClassCastException`. Although `ClassCastException` is a `Runtime Exception` and should not normally be caught, this could be considered an appropriate situation where it should be handled. We can rewrite the method as below.

```
double computeTax(Investment investment) {
  double amount;
  try {
    Deposit deposit = (Deposit) investment;
    amount = deposit.getInterest();
    // code for computing tax on amount
  } catch(ClassCastException cce) {
    try {
      Stock stock = (Stock) investment;
      amount = stock.getInterest();
      // code for computing tax on amount
    } catch(ClassCastException cce) {
      cce.printStackTrace();
    }
  }
  // return tax
}
```

The example above seems to suggest that downcasting and the `instanceof` operator can be used interchangeably. Although they are functionally equivalent, there is a stylistic difference in that exceptions, ideally, should not be thrown unless an exceptional situation occurs. In Chap. 10 we find a situation where downcasting is a natural solution to the problem at hand, and in Chap. 11 we have an example of a situation where the `instanceof` operator provides an elegant solution.

4.5 Graphical User Interfaces: Programming Support

In this section we discuss the basics of creating graphical user interfaces (GUI) in Java. We would like to emphasise the word 'basics'. The goal is to help the reader create simple GUIs and provide him/her with enough knowledge to explore and understand the extensive functionality provided by Java in this area.

Java GUI programs can take two forms: **applets** and **applications**. Applets are programs that need a web browser to live in; in other words, the applet occupies part of a web page. When a page containing an applet is downloaded, the applet comes along with the web page and gets executed by the browser. This helps provide more functionality than is otherwise possible using just text and graphics. We do not cover applets in this book.

GUI applications are standalone programs that can be executed like any other program but providing a graphical interface. They are only slightly more complicated to program than applets. With a knowledge of GUI applications, the reader should have little difficulty in learning to create applets.

4.5.1 The Basics

As a first step in grasping the fundamentals of GUI creation, let us take a simple GUI application and understand it. For this, consider the user interface given in Fig. 4.1.

Fig. 4.1 A sample GUI screen

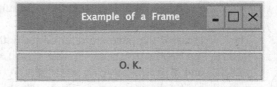

Let us break the shown interface into several parts.

1. An outer window with the title 'Example of a Frame', the minimise, maximise, and close buttons.
2. A white box, in which, although not obvious from the picture, the user can enter some text.
3. A button labelled 'O.K'.

Next, we will see the major steps in creating the interface from a programmer's perspective.

1. Create the window: The system will do most of the hard work. The programmer essentially says that a window is needed; the title for the window also can be supplied. The system draws the outline, the title bar, and supplies the three buttons: close, minimise, and maximise.
   A common class used for creating the window is JFrame. A possible code for creating the window is

   ```
   new JFrame("Example of a Frame");
   ```

2. Create the two widgets, the text box and the button. The text box is created using the Java class JTextField, and the button is created using the class JButton. The system, once again, will perform the operations necessary to draw the two widgets.
   The first line in the following code fragment creates the button. Notice that we pass the label for the button while constructing it. The second line obviously constructs the text field. The parameter for the text field contains the length in characters for this widget. (We would like to note that the resulting text field's size may not precisely fit the number of characters specified as parameter.)

   ```
   JButton button1 = new JButton("O.K.");
   JTextField textField1 = new JTextField(20);
   ```

3. Next, we put the widgets in the frame. The frame has several **panes**. The widgets are stored in what is termed the **content pane.** While adding, we need to specify where the widgets should be added. By default, the content pane of a frame is divided into five parts as shown in Fig. 4.2.
   The five areas of the pane are referred to by the constants BorderLayout. SOUTH, BorderLayout.NORTH, BorderLayout.WEST, BorderLayout .EAST, and BorderLayout.CENTER. A widget is added by issuing the method add on the content pane object, which is obtained by issuing the method getContentPane on the frame. The add method requires the widget reference and the area of the pane; If no area is specified, the widget is stored in the centre area. Thus, in the code below, the text field is stored in the centre, whereas the button is stored in the south.

Fig. 4.2 Border layout

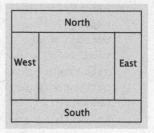

```
        frame.getContentPane().add(textField1);
        frame.getContentPane().add(button1, BorderLayout.SOUTH);
```

4. Until this time, the frame is not visible. The last step in this example is to display it. This is done by first issuing the `pack` method on the frame so that it is sized to fit the preferred size of the widgets based on the current layout.

```
        frame.pack();
        frame.setVisible(true);
```

The complete code for the example is given below.

```
import javax.swing.*;
import java.awt.*;
public class FrameDemo {
  public static void main(String[] s) {
    JFrame frame = new JFrame("Example of a Frame");
    JButton button1 = new JButton("O.K.");
    JTextField textField1 = new JTextField(20);
    frame.getContentPane().add(textField1);
    frame.getContentPane().add(button1, BorderLayout.SOUTH);
    frame.pack();
    frame.setVisible(true);
  }
}
```

The classes `JFrame`, `JTextField`, and `JButton` are in the package `javax.swing`, whereas `BorderLayout` resides in `java.awt`.

Another way of getting the same result is to make `FrameDemo` a subclass of `JFrame` and have the button and text field as fields. The code is given below.

```
import javax.swing.*;
import java.awt.*;
public class FrameDemo2 extends JFrame {
  private JButton button1;
  private JTextField textField1;
```

```
public FrameDemo2(String title) {
  super(title);
  button1 = new JButton("O.K.");
  textField1 = new JTextField(20);
  getContentPane().add(textField1);
  getContentPane().add(button1, BorderLayout.SOUTH);
  pack();
  setVisible(true);
}
public static void main(String[] s) {
  new FrameDemo2("Example of a Frame");
}
}
```

4.5.2 Event Handling

The program we developed in the previous section does not really do anything useful. The three buttons, minimise, maximise, and close, work, but that functionality is provided by the system itself.

To make a Java GUI application do anything useful when users interact with it, we need to handle events. Whenever the user does something on the widgets, for example clicking a button or hitting the enter key while the cursor is in a text field, the system generates what are known as **events.** The default action for events is to do nothing. The programmer must decide what should happen when events occur.

Event handling is best explained via an example. Taking a button click as an example, we first note that such an event generates an action event, represented by the class ActionEvent in the package java.awt.event. However, that event does not result in any meaningful action unless some object **listens** to it and takes some action in response.

To process action events, therefore, two things must happen.

1. An object must become a listener to an action event by implementing the interface ActionListener (in the package java.awt.event). An example is given below.

```
public class SomeClass implements ActionListener {
```

Java then knows that objects of type SomeClass are capable of handling action events. The interface itself is implemented by coding the method action Performed, which is the only method in ActionListener. This method has just one parameter, which is of type ActionEvent and represents the event.

```
public class SomeClass implements ActionListener {
  // fields and other methods
  public void actionPerformed(ActionEvent event) {
    // code to process the event
  }
}
```

2. It is not enough for a class (and thus objects of the class) to have the ability to process events; it must also request that it be told of those events. Suppose that button1 is of type JButton. Then the following code in SomeClass requests that objects of type SomeClass be notified when action events occur on that button.

```
button1.addActionListener(this);
```

Let us now modify the GUI program, FrameDemo2, so that whenever the button is clicked, the program displays some message. We will make it a little more interesting by actually displaying how many times the button was clicked.

For this, we need to remember the number of times the button was clicked; this is done by introducing a field in FrameDemo2. The code for actionPerformed is then

```
public void actionPerformed(ActionEvent event) {
  textField1.setText("You clicked " + ++count + " times so far.");
}
```

A shortcoming of the program is that when the close button is clicked, the frame disappears, but the process itself remains. What really happens is that the GUI part of the application has exited but the non-GUI part is still alive. Clicking on the close button is a type of event called window event. As you might expect, there is a class called WindowEvent, and, you guessed it right, an interface called WindowListener, again in the package java.awt.event.

However, there are seven methods in this interface. They correspond to actions on the window such as making it an icon, activating it, closing it, etc. Only one of these actions is relevant, which is handled by putting some code within the method called windowClosing as shown next.

```
public void windowClosing(WindowEvent event) {
  System.exit(0);
}
```

The complete code for the new version is given below.

```
import javax.swing.*;
import java.awt.*;
import java.awt.event.*;
public class FrameDemo2 extends JFrame implements
                     ActionListener, WindowListener {
  private JButton button1;
  private JTextField textField1;
  private int count;
  public FrameDemo2(String title) {
    super(title);
    button1 = new JButton("O.K.");
    textField1 = new JTextField(20);
    getContentPane().add(textField1);
    getContentPane().add(button1, BorderLayout.SOUTH);
    button1.addActionListener(this);
    addWindowListener(this);
    pack();
    setVisible(true);
  }
  public void windowOpened(WindowEvent event) {
  }
  public void windowIconified(WindowEvent event) {
  }
  public void windowDeiconified(WindowEvent event) {
  }
  public void windowClosed(WindowEvent event) {
  }
  public void windowActivated(WindowEvent event) {
  }
  public void windowDeactivated(WindowEvent event) {
  }
  public void windowClosing(WindowEvent event) {
    System.exit(0);
  }
  public void actionPerformed(ActionEvent event) {
    textField1.setText("You clicked " + ++count + " times so far.");
  }
  public static void main(String[] s) {
    new FrameDemo2("Example of a Frame");
  }
}
```

Another type of widget that we will use in this book is a **label**, which displays a piece of text or an image. It cannot be used by the user to enter information.

Here is how to create a label.

```
JLabel nameLabel = new JLabel("Name:");
```

The usual method of adding widgets applies to labels as well.

4.5.3 *More on Widgets and Layouts*

Let us now extend the program to have two buttons side by side in the 'southern' part of the frame. Our goal here is to display different messages when the two buttons are pressed.

The problem presents two difficulties:

1. We can put only one widget directly in `BorderLayout.SOUTH`.
2. We need to know which button is clicked.

To handle the first situation, we introduce a new container called a panel, available via the class `JPanel`. Suppose that `button1` and `button2` are `JButton` objects. Then, we create a `JPanel` object and put the buttons in it, and then put the panel itself in the content pane as shown below.

```
JPanel panel = new JPanel();
panel.add(button1);
panel.add(button2);
getContentPane().add(panel, BorderLayout.SOUTH);
```

Notice that we issue the `add` method on the panel object itself because it has a much simpler organisation than `JFrame`. Panels add the widgets from left to right.

To handle clicks, we need to listen to their occurrences on both buttons. The method `actionPerformed` must be modified to determine which action event—click on `button1` or `button2`—has occurred. The identity of the button is established by asking the event object itself. Every event supports a method called `getSource` that returns a reference to the object that generated the event. The code is thus

```
if (event.getSource() == button1) {
  textField1.setText("Hello");
} else if (event.getSource() == button2) {
  textField1.setText("Hi");
}
```

The complete program is

```
import javax.swing.*;
import java.awt.*;
import java.awt.event.*;
public class FrameDemo3 extends JFrame implements
                    ActionListener, WindowListener {
  private JButton button1;
  private JButton button2;
  private JTextField textField1;
```

```java
public FrameDemo3(String title) {
  super(title);
  button1 = new JButton("Print Hello");
  button2 = new JButton("Print Hi");
  JPanel panel = new JPanel();
  panel.add(button1);
  panel.add(button2);
  textField1 = new JTextField(20);
  getContentPane().add(textField1);
  getContentPane().add(panel, BorderLayout.SOUTH);
  button1.addActionListener(this);
  button2.addActionListener(this);
  addWindowListener(this);
  pack();
  setVisible(true);
}
public void windowOpened(WindowEvent event) {
}
public void windowIconified(WindowEvent event) {
}
public void windowDeiconified(WindowEvent event) {
}
public void windowClosed(WindowEvent event) {
}
public void windowActivated(WindowEvent event) {
}
public void windowDeactivated(WindowEvent event) {
}
public void windowClosing(WindowEvent event) {
  System.exit(0);
}
public void actionPerformed(ActionEvent event) {
  if (event.getSource() == button1) {
    textField1.setText("Hello");
  } else if (event.getSource() == button2) {
    textField1.setText("Hi");
  }
}
public static void main(String[] s) {
  new FrameDemo3("Example of a Frame");
}
}
```

4.5.4 Drawing Shapes

Suppose we want to draw shapes such as squares and circles in a window. This can be accomplished by first creating a JFrame and then storing a JPanel object within it. Whenever Java thinks the window should be refreshed (examples: the program is de-iconified; the window becomes uncovered) or when the application code makes an explicit request that the window be refreshed, a method called paintComponent within the frame is executed, which calls the paintComponent method in the JPanel class. The method returns nothing (void) and has a single parameter of type Graphics. Here is an example:

```
public void paintComponent(Graphics g) {
   g.drawRect(30, 75, 100, 50);
   g.drawOval(30, 40, 50, 50);
}
```

The first statement in the method draws a rectangle 100 pixels wide and 50 pixels high. The left edge of the rectangle is 30 pixels from the left edge of the frame and the top edge is 75 pixels from the top of the frame. Within a graphics window, the coordinate values increase as we move from left to right and from top to bottom.

The second statement draws a circle using a method that can draw an oval. The third and fourth coordinates are the width and height of the oval, both of which are the same, so we end up with a circle. The circle fits within a rectangle whose left edge is 30 pixels from the left edge of the frame and top edge is 40 pixels from the top of the frame.

The code for the panel that is stored in the frame is given below.

```
private class DrawingPanel extends JPanel {
   public void paintComponent(Graphics g) {
       g.drawRect(30, 75, 100, 50);
       g.drawOval(30, 40, 50, 50);
   }
}
```

The following code instantiates the panel and adds it to the frame.

```
getContentPane().add(new DrawingPanel());
```

4.5.5 Displaying a Piece of Text

To display a piece of text, the drawString method can be used. Suppose we wish to display the text OOAD on the screen. In addition to the text, we need to specify the

x and y coordinates of the starting point as parameters to the `drawString` method, which is invoked on the `Graphics` object.

```
g.drawString("Java", 100, 200);
```

The above line causes `Java` to be displayed starting at the point whose x coordinate is 100 and y coordinate is 200. The display uses the graphics object's current settings of font and colour. The reader may wish to consult the Java documentation to get more details.

4.6 Long-Term Storage of Objects

Most, if not all, business systems need to maintain data for long periods of time. Since main memory is volatile and the amount of data that needs to be maintained is large compared to the amount of main memory, many application systems store most of the data on secondary storage and retrieve it as needed.

Files on disk are represented as objects in an object-oriented program. Suppose that we have a file named `f1` on disk, which we would like to read in an object-oriented program. For this, we create an object that gets associated with the file. When the object is manipulated, the file gets manipulated accordingly. The idea is shown in Fig. 4.3. Here object `o1` represents the file `f1`, which resides on disk. The file can be read, written, etc. by manipulating the object.

To put this idea into practice, we need to find a class that can be instantiated to get objects such as `o1`. Usually, such classes are part of the application programming interface supported by the language. For example, in Java there is a class called `ObjectInputStream`, using which we can read files containing objects.

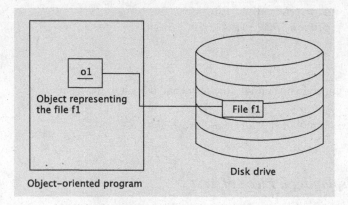

Fig. 4.3 Representation of a file as an object

As we will see later, we run into some difficulties when we read and write objects. To ease the process, we first show how to store and retrieve contents of primitive variables (like `int` and `char`).

The first step is to establish a connection with the disk file. An examination of the package `java.io` shows several possible classes that will let us create such objects. One of these is `FileOutputStream`. The documentation says that this class 'is meant for writing streams of raw bytes such as image data', which implies that we will need the support of other classes as well.

In any case, the code

```
FileOutputStream file = new FileOutputStream("someData");
```

will create a file named `someData` in the current directory.

An examination of the class reveals no useful methods for writing primitive variables. For that, there is a class called `ObjectOutputStream`, which can be constructed as below.

```
ObjectOutputStream output = new ObjectOutputStream(file);
```

One of the constructors for `ObjectOutputStream` accepts an `OutputStream` object as a parameter, and as shown in Fig. 4.4, `FileOutputStream` is a subclass of `OutputStream`.

We are using the constructor `ObjectOutputStream(OutputStream out)`. We now proceed to write several types of variables into this file.

```
int i = 7;
char c = 'q';
boolean b = true;
double d = 3.14;
output.writeInt(i);
output.writeChar(c);
output.writeBoolean(b);
output.writeDouble(d);
output.close();
```

Fig. 4.4 FileOutputStream
and OutputStream

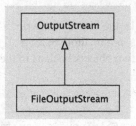

To read back what we wrote, we need to create an object of type ObjectInput Stream. The object can be constructed by first creating a FileInputStream object and passing that object to the constructor of ObjectInputStream.

```
FileInputStream file = new FileInputStream("someData");
ObjectInputStream input = new ObjectInputStream(file);
```

Next, we read the variables using the object input.

```
int i = input.readInt();
char c = input.readChar();
boolean b = input.readBoolean();
double d = input.readDouble();
```

4.6.1 Storing and Retrieving Objects

In this section we address the difficulties that we run into when we try to store objects on disk.

Let us revisit the code we wrote in the previous section and compare the nature of primitive types and objects. The Java API has methods such as writeInt() and readInt() because int is a primitive type in the language. In contrast, user-defined classes such as Television or Account are not known to the language designer, so there no methods such as writeAccount or readTelevision in the Java API. The set of application classes is infinite, so it is impossible to support a separate method for reading and writing instances of all these classes!

What is more realistic in a language is to have methods that write any object. So what we can do in the language is write code such below.

```
Television television = new Television();
Account account = new Account();
FileOutputStream file = new FileOutputStream("objectData");
ObjectOutputStream output = new ObjectOutputStream(file);
output.writeObject(television);
output.writeObject(account);
```

In the above, we write a Television object and a Account object using the same method writeObject. When we read, we should expect to retrieve these two objects back as in the code below.

```
Television television;
Account account;
FileInputStream file = new FileInputStream("objectData");
```

```
ObjectInputStream input = new ObjectInputStream(file);
television = input.readObject();
account = input.readObject();
```

4.6.2 Issues in Storing and Retrieving Objects

To gain a basic understanding of how to store and retrieve objects, we need to consider several issues.

Reconstruction

How is the system to reconstruct the object? To see the problem, it is instructive to look at the process of storing and retrieving a variable of a primitive type, say, an `int`. Assume that an `int` variable is represented using the 32 bit, 2's-complement notation. The bit pattern can be written to disk exactly as it appears in main memory. The result is that secondary storage will now contain 32 bits representing an integer. Suppose that the `int` variable contains the value 7. The value in disk will contain the following bit pattern:

```
0000 0000 0000 0000 0000 0000 0000 0111
```

When code such as `int a = input.readInt()` is executed to retrieve the value from the file, the system knows that it must look for a 32-bit sequence of data and interpret it as an integer. So, it reads that many bits from disk and stores them in the variable a.

On the other hand, not all objects have the same length and format. So, when an object is to be read back, information about how much to read and what the bits mean should be available.

Complexity

Consider the following class definitions.

```java
public class StaffMember {
  private String name;
  private String phone;
  private Department department;
  // constructors and methods
}

public class Department {
  private String departmentName;
  private StaffMember manager;
```

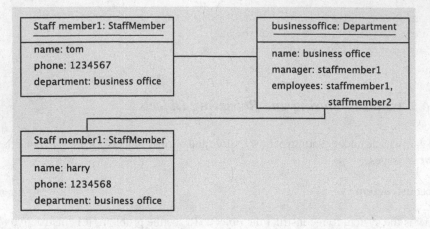

Fig. 4.5 A situation for storing objects

```
    private List employees;
    // constructors and methods
}
```

Even with these relatively simple classes, we can get into tricky situations as shown in the object diagram in Fig. 4.5. There are two staff members, denoted by the two objects staffmember1 and staffmember2. They correspond to employees 'Tom' and 'Harry' with phone numbers 1234567 and 1234568 respectively. Both staff members belong to the same department, Business Office. The business office's manager is Tom and it currently has just two members: Tom and Harry.

The structure is represented using a directed graph in Fig. 4.6, with the objects represented by vertices and references represented by links. Vertices v1 and v2 correspond to the two staff members and vertex v3 represents the business office. The arrows represent references maintained in the objects: for example, the arrow from v1 to v3 indicates that the object for Tom maintains a reference to the object corresponding to the business office.

A little thought reveals some difficulties in storing structures such as the above.

1. The structure is recursive. When we store v1, we need to copy v3 as well, but storing v3 requires that we copy v1. This cyclic nature of the relationship needs to be addressed so that we do not get into an infinite loop.
2. A single object may be referred to from more than one object. For example, v3 is referred to from both v1 and v2. When we write out v1 in Fig. 4.6, for example, we store an instance of v3. When we copy v2 to disk, a naive approach will store v3 once again, as in Fig. 4.7. (The figure does not show all the arcs.) Apart from wasting resources, storing multiple copies of an object means that while reading the data back, these multiple copies will be retrieved, and the resulting configuration after retrieval will be inconsistent with what existed in memory

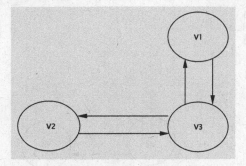

Fig. 4.6 Modelling the object structure using a directed graph

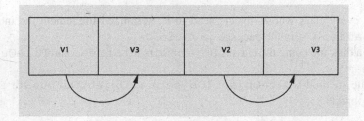

Fig. 4.7 Incorrect storage of the objects shown in Fig. 4.6

prior to the save. After the data in Fig. 4.7 is read back from disk, we end up with the configuration in Fig. 4.8, which is incorrect.

Clearly, a great deal of sophistication is demanded of the application programs to store objects on disk. Typically, we would like to avoid introducing such intricate code into our programs. Since many applications require such a functionality, it is better if such a facility were supported by the language itself. To handle this common problem, the Java designers have come up with a facility known as **serialization**.

4.6.3 The Java Serialization Mechanism

The problems we have discussed can be handled by using the Java serialization mechanism.[1] The major steps in storing a disk avoiding the problems we have discussed are given below. We omit some of the subtle issues involved in the process, deferring these aspects to Chap. 7.

---

[1] The serialization mechanism is a little more general than simply writing objects to disk. It can be thought of as a mechanism to construct a linear representation of a set of objects which can be used for a multitude of purposes.

Fig. 4.8 Reconstructed
relationships based on data
retrieved from disk (see
Fig. 4.7)

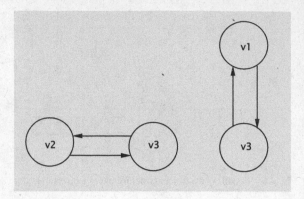

1. Make every class whose objects need to be serialized implement the interface
   `Serialisable` in the package `java.io`.
2. Open a disk file using the classes `ObjectOutputStream` and `FileOutput`
   `Stream`.
3. Use the method `writeObject(Object)` in `ObjectOutputStream` to
   store objects.

The process of writing out objects using the above approach is called **serialization.**
   The reverse process, whereby data written through serialization is read back to
memory is called **deserialization**; this is effected as below.

1. Open a disk file using the classes `ObjectInputStream` and `FileInput`
   `Stream`.
2. Use the method `readObject` in `ObjectInputStream` to read objects. The
   objects are assigned to variables of the appropriate type. (It is necessary to cast
   each object before assignment.)
3. Objects must be read back in the order in which they were written.

The `Serializable` interface contains no methods, so it is just a 'marker' to
inform the system that the corresponding class is Serializable. Objects of type
`Department` and `StaffMember` can be serialized by simply declaring them
to be `Serializable`. This is because they contain instance fields, each of which
is defined to be `Serializable`. We do this as below.

```
import java.io.Serializable;
public class StaffMember implements Serializable {
  // fields and methods of StaffMember
}
import java.io.Serializable;
public class Department implements Serializable {
  // fields and methods of Department
}
```

The two `StaffMember` objects and the `Department` object can be serialized as below.

```
FileOutputStream file = new FileOutputStream("objectData");
ObjectOutputStream output = new ObjectOutputStream(file);
// Create the StaffMember and Department objects
output.writeObject(departmentObject);
```

Since `departmentObject` contains references to the two staff members, storing it results in the serialization of the staff members as well.

Deserialization can be done as follows:

```
FileInputStream file = new FileInputStream("objectData");
ObjectInputStream input = new ObjectInputStream(file);
Department aDepartment = (Department) input.readObject();
Staffmember member1 = (StaffMember) aDepartment.employees(0);
Staffmember member2 = (StaffMember) aDepartment.employees(1);
```

Although the above code looks simple enough, things do not always work out as easily as might be implied. A major point is that it may not make sense to serialise certain objects. Fields defined as `static` are not automatically serialized by the Java serialization mechanism although application code may explicitly serialise them via its own code. There are also many Java library classes that are *not* serializable. An example would be the abstract class `java.awt.Graphics` discussed in the last section. Instances of concrete subclasses of `Graphics` such as `Graphics2D` are created by the system and supplied to application programs for drawing on the screen. A `Graphics` object can be thought of as a collection of the brush (or pen), colour palette, font, etc. Every time the program needs to redraw the screen, the system supplies it with a new `Graphics` object. Once the program completes the drawing operation, the object is no longer applicable, and a new one will be supplied for a subsequent rendering.

These and some subtle issues related to serialization will be discussed in Chap. 7.

4.7 Discussion and Further Reading

While many of the topics discussed in this chapter may seem very specific to the Java language, we would like to state that they are really Java implementations of well-established concepts in the literature. A sound understanding of the concepts presented here would help the reader learn equivalent technologies in other languages and systems such as C# and `.net`. It seems that many object-oriented languages such as Java and C# tend to borrow ideas from each other. So studying a popular object-oriented language well usually helps in understanding the features of another.

Like most other features in the Java language, the sheer size of the GUI library (packages and associated classes) can be intimidating to someone new to this style of programming. The best strategy to understanding the system is to master the basic principles: creation of a window, adding widgets, techniques of using the layout managers, processing events and so on. There are just too many classes and the reader will probably learn quickly that attempts to memorise the methods and their signatures are usually futile.

The members of packages such as `java.awt`, `javax.swing`, etc., is a collection of abstract and concrete classes that collaborate to provide the ability to produce a window on the screen. The window has no specific application-related capability because it is something to be determined, designed and implemented by users and application software designers and implementers. The idea is that the JDK classes themselves form a reusable design that the application development community may adapt as it deems fit. Such a reusable collection of classes is called a **framework**.

In the same vein, we would also like to emphasise the importance of being productive: in the software engineering arena, this translates to being able to gain a good understanding of the problem to be solved and provide speedy solutions. Since technology changes fairly quickly, it is important to understand the general principles behind specific features available in a language and, at the same time, be an effective toolsmith, which means the ability to use available tools to craft solutions rather than 'reinvent the wheel'.

As alluded to in the footnotes, the technique of serialization can be applied for purposes other than storing objects on the disk. Notice that in serialization we write objects to an `ObjectOutputStream` object, producing in effect a sequence of bits that represent one or more objects. We stored the serialized version of the objects on disk by directing the stream (`ObjectOutputStream` object) to a `FileOutputStream` object. Instead, we could transfer these bits to any Java Virtual Machine (JVM), perhaps even over a network to a JVM running on a geographically distant site. This technique is employed for implementing distributed object-oriented systems and the corresponding technology is called **Remote Method Invocation (RMI)**. We will discuss RMI in Chap. 12.

Projects

1. Consider the following interface:

```java
import java.util.*;
public interface Deque {
    public boolean addAtTail(Object value);
    public Object removeElementAtTail();
    public Object getElementAtTail();
    public boolean addAtHead(Object value);
    public Object removeElementAtHead();
```

```
    public Object getElementAtHead();.
    public int size();
    public void clear();
    public Iterator iterator();
}
```

The interface represents a double-ended queue in which members can be added and removed at either end. The method names should convey the semantics of the operations. Implement the interface using the class `java.util.LinkedList`.

2. This project requires you to explore the Java GUI framework on your own, determine the appropriate classes to use, and write two Java classes that create a GUI program. The first class `CourseProcessor` is the GUI interface, and the second class `Course` stores information about a single course.

The program accepts and stores information about courses offered in six departments: Computer Science, Mathematics, Chemistry, Physics, Botany, and Zoology.

The user can do the following.

(a) Enter information about a course by selecting a department name from a combo box, typing in the course number, name, number of credits and then pressing the enter button. The interface checks that the entries are non-empty (display error message otherwise) and then creates a `Course` object using the information and then stores the object in a `java.util.Vector` object.

(b) Ask to list all courses by clicking on a button labelled display (all). All the objects in the `Vector` object are displayed. There is a scrollbar that allows viewing records that cannot be displayed in the given space. Also, note the department codes such as CS and MATH inserted by the program.

(c) Ask to list courses of a given department by clicking on a button labelled display (dept.). Courses for the selected department (via the combo box) in the `Vector` object are displayed.

(d) Quit instantly by clicking on the window's 'close' button, or close (after a confirm dialog) via an 'exit' button within the frame.

Department codes Store the codes associated with departments in static arrays in the class `Course`. This mapping should not be duplicated and should be used consistently and reliably within your code. The codes are given below.

Computer Science	CS
Physics	PHY
Chemistry	CHEM
Mathematics	MATH
Botany	BOT
Zoology	ZOO

3. Write a program that draws shapes that look like houses. A house is made up of a rectangle, on top of which is placed a triangle. You need to write two classes: one that represents a single house and another that creates and draws the houses. It should be possible to specify the size of the house. You may make assumptions on the relationships between the length and height of a house.

4. Write a Java program that accepts the names of a set of files while it is started from the command line and processes these files as specified below.

    (a) The user must supply at least two file names. Thus, the following are among the infinite number of valid commands.

```
java Processor infile outfile
java Processor infile1 infile2 outfile
java Processor infilea infileb infilec myoutfile
```

    The following are invalid.

```
java Processor
java Processor fileName
```

    For invalid commands, the program prints an error message and terminates.

    (b) The very last parameter is the name of an output file. All the other file names are input files. All are pure text files (no binary data) and you may assume that the output file is also not specified as an input file. Thus, you do not have to worry about situations such as

```
java Processor infilea infileb infilec infileb
```

    (c) Each of the input files is read and copied to the output. The files are opened and read in the specified order.

    (d) If one of the input files is missing, it is skipped and the next input file, if any, is processed.

    (e) If there is a problem opening the output file, the program displays an error message and exits.

    (f) Each line of each input file is read and copied to the output file. Just prior to copying a line to the output, the name of the input file, the line number in the input file and the line number in the output file are all given as output.

4.8 Exercises

1. Take a look at the package java.util.* and the documentation for the classes Vector, LinkedList and ArrayList. Compare them for their features, the interfaces they implement and the class hierarchy that leads to each of them.

2. The following code attempts to write an instance of C1 followed by an instance of C2 onto disk and recreate the objects by reading the data from disk. However, there are errors in the code. Correct them.

```
import java.io.Serializable;
public class C1 implements Serializable {
}
import java.io.Serializable;
public class C2 {
}

import java.io.*;
public class C3 {
public static void main(String[] s) {
    FileOutputStream fos = new FileOutputStream("f1");
    ObjectOutputStream oos = new ObjectOutputStream(fos);
    C1 c1 = new C1();
    C2 c2 = new C2();
    oos.writeObject(c1);
    oos.writeObject(c2);
    FileInputStream fis = new FileInputStream("f1");
    ObjectInputStream ois = new ObjectInputStream(fis);
    C2 anotherC2 = (C2) ois.readObject();
    C1 anotherC1 = (C1) ois.readObject();
    }
}
```

3. The Java compiler flags an error if a checked exception is not caught. Study Java documentation to see how Java determines whether a certain exception is a checked exception or not.

4. An example of an unchecked exception is NumberFormatException. Come up with an example where it is advisable to catch exceptions of this type.

Part II
Introduction to Object-Oriented Analysis, Design, Implementation and Refactoring

Chapter 5
Elementary Design Patterns

As one may expect, a software engineer who has had experience developing a number of application systems is able to utilise the expertise gained in future projects. Although two applications may not be alike and may exhibit relatively little similarity at the outset, delving deeper into the design may reveal a number of similar issues. Working on a variety of projects, a software engineer gets exposure to problems that are common to multiple scenarios, which hones his/her ability to identify repeated instances of problems and spell out solutions for them fairly quickly. From an object-oriented perspective, what it means is that two different applications may provide design issues that are alike; the solutions may involve the development of a set of classes with similar functionalities and relationships. Thus the class structures for the two subproblems may end up being the same although there may be differences in details.

An example from the imperative paradigm may help the reader better understand the above discussion. Consider two applications, one a university course registration system and the other a human resource (HR) system for some organisation. In the first example we may wish to provide screens which allow a student to register for classes that can be selected from a list. Let us say that we will list courses sorted according to the departments in the university and that within the department, the courses will be listed in ascending order of course identifiers—this information is to be retrieved from disk before it can be displayed. In the second application, let us assume that we want to retrieve employee-related information from disk and print the information in the sorted order of departments, and within each department in the ascending order of employee names. Although the applications are quite different, the scenarios have similarity: both involve reading information which is data related to some application from disk and then sorting the data based on some fields in it. An efficient sorting mechanism should be used in both cases. We could envisage similar processing in many other applications as well. A professional who has some experience in application design and is conversant with such scenarios should be

© Universities Press (India) Private Ltd. 2015

B. Dathan and S. Ramnath, *Object-Oriented Analysis, Design and Implementation*,
Undergraduate Topics in Computer Science, DOI 10.1007/978-3-319-24280-4_5

able to identify the proper approach to be taken for solving the problem and employ it effectively.

In object-oriented systems, we break up the system into objects and develop classes that serve as blueprints for creating objects. Therefore, unlike the imperative world where we need to recognise the appropriate algorithms for solving a problem, the task in object-oriented systems is to recognise the necessary classes, interfaces and relationships between them for solving a specific design problem. Such an approach, which can then be tailored to solve similar design problems that recur in a multitude of applications, is called a **design pattern**.

Here are some quotes from the literature:

> Design patterns are partial solutions to common problems such as separating an interface from a number of alternate implementations, wrapping around a set of legacy classes, protecting a caller from changes associated with specific problems. A design pattern is composed of a small number of classes that, through delegation and inheritance, provide a robust and modifiable solution. These classes can be adapted and refined for the specific system under construction [1].

> A pattern is a way of doing something, or a way of pursuing an intent [2].

A number of design patterns are known, and as one may expect, they vary in the level of difficulty of comprehending and employing them. In this chapter we study three design patterns. Although the patterns we treat here are relatively simple, they also are quite popular and useful. So the reader is likely to find them being utilised in applications and may use them often in his/her own code.

In Sect. 5.2, we study the Iterator pattern which helps us traverse a collection with no regard to the way the collection is organised. The second pattern, Singleton, is discussed in Sect. 5.3. This pattern is used when it is known that we should have exactly one instance of a certain class. The main utility of this pattern is thus in its ability to support data integrity. Finally, we study the Adapter pattern which helps us develop new classes that satisfy an interface by exploiting the functionality of the existing classes.

5.1 Iterator

In many applications we need to maintain collections which are objects that store other objects. For example, a telephone company system could have a collection object that stores an object for each of its customers; an airline system is likely to maintain information about each of its flights and the references to them may be stored in a collection object. Depending on the type of application, the actual data structure employed may differ. In Chap. 3 we talked about collections in general, and in Chap. 4 we discussed collection classes such as `java.util.LinkedList`.

Popular data structures that implement collections include linked lists, queues, stacks, double-ended queues, binary search trees, B-Trees and hash tables.

Let us imagine a collection implemented as a list that stores instances of type `Object`. The list provides several methods for accessing the elements including the following:

1. `size()`, which returns the number of elements in the list.
2. `get(int index)`, which returns the element at a specific position given by `index`.

Consider a client that maintains a list of `Object`s as below:

```
private ListImplementation1 elements;
```

If the client needs to process all of the objects in the collection, it needs to set up a loop to access every element.

```
for (int index = 0; index < elements.size(); index++) {
  Object object = elements.get(index);
  // process object
}
```

Assume that after the system development we determine that an alternate implementation of the collection is warranted. The client code is modified so that the elements are a list of type `ListImplementation2`:

```
private ListImplementation2 elements;
```

Suppose that `ListImplementation2` does not support either of the above two methods, `size()` and `get(int index)`. Instead, the supported operations include:

1. `reset()`: makes the collection ready to return elements.
2. `next()`: returns an element from the collection in no specific order. Every element is returned exactly once. The method returns `null` if there are no more elements.

Obviously, the client code that iterated using `size` and `get(int index)` need to be rewritten. One way to iterate would be:

```
Object object;
for (elements.reset(), object = elements.next(); object != null;
                       object = elements.next()) {
  // process object
}
```

This requires modification of code within the client, which is not very desirable. Although changes are inevitable in most systems, alterations in implementation of a subsystem should not necessitate modifications of other subsystems. In other words, the system should be loosely coupled. Otherwise, the cost of maintenance can be high.

In fact, the above cost can be completely avoided if we ensure that interfaces supported by classes never change. In the example we have been discussing, this means that `ListImplementation1` and `ListImplementation2` both support a common set of methods.

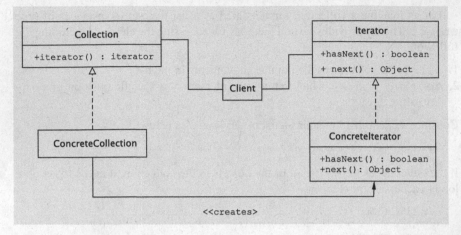

Fig. 5.1 Iterator structure

Another way to ensure less coupling between the client and the collection class would be to require that collection traversal be implemented by employing a special type of object which provides a standard way of iterating over the elements, independent of the internal organisation of the collection. Every collection is then required to return an **iterator** object, which provides these standard methods to traverse the collection.

For example, if `myCollection` refers to an object of type `Collection`, the expression

```
myCollection.iterator()
```

returns an iterator object.

The iterator supports a method called `next()`, which returns an element from the collection each time it is called. No element is returned more than once and if enough calls are made, all elements will be returned. The caller may check whether all elements have been returned by using the method `hasNext()`, which returns `true` if not all elements have been returned.

Thus, in our scheme, we have the following classes and interfaces as shown in Fig. 5.1.

1. `Collection`, an interface that allows the usual operations to add and delete objects, plus the method `iterator()` that returns an iterator object.
2. `Iterator`, an interface that supports the operations `hasNext()` and `next()` described earlier.
3. Implementation of the `Collection` interface: obviously, every implementation must implement the `iterator` method by creating an `Iterator` object and returning it.
4. Implementation of the `Iterator` interface: this class must cooperate with the code in (3) above to properly access and return the elements of the collection.
5. Client code that uses the collection.

Let us look at the class `LinkedList` in Java, which implements `Collection` and supports the `iterator` method.

```
Collection collection = new LinkedList();
collection.add("Element 1");
collection.add(new Integer(2));
for (Iterator iterator = collection.iterator(); iterator.hasNext(); ) {
  System.out.println(iterator.next());
}
```

The first line creates a `LinkedList` object whose reference is stored in the variable `collection`. We add two elements to the collection, a `String` object and an `Integer` object. Every object of type `Collection` supports the `iterator` method, and this method is invoked in the initialisation of the `for` loop. The returned object `iterator` is of the type `Iterator`. Before entering the loop the first time or in any succeeding iteration, we make sure that we have not processed all the elements. The method call `iterator.hasNext()` returns `true` if there is at least one element in the collection not yet retrieved since the `iterator` was created. Such a collection element is retrieved in the body of the loop by the call `iterator.next()`. In this code, we simply print the elements. Thus, we will end up printing `Element 1` and `2` in successive lines.

Changes are inevitable in almost all applications, so we must ensure that these changes do not have widespread ramifications. If every collection class implements the `iterator` method that returns an object of type `Iterator`, clients can use the iterator object to traverse the collection making the process independent of the collection implementation. This insulates the client code from changes in the collection class.

One natural question that may arise in this context is the following: *why is it necessary to return an iterator?* One could argue that it is enough to ensure that every collection supports the methods `hasNext` and `next`. This argument has some validity, but the drawback of this approach is that the design and implementation of the collection class itself becomes more complicated. In addition to managing the elements in the collection, the collection class will have to keep track of every client that navigates the elements. This results in the design being less cohesive. As we shall see in the implementation below, the iterator pattern provides a clean solution to this by separating each traversal process from the collection itself.

5.1.1 Iterator Implementation

In this section we describe how to implement an iterator in Java. Suppose we have the interface `Queue`, which allows adding and removing of objects using the queue discipline (FIFO).

```
public interface Queue {
  public boolean add(Object value);
  public Object remove();
}
```

We implement the above interface in `LinkedQueue`. The inner class `Node` stores an object and the reference to the next element in the linked list. The head and tail of the Queue are stored in the variables `head` and `tail` respectively.

```java
import java.util.*;
public class LinkedQueue implements Queue {
  private Node head;
  private Node tail;
  private int numberOfElements;
  private class Node {
    private Object data;
    private Node next;
    private Node(Object object, Node next) {
      this.data = object;
      this.next = next;
    }
    public Object getData() {
      return data;
    }
    public void setNext(Node next) {
      this.next = next;
    }
    public Node getNext() {
      return next;
    }
  }
  // Queue methods
}
```

The add method creates an instance of `Node` and inserts it at the tail of the list. The code is straightforward.

```java
public boolean add(Object value) {
  Node node = new Node(value, null);
  if (tail == null) {
    tail = head = node;
  }
  else {
    tail.setNext(node);
    tail = node;
  }
  numberOfElements++;
  return true;
}
```

The `remove` method also employs the standard approach to deleting from a queue. Before changing the value of `head`, we retrieve the contents of the first node in the queue so we can return the deleted element.

```java
public Object remove() {
  if (head == null) {
    return null;
  }
  Object value = head.getData();
  head = head.getNext();
  if (head == null) {
    tail = null;
  }
```

```
      numberOfElements--;
      return value;
   }
// The iterator method returns a new Iterator.
   public Iterator iterator() {
      return new QueueIterator();
   }
```

The iterator is implemented as an inner class. In the interface java.util. Iterator, there are three methods: hasNext, next, and remove, the last operation being optional. The Iterator object must maintain the list of elements in the queue that are not yet returned to the client. For this we take advantage of the fact that the LinkedQueue class itself has a linked list and that list is accessible from the code within QueueIterator. However, the iterator class must not modify the field head in LinkedQueue; for this, we maintain a field called cursor within QueueIterator. This field is initialised to head when the iterator object is created.

```
      private class QueueIterator implements Iterator {
         private Node cursor;
         public QueueIterator() {
            cursor = head;
         }
         // hasNext, next, and remove
      }
```

Our plan is to return the elements as they appear in the queue. Therefore, the code for hasNext is quite simple: we just need to make sure that cursor is not null. Hence, we have

```
      public boolean hasNext() {
         return cursor != null;
      }
```

To retrieve the next element, we must first make sure that there is at least one element not supplied to the client. That is, hasNext() does not return a null value. Then, we just move one element forward by setting cursor to cursor.getNext().

```
      public Object next() {
         if (!hasNext()) {
            return null;
         }
         Object object = cursor.getData();
         cursor = cursor.getNext();
         return object;
      }
```

Finally, the implementation of the remove method is the simplest of all because we decided not to support this functionality! As a result, the method body is empty.

```
      public void remove() {
      }
```

The above implementation shows the clean separation between the collection and the iterator. Another advantage of this approach is that we incur no additional complexity if there are multiple iterators being employed simultaneously, as the following code illustrates.

```
Collection collection = new LinkedList();
collection.add(new Integer(1));
collection.add(new Integer(2));
for (Iterator iterator1 = collection.iterator(); iterator1.hasNext(); ) {
  Integer int1 = (Integer) iterator1.next();
  int count = 0;
  for (Iterator iterator2 = collection.iterator(); iterator2.hasNext(); ) {
    Integer int2 = (Integer) iterator2.next();
    if (int1.equals(int2)) {
      count++;
    }
  }
  System.out.println(int1 + count);
}
```

5.2 Singleton

As a second example of a scenario that repeats across applications, we note that in many situations we want to ensure that there is just one object of a certain class. For example, although a computer system may have many printers, there is usually only one spooler. A company has only one president. A single-processor system obviously can have only one CPU.

To create a class that can only be instantiated once, we note that the constructor cannot have the `public` access specifier. Instead, we provide a method called `instance()` that returns the only instance of the class.

```
public class B {
  private static B singleton;
  private B() {
  }
  public static B instance() {
    if (singleton == null) {
      singleton = new B();
    }
    return singleton;
  }
  // application code
}
```

The major observation to be made here is that to get the only instance of class B, a client invokes the static method `instance`. This is because the constructor is private, so the code from outside the class cannot instantiate B. When the class is loaded, the field `singleton` will be set to `null`. In the very first call to `instance`, an instance of B is created and the reference stored in `singleton`. Further calls to `instance` result in no new allocations, and the value in `singleton` is returned.

Notice some of the other major features of the implementation:

1. Clients need not maintain a variable to keep track of the instance. Simply by invoking the static method `instance`, the instance can be retrieved.
2. The class can be subclassed. The subclasses themselves may be singletons.
3. Instead of using a singleton, one may have a class with static methods. But since static methods are not virtual, subclassing will not be able to override these methods.

5.2.1 Subclassing Singletons

In some applications it is necessary to develop subclasses of a singleton class where the subclasses themselves are singletons. For an example of such a system, consider a distributed system with one or more server machines and many client sites. A server machine runs several server processes. In our example, we have exactly four processes.

1. A general-purpose server that provides many services including time, directory, file, replication and name services. However, some of these services are somewhat primitive in nature.
2. A directory server that provides sophisticated directory service.
3. A file server that allows reading and updating of data.
4. A file server that allows only reading; only new files can be written.

Since the general-purpose server already provides the basic support for directory and file management, it seems reasonable to assume that the specialised classes for instantiating the directory and file servers are subclasses of the class for the general-purpose server. All the classes are singletons.

For a second example, consider a large corporation with offices all around the world. The corporate headquarters is located in, say, New York. Every country in which the corporation operates has its own separate national headquarters to control operations within that country. For instance, the company may operate in France and have its headquarters in Paris. A sample hierarchy is given in Fig. 5.2.

Let us further assume that the functionality of each of the national headquarters is quite similar to the functionality of the corporate headquarters. However, there are differences between the corporate headquarters and individual national headquarters (in matters such as labour and other laws, currency, etc.).

Thus, we implement the above system using a singleton class for the corporate headquarters and a separate singleton subclass for each of the national headquarters.

In general, the problem of interest in this context boils down to the following: We need to implement two classes, B and D where B is the superclass of D, and both classes are singletons.

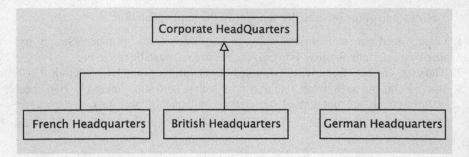

Fig. 5.2 Singleton hierarchy

Consider the implementation of B as we had it in Sect. 5.2. Suppose we attempt to implement D as below.

```
public class D extends B {
  private static D singleton;
  private D() {
  }
  public static D instance() {
    if (singleton == null) {
      singleton = new D();
    }
    return singleton;
  }
  // application code
}
```

This code has a problem: since B has a private constructor, it is impossible for D to be instantiated. The constructor of D makes an implicit call to the no-argument constructor of the superclass, B, and the compiler blocks this because the superclass's constructor is private.

The solution developed below recognises the fact that the instantiation of B has to be done differently when we have a singleton hierarchy.

1. B is instantiated through the `instance` method. The class does not have any public constructors.
2. For D to be instantiated, it is necessary that some constructor of B be accessible from the code within D. Since this constructor cannot be public, it follows that the constructor be protected. Therefore, we have

```
public class B {
  private static B singleton;
  protected B() {
  }
  public static B instance() {
    if (singleton == null) {
      singleton = new B();
    }
    return singleton;
  }
```

```
    // more application code
  }
  public class D extends B {
    private static D singleton;
    protected D() {
    }
    public static D instance() {
      if (singleton == null) {
        singleton = new D();
      }
      return singleton;
    }
    // more application code
  }
```

3. The code has the flaw that the code within class D can instantiate multiple instances of B, violating the fundamental property of a singleton class.

   Therefore, we must control the behavior when B's constructor is invoked from D. This can achieved by using the Java reflection mechanism, which, as we saw earlier, allows Java code to discover the properties and behaviour of an object at the execution time. In particular, this mechanism allows, at runtime, the discovery of the name of the class to which an object belongs, the names of the supported interfaces, field names, methods and constructors. Let C be a class and p a reference created as below.

   ```
   C p = new C();
   ```

   Since the expression p.getClass().getName() returns 'C', we can modify the class B as below.

   ```
   import java.lang.reflect.*;
   public class B {
     private static B singleton;
     protected B() {
       if (getClass().getName().equals("B")) {
         throw new Exception();
       }
     }
     public static B instance() {
       if (singleton == null) {
         singleton = new B();
       }
       return singleton;
     }
     // more application code
   }
   ```

Any attempt to instantiate B directly will now fail because the invocation will have to go through the protected method, which throws an exception whenever B is instantiated. Our solution requires that the constructor knows what kind of object is being created at the execution time by calling for RTTI, which, in this case, is obtained through reflection. In this situation, the instanceof operator does not suffice; every instance of D is an instance of B and the resulting constructor would not allow the creation of any object whatsoever.

4. The above modification introduces the problem that instances of B cannot be created at all! (When the `instance()` method of B invokes the constructor, an exception is thrown.) This is corrected by introducing a private constructor. Since constructors must have differing signatures, we introduce an artificial parameter to this constructor. This step thus yields

```java
import java.lang.reflect.*;
public class B {
  private static B singleton;
  protected B() throws Exception {
    if (getClass().getName().equals("B")) {
      throw new Exception();
    }
  }
  private B(int i) {
  }
  public static B instance() {
    if (singleton == null) {
      singleton = new B(1);
    }
    return singleton;
  }
  // more application code
}
```

The descendants of B use the protected constructor, but only to create instances of B that are embedded in instances of the descendants, which cannot be independently accessed. Only one explicitly constructed instance of B exists, which is done using the private constructor.

5.3 Adapter

Suppose that during the design stage of a piece of software we formalise an interface, i.e., come up with a set of methods that we want implemented. Assume that we have available to us a class whose application programming interface (API)—the set of methods available to clients—is similar to the demands we have identified, but still does not quite match the interface we arrived at. Rather than implement the interface completely from scratch, which may entail considerable expenditure in terms of time and money, we may be better off by tweaking the existing class. However, modifying the class directly to arrive at the new functionality is also not the best approach for two fairly obvious reasons:

1. We need to understand the details of the implementation of the given class, which may be expensive.
2. Future changes to the original class to fix bugs, enhance functionality, etc., will not be available in the interface's implementation.

Therefore, we need a better strategy for this problem.

Before discussing a better solution, let us specify the problem a little more formally. We have a class C that supports a set, say, M_C, of methods. We assume that we need to implement interface I that contains a set, M_I, of methods. By some measure, let us say that M_I resembles M_C, but the methods in the two sets are not quite the same. The problem is to figure out the best way to arrive at an implementation for the interface I given the fact that there are similarities between the methods in M_I and M_C.

This is a problem that frequently occurs in practice. As toolsmiths, it is important for us not to start from scratch nor delve into other's ventures that require an inordinate investment of time and money, if at all possible. The strategy that we have in mind is to develop a class A that implements I, whereby each method in M_I is realised by a combination of calls to a subset of the methods in M_C.

The approach outlined above is known as the adapter pattern. Its main function is to adapt an existing module to implement a given application interface. For obvious reasons, it promotes code reuse.

The structure of the pattern is shown in Fig. 5.3. The interface Client Interface corresponds to the interface I in the above discussion, and the client wants to invoke methods in this interface. For this purpose, the client maintains a reference to an Adapter instance, which implements the methods in ClientInterface. Notice that method1 and method2 form the set M_I in our earlier discussion. The class Adaptee is an existing class (C in our discussion) and the set of methods formed by adapteeMethod1 and adapteeMethod2 corresponds to the set M_C.

In our strategy, the adapter creates and maintains a reference to an adaptee instance. Now, suppose the client wants to invoke method method1 in ClientInterface. The adapter satisfies the request by using the methods of the adaptee.

As an example, suppose we are given the interface Deque. A Deque instance is a collection of objects in which elements can be added and deleted at either end. Moreover, the interface also supports methods to peek at the head and tail of the

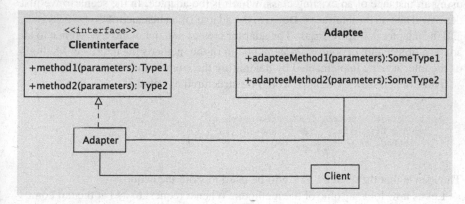

Fig. 5.3 Object adapter structure

collection (getElementAtHead and getElementAtTail), determine the size (size), delete all elements (clear), and return an iterator (iterator).

```
import java.util.*;
public interface Deque {
  public boolean addAtTail(Object value);
  public Object removeElementAtTail();
  public Object getElementAtTail();
  public boolean addAtHead(Object value);
  public Object removeElementAtHead();
  public Object getElementAtHead();
  public int size();
  public void clear();
  public Iterator iterator();
}
```

In Java, we have the class LinkedList in which elements can be added, deleted, or peeked at any position: (add(int index, E element), remove(int index), and get(int index)); the size can be determined (size), all elements can be deleted(clear) and, an iterator on the collection can be retrieved (iterator). However, there are two disadvantages to using the LinkedList class in place of a Deque implementation.

1. In some cases, the method names are different from the ones in the Deque interface.
2. The class is more general than the demands of the Deque interface. For instance, the remove(int index) method can be used to delete an element at any position, not just at the head or tail. This violates the Deque discipline.

Nonetheless, a subset of the LinkedList class methods have enough similarity with the methods of Deque that we can use the former in the interface's implementation. Let us assume that Deque is implemented in a class named DequeImpl.

The adapter pattern comes in handy for the purpose. There are two forms of the pattern; **object adapter**s and **class adapter**s. In this example, we use an object adapter. An object adapter creates an adapter class that implements a given interface using an instance of an existing class, which is the adaptee. In the scenario we just described above, the interface is Deque, the adaptee is an instance of LinkedList, and the adapter is DequeImpl. The adapter creates and maintains a reference to an adaptee object and, of course, implements all of the methods the interface. Methods of the interface are implemented by delegating the work to the adaptee object.

Thus, the class DequeImpl would be structured as below.

```
import java.util.*;
public class DequeImpl implements Deque {
  private List list = new LinkedList();
  // methods as dictated by Deque
}
```

The idea is that the object list will be used to store the deque.

Let us now look at some of the methods. When a request to add at the tail comes in, we simply insert it at the tail of the List object. This is done by invoking the add method in List. Thus, the code for addAtTail is

```
public boolean addAtTail(Object value) {
  return list.add(value);
}
```

Similarly, removing from the tail is accomplished by invoking the `remove` method in `List` as below.

```
public Object removeElementAtTail() {
  if (list.size() > 0) {
    return list.remove(list.size() - 1);
  }
  return null;
}
```

Notice that we need to protect the code; so, we must ensure that the list contains at least one element before invoking the remove operation.

The code for accessing the tail element is

```
public Object getElementAtTail() {
  if (list.size() > 0) {
    return list.get(list.size() - 1);
  }
  return null;
}
```

The methods for processing the head element are similar.

Methods for getting the size, iterator and clearing the `Deque` object are quite simple.

```
public int size() {
  return list.size();
}
public void clear() {
  list.clear();
}
public Iterator iterator() {
  return list.iterator();
}
```

The `equals` method can be implemented by comparing the `Deque` object with another object, element by element.

```
public boolean equals(Object object) {
  Deque other = (Deque) object;
  if (other.size() != this.size()) {
    return false;
  }
  Iterator thisIterator = this.iterator();
  Iterator otherIterator = other.iterator();
  while (thisIterator.hasNext() && otherIterator.hasNext()) {
    if (!(thisIterator.next().equals(otherIterator.next()))) {
      return false;
    }
  }
  return true;
}
```

Note that in the above example we keep a reference to the List object within Deque rather than extend an implementation of List. We are thus adapting the List object, and hence the pattern is called an object adapter. The methods of List are unavailable to the user of DequeImpl.

In contrast, we could have extended LinkedList and called the methods of the superclass to carry out the actions of the Deque interface. Such an adapter is called a **class adapter**. This is not as flexible as the object-based approach because we are extending a specific class and that decision is made at compile time. The object adapter has the advantage that the choice of the adaptee class can be postponed until execution time. Moreover, in the case of the class adapter, all of the public methods of the extended class are exposed to the client. The downside to an object adapter is that it introduces one more object into the system.

5.4 Discussion and Further Reading

A major goal of employing design patterns is to cater to the changes that may become necessary during the lifetime of a system. Changes are inevitable in any application system and systems must be designed so that they can handle changes in specifications with minimum fuss: any specification change should result in the modification of a small number of classes with no wide ramifications within the system. An implementation based on a design that cannot accommodate changes very well is likely to have a short life or will be too expensive to maintain.

Using design patterns can also help in the understanding of designs more quickly because they are well-understood solutions to frequently occurring problems. For instance, if we say that a certain part of the system is built using the adapter pattern, we can immediately understand how classes and interfaces in that part of the system are organised.

Although several design patterns are quite easy to understand, there are some that are quite difficult. Regardless of the difficulty, most design patterns use a combination of some of the following approaches.

1. Program to a type. If at all possible, commit to a class as late as possible. This allows us to use the appropriate implementation at execution time. Since implementations can change during a system's lifetime, this strategy helps to ensure that we are adapting to changes as they occur. For example, in the following code we define mySet as of type Set rather than as HashSet or TreeSet, which are implementations.

```
Set mySet;
// code
mySet = new HashSet();
```

2. To make the above point feasible, ensure that the specifications are spelled out using interfaces.

3. Use composition and inheritance appropriately. When it is required that we inherit the type and implementation of a specific class, use inheritance. In many situations, however, we can get around this requirement and use composition.
4. Isolate what can vary and encapsulate it. Define a suitable interface for the varying entity. The code in the rest of the system can then use the idea in (1) above to refer to the actual object that implements the interface. If changes require creating a new class for the interface, the code that references the old object can easily switch to an instance of the new class.

The reader should look for the above principles while studying design patterns.

Understanding design patterns is a relatively easy task compared to identifying situations where these patterns are applicable. A first step toward meeting this challenging task can be taken by a thorough understanding of the patterns (study good examples) and convincing oneself of the fact that the ideas used are indeed useful. After that a little bit of experience in using the patterns in a few situations should make the process simpler. Once again, it appears that patterns that are simpler to understand are also easier to apply.

The best source of reference for design patterns is the classic catalog of the patterns by Gamma, Helm, Johnson, and Vlissides (aka Gang of Four, abbreviated GoF) *Design Patterns: Elements of Reusable Object-Oriented Software* [3]. This was the first book that talked about the fundamental patterns (23 of them). A number of other books [4–6] that explain the patterns are also available in the market, but the GoF book remains unmatched for its elegance and precision.

Projects

1. The following interface DateInterface contains a subset of the methods in the class java.util.Date. We have indicated what the methods do mostly by quoting from the documentation in Sun's JDK. (For more details of what the methods do, please see the JDK documentation.)

```
public interface DateInterface {
  // Returns the year minus 1900
  public int getYear();
  // Sets the year
  public void setYear(int year);
  /* Returns the month represented by this date. The value is
between 0 and 11. */
  public int getMonth();
  // sets the month
  public void setMonth(int month);
  // returns the day of the month
  public int getDate();
  // sets the day of the month
  public void setDate(int date);
  //  Returns the day of the week
  public int getDay();
  // Returns the hour between 0 and 23
  public int getHours();
  // Sets the hour
  public void setHours(int hours);
  //  Returns the number of minutes past the hour
```

```
public int getMinutes();
// Sets the minutes of this Date object
public void setMinutes(int minutes);
//   Returns the number of seconds past the minute
public int getSeconds();
//   Sets the seconds of this Date object
public void setSeconds(int seconds);
/*  Returns the number of milliseconds since January 1, 1970,
00:00:00 GMT */
// represented by this Date object.
public long getTime();
//   Sets this Date object to represent a point in time that is time
//   milliseconds after January 1, 1970 00:00:00 GMT.
public void setTime(long time);
}
```

Your task is to implement the above interface using the adapter pattern. For this, locate a class other than `java.util.Date` to be used as the adaptee. Implement some suitable constructors as well.

2. Study the class `java.util.StringTokenizer`. Implement the following interface, `PushbackTokenizer`, as a class adaptor with `StringTokenizer` as the adaptee.

```
public interface PushbackTokenizer {
// Returns the next token
  public String nextToken();
// Returns true if and only if there are more tokens
  public boolean hasMoreTokens();
/* The token read is pushed back, so it can be read again
using nextToken.*/
  public void pushback();
}
```

5.5 Exercises

1. The interface `java.util.Iterator` contains an additional method `remove()`. Study what this method does and explain any difficulties that you forsee if this is implemented.
2. Implement a list class that implements the following interface:

```
// add at the tail
public void add(Object object);
// add at the given position
public void add(Object object, int index);
// delete and return the element at the given position;
// return null if no such element exists
public Object delete(int index);
// return the number of elements in the list.
public int size();
// return an object of type java.util.ListIterator
public ListIterator listIterator();
```

3. Look up Java documentation for details on the `clone` method. Suppose that a singleton class implements the `clone()` method. How does it affect the integrity of the system? Discuss how you may circumvent these difficulties.
4. We have already noted that the singleton pattern can be realised by having a class that contains nothing but a set of static methods. Find a real-life example of a singleton class and show that this observation is true. Next, identify a pair of classes in which one is a subclass of the other and both are singletons. Attempt to use the 'static methods approach' to make them singletons and convince yourself of the difficulties.
5. Identify singleton classes in a university that maintains several separate collections including the following for storing the list of faculty members, the list of students, the list of staff members, and one that maintains a list of these collections themselves.
6. Compare and contrast the interfaces `Enumeration` and `Iterator` in `java.util`.
7. Suppose that we would like to implement a Java interface using the class adapter pattern. However, exposing some methods of the adaptee could result in loss of integrity. Suggest a way to hide such methods.
8. What are the proper methods for a `Stack` object? With this background, examine the design of the `java.util.Stack` class and see if it the design is sound.

References

1. B. Bruegge, A.H. Dutoit, *Object-Oriented Software Engineering* (Prentice Hall, New Jersey, 2000)
2. B. Goetz, Java theory and practice: Be a good (event) listener. guidelines for writing and supporting event listeners, http://www.ibm.com/developerworks/, July 2005
3. E. Gamma, R. Helm, R. Johnson, J. Vlissides, *Design Patterns: Elements of Reusable Object-Oriented Software* (Addison-Wesley, Boston, 1994)
4. S.J. Metsker, *Design Patterns Java Workbook* (Addison-Wesley, Boston, 2002)
5. A. Shalloway, J.R. Trott. *Design Patterns Explained A New Perspective on Object-Oriented Design* (Addison-Wesley, Boston, 2004)
6. E. Freeman, E. Robson, B. Bates, K. Sierra, *Head First Design Patterns (Head First)* (O'Reilly, California, 2004)

Chapter 6
Analysing a System

In Chaps. 6–8, we examine the essential steps in object-oriented software development: analysis, design, and implementation. To illustrate the process, we study a relatively simple example—a piece of software to manage a small library—whose function is limited to that of lending books to its members, receiving them back, doing the associated operations such as querying, registering members, etc., and keeping track of these transactions. In the course of these chapters, we go through the entire process of analysing, designing and implementing this system.

The software construction process begins with an analysis that determines the requirements of the system, which is what we introduce in this chapter. At this stage the focus is on determining what the system must perform without regard to the methodology to be employed. This process is carried out by a team of analysts, perhaps familiar with the specific type of application. The requirements are spelled out in a document known variously as the 'Requirements Specification', 'System Requirements', etc. Using these, the system analyst creates a model of the system, enabling the identification of some of the components of the system and the relationships between them. The end product of this phase is a *conceptual model* for the system which describes the functionality of the system, identifies its conceptual entities and records the nature of the associations between these entities.

Once the analysis has been satisfactorily completed, we move on to the design phase, which is addressed in the first part of Chap. 7. The design starts with a detailed breakdown of how the system will emulate the behaviour outlined in the model. In the course of this breakdown, all the parts of the system and their responsibilities are clearly identified. This step is followed by determining the software and hardware structures needed to implement the functionality discovered in the analysis stage. In the object-oriented world, this would mean deciding on the language or languages to be used, the packages, the platform, etc. The second part of Chap. 7 looks at implementation, wherein we discuss the lower-level issues, language features employed, etc.

A question that a conscientious beginner often ponders is: *Did I do a good job of the design?* or *Is my design really object-oriented?* Indeed, in the real world, it is often the case that designs conform to object-oriented principles to varying degrees.

© Universities Press (India) Private Ltd. 2015   129
B. Dathan and S. Ramnath, *Object-Oriented Analysis, Design and Implementation*,
Undergraduate Topics in Computer Science, DOI 10.1007/978-3-319-24280-4_6

Fortunately, in addition to the broad guidelines for what constitutes a good object-oriented design, there are some more specific rules that can be applied to look for common mistakes and correct them. These rules, known as *refactoring rules*, are more commonly presented as a means for improving the design of the existing code. They are, however, just as useful to check the design of a system before it is fully implemented. In Chap. 8, we introduce the concept of refactoring and apply these rules to our small system.

As our main focus in this book is the elaboration of the process of analysis, design, and implementation, we will bypass many software engineering and project management issues. We will not dwell on conceptual frameworks such as agile software development for managing the software development life cycle. We use UML notations in an appropriate manner that is sufficient to describe our design, but do not cover these exhaustively. For a detailed exposition on these topics, the reader is referred to the works cited at the end of each chapter.

6.1 Overview of the Analysis Phase

To put it in a simple sentence, the major goal of this phase is to address this basic question: what should the system do? A typical computer science student writes a number of programs by the time he/she graduates. Typically, the program requirements are written up by the instructor: the student does some design, writes the code, and submits the program for grading. To some extent, the process of understanding the requirements, doing the design, and implementing that design is relatively informal. Requirements are often simple and any clarifications can be had via questions in the classroom, e-mail messages, etc.

The above simple-minded approach does not quite suffice for 'real-life' projects for a number of reasons. For one reason, such systems are typically much bigger in scope and size. They also have complex and ambiguously-expressed requirements. Third, there is usually a large amount of money involved, which makes matters quite serious. For a fourth reason, hard as it may be for a student to appreciate it, project deadlines for these 'real-life' projects are more critical. (Users are fussier than instructors!)

However, as in the case of the classroom assignment, there are still two parties: the user community, which needs some system to be built and the development people, who are assigned to do the work. The process could be split into three activities:

1. Gather the requirements: this involves interviews of the user community, reading of any available documentation, etc.
2. Precisely document the functionality required of the system.
3. Develop a conceptual model of the system, listing the conceptual classes and their relationships.

It is not always the case that these activities occur in the order listed. In fact, as the analysts gather the requirements, they will analyse and document what they have collected. This may point to holes in the information, which may necessitate further requirements collection.

6.2 Stage 1: Gathering the Requirements

The purpose of *requirements analysis* is to define what the new system should do. The importance of doing this correctly cannot be overemphasized. Since the system will be built based on the information garnered in this step, any errors made in this stage will result in the implementation of a wrong system. Once the system is implemented, it is expensive to modify it to overcome the mistakes introduced in the analysis stage.

Imagine the scenario when you are asked to construct software for an application. The client may not always be clear in his/her mind as to what should be constructed. One reason for this is that it is difficult to imagine the workings of a system that is not yet built. Only when we actually use a specific application such as a word processor do we start realising the power and limitations of that system. Before actually dealing with it, one may have some general notions of what one would like to see, but may find it difficult to provide many details.

Incompleteness and errors in specifications can also occur because the client does not have the technical skills to fully realise what technology can and cannot deliver. Once again, the general concepts can be stated, but specifics are harder. A third reason for omissions is that it is all too common to have a client who knows the system very well and consequently either assumes a lot of knowledge on the part of the analyst or simply skips over the 'obvious details'.

Requirements for a new system are determined by a team of analysts by interacting with teams from the company paying for the development (clients) and the user community, who ultimately uses the system on a day-to-day basis. This interaction can be in the form of interviews, surveys, observations, study of existing manuals, etc.

Broadly speaking, the requirements can be classified into two categories:

- *Functional requirements* These describe the interaction between the system and its users, and between the system and any other systems, which may interact with the system by supplying or receiving data.
- *Non-functional requirements* Any requirement that does not fall in the above category is a non-functional requirement. Such requirements include response time, usability and accuracy. Sometimes, there may be considerations that place restrictions on system development; these may include the use of specific hardware and software and budget and time constraints.

It should be mentioned that initiating the development cycle for a software system is usually preceded by a phase that includes the initial conception and planning. A developer would be approached by a client who wishes to have a certain product developed for his/her business. There would be a *domain* associated with the business, which would have its own jargon. Before approaching the developer, one would assume that the client has determined that a need for a product exists. Once all these issues are sorted out, the developer(s) would meet with the client and, perhaps several would-be end-users, to determine what is expected of the system. Such a process would result in a list of requirements of the system.

As mentioned at the beginning of this chapter, we study the development process by analysing, designing, and implementing a simple library system; this is introduced next.

6.2.1 Case Study Introduction

Let us proceed under the assumption that developers of our library system have available to them a document that describes how the business is conducted. This functionality is described as a list of what are commonly called *business processes*.

The business processes of the library system are listed below.

- **Register new members** The library receives applications from people who want to become library members, whom we alternatively refer to as **users**. While applying for membership, a person supplies his/her name, phone number and address to the library. The library assigns each member a unique identifier (ID), which is needed for transactions such as issuing books.
- **Add books to the collection** We will make the assumption that the collection includes just books. For each book the library stores the title, the author's name, and a unique ID. (For simplicity, let us assume that there is only one author per book. If there are multiple authors, let us say that the names will have to be concatenated to get a pretty huge name such as 'Brahma Dathan and Sarnath Ramnath'. As a result, to the system, it appears that there is just one author.)
  When it is added to the collection, a book is given a unique identifier by the clerk. This ID is based on some standard system of classification.
- **Issue a book to a member (or user)** To check out books, a user (or member) must identify himself to a clerk and hand over the books. The library remembers that the books have been checked out to the member. Any number of books may be checked out in a single transaction.
- **Record the return of a book** To return a book, the member gives the book to a clerk, who submits the information to the system, which marks the book as 'not checked out'. If there is a hold on the book, the system should remind the clerk to set the book aside so that the hold can be processed.
- **Remove books from the collection** From time to time, the library may remove books from its collection. This could be because the books are worn-out, are no longer of interest to the users, or other sundry reasons.
- **Print out a user's transactions** Print out the interactions (book checkouts, returns, etc.) between a specific user and the library on a certain date.

- **Place/remove a hold on a book** When a user wants to put a hold, he/she supplies the clerk with the book's ID, the user's ID, and the number of days after which the book is not needed. The clerk then adds the user to a list of users who wish to borrow the book. If the book is not checked out, a hold cannot be placed. To remove a hold, the user provides the book's ID and the user's ID.
- **Renew books issued to a member** Customers may walk in and request that several of the books they have checked out be renewed (re-issued). The system must display the relevant books, allow the user to make a selection, and inform the user of the result.
- **Notify member of book's availability** Customers who had placed a hold on a book are notified when the book is returned. This process is done once at the end of each day. The clerk enters the ID for each book that was set aside, and the system returns the name and phone number of the user who is next in line to get the book.

In addition, the system must support three other requirements that are not directly related to the workings of a library, but, nonetheless, are essential.

- A command to save the data on a long-term basis.
- A command to load data from a long-term storage device.
- A command to quit the application. At this time, the system must ask the user if data is to be saved before termination.

To keep the process simple, we restrict our attention for the time being to the above operations. A real library would have to perform additional operations like generating reports of various kinds, impose fines for late returns, etc. Many libraries also allow users to check out books themselves without approaching a clerk. Whatever the case may be, the analysts need to learn the existing system and the requirements. As mentioned earlier, they achieve this through interviews, surveys, and study.

Our goal here is to present the reader with the big picture of the entire process so that the beginner is not overwhelmed by the complexity or bogged down in minutiae. Keeping this in mind, we will be designing a system that the reader may find somewhat simplistic, particularly if one compares this with the kinds of features that a 'real' system in today's market can provide. While there is some truth to this observation, it should be noted that the simplification of the system has been done with a view to reducing unnecessary detail so that we can focus instead on the development process, elaborate on the use of tools described previously, and explain through an example how good design principles are applied. In the course of applying the above, we come with a somewhat simplified *sample development process* that may be used as a template by someone who is getting started on this subject.

Assuming that we have a good grasp of the requirements, we need to document the functional requirements of the application and determine the system's major entities and their relationships. As mentioned earlier, the steps may be, and are often, carried out as an iterative, overlapping process; for pedagogical reasons, we discuss them as a sequence of distinct activities.

Analysing a System

6.3 Functional Requirements Specification

It is important that the requirements be precisely documented. The requirements specification document serves as a contract between the users and the developers. When it is time to deliver the system, there should be no confusion as to what the expectations are. Equally or perhaps even more important, it also tells the designers the expected functionality of the system. Moreover, as we attempt to create a precise documentation of the requirements, we will discover errors and omissions.

An accepted way of accomplishing this task is the *use case analysis*, which we study now.

6.3.1 Use Case Analysis

Use case analysis is a case-based way of describing the uses of the system with the goal of defining and documenting the system requirements. It is essentially a narrative describing the sequence of events (actions) of an external agent (actor) using the system to complete a process. It is a powerful technique that describes the kind of functionality that a user expects from the system. Use cases have two or more parties: *agents* who interact with the system and the *system* itself. In our simple library system, the members do not use the system directly. Instead, they get services via the library staff.

To initiate this process, we need to get a feel for how the system will interact with the end-user. We assume that some kind of a user-interface is required, so that when the system is started, it provides a menu with the following choices:

1. Add a member
2. Add books
3. Issue books
4. Return books
5. Remove books
6. Place a hold on a book
7. Remove a hold on a book
8. Process Holds: Find the first member who has a hold on a book
9. Renew books
10. Print out a member's transactions
11. Store data on disk
12. Retrieve data from disk
13. Exit

The above menu gives us the list of ways in which the system is going to be used. There are some implicit requirements associated with these operations. For instance, when a book is checked out, the system must output a due-date so that the clerk can stamp the book. This and other such details will be spelled out when we elaborate on the use cases.

The actors in our system are members of the library staff who manage the daily operations. This idea is depicted in the use case diagram in Fig. 6.1, which gives an overview of the system's usage requirements. Notice that even in the case of issuing books, the functionality is invoked by a library staff member, who performs the actions on behalf of a member.

We are about to take up the task of specifying the individual use cases. In order to keep the discussion within manageable size and not lose focus, we make the following assumption: While the use cases will state the need for the system to display different messages prompting the user for data and informing the results of operations, the user community is not fussy about the minute details of what the messages should be; any meaningful message is acceptable. For example, we may specify in a use case that the system 'informs the clerk if the member was added'. The actual message could be any one of a number of possibilities such as 'Member added', or 'Member registered', etc.

Use case for registering a user Our first use case is for registering a new user and is given in Table 6.1. Recall from our discussion in Chap. 2 that use cases are specified

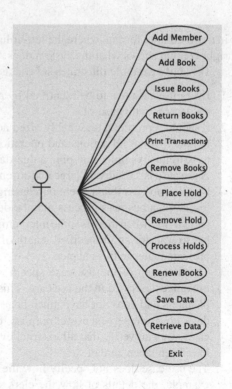

Fig. 6.1 Use case diagram for the library system

Table 6.1 Use case Register New Member

Actions performed by the actor	Responses from the system
1. The customer fills out an application form containing the customer's name, address, and phone number and gives this to the clerk	
2. The clerk issues a request to add a new member	
	3. The system asks for data about the new member
4. The clerk enters the data into the system	
	5. Reads in data, and if the member can be added, generates an identification number (which is not necessarily a number in the literal sense just as social security numbers and phone numbers are not actually numbers) for the member and remembers information about the member. Informs the clerk if the member was added and outputs the member's name, address, phone and id
6. The clerk gives the user his identification number	

in a two-column format, where the left-column states the actions of the actor and the right-column shows what the system does.

The above example illustrates several aspects of use cases.

1. Every use case has to be identified by a name. We have given the name Register New Member to this use case.
2. It should represent a reasonably-sized activity in the organisation. It is important to note that not all actions and operations should be identified as use cases. As an extreme example, stamping a due-date on the book should not be a use case. A use case is a relatively large end-to-end process description that captures some business process that a client purchasing the software needs to perform. In some instances, a business process may be decomposed into more than one use case, particularly when there is some intervening real-world event(s) for which the agent has to wait for an unspecified length of time. An example of such a situation is presented later in this chapter.
3. The first step of the use case specifies a 'real-world' action that triggers the exchange described in the use case. This is provided mainly for the sake of completeness and does not have much bearing on the actual design of the system. It does, however, serve a useful purpose: by looking at the first steps of all the use cases, we can verify that all external events that the system needs to respond to have been taken care of.
4. The use case does not specify how the functionality is to be implemented. For example, the details of how the clerk enters the required information into the

system are left unspecified. Although we assume that the user interacts with the system through the menu, which was briefly described earlier, we do not specify the details of this mechanism. The use case also does not state how the system accomplishes the task of registering a user: what software components form the system, how they may interact, etc.

5. The use case is not expected to cover all possible situations. While we would expect that the sequence of events that are specified in the above use case is what would actually happen in a library when a person wants to be registered, the use case does not specify what the system should do if there are errors. In other words, the use case explains only the most commonly-occurring scenario, which is referred to as the *main flow*. Deviations from the main flow due to occurrences of errors and exceptions are not detailed in the above use case.

Use case for adding books Next, we look at the use case for adding new books in Table 6.2. Notice that we add more than one book in this use case, which involves a repetitive process captured by a *go-to* statement in the last step. Notice that details of how the identifier is generated are not specified. From the point of view of the system analyst, this is something that the actor is expected to take care of independently.

Use case for issuing books Consider the use case where a member comes to the check-out counter to issue a book. The user identifies himself/herself to a clerk, who checks out the books for the user. It proceeds as in Table 6.3.

There are some drawbacks to the way this use case is written. One is that it does not specify how due-dates are computed. We may have a simple rule (example: due-dates are one month from the date of issue) or something quite complicated

Table 6.2 Use case Adding New Books

Actions performed by the actor	Responses from the system
1. Library receives a shipment of books from the publisher	
2. The clerk issues a request to add a new book	
	3. The system asks for the identifier, title, and author name of the book
4. The clerk generates the unique identifier, enters the identifier, title, and author name of a book	
	5. The system attempts to enter the information in the catalog and echoes to the clerk the title, author name, and id of the book. It then asks if the clerk wants to enter information about another book
6. The clerk answers in the affirmative or in the negative	
	7. If the answer is in the affirmative, the system goes to Step 3. Otherwise, it exits

Table 6.3 Use case Book Checkout

Actions performed by the actor	Responses from the system
1. The member arrives at the check-out counter with a set of books and supplies the clerk with his/her identification number	
2. The clerk issues a request to check out books	
	3. The system asks for the user ID
4. The clerk inputs the user ID to the system	
	5. The system asks for the ID of the book
6. The clerk inputs the ID of a book that the user wants to check out	
	7. The system records the book as having been issued to the member; it also records the member as having possession of the book. It generates a due-date. The system displays the book title and due-date and asks if there are any more books
8. The clerk stamps the due-date on the book and replies in the affirmative or negative	
	9. If there are more books, the system moves to Step 5; otherwise it exits
10. The customer collects the books and leaves the counter	

(example: due-date is dependent on the member's history, how many books have been checked out, etc.). Putting all these details in the use case would make the use case quite messy and harder to understand. Rules such as these are better expressed as **Business Rules**. A business rule may be applicable to one or more use cases.

The business rule for due-date generation is simple in our case. It is Rule 1 given in Table 6.4 along with all other rules for the system.

Table 6.4 Rules for the library system

Rule number	Rule
Rule 1	Due-date for a book is one month from the date of issue
Rule 2	All books are issuable
Rule 3	A book is removable if it is not checked out and if it has no holds
Rule 4	A book is renewable if it has no holds on it
Rule 5	When a book with a hold is returned, the appropriate member will be notified
Rule 6	Holds can be placed only on books that are currently checked out

A second problem with the use case is that as written above, it does not state what to do in case things go wrong. For instance,

1. The person may not be a member at all. How should the use case handle this situation? We could abandon the whole show or ask the person to register.
2. The clerk may have entered an invalid book id.

To take care of these additional situations, we modify the use case as given in Table 6.5. We have resolved these issues in Step 7 by having the system check whether the book is issuable, which can be expressed as a business rule. This could check one (or more) of several conditions: *Is the member in good standing with the library? Is there some reason the book should not be checked out? Has the member checked out more books than permitted (if such limits were to be imposed)?* The message displayed by the system in Step 7 informs the clerk about the result of the transaction. In a real-life situation, the client will probably want specific details of

Table 6.5 Use case Book Checkout revised

Actions performed by the actor	Responses from the system
1. The member arrives at the check-out counter with a set of books and supplies the clerk with his/her identification number	
2. Clerk issues a request to check out books	
	3. The system asks for the user ID
4. Clerk inputs the user ID to the system	
	5. If the ID is valid, the system asks for the ID of the book; otherwise it prints an appropriate message and exits the use case
6. The clerk inputs the identifier of a book that the user wants to check out	
	7. If the ID is valid and the book is issuable to the member, the system records the book as having been issued to the member; It records the member as having possession of the book and generates a due-date as in Rule 1. It then displays the book's title and due-date. If the book is not issuable as per Rule 2, the system displays a suitable error message. The system asks if there are more books
8. The clerk stamps the due-date, prints out the transaction (if needed) and replies positively or negatively	
	9. If there are more books for checking out, the system goes back to Step 5; otherwise it exits
10. The clerk stamps the due date and gives the user the books checked out. The customer leaves the counter	

what went wrong; if they are important to the client, these details should be expressed in the use case. Since our goal is to cover the basics of requirements analysis, we sidestep the issue.

Let us proceed to write more use cases. For the most part, these are quite elementary, and the reader may well choose to skip the details or try them out as an exercise.

Use case for returning books Users return books by leaving them on a library clerk's desk; the clerk enters the book ids one by one to return them. Table 6.6 gives the details of the use case. Here, as in the use case for issuing books, the clerk may enter incorrect information into the system, which the use case handles. Notice that if there is a hold on the book, that information is printed for use by the clerk at a later time.

Use cases for removing (deleting) books, printing member transactions, placing a hold, and removing a hold The next four use cases deal with the scenarios for removing books (Table 6.7), printing out member transactions (Table 6.8), placing a hold (Table 6.9), and removing a hold (Table 6.10). In the second of these, the system does not actually print out the transactions, but only displays them on the interface. We are assuming that the necessary facilities to print will be a part of the underlying platform.

In Step 5 in Table 6.7, we allow for the possibility that the deletion may fail. In this event, we assume that there will be some meaningful error message so that the clerk can take corrective action. We shall revisit this issue when we discuss the design and implementation in the next chapter.

Table 6.6 Use case Return Book

Actions performed by the actor	Responses from the system
1. The member arrives at the return counter with a set of books and leaves them on the clerk's desk	
2. The clerk issues a request to return books	
	3. The system asks for the identifier of the book
4. The clerk enters the book identifier	
	5. If the identifier is valid, the system marks that the book has been returned and informs the clerk if there is a hold placed on the book; otherwise it notifies the clerk that the identifier is not valid. It then asks if the clerk wants to process the return of another book
6. The clerk answers in the affirmative or in the negative and sets the book aside in case there is a hold on the book (see Rule 5)	
	7. If the answer is in the affirmative, the system goes to Step 3. Otherwise, it exits

Table 6.7 Use case Removing Books

Actions performed by the actor	Responses from the system
1. Librarian identifies the books to be deleted	
2. The clerk issues a request to delete books	
	3. The system asks for the identifier of the book
4. The clerk enters the ID for the book	
	5. The system checks if the book can be removed using Rule 3. If the book can be removed, the system marks the book as no longer in the library's catalog. The system informs the clerk about the success of the deletion operation. It then asks if the clerk wants to delete another book
6. The clerk answers in the affirmative or in the negative	
	7. If the answer is in the affirmative, the system goes to Step 3. Otherwise, it exits

Table 6.8 Use case Member Transactions

Actions performed by the actor	Responses from the system
1. The clerk issues a request to get member transactions	
	2. The system asks for the user ID of the member and the date for which the transactions are needed
3. The clerk enters the identity of the user and the date	
	4. If the ID is valid, the system outputs information about all transactions completed by the user on the given date. For each transaction, it shows the type of transaction (book borrowed, book returned or hold placed) and the title of the book
5. Clerk prints out the transactions and hands them to the user	

There may be some variations in the way these scenarios are played out. When placing or removing a hold, the library staff may actually want to see a message that the operation was successfully completed. These requirements would modify the manner in which the system responds in these use cases. While such information should be gleaned from the client as part of the requirements analysis, it is often necessary to go back to the client after the use cases are written, to ensure that the system interacts in the desired manner with the operator.

Table 6.9 Use case Place a Hold

Actions performed by the actor	Responses from the system
1. The clerk issues a request to place a hold	
	2. The system asks for the book's ID, the ID of the member, and the duration of the hold
3. The clerk enters the identity of the user, the identity of the book and the duration	
	4. The system checks that the user and book identifiers are valid and that Rule 6 is satisfied. If yes, it records that the user has a hold on the book and displays that; otherwise, it outputs an appropriate error message

Table 6.10 Use case Remove a Hold

Actions performed by the actor	Responses from the system
1. The clerk issues a request to remove a hold	
	2. The system asks for the book's ID and the ID of the member
3. The clerk enters the identity of the user and the identity of the book	
	4. The system removes the hold that the user has on the book (if any such hold exists), prints a confirmation and exits

Table 6.11 Use case Process Holds

Actions performed by the actor	Responses from the system
1. The clerk issues a request to process holds (so that Rule 5 can be satisfied)	
	2. The system asks for the book's ID
3. The clerk enters the ID of the book	
	4. The system returns the name and phone number of the first member with an unexpired hold on the book. If all holds have expired, the system responds that there is no hold. The system then asks if there are any more books to be processed
5. If there is no hold, the book is then shelved back to its designated location in the library. Otherwise, the clerk prints out the information, places it in the book and replies in the affirmative or negative	
	6. If the answer is yes, the system goes to Step 2; otherwise it exits

Use case for processing holds Given in Table 6.11, this use case deals with processing the holds at the end of each day. In this case, once the contact information for the member has been printed out, we assume that the library will contact the member. The member may not come to collect the book within the specified time, at which point the library will try to contact the next member in line. All this is not included in the use case. If we were to do so, the system would, in essence, be waiting on the user's response for a long period of time. We therefore leave out these steps and when the next user has to be contacted, we simply process holds on the book once again.

How do Business Rules Relate to Use Cases?

Business rules can be broadly defined as the details through which a business implements its strategy. Business analysts perform the task of gathering business rules, and these belong to one of four categories:

- **Definitional rules** which explain what is meant when a certain word is used in the context of the business operations. These may include special technical terms, or common words that have a particular significance for the business. For instance the term *Book* in the context of the library refers to a book owned by the library.
- **Factual rules** which explain basic things about the business's operations; they tell how the terms connect to each other. A library, for instance, would have rules such as 'Books are issued to Members,' and 'Members can place holds on Books'.
- **Constraints** which are specific conditions that govern the manner in which terms can be connected to each other. For instance, we have a constraint that says 'Holds can be placed only on Books that are currently checked out'.
- **Derivations** which are knowledge that can be derived from the facts and constraints. For instance, a bank may have the constraint, "The balance in an account cannot be less than zero," from which we can derive that if an amount requested for withdrawal is more than the balance, then the operation is not successful.

When writing use cases, we are mainly concerned with constraints and derivations. Typically, such business rules are in-lined with the logic of the use-case. The use-case may explicitly state the test that is being performed and cite the appropriate rule, or may simply mention that the system will respond in accordance with a specific rule.

In addition to the kinds of rules we have presented for this case study, there are always implicit rules that permeate the entire system. A common example of this is validation of input data; a zip code, for instance, can be validated against a database of zip-codes. Note that this rule does not deal with how entities are connected to one another, but specifies the required properties of a data element. Such constraints do not belong in use cases, but could be placed in classes that store the corresponding data elements.

Use case for renewing books This use case (see Table 6.12) deals with situations where a user has several books checked out and would like to renew some of these. The user may not remember the details of all of them and would perhaps like the system to prompt him/her. We shall assume that users only know the titles of the books to be renewed (they do not bring the books or even the book ids to the library) and that most users would have borrowed only a small number of books. In this situation, it is entirely appropriate for the system to display the title of each book borrowed by the user and ask if that book should be renewed.

Table 6.12 Use case Renew Books

Actions performed by the actor	Responses from the system
1. Member makes a request to renew several of the books that he/she has currently checked out	
2. Clerk issues a request to renew books	
	3. System asks for the member's ID
4. The clerk enters the ID into the system	
	5. System checks the member's record to find out which books the member has checked out. If there are none, the system prints an appropriate message and exits; otherwise it moves to Step 6
	6. The system displays the title of the next book checked out to the member and asks whether the book should be renewed
7. The clerk replies yes or no	
	8. The system attempts to renew the book using Rule 4 and reports the result. If the system has displayed all checked-out books, it reports that and exits; otherwise the system goes to Step 6

It may be the case that a library has additional rules for renewability: if a book has a hold or a member has renewed a book twice, it might not be renewable. In the above interaction, the system displays all the books and determines the renewability only if the member wishes to renew the book. A different situation could arise if we require that the system display only the renewable books. (The system would have to have a way for checking renewability without actually renewing the book, which places additional requirements on the system's functionality.) For our simple library, we go with the scenario described in Table 6.5.

6.4 Defining Conceptual Classes and Relationships

As we discussed earlier, the last major step in the analysis phase involves the determination of the conceptual classes and the establishment of their relationships. For example, in the library system, some of the major conceptual classes include members and books. Members borrow books, which establishes a relationship between them.

We could justify the usefulness of this step in at several ways:

1. **Design facilitation** Via use case analysis, we determined the functionality required of the system. Obviously, the design stage must determine how to implement the functionality. For this, the designers should be in a position to determine the classes that need to be defined, the objects to be created, and how the objects interact. This is better facilitated if the analysis phase classifies the entities in the application and determines their relationships.
2. **Added knowledge** The use cases do not completely specify the system. Some of these missing details can be filled in by the class diagram.
3. **Error reduction** In carrying out this step, the analysts are forced to look at the system more carefully. The result can be shown to the client who can verify its correctness.
4. **Useful documentation** The classes and relationships provide a quick introduction to the system for someone who wants to learn it. Such people include personnel who join the project to carry out the design or implementation or subsequent maintenance of the system.

In practice, an analyst will probably use multiple methods to come up with the conceptual classes and their relationships. In this case study, however, we use a simple approach: we examine the use cases and pick out all the nouns in the description of the requirements. For example, from the text of the use case for registering new users, we can pick out the nouns.

Guidelines to Remember When Writing Use Cases

- A use case must provide something of value to an actor or to the business: when the scenario described in the use case has played out, the actor has accomplished some task. The system may have other functions that do not provide value; these will be just steps within a use case. This also implies that each use case has at least one actor.
- Use cases should be *functionally cohesive,* i.e., they encapsulate a single service that the system provides.
- Use cases should be *temporally cohesive.* This notion applies to the time frame over which the use case occurs. For instance, when a book with a hold is returned, the member who has the hold needs to be notified. The notification is done after some delay; due to this delay, we do not combine the two operations into one use case. Another example could be a university registration system—when a student registers for a class, he or she should be billed. Since the billing operation is not temporally cohesive with the registration, the two constitute separate use cases.
- If a system has multiple actors, each actor must be involved in at least one, and typically several use cases. If our library allowed members to check out books by themselves, "member" is another possible actor.
- The model that we construct is a *set* of use cases, i.e., there is no relationship between individual use cases.
- Exceptional exit conditions are not handled in use cases. For instance, if a system should crash in the middle of a use case, we do not describe what the system is supposed to do. It is assumed that some reasonable outcome will occur.
- Use cases are written from the point of view of the actor in the active voice.
- A use case describes a scenario, i.e., tells us what the visible outcome is and does not give details of any other requirements that are being imposed on the system.
- Use cases change over the course of system analysis. We are trying to construct a model and consequently the model is in a state of evolution during this process. Use cases may be merged, added or deleted from the model at any time.

Here is the text of that use case, once again, with all nouns bold-faced:

(1) The **customer** fills out an **application form** containing the **customer's name**, **address**, and **phone number** and gives this to the **clerk**. (2) The **clerk** issues a **request** to add a new **member**. (3) **The system** asks for **data** about the new **member**. (4) The **clerk** enters the **data** into the **system**. (5) Reads in **data**, and if the **member** can be added, generates an **identification number** for the **member** and remembers

information about the **member**. Informs the clerk if the member was added and outputs the **member's name, address, phone**, and **id**. (6) The **clerk** gives the **user** his **identification number**.

Let us examine the nouns. First, let us eliminate duplicates to get the following list: **customer, application form, customer's name, address, phone number, clerk, request, system, data, identification number, member, user, member information**, and **member's name**. Some of the nouns such as **member** are composite entities that qualify to be classes.

While using this approach, we must remember that natural languages are imprecise and that synonyms may be found. We can eliminate the others as follows:

1. **customer**: becomes a member, so it is effectively a synonym for member.
2. **user**: the library refers to members alternatively as users, so this is also a synonym.
3. **application form** and **request**: application form is an external construct for gathering information, and request is just a menu item, so neither actually becomes part of the data structures.
4. **customer's name, address**, and **phone number**: They are attributes of a customer, so the Member class will have them as fields.
5. **clerk**: is just an agent for facilitating the functioning of the library, so it has no software representation.
6. **identification number**: will become part of a member.
7. **data**: gets stored as a member.
8. **information**: same as data related to a member.
9. **system**: refers to the collection of all classes and software.

The noun **system** implies a conceptual class that represents all of the software; we call this class Library. Although we do not have as yet any specifics of this class, we note its existence and represent it in UML without any attributes and methods (Fig. 6.2). (Recall from Chap. 2 that a class is represented by a rectangle.)

A member is described by the attributes name, address, and phone number. Moreover, the system generates an identifier for each user, so that also serves as an attribute. The UML convention is to write the class name at the top with a line below it and the attributes listed just below that line. The UML diagram is shown in Fig. 6.3.

Fig. 6.2 UML diagram for the class Library

Fig. 6.3 UML diagram for the class Member

Recall the notion of association between classes, which we know from Chaps. 2 and 3 as a relationship between two or more classes. We note several examples of association in our case study. The use case Register New Member (Table 6.1) says that the system 'remembers information about the member'. This implies an association between the conceptual classes Library and Member. This idea is shown in Fig. 6.4; note the line between the two classes and the labels 1, *, and 'maintains a collection of' just above it. They mean that one instance of the Library maintains a collection of zero or more members.

Obviously, members and books are the most central entities in our system: the sole reason for the library's existence is to provide service to its members and that is effected by letting them borrow books. Just as we reasoned for the existence of a conceptual class named Member, we can argue for the need of a conceptual class called Book to represent a book. It has attributes id, title, and author. A UML description of the class is shown in Fig. 6.5. It should come as no surprise that an association between the classes Library and Book, shown in Fig. 6.6, is also needed. We show that a library has zero or more books. (Normally, you would expect a library to have at least one book and at least one member; But our design takes no chances!)

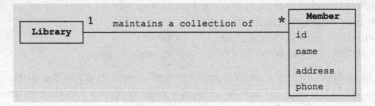

Fig. 6.4 UML diagram showing the association of Library and Member

Fig. 6.5 UML diagram for the class Book

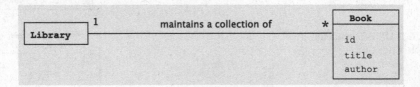

Fig. 6.6 UML diagram showing the association of Library and Book

Some associations are *static*, i.e., permanent, whereas others are *dynamic*. Dynamic associations are those that change as a result of the transactions being recorded by the system. Such associations are typically associated with verbs.

As an example of a dynamic association, consider members borrowing books. This is an association between Member and Book, shown in Fig. 6.7. At any instant in time, a book can be borrowed by one member and a member may have borrowed any number of books. We say that the relationship Borrows is a one-to-many relationship between the conceptual classes Member and Book and indicate it by writing 1 by the side of the box that represents a user and the * near the box that stands for a book.

This diagram actually tells us more than what the Issue Book use case does. That use case does not say some of the considerations that come into play when a user borrows a book: for example, how many books a user may borrow. We might have forgotten to ask that question when we learned about the use case. But now that we are looking at the association and are forced to put labels at the two ends, we may end up capturing missing information. In the diagram of Fig. 6.7, we state that there is no limit. It also states that two users may not borrow the same book at the same time. Recollect from Chap. 3 that an association does not imply that the objects of the classes are always linked together; we may therefore have a situation where no book in the library has been checked out.

Another action that a member can undertake is to place a hold on a book. Several users can have holds placed on a book, and a user may place holds on an arbitrary number of books. In other words, this relationship is many-to-many between users and books. We represent this in Fig. 6.8 by putting a * at both ends of the line representing the association.

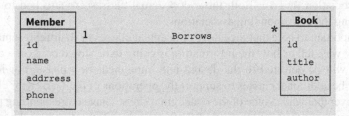

Fig. 6.7 UML diagram showing the association Borrows between Member and Book

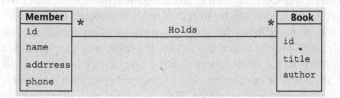

Fig. 6.8 UML diagram showing the association Holds between Member and Book

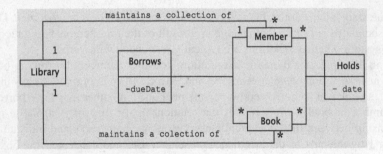

Fig. 6.9 Conceptual classes and their associations

We capture all of the conceptual classes and their associations into a single diagram in Fig. 6.9. To reduce complexity, we have omitted the attributes of Library, Member, and Book. As seen before, a relationship formed between two entities is sometimes accompanied by additional information. This additional information is relevant only in the context of the relationship. There are two such examples in the inter-class relationships we have seen so far: when a user borrows a book and when a user places a hold on a book. Borrowing a book introduces new information into the system, viz., the date on which the book is due to be returned. Likewise, placing a hold introduces some information, viz., the date after which the book is not needed. The lines representing the association are augmented to represent the information that must be stored as part of the association. For the association Borrows and the line connecting Member and Book, we come up with a conceptual class named Borrows having an attribute named dueDate. Similarly, we create a conceptual class named Holds with the attribute called date to store the information related to the association Holds. Both these conceptual classes are attached to the line representing the corresponding associations.

It is important to note that the above conceptual classes or their representation do not, in any way, tell us how the information is going to be stored or accessed. Those decisions will be deferred to the design and implementation phase. For instance, there may be additional classes to support the operations of the Library class. We may discover that while some of the conceptual classes have corresponding physical realisations, some may disappear and the necessary information may be stored as fields distributed over multiple classes. We may discover that while some of the conceptual classes have corresponding physical realisations, some may disappear and the necessary information may be stored as fields distributed over multiple classes. We may choose to move fields that belong to an association elsewhere. For instance, the field dueDate may be stored as a field of the book or as a separate object, which holds a reference to the book object and the user object involved. Upon making that choice, the designer decides how the conceptual relationship between User and Book is going to be physically realised. The conceptual class diagram is simply that: **conceptual**.

6.5 Using the Knowledge of the Domain

Domain analysis is the process of analysing related application systems in a domain so as to discover what features are common between them and what parts are variable. In other words, we identify and analyse common requirements from a specific application domain. In contrast to looking at a certain problem completely from scratch, we apply the knowledge we already have from our study of similar systems to speed up the creation of specifications, design, and code. Thus, one of the goals of this approach is reuse.

Any area in which we develop software systems qualifies to be a **domain**. Examples include library systems, hotel reservation systems, university registration systems, etc. We can sometimes divide a domain into several interrelated domains. For example, we could say that the domain of university applications includes the domain of course management, the domain of student admissions, the domain of payroll applications, and so on. Such a domain can be quite complex because of the interactions of the smaller domains that make up the bigger one.

Before we analyse and construct a specific system, we first need to perform an exhaustive analysis of the class of applications in that domain. In the domain of libraries, for example, there are things we need to know including the following.

1. The environment, including customers and users. Libraries have loanable items such as books, CDs, periodicals, etc. A library's customers are members. Libraries buy books from publishers.
2. Terminology that is unique to the domain. For example, the Dewey decimal classification (DDC) system for books.
3. Tasks and procedures currently performed. In a library system, for example:
   (a) Members may check out loanable items.
   (b) Some items are available only for reference; they cannot be checked out.
   (c) Members may put holds on loanable items.
   (d) Members will pay a fine if they return items after the due date.

Finding the Right Classes

In general, finding the right classes is non-trivial. It must be remembered that this process is iterative, i.e., we start with a set of classes and complete a conceptual design. In the process of walking through the use case implementations, we may find that some classes have to be dropped and some others have to be added. Familiarity with Design Patterns also helps in recognizing the classes. The following thumb rules and caveats come in handy:

- In general, do not build classes around functions. There are exceptions to this rule as we will see in Chap. 9. Write a class description. If it reads 'This class performs...' we most likely have a problem. If class name is imperative, e.g., print, parse, etc., it is likely that either the class is wrong or the name is wrong.
- Remember that a class usually has more than one method; otherwise it is probably a method that should be attached to some other class.
- Do not form an inheritance hierarchy too soon unless we have a pre-existing taxonomy. (Inheritance is supposed to be a relationship among well-understood abstractions.)
- Be wary of classes that have no methods, (or only query methods) because they are not frequent. Some situations in which they occur are:
  (i) representing objects from outside world, (ii) encapsulating facilities, constants or shared variables, (iii) applicative classes used to describe non-modifiable objects, e.g., integer class in Java generates new integers, but does not allow modification of integers.
- Check for the following properties of the ideal class: (i) a clearly associated abstraction, which should be a data abstraction (as opposed to a process abstraction), (ii) a descriptive noun/adjective for the class name, (iii) a non-empty set of runtime objects, (iv) queries and commands, (v) abstract properties that can be described as pre/post conditions and invariants.

One of the major activities of this analysis is discovering the business rules, the rules that any properly-functioning system in that domain must conform to.

Where does the knowledge of a specific domain come from? It could be from sources such as surveys, existing applications, technical reports, user manuals, and so on. As shown in Fig. 6.10, a domain analyst analyses this knowledge to come up with specifications, designs, and code that can be reused in multiple projects.

Clearly, a significant amount of effort has to be expended to domain analysis before undertaking the specific problem. The benefit is that after the initial investment of resources, the products (such as specifications, designs, code, test data, etc.) can be reused for the development of any number of applications in that domain. This reduces development time and cost.

Fig. 6.10 Domain analysis

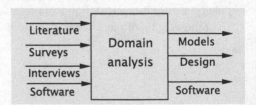

6.6 Discussion and Further Reading

A detailed treatment of object-oriented analysis methods can be found in [1]. The rules for finding the right classes are condensed from [2].

Obtaining the requirements specification is typically part of a larger '*plan and elaborate phase*' that would be an essential component of any large project. In addition to specification of requirements, this phase includes such activities as the *initial conception, investigation of alternatives, planning, budgeting* etc. The end product of this phase will include such documents as the *Plan* showing a schedule, resources, budget etc., a *preliminary investigation report* that lists the motivation, alternatives, and business needs, *requirements specification*, a *glossary* as an aid to understanding the vocabulary of the domain, and, perhaps, a *rough conceptual model*. Larger systems typically require more details before the analysis can proceed.

Use case modeling is one of the main techniques of a more general field of study called *usage modeling*. Usage modeling employs the following techniques: *essential use cases, system use cases, UML use case diagrams, user stories* and *features* [3]. What we have discussed here are essential use cases, which deal only with the fundamental business task without bringing technological issues into account. These are used to explore usage-based requirements.

Making sure that our use cases have covered all the business processes is in itself a non-trivial task. This area of study, called *business process modeling*, employs tools such as *data flow diagrams, flowcharts,* and *UML Activity Diagrams* [3] and is used to create process models for the business.

There are several UML tools available for analysis, and new variants are being constantly developed. What a practitioner chooses often depends on the development package being employed. A good, compact reference to the entire language can be found in [4]. The use case table and the class diagram with associations exemplify the very basic tools of object-oriented analysis.

There is no prescribed analysis or design technique that software designer must follow at all costs. There are several methodologies in vogue, and these ideas continue to evolve over time. In [5] it has been pointed out that while some researchers and developers are of the opinion that object-oriented methodologies are a revolutionary change from the conventional techniques, others have argued that object-oriented techniques are nothing but an elaboration of structured design. A comparative study of various object-oriented and conventional methodologies is also presented in that article.

Projects

1. **A database for a warehouse** A large warehousing corporation operates as follows:

    (a) The warehouse stocks several products, and there are several manufacturers for each product.

(b) The warehouse has a large number of registered clients. The clients place orders with the warehouse, which then ships the goods to the client. This process is as follows: the warehouse clerk examines the client's order and creates an invoice, depending on availability of the product. The invoice is then sent to the shop floor where the product is packed and shipped along with the invoice. The unfilled part of the order is placed in a waiting list queue.

(c) When the stock of any product runs low, the warehouse orders that product from one of the manufacturers, based on the price and terms of delivery.

(d) When a product shipment is received from a manufacturer, the orders in the waiting list are filled in first. The remainder is added to the inventory.

The business processes: The warehouse has three main operational business processes, namely,

(a) receiving and processing an order from a client,
(b) placing an order with the manufacturer,
(c) receiving a shipment,
(d) receiving payment from a client.

Let us examine the first of these. When an order is received from a client, the following steps are involved:

(a) Clerk receives the order and enters the order into the system.
(b) The system generates an invoice based on the availability of the product(s).
(c) The clerk prints the invoice and sends it over to the storage area.
(d) A worker on the floor picks up the invoice, retrieves the product(s) from the shelves and packs them, and ships the goods and the invoice to the client.
(e) The worker requests the system to mark the order as having been shipped.
(f) The system updates itself by recording the information.

This is an interesting business process because of the fact that steps of printing the invoice and retrieving the product from the shelves are performed by different actors. This introduces an indefinite delay into the process. If we were to translate this into a single end-to-end use case, we have a situation where the system will be waiting for a long time to get a response from an actor. It is therefore appropriate to break this up into two use cases as follows:

1. Use case create-invoice.
2. Use case fill-invoice.

In addition to these operational business processes, the warehouse will have several other querying and accounting processes such as:

(a) Registering a new client.
(b) Adding a new manufacturer for a certain product.
(c) Adding a new product.
(d) Printing a list of clients who have defaulted on payments.
(e) Printing a list of manufacturers who are owed money by the warehouse, etc.

Write the use cases, and determine the conceptual classes and their relationships.

2. **Managing a university registration system**

   A small university would like to create a registration system for its students. The students will use this system to obtain information about courses, when and where the classes meet, register for classes, print transcripts, drop classes, etc. The faculty will be using this system to find out what classes they are assigned to teach, when and where these classes meet, get a list of students registered for each class, and assign grades to students in their classes. The university administrative staff will be using this database to add new faculty and students, remove faculty and students who have left, put in and update information about each course the university ofers, enter the schedules for classes that are being offered in each term, and any other housekeeping tasks that need to be performed.

   Your task is to analyse this system, extract and list the details of the various business processes, develop the use cases, and find the conceptual classes and their relationships.

   In finding the classes for this system, one of the issues that comes up is that of distinguishing a course from an offering of the course. For instance 'CS 430: Principles of Object-Oriented Software Construction' is a course listed in the university's course bulletin. The course is offered once during the fall term and once during the spring term. Each offering may be taught at a different time and place, and in all likelihood will have a different set of students. Therefore, all offerings have some information in common and some information that is unique to that offering. How will you choose a set of classes that models all these interactions?

3. **Creating an airline reservation and staff scheduling database**

   An airline has a weekly flight schedule. Associated with each flight is an aircraft, a list of crew, and a list of passengers. The airline would like to create and maintain a database that can perform the following functions:

   For passengers Add a passenger to the database, reserve a seat on a flight, print out an itinerary, request seating and meal preferences, and update frequent flier records.

   For crew Assign crew members to each flight, allow crew members to view their schedule, keep track of what kinds of aircraft the crew member has been trained to operate.

   For flights Keep track of crew list, passenger list, and aircraft to be used for that flight.

   For aircraft Maintain all records about the aircraft and a schedule of operation.

   Make an exhaustive list of queries that this system may be required to answer. Carry out a requirements analysis for the system and model it as a collection of use cases. Find the conceptual classes and their relationships.

6.7 Exercises

1. In the use case Issue Book, the system displays the transaction details with each book. Modify this so that there is only one display of transactions at the very end of the process.
2. (Discussion) In a real library, there would be several other kinds of query operations that would be performed. Carry out a brainstorming exercise to come up with a more complete list of use cases for a real library system.
3. A hotel reservation system supports the following functionality:

   (a) Room reservation
   (b) Changing the properties of a room (for example, from non-smoking to smoking)
   (c) Customer check-in
   (d) Customer check-out

   Come up with system use cases for the above functionality.
4. We are building a system to track personal finances. We plan an initial version with minimal functionality: tracking the expenditures. (Each expenditure has a description, date and amount.) We show below the use case for creating a new expenditure item and a new income item.

Actor	System
(1) Inputs a request to create a new expenditure item	
	(2) Asks for description, date, and amount
(3) Supplies the data	
	(4) Creates an expenditure item and notifies the user

Actor	System
(1) Inputs a request to create a new income item	
	(2) Asks for description, date, and amount
(3) Supplies the data	
	(4) Creates an income item and notifies the user

   (a) The use cases are quite weakly specified. In what ways? (Hint: Compare with the addition of a new member or book in the library system.)
   (b) What are the alternate flows in the use cases? Modify the two use cases to handle the alternate flows.
   (c) Identify the conceptual classes.

5. Consider the policies maintained by an automobile insurance company. A policy has a primary policy holder, a set of autos insured, and a list of people who are covered by the insurance. From your knowledge of insurance, come up with system use cases for

   (a) creating a new policy
   (b) adding a new person to a policy
   (c) adding a new automobile to a policy
   (d) recording a claim.

6. Consider an information system to be created for handling the business of a supermarket. For each of the following, state if it is a possible class. If not, explain why not. Otherwise, why would you consider it to be a class? What is its role in the system?

   (a) Customer
   (b) Vegetable
   (c) Milk
   (d) Stock
   (e) Canned food
   (f) Quantity on hand for a product

7. A company has several projects, and each employee works in a single project. The human resource system evaluates the personnel needs of each project and matches them against the personnel file to find the best possible employees to be assigned to the project. Come up with the conceptual classes by conducting use case analysis.

8. Explain why mistakes made in the requirements analysis stage are the costliest to correct.

9. Among the following requirements, which are functional and which are non-functional?

   (a) Paychecks should be printed every two weeks.
   (b) Database recovery should not take more than one hour.
   (c) The system should be implemented using the C++ language.
   (d) It should be possible to selectively print employee checks.
   (e) Employee list should be displayed in lists of size 10.

10. Suppose the library system has to be augmented so that it can support inter-library loans. That is, a customer can ask the clerk if a certain book, which is not locally available, is available in some other library. What changes are needed (classes and use cases) to incorporate this new functionality?

11. In Problem 6, assume that a customer may pay with cash, check, or credit/debit cards. Should this aspect be taken into consideration while developing the use case for purchasing grocery? Justify your answer.

12. Again, in Problem 6, suppose that a user may check out by interacting with a sales clerk or independently in an automated checkout counter. Should there be two versions of the grocery purchase use case? Explain.
13. What are the advantages of ignoring implementation-related aspects while performing analysis?

References

1. C. Larman, *Applying UML and Patterns* (Prentice Hall PTR, 1998)
2. B. Meyer, *Object-Oriented Software Construction* (Prentice Hall, 1997)
3. S. Ambler, *The Object Primer: Agile Model-Driven Development with UML 2.0* (Cambridge University Press, 2004)
4. M. Fowler, K. Scott, *UML Distilled* (Addison-Wesley Longman, 1997)
5. R. Fichman, C. Kemerer, *Object-Oriented and Conventional Analysis and Design Methodologies* (IEEE Computer Society Press, 1995)

Chapter 7
Design and Implementation

Having done an analysis of the requirements, we proceed to the design stage. In this step, we use the class structure produced by the analysis to design a system that behaves in the manner specified by the model. The main UML tool that we employ here is the sequence diagram. In a sequence diagram, the designer specifies the details of how the behaviour specified in the model will be realised. This process requires the system's actions to be broken down into specific tasks, and the responsibility for these tasks to be assigned to the various players in the system. In the course of assigning these responsibilities, we determine the public methods of each class, and also describe the function performed by each method. Since the stage after design is implementation, which is coding, testing, and debugging, it is imperative that we have a full understanding of how the required functionality will be realised through code. The designer thus breaks down the system into smaller units and provides enough information so that a programmer can code and test each unit separately.

After the design is complete, we proceed to the implementation stage. As the coding is being done, the programmer should follow good coding and testing practices. We do not emphasise these principles here, since these are concepts common to any software design methodology. Our implementation will be done in Java. Any new language concepts that need elaboration are dealt with in the context where we employ them.

7.1 Design

During the design process, a number of questions need to be answered:

1. On what platform(s) (hardware and software) will the system run? For example, will the system be developed for just one platform, say, Windows running on 386-type processors? Or will we be developing for other platforms such as Unix?

© Universities Press (India) Private Ltd. 2015

159

B. Dathan and S. Ramnath, *Object-Oriented Analysis, Design and Implementation*,
Undergraduate Topics in Computer Science, DOI 10.1007/978-3-319-24280-4_7

2. What languages and programming paradigms will be used for implementation? Often, the choice of the language will be dictated by the expertise the company has. But sometimes the functionality will also heavily influence the choice of the language. For example, a business application may be developed using an object-oriented language such as Java or C++, but an artificial intelligence application may be programmed in LISP or Prolog. (In this chapter, we are assuming an object-oriented system.)
3. What user interfaces will the system provide? These include GUI screens, print-outs, and other devices (for example, library cards).
4. What classes and interfaces need to be coded? What are their responsibilities?
5. How is data stored on a permanent basis? What medium will be used? What model will be used for data storage?
6. What happens if there is a failure? Ideally, we would like to prevent data loss and corruption. What mechanisms are needed for realising this?
7. Will the system use multiple computers? If so, what are the issues related to data and code distribution?
8. What kind of protection mechanisms will the system use?

Since our focus in this book is on software design and development using the object-oriented paradigm using the Java programming language, we will not be distracted by considerations of the exact platform on which the system will run. Our major focus throughout the book is the identification of the software structure: *the classes and interfaces that make up the system.* Although we discuss User Interface (UI) design and long-term storage issues, we do not address protection and recovery mechanisms since the development of these is largely orthogonal to the issues that we are attempting to address. In general, systems typically employ some combination of application software, firewalls, database management system support, manual procedures, etc., to provide the necessary mechanisms for protection, concurrency control and recovery. The choices made when designing solutions for these issues should have little or no impact on the design of the application software itself.

7.1.1 Major Subsystems

The first step in our design process is to identify the major subsystems. We can view the library system as composed of two major subsystems:

1. **Business logic** This part deals with input data processing, data creation, queries, and data updates. This module will also be responsible for interacting with external storage, storing and retrieving data.
2. **User interface** This subsystem interacts with the user, accepting and outputting information.

It is important to design the system such that the above parts are separated from each other so that they can be varied independently. That way, we get good cohesion within each module. Our focus in this chapter is mainly on the design and implementation of the business logic. At the end of the chapter, we put together a rudimentary UI. We also implement a mechanism for storing and retrieving data by interacting with external storage devices. While the UI and external storage management modules are adequate to carry out functional testing of our system, a more sophisticated design (and implementation) would be in order for a full-blown system.

7.1.2 Creating the Software Classes

The next step is to create the **software classes**. During the analysis, after defining the use case model, we came up with a set of conceptual classes and a conceptual class diagram for the entire system. As mentioned earlier, these come from a conceptual or essential perspective. The software classes are more 'concrete' in that they correspond to the software components that make up the system. In this phase there are two major activities.

1. Come up with a set of classes.
2. Assign responsibilities to the classes and determine the necessary data structures and methods.

In general, it is unlikely that we can come up with a design simply by doing these activities exactly once. Several iterations may be needed and classes may need to be added, split, combined, or eliminated.

As we are having just a rudimentary text-based interface, the UI subsystem will consist of a single class, aptly named `UserInterface`. The classes for the business logic module will be the ones instrumental in implementing the system requirements described in the use case model. In our analysis, we came up with a set of *conceptual* classes and relationships. It is, therefore, reasonable that as a 'first guess' for the required software classes for the business logic, we pick these conceptual classes. A closer scrutiny of these is now in order.

1. **Member and Book** These are central concepts. Each `Member` object comprises several attributes such as name and address, stays in the system for a long period of time and performs a number of useful functions. Books stay part of the library over a long time and we can do a number of useful actions on them. We need to instantiate books and members quite often. Clearly, both are classes that require representation in software.
2. **Library** Do we really need to make a class for this? To answer the question, let us ask what the real library—not a possible object—has. It keeps track of books and members. When a member thinks of a library, he/she thinks of borrowing and returning books, placing and removing holds, i.e., the *functionality* provided by the library. To model a library with software, we need to mimic this functionality, which we did by creating a use case model. The use case behaviour is what is exhibited by the UI, and to meet the required specifications, the UI must perform

some other computations that involve the module that implements the business logic. One of the important principles of object-oriented design is that every computation must be represented as an application of a method on a given object, which is then treated as the current object for the computation. All the computation required of the business logic module must be executed on some current object; that object is a `Library`. This requires that `Library` be a class in its own right, and the operations required of the business logic module correspond to the methods of this class.

Although details of its functionality remain to be determined by examining the use cases, with some thought we can come up with two important aspects of the `Library` class. As we have seen in Chap. 6, the `Library` instance must keep track of the members of the library as well as the books, which obviously imply maintenance of two collection objects. The functionality of these two collections is again to be determined, but it is likely that we need two different classes, `MemberList` and `Catalog`, which may be alike in certain respects.[1] These two collections last as long as the library itself, and we make modifications to them very frequently. The actions that we perform are not supported by programming languages although there may be some support in the associated packages such as the list classes in the Java Development Kit. All these would suggest that they be classes. However, we create them just once. As we know from Chap. 5, a class that has just one instance is called a *singleton*. Both `MemberList` and `Catalog` are singletons.

3. **Borrows** This class represents the one-to-many relationship between members and books. *In typical one-to-many relationships, the association class can be efficiently implemented as a part of the two classes at the two ends.* To verify this for our situation, for every pair of member *m* and book *b* such that *m* has borrowed *b*, the corresponding objects simply need to maintain a reference to each other. Since a member may borrow multiple books, this arrangement entails the maintenance of a list of `Book` objects in `Member`, but since there is only a single borrower for a book, each `Book` object needs to store a reference to only one instance of `Member`. Further examining the role played by the information in `Borrows`, we see that when a book is checked out, the due date can be stored in `Book`. In general, this means that all attributes that are unique to the relationship may be captured by storing information at the 'many' end of the relationship. When the book is returned, the references between the corresponding `Member` and `Book` objects as well as the due date stored in `Book` can be 'erased.'

This arrangement efficiently supports queries arising in almost any situation: a user wanting to find out when her books are due, a staff member wanting to know the list of books borrowed by a member, or an anxious user asking the librarian when he can expect the book on which he placed a hold. In all these situations we have operations related to some `Member` and `Book` objects.

---

[1] Although we use the name `MemberList`, we do not imply that this class has to be organised as a list.

4. **Holds** Unlike `Borrows`, this class denotes a many-to-many relationship between the `Member` and `Book` classes. *In typical many-to-many relationships, implementation of the association without using an additional class is unlikely to be clean and efficient.* To attempt to do this without an additional class in the case of holds, we would need to maintain within each `Member` object references to all `Book` instances for which there is a hold, and keep 'reverse' references from the `Book` objects to the `Member` objects. This is, however, incomplete because we also need to maintain for each hold the number of days for which it is valid. But there is no satisfactory way of associating this attribute with the references. We could have queries like a user wanting a list of all of his holds that expire within 30 days. The reader can verify that implementations without involving an additional class will be messy and inefficient.

It is, therefore, appropriate that we have a class for this relationship and make the `Hold` object accessible to the instances of `Member` and `Book`.

As we look at ways to implement the use cases, it often happens that we eliminate some of these classes, discover more, and determine the attributes and methods for all of the concrete classes.

7.1.3 Assigning Responsibilities to the Classes

Having decided on an adequate set of software classes, our next task is to assign responsibilities to these. Since the ultimate purpose of these classes is to enable the system to meet the responsibilities specified in the use case, we shall work with these system responsibilities to find the class responsibilities. The next step is, therefore, to spell out the details of how the system meets its responsibilities by devolving these down to the software classes, and the UML tool that we employ to describe this devolution is the sequence diagram.

It should be noted that the sequence diagram is only a concise, visual way of *representing* the devolution, and we need to make our design choices *before* we start drawing our arrows. For each system response listed in the right-hand column of the use case tables, we need to specify the following:

- The sequence in which the operations will occur.
- How each operation will be carried out.

For the first item above, we need a complete algorithm; the second item describes which classes will be involved in each step of the algorithm and how the classes will be engaged. In specifying the second item, we spell out detailed definitions of the classes: the methods that need to be invoked and the parameters that should be passed to these methods. The first item specifies what is done in each step; since each step is a method call, we are specifying what each method is supposed to accomplish. In the course of figuring out how the method computes what is needed, we make other design choices. In the end, all of these things come together to give us a complete system.

Register Member

The sequence diagram for the use case for registering a member is shown in Fig. 7.1. The clerk issues a request to the system to add a new member. The system responds by asking for the data about the new member. This interaction occurs between the library staff member and the `UserInterface` instance. The clerk enters the requested data, which the `UserInterface` accepts.

Obviously, at this stage the system has all the data it needs to create a new `Member` object. The role of the UI is to interact with the user and not to perform business logic. So if the UI were to assume all responsibility for creating a `Member` object and adding that object to the `Library` instance, the consequence will be unnecessary and unwanted coupling between the business logic module and the UI class. We would like to retain the ability to develop the UI knowing as little as possible about the application classes. For this purpose, it is ideal to have a method, viz., `addMember`, within `Library` to perform the task of creating a `Member` and storing it in `MemberList`. All that `UserInterface` needs to do is pass the three pieces of information—name, address, and phone number of the applicant—as parameters to the `addMember` method, which then assumes full responsibility for creating and adding the new member.

Let us see details of the `addMember` method. The algorithm here consists of three steps:

1. Create a `Member` object.
2. Add the `Member` object to the list of members.
3. Return the result of the operation.

To carry out the first two steps, we have two options:

Option 1 Invoke the `Member` constructor from within the `addMember` method of `Library`. The constructor returns a reference to the `Member` object and an operation, `insertMember`, is invoked on `MemberList` to add the new member.

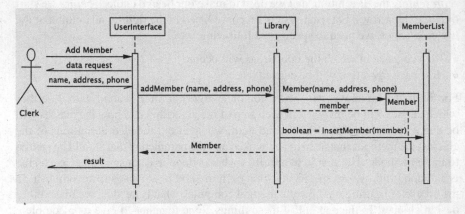

Fig. 7.1 Sequence diagram for adding a new member

Option 2 Invoke an `addNewMember` method on `MemberList` and pass as parameters all the data about the new member. `MemberList` creates the `Member` object and adds it to the collection.

Let us examine what the purpose of the `MemberList` class is: *to serve as a container for storing a large number of members, adding new ones, removing existing ones, and performing search operations.* The container should not, therefore, concern itself with details of a member, especially, its attributes. If we choose Option 2, `addNewMember` must take in as parameters the details of a member (name, address, and phone) so that it can call the constructor of the `Member` class. This introduces unnecessary coupling between `MemberList` and `Member`. As a result, if changes are later made to the `Member` constructor, these will also affect `MemberList`, even though the intended functions of `MemberList` do not warrant these changes.

Therefore, we prefer Option 1 to implement the `addMember` method.

The last step is to return the result so that `UserInterface` can adequately inform the actor about the success of the operation. The requirements for this are spelled out in Step 5 in Table 6.1, which reads: '(The system) informs the clerk if the member was added and outputs the member's name, address, phone, and id.' This can be achieved if `Library` returns a reference to the `Member` object that was created. If the reference is `null`, the UI informs the actor that the operation was unsuccessful; otherwise, the necessary information is accessed from the `Member` object and reported.

Add Books

The next sequence diagram that we show is for the Add Books use case. This use case allows the insertion of an arbitrary number of books into the system. In this case, when the request is made by the actor, the system enters a loop. Since the loop involves interacting repeatedly with the actor, the loop control mechanism is in the UI itself. The first operation is to get the data about the book to be added. The algorithm here consists of the following steps: (i) create a `Book` object, (ii) add the `Book` object to the catalog and (iii) return the result of the operation. This is handled in a manner similar to the previous use case.

The UI returns the result and continues until the actor indicates an exit. This repetition is shown diagrammatically by a special rectangle that is marked `loop`. All activities within the rectangle are repeated until the clerk indicates that there are no more books to be entered (Fig. 7.2).

In the last two sequence diagrams, note that `Library`, `MemberList` and `Catalog` are in the top row. Placing the entity in the top row indicates that it is in existence at the beginning of the process. This contrasts with the entities corresponding to `Member` and `Book`, which do not exist at the start, but are created by invoking constructors. This is indicated by placing the boxes labelled 'Member' and 'Book' respectively at the end of the arrow representing the call to the constructor. This box is at a lower level, to signify the later point in time when the entity comes into existence.

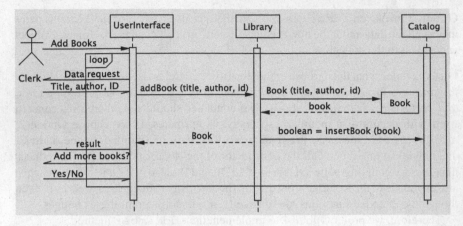

Fig. 7.2 Sequence diagram for adding books

Issue Books

The sequence diagram for the Issue Books use case is given next (Fig. 7.3). When a book is to be checked out, the clerk interacts with the UI to input the user's ID. The system has to first check the validity of the user. This is accomplished by invoking the method searchMembership on the Library.

Two options suggest themselves for implementing the search:

- **Option 1** Get an enumeration of all Member objects from MemberList, get the ID from each and compare with the target ID.
- **Option 2** Delegate the entire responsibility to MemberList.

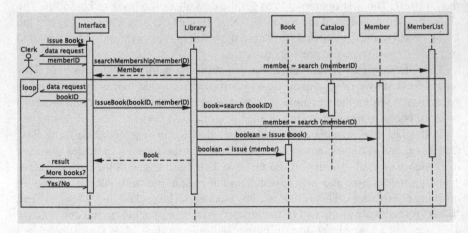

Fig. 7.3 Sequence diagram for issuing books

Option 1 places too much detail of the implementation in Library, which is undesirable. Option 2 is more attractive because search is a natural operation that is
performed on a container. The flip-side with the second option is that in a naive
implementation, MemberList will now become aware of implementation details
of Member (that memberID is a unique identifier, etc) causing some unwanted coupling between (Member) and the container class (MemberList). This coupling is
not a serious concern because it can be removed using generics as we shall see in the
next chapter.

UserInterface receives a reference to the Member object from Library
and then queries the actor for the ID of the book. In Library, we are providing a
method that issues a single book to a user. UserInterface invokes this method
repeatedly in order to issue several books to the user, each time passing the member's
ID and the book's ID as parameters. Once again, searching for the Book object is
delegated to Catalog. Next, the Book and Member objects are updated to indicate
that the book is checked out to the member (and that the member is in possession
of the book). Notice that the Library class orchestrates the whole show and also
acts as a go-between for all operations that the UserInterface requests from the
business logic module.

It may be tempting for a beginner to directly access the Member object from
UserInterface, pass the book's ID as a parameter and thereby initiate the issuing process. To understand why this is a bad idea, imagine that at later time, the
business logic associated with issuing a book changes. This change could potentially
force changes in the UserInterface class, i.e., *classes outside the core library
subsystem are affected.* As a general rule, we avoid exposing details of business logic
implementation to the UI. Likewise, one may be tempted to send bookID to Member
and handle all the details within Member; this would mean that Member searches
Catalog, creating a dependency between these classes. These other approaches,
therefore, expose system details to the UI and create tight coupling between the
classes, thus hurting reuse.

Another question we need to address is this: *Where should the responsibility for
generating the due-date lie?* In our simple system, the due-date is simply one month
from the date of issue, and it is not determined by other factors such as member
privileges. Consequently computing the due-date is a simple operation that can be
done in any of the objects, but since we are storing the due-date as a field in Book,
we will assign this responsibility to Book.

As before, we must decide the return type of the method issueBook. The use
case requires of the system that it generates a due-date. The system displays the book
title and due-date and asks if there are any more books. This can be easily done by
returning a reference to the Book object. The operation is reported as unsuccessful
if the reference is null.

Return Books

The Return Book use case is implemented in Fig. 7.4 as a sequence diagram. For
each book returned, the returnBook method of the Library class obtains the

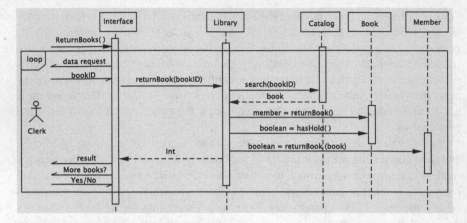

Fig. 7.4 Sequence diagram for returning books

corresponding Book object from Catalog. The returnBook method is invoked using this Book object, and this method returns the Member object corresponding to the member who had borrowed the book. The returnBook method of the Member object is now called to record that the book has been returned. This operation has three possible outcomes that the use case requires the system to distinguish (Step 5 in Table 6.5):

1. *The book's ID was invalid,* which would result in the operation being unsuccessful;
2. *the operation was successful;*
3. *The operation was successful and there is a hold on the book.* The value returned by returnBook must enable UserInterface to make the distinction between these. This is done by having Library return a result code, which could simply be one of three suitably named integer constants.

Remove Books

The diagram in Fig. 7.5 shows the sequence diagram for removing books from the collection. Here, as discussed in the use case, we remove only those books that are not checked out and do not have a hold. This logic for deciding whether the book is removable is in the removeBook method in Library. This method checks each property of the book in question and if all properties are satisfied, the remove method in Catalog is invoked, which then removes the book. The square brackets before the invocation of remove contain the condition 'can delete book', indicating that the book is deleted only if this condition is met. Library returns a specific code for each possible outcome, which UserInterface translates into an appropriate message.

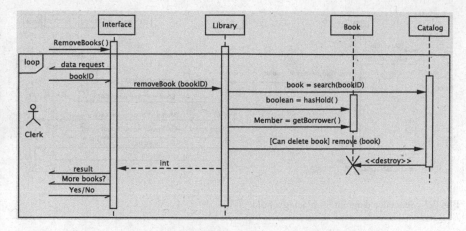

Fig. 7.5 Sequence diagram for removing books

Member Transactions

Following the earlier examples, it is no surprise that the end-user (clerk) interacts with the Library class to print out the transactions of a given member. From the descriptions given so far, the reader should have gained enough skill to interpret most of the sequence diagram in Fig. 7.6.

The Member class stores the necessary information about the transactions, but the UI would be the one to decide the format. It would, therefore, be desirable to provide the information to the UI as a collection of objects, each object containing the information about a particular transaction. This can be done by defining a class Transaction that stores the type of transaction (issue, return, place, or remove hold), the date, and the title of the book involved. Member stores a list of transactions, and the method getTransactions returns an enumeration (Iterator) of the

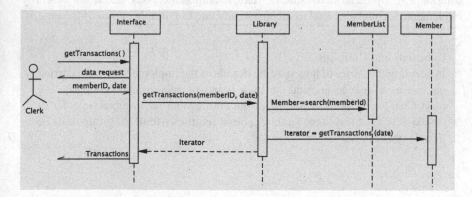

Fig. 7.6 Sequence diagram for printing a member's transactions

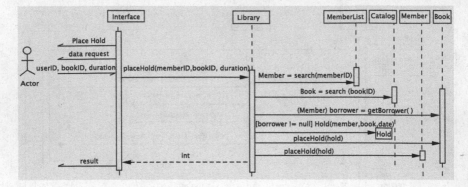

Fig. 7.7 Sequence diagram for placing a hold

Transaction objects whose date matches the one specified. Library returns this to the UI, which extracts and displays the needed information.

Place Hold

As discussed earlier, we create a separate Hold class for representing the holds placed by members. Each Hold object stores references to a Member object and a Book object, and the date when the hold expires (see Fig. 7.7).

When a clerk issues request to the library to place a hold on behalf of a member for a certain book, the Library object itself creates an instance of Hold and makes both the Book and Member instances involved to store references to it. The UI is informed of the outcome by a result code.

It is instructive to consider what alternate implementations may be used for storing the holds. One possibility is that both Book and Member create their own individualised Hold objects, with a BookHold class storing the date and a reference to Member and MemberHold storing the date and a reference to Book. Such a solution is less preferable because it creates additional classes, and if not carefully implemented, could also lead to inconsistency due to multiple copies of the date.

Cohesion and Coupling

In deciding the issues of how specific details of the implementation are carried out, we have to keep in mind the twin issues of cohesion and coupling. We must have *good cohesion* among all the entities that are grouped together or placed within a subsystem. Simultaneously, entities within the group must be *loosely coupled*.

In our example, when issuing a book, we have chosen to implement the system so that the Library calls the issue methods of Book and Member. Contrast this with a situation where Book calls the issue method of Member; in such a situation, the code in Book depends on the method names of Member, which causes tight coupling between these two classes. Instead, we have chosen a solution where each of these classes is somewhat tightly coupled with Library, but there is very loose coupling between any other pair of classes. This means that when the system has to adapt to changes in any class, this can be done by modifying Library only. Library, therefore, serves as 'glue' that holds the system together and simultaneously acts an interlocutor between the entities in the library system.

We have also consciously chosen to separate the design of the business module from the UI through which the actors will interact with the system. This is to ensure good cohesion within the system's 'back-end'.

A related question that we face at a lower level is that of how responsibilities are being assigned. We ask this question when a class is being designed. Responsibilities are assigned to classes based on the fields that the class has. These responsibilities turn into the methods of the class. The principle that we are following here can be tersely summarised in an Italian saying (attributed to Bertrand Meyer), *'The shoemaker must not look past the sandal'*. In other words, the only responsibilities assigned to an object/class should be the ones that are relevant to the data abstraction that the class represents. This, in turn, ensures that we avoid unnecessary coupling between classes.

Process Holds

The input here is only the ID for the book, from which we get the next hold that has not expired. In this process, the book would quite likely find some holds that are not valid. These holds should obviously be removed from the system and the responsibility for this clean up is assigned to the getNextHold() method in Book. The Library gets a reference to the Member object from Hold (see Fig. 7.8) and returns this to the UI.

Remove Hold

The sequence diagram is given in Fig. 7.9. A request is issued to Library via the method removeHold. Library retrieves the corresponding Member and Book objects using MemberList and Catalog and then invokes the removeHold method on these objects to delete their references to the Hold object.

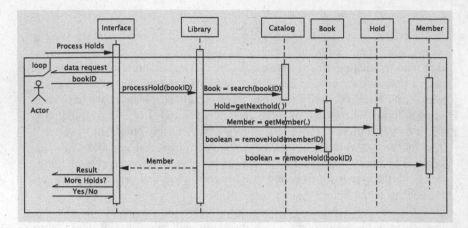

Fig. 7.8 Sequence diagram for processing holds

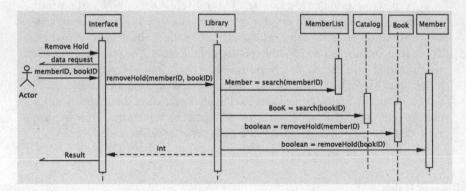

Fig. 7.9 Sequence diagram for removing a hold

Renew Books

Figure 7.10 details the implementation for renewing books. This process involves interactively updating the information on several members of a collection. We can accomplish this by allowing UserInterface to get an enumeration (Iterator) of the items in the collection, getting responses on each from the user and invoking the methods on the library to update the information.

The Library class thus provides a set of methods for the UI and serves as a single point of entry to and exit from the business logic module. This is a useful approach in many situations, so it is given a special name: **Facade.** All updates are done by invoking methods on the facade and not by directly manipulating the objects in the enumeration. Such direct manipulation would place some of the business logic in the UI and also hurt reuse as we have observed earlier.

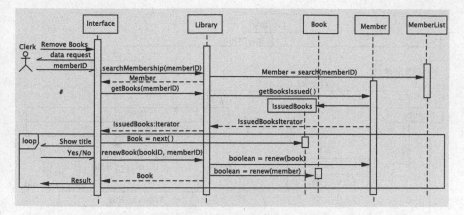

Fig. 7.10 Sequence diagram for renewing books

7.1.4 Class Diagrams

Hopefully, at this stage, we have come up with all the software classes. To review:

1. Library
2. MemberList
3. Catalog
4. Member
5. Book
6. Hold
7. Transaction

The relationships between these classes is shown in Fig. 7.11. Note that Hold is not shown as an association class, but an independent class that connects Member and Book. The new class Transaction is added to record transactions; this has a dependency on Book since it stores the title of the book.

By inspecting the sequence diagrams, we can collect the methods of each of these classes, and draw a class diagram for each. In specifying the types of attributes, we have to make language-specific choices; in the process of doing this we transition from the software classes to the **implementation** classes.

We first examine the methods and then arrive at the attributes by examining the methods.

Class Diagram for Library

The methods are simply a collection of methods with their parameters as given in the sequence diagrams. However, we have specified their return types, which were not clearly specified in the sequence diagrams. Whenever something is added to the system such as a member or a book or a hold, some information about the added object is returned, so that the clerk can verify that the data was correctly recorded.

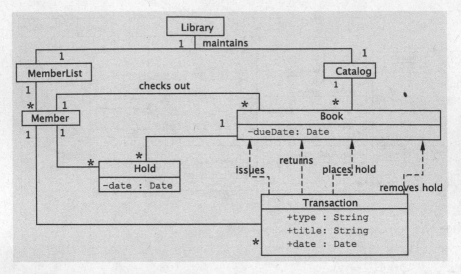

Fig. 7.11 Relationships between the software classes

Library
- members: MemberList
- books: Catalog
+ addBook(title:String, author: String, id :String): Book
+ addMember(name: String, address:String, phone:String):Member
+ issueBook (bookId:String,memberIdLString): Book
+ returnBook (bookId:String): int
+ removeBook(bookIdLString):int
+ placeHold(memberId:String,bookId:String,duration:int):int
+ processHold(bookId:String): Member
+ removeHold (memberId:String, bookId:String): int
+ searchMembership(memberId: String): Member
+ renewBook(memberId:String,bookId:String):Book
+ getTransactions(memberId:String,date:Calendar): Iterator
+ getBooks (memberId: String):Iterator

Fig. 7.12 Class diagram for Library

We have already seen that the class must maintain references to Catalog and MemberList. See Fig. 7.12 for the class diagram.

Class Diagram for Member

Once again, we get our methods and attributes by examining the sequence diagrams. In our design, we make the Member class generate the member ID. We need a mechanism to ensure that no two members get the same ID, i.e., there has to be some

Member
– name: String – address: String – phone: String – booksOnHold: List – transaction: List
+ Member (name:String,address:String,phone:String):Member + issue(book:Book): boolean + returnBook (book:Book):boolean + renew(book:Book):boolean + placeHold(hold:Hold): void + removeHold(bookId:String):boolean + getName(): String + getAddress(): String + getPhone(): String + getId(): String + setName(name:String): void + setPhone(phone:String):void + setAddress(address:String): void + getTransactions(date:Calendar):Iterator + getBooksIssued(): Iterator

Fig. 7.13   Class diagram for Member

central place where we keep track of how ids are generated. It would be tempting to do this in the Library class, but the right solution would be to make it a static method in the Member class. This gives us decentralised control and places responsibilities close to the data. The class diagram is given in Fig. 7.13.

Class Diagram for Book

The approach to developing the class diagram for Book parallels that of the approach for the Member class. As in the other cases, we now add the attributes. However, there are no setters for the Book class because we don't expect to change anything in a Book object (see Fig. 7.14).

Class Diagram for Catalog

Typical operations on a list would be add, remove, and search for objects. Proceeding as in the case for the Library class, we obtain the methods shown in Fig. 7.15.

The only attribute that we come up with is a List object that stores Book objects. The reader will also notice the method getBooks, whose return type is Iterator. This enables the Library to get an enumeration of all the books so that any specialised operations that have to be applied to the collection are facilitated.

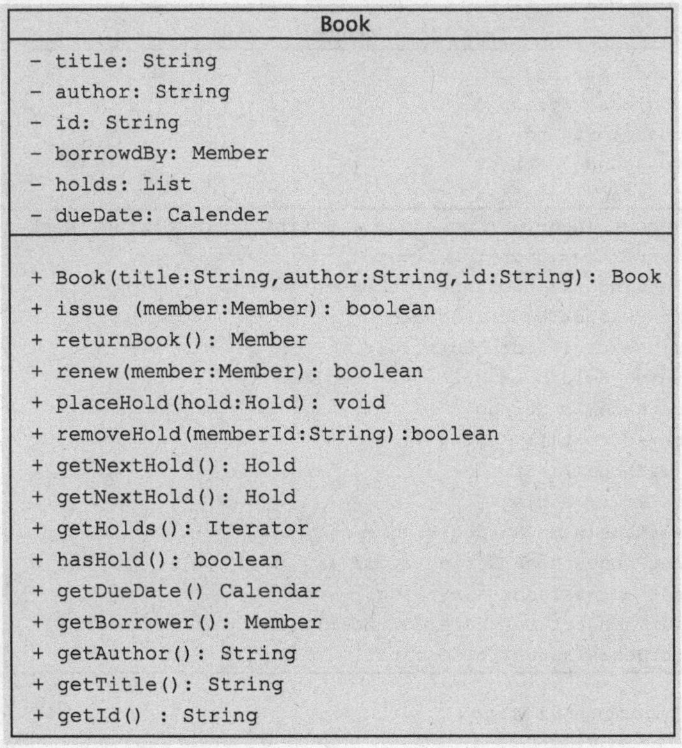

Book
− title: String
− author: String
− id: String
− borrowdBy: Member
− holds: List
− dueDate: Calender
+ Book(title:String,author:String,id:String): Book
+ issue (member:Member): boolean
+ returnBook(): Member
+ renew(member:Member): boolean
+ placeHold(hold:Hold): void
+ removeHold(memberId:String):boolean
+ getNextHold(): Hold
+ getNextHold(): Hold
+ getHolds(): Iterator
+ hasHold(): boolean
+ getDueDate() Calendar
+ getBorrower(): Member
+ getAuthor(): String
+ getTitle(): String
+ getId() : String

Fig. 7.14 Class diagram for the Book class

Fig. 7.15 Class diagram for
the Catalog class

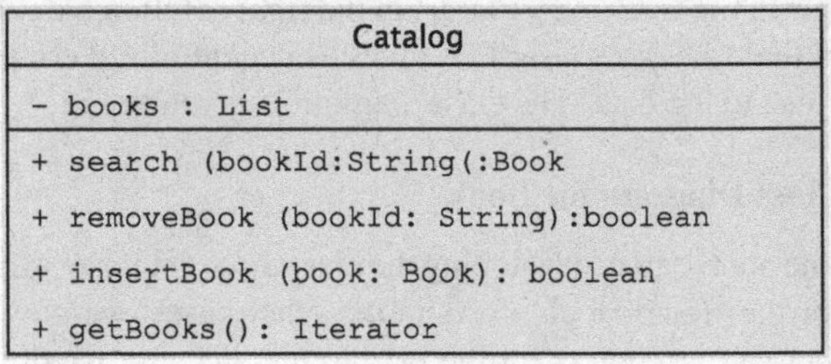

Catalog
− books : List
+ search (bookId:String(:Book
+ removeBook (bookId: String):boolean
+ insertBook (book: Book): boolean
+ getBooks(): Iterator

Class Diagram for MemberList

The derivation of this is fairly straightforward after developing the Catalog class
and is shown in Fig. 7.16. Since we never asked for the functionality of removing a
member, there is no such method in the class. We need an attribute of type List to
store the members.

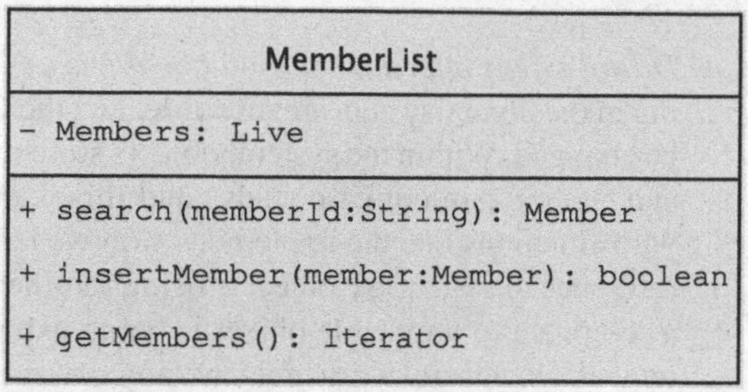

Fig. 7.16 Class diagram for
the MemberList class

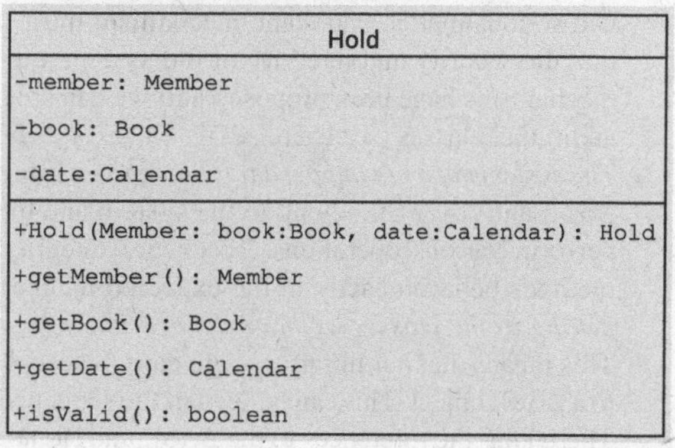

MemberList
− Members: Live
+ search(memberId:String): Member   + insertMember(member:Member): boolean   + getMembers(): Iterator

Fig. 7.17 Class diagram for
Hold

Hold
-member: Member   -book: Book   -date:Calendar
+Hold(Member: book:Book, date:Calendar): Hold   +getMember(): Member   +getBook(): Book   +getDate(): Calendar   +isValid(): boolean

Class Diagram for Hold

Besides the accessors, getMember, getBook, and getDate, the class diagram
for Hold (Fig. 7.17) shows the isValid method, which checks whether a certain
hold is still valid.

Exporting and Importing Objects
The classes that we have implemented for the business logic form an object-
oriented system, which can be accessed and modified through the methods of
Library. When dealing with object-oriented systems, one must keep in mind
that there are often several references to one object, stored in multiple locations.
For instance, a reference to every Member object is stored in MemberList,
but when the member checks out a book, the Book object also holds a reference.
In a lot of situations it is convenient to have a query return a reference to an
object. This multiplicity of references means that we need to observe some
caveats to ensure that data integrity is not compromised. In the context of
importing and exporting references through the facade, the following deserve
mention.

- *Do not export references to mutable objects.* All the objects that we are creating in the library system are **mutable**, i.e., the values stored in their fields can be changed. Within the system, objects store references to each other (Book and Member in our case study) and this is unavoidable. Our worries start with situations like the implementation we have for Issue Books, in which a reference to a Member object is being returned to UserInterface. Here a reference to a mutable object is being exported from the library subsystem, and in general we do not have any control over how this reference could be (mis)used. In a system that has to be deployed for widespread use, this is a serious matter, and some mechanism must be employed to make sure that the security and integrity of the system are not compromised. Several mechanisms have been proposed and we can create simple ones by defining additional classes (see exercises).

- *The system must not import a reference to an* **internal** *object.* Objects of type Book and Member belong to the system and their methods are invoked to perform various operations. To ensure integrity, it is essential that these methods behave exactly in the expected manner, i.e., *the objects involved belong to the classes we have defined and not any malicious descendants.* This means that our library system cannot accept as a parameter a reference to a Book object. This can be seen in the sequence diagram for Renew Books. The UI has the references to the Book and Member objects, but the Library does not accept these as parameters for renewBook. Working with the ID may mean an additional overhead to search for the object reference using the ID, but it certifies that when the renew methods are invoked, these are on objects that belong to the system.

Class Diagram for Transaction

The class diagram is shown in Fig. 7.18. Note that we have to store the date for each transaction, i.e., we need to choose an appropriate type for this attribute. Java's util package has a class Calendar that provides the needed functionality.

7.1.5 User Interface

As discussed earlier, our UI provides a menu with the following options:

1 Add a member
2 Add books
3 Issue books
4 Return books
5 Renew books

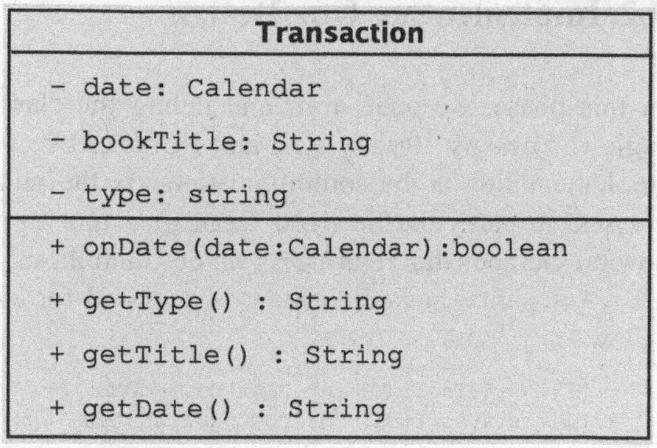

Fig. 7.18 Class diagram for
Transaction

Transaction
– date: Calendar
– bookTitle: String
– type: string
+ onDate(date:Calendar):boolean
+ getType() : String
+ getTitle() : String
+ getDate() : String

6 Remove books
7 Place a hold on a book
8 Remove a hold on a book
9 Process holds
10 Print a member's transactions on a given date
11 Save data for long-term storage
12 Retrieve data from storage
0 Exit
13 Help

Initially, the system will display a menu. The user can enter a number from 0 through 13 indicating the operation. (The options 0 and 13 will be used to exit the system and display the help screen respectively.) Parameters required for the operation will be prompted. The result of the operation is then displayed.

All input/output will be via simple text interface.

7.1.6 Data Storage

Ultimately, most applications will need to store data on a long-term basis. In a full-blown system, data is usually stored in a database, and this data is managed by a database management system. To avoid digressing, however, we will adopt a simple approach to store data on a long-term basis. Recall that we had decided to include the following commands in our UI.

1. A command to save the data on a long-term basis.
2. A command to load data from a long-term storage device.

When the first command is executed, we will copy all of the data onto secondary storage. Similarly, when the second command is executed, the data stored on the storage device is copied to recreate the object.

7.2 Implementing Our Design

In this phase, we code, test, and debug the classes that implement the business logic (`Library`, `Book`, etc.) and `UserInterface`. An important issue in the implementation is the communication via the return values between the different classes: in particular between `Library` and `UserInterface`; `Library` has several methods that return `int` values, and these values must be interpreted by the UI.[2] A separate named constant is declared for each of these outcomes as shown below.

```
public static final int BOOK_NOT_FOUND  = 1;
public static final int BOOK_NOT_ISSUED = 2;
// etc.
```

These are declared in `Library`.

7.2.1 Setting Up the Interface

We are now ready to complete our development by writing the code. The main program resides in the class `UserInterface`. When the main program is executed, an instance of the UserInterface is created (a singleton).

```
public static void main(String[] s) {
  UserInterface.instance().process();
}

public static UserInterface instance() {
  if (userInterface == null) {
    return userInterface = new UserInterface();
  } else {
    return userInterface;
  }
}
```

The private constructor checks whether a serialized version of the `Library` object exists. (We assume that it is stored in a file called 'LibraryData'.) The `File` class in Java is a convenient mechanism to check the existence of files. The user is given an option to retrieve any serialized version of the `Library` object. (We will explain later how the problem of safely combining serialization and singletons is tackled.) In any case, `UserInterface` gets an instance of `Library`.

```
private UserInterface() {
  File file = new File("LibraryData");
  if (file.exists() && file.canRead()) {
    if (yesOrNo("Saved data exists. Use it?")) {
      retrieve();
    }
```

---

[2]The implementation has additional methods to aid testing: methods to display books, members, etc. We do not discuss these methods here.

```
    }
    library = Library.instance();
}
```

Following this, the `process` method of `UserInterface` is executed, which initialises a loop that provides the user with a list of options. This code snippet is given below.

```
public void process() {
  int command;
  help();
  while ((command = getCommand()) != EXIT) {
    switch (command) {
      case ADD_MEMBER:    addMember();
                          break;
      case ADD_BOOKS:     addBooks();
                          break;
      case ISSUE_BOOKS:   issueBooks();
                          break;
      // several lines of code not shown
      case HELP:          help();
                          break;
    }
  }
}
```

The `help` method displays all the options with the corresponding numeric choices. In addition to the methods for each of the menu items, `UserInterface` also has methods `getToken`, `getNumber`, `getDate`, and `getCommand` for reading the user input. An examination of the sequence diagrams shows the need to query the user in multiple situations for a 'Yes' or 'No' answer to different questions. For this, we have also coded a method `yesOrNo` with a `String` parameter to prompt the user. We can now follow our sequence diagrams to implement the methods. Some of these are explained below.

7.2.2 Adding New Books

The `addBooks` method in `UserInterface` is shown below:

```
public void addBooks() {
  Book result;
  do {
    String title = getToken("Enter book title");
    String author = getToken("Enter author");
    String bookID = getToken("Enter id");
    result = library.addBook(title, author, bookID);
    if (result != null) {
      System.out.println(result);
    } else {
      System.out.println("Book could not be added");
    }
    if (!yesOrNo("Add more books?")) {
```

```
      break;
    }
  } while (true);
}
```

The loop is set up in UserInterface, all the input is collected, and the addBook method in Library is invoked. Following the sequence diagram, this method is implemented in Library as follows:

```
public Book addBook(String title, String author, String id) {
  Book book = new Book(title, author, id);
  if (catalog.insertBook(book)) {
    return (book);
  }
  return null;
}
```

In the above code, the constructor for Book is invoked and the new book is added to the catalog. The Catalog (which is also a singleton) is an adapter for the LinkedList class, so all it does is to invoke the add method in Java's LinkedList class, as shown below.

```
public class Catalog {
  private List books = new LinkedList();
  // some code not shown
  public boolean insertBook(Book book) {
    return books.add(book);
  }
}
```

7.2.3 Issuing Books

Once again, UserInterface gets the member's ID and sets up the loop. Here, UserInterface remembers the member's ID throughout the process. The issue Book method of Library is repeatedly invoked and the response to the actor is generated based on the value returned by each invocation.

```
public void issueBooks() {
  Book result;
  String memberID = getToken("Enter member id");
  if (library.searchMembership(memberID) == null) {
    System.out.println("No such member");
    return;
  }
  do {
    String bookID = getToken("Enter book id");
    result = library.issueBook(memberID, bookID);
    if (result != null){
      System.out.println(result.getTitle()+ "   " + result.getDueDate());
    } else {
      System.out.println("Book could not be issued");
    }
    if (!yesOrNo("Issue more books?")) {
```

```
        break;
    }
  } while (true);
}
```

The `issueBook` method in `Library` does the necessary processing and returns a reference to the issued book.

```
public Book issueBook(String memberId, String bookId) {
  Book book = catalog.search(bookId);
  if (book == null) {
    return(null);
  }
  if (book.getBorrower() != null) {
    return(null);
  }
  Member member = memberList.search(memberId);
  if (member == null) {
    return(null);
  }
  if (!(book.issue(member) && member.issue(book))) {
    return null;
  }
  return(book);
}
```

The `issue` methods in `Book` and `Member` record the fact that the book is being issued. The method in `Book` generates a due date for our simple library by adding one month to the date of issue.

```
public boolean issue(Member member) {
  borrowedBy = member;
  dueDate = new GregorianCalendar();
  dueDate.setTimeInMillis(System.currentTimeMillis());
  dueDate.add(Calendar.MONTH, 1);
  return true;
}
```

`Member` is also keeping track of all the transactions (issues and returns) that the member has completed. This is done by defining the class `Transaction`.

```
import java.util.*;
import java.io.*;
public class Transaction implements Serializable {
  private String type;
  private String title;
  private Calendar date;
  public Transaction (String type, String title) {
    this.type = type;
    this.title = title;
    date = new GregorianCalendar();
    date.setTimeInMillis(System.currentTimeMillis());
  }
  public boolean onDate(Calendar date) {
    return ((date.get(Calendar.YEAR) == this.date.get(Calendar.YEAR)) &&
            (date.get(Calendar.MONTH) == this.date.get(Calendar.MONTH)) &&
            (date.get(Calendar.DATE) == this.date.get(Calendar.DATE)));
  }
```

```
public String getType() {
  return type;
}
public String getTitle() {
  return title;
}
public String getDate() {
  return date.get(Calendar.MONTH) + "/" + date.get(Calendar.DATE) + "/"
                                     + date.get(Calendar.YEAR);
}
public String toString(){
  return (type + "   " + title);
}
}
```

With each book issued, a record is created and added to the list of transactions, as shown in the following code snippet from Member.

```
private List booksBorrowed = new LinkedList();
private List booksOnHold = new LinkedList();
private List transactions = new LinkedList();

public boolean issue(Book book) {
  if (booksBorrowed.add(book)){
    transactions.add(new Transaction ("Book issued ", book.getTitle()));
    return true;
  }
  return false;
}
```

7.2.4 Printing Transactions

Library provides a query that returns an Iterator of all the transactions of a member on a given date, and this is implemented by passing the query to the appropriate Member object. The method getTransactions in Member filters the transactions based on the date and returns an Iterator of the filtered collection.

```
public Iterator getTransactions(Calendar date) {
  List result = new LinkedList();
  for (Iterator iterator = transactions.iterator(); iterator.hasNext(); ) {
    Transaction transaction = (Transaction) iterator.next();
    if (transaction.onDate(date)) {
      result.add(transaction);
    }
  }
  return (result.iterator());
}
```

Library returns null when the member is not in MemberList; otherwise an iterator to the filtered collection is returned. The UI extracts the necessary information and displays it in the preferred format.

```
public void getTransactions() {
  Iterator result;
  String memberID = getToken("Enter member id");
```

```
       Calendar date  = getDate("Please enter the date for which you want " +
                                  "records as mm/dd/yy");
       result = library.getTransactions(memberID,date);
       if (result == null) {
         System.out.println("Invalid Member ID");
       } else {
         while(result.hasNext()) {
           Transaction transaction = (Transaction) result.next();
           System.out.println(transaction.getType() + "   "   +
                              transaction.getTitle() + "\n");
         }
         System.out.println("\n  There are no more transactions \n" );
       }
     }
```

7.2.5 Placing and Processing Holds

When placing a hold, the information about the hold is passed to Library, which
checks the validity of the information and creates a Hold object. In our implementation, the Member and Book objects store the reference to the Hold object. The
placeHold method in both Book and Member simply appends the new hold to
the list. (The code for Book is shown below.)

```
private List holds = new LinkedList();
public void placeHold(Hold hold) {
   holds.add(hold);
}
```

One problem with this simple solution is that unwanted holds can stay in the system
forever. To prevent this, we may want to delete all invalid holds periodically, perhaps
just before the system is saved to disk. This is left as an exercise.

The list booksOnHold in Member keeps a collection of all the active holds the
member has placed. In the Member class we also generate a transaction whenever a
hold is placed.

```
public void placeHold(Hold hold) {
   transactions.add(new Transaction ("Hold Placed", hold.getBook().getTitle()
   ));  booksOnHold.add(hold);
}
```

To process a hold, Library invokes the getNextHold method in Book, which
returns the first valid hold.

```
public Hold getNextHold() {
   for (ListIterator iterator = holds.listIterator(); iterator.hasNext();) {
     Hold hold = (Hold) iterator.next();
     iterator.remove();
     if (hold.isValid()) {
       return hold;
     }
   }
   return null;
}
```

The `Hold` class is shown below. There are no modifiers for the attributes, since a hold cannot be changed once it has been placed. The method `isValid()` checks if the hold is still valid.

```
public class Hold implements Serializable {
  private Book book;
  private Member member;
  private Calendar date;
  public Hold(Member member, Book book, int duration) {
    this.book = book;
    this.member = member;
    date = new GregorianCalendar();
    date.setTimeInMillis(System.currentTimeMillis());
    date.add(Calendar.DATE, duration);
  }
  public Member getMember() {
    return member;
  }
  public Book getBook() {
    return book;
  }
  public Calendar getDate() {
    return date;
  }
  public boolean isValid() {
    return (System.currentTimeMillis() < date.getTimeInMillis());
  }
}
```

Once the reference to the `Hold` object has been found in the Book, the hold is removed from the book and from the corresponding member as well. The book's ID is passed to the `removeHold` method in `Member`, which is shown below.

```
public boolean removeHold(String bookId) {
  boolean removed = false;
  for (ListIterator iterator = booksOnHold.listIterator();
                                iterator.hasNext(); ) {
    Hold hold = (Hold) iterator.next();
    String id = hold.getBook().getId();
    if (id.equals(bookId)) {
      transactions.add(new Transaction ("Hold Removed ",
                                      hold.getBook().getTitle()));
      removed = true;
      iterator.remove();
    }
  }
  return removed;
}
```

As is evident from the pieces of code shown above, the translation from sequence diagrams to code is a fairly straightforward task. This is what one should expect. In fact, the sequence diagrams in software design perform a role analogous to blueprint in engineering design. Once the sequence diagrams are complete, there is very little left to explain or discuss. If it were otherwise, that would reflect poorly on the process being followed.

Memory Management in Object-Oriented Systems

Proliferation of objects contributes in large part to the degradation of performance in object-oriented systems, which means that objects must be removed from the system in an expedient manner as soon as they have served their purpose. Objects are typically allocated in the process memory space known as the *heap*. In Java, memory allocated to an object in the heap is not reclaimed until all references to the object are set to null. Some languages such as C++ allow and require the user to employ a specific operator in order to free up the space allocated to an object.

The availability of automatic reclamation of storage in Java is often touted as a boon, and it indeed is: it ensures that there are no *dangling references* or *memory leaks* in the traditional sense of these two terms. But it does not absolve the programmer from his/her responsibilities to ensure proper memory management. The reader must be aware that memory shortage and data integrity issues, which are respectively the consequences of memory leaks and dangling pointers, may manifest themselves because of design and coding errors.

The problem of memory shortage may still arise in a Java program because we may forget to set to null every reference to an object that should be deleted: the language's garbage collection mechanism must be given a chance to kick in, and that will not happen without some cooperation from the application code. Removing objects can be a tricky exercise and to ensure reliable performance, a systematic process is needed for removing the unwanted ones. As systems become more complex, we have more intricate relationships between objects, which, in turn, make the unwanted objects harder to detect. In our example, Book and Member objects are relatively stable and introduced into the system in a fairly controlled manner. Hold objects, on the other hand, are more ephemeral and can be easily added and removed,which means that there is a potential for their numbers to explode. In the library system, we suggest that this be fixed by removing invalid holds periodically.

Dangling pointers, which imply invalid object references, could ultimately lead to illegal data access and failure. Careless design and development may result in the very same fate in a Java program. While deleting the reference to an object from one part of the system, we must be careful to ensure that any remaining references to the object from other parts of the system will not lead to inconsistencies. When deleting an object from a collection, we typically obtain a reference to the object by searching the container. If there are references to a deleted object stored in other active objects, we may up with *mutual inconsistency*. For instance, assume that we remove a book *b* from the catalog by deleting the reference to the appropriate Book object from Catalog. Furthermore, suppose that *b* has a hold *h* on it.

This could lead to the situation where we obtain the reference to the Book object (corresponding to *b*) from the Hold object (corresponding to *h*) and use *b*'s ID at a later point to search the catalog; obviously, this search will lead to an unexpected failure! There are two possible solutions to overcome this problem: *(i) delete the corresponding Hold object* while removing the book from the catalog or *(ii) remove the reference from Catalog only if there are no holds and the book is not currently checked out.* In our implementation, we have chosen the second solution.

7.2.6 Storing and Retrieving the Library Object

Java Serialization

Our approach to long-term storage of the library data uses the Java *serialization* mechanism. In Chap. 4 we saw that the methods readObject() and writeObject (Object) in ObjectInputStream and ObjectOutputStream respectively can be used to read and write objects and that this can be easily done for simple cases by having the corresponding class implement the Serializable interface.

In our current example, Book and Hold can be serialized by simply declaring them to be Serializable. This is because they contain instance fields each of which is defined to be Serializable. (The reader can verify this by examining the documentation of the Java classes we use, such as GregorianCalendar and LinkedList and the definition of Book and Hold.) Member, MemberList, Catalog, and Library need more work because they all have static fields in them. The default serialization mechanism in Java does not store static fields.

Storing the Data

What should we do to store the entire data? To answer this question, observe that Library has references to both the Catalog and MemberList objects, which, in turn, have references to the Book and Member objects respectively; the Hold objects are referred to by the Book objects and the Member objects. Thus, if we simply store the Library object, all of the data will be stored. As in our earlier use cases, we would like to keep these details out of the UI, and so UserInterface has a save method that simply invokes a save method on the Library object.

```
private void save() {
  if (library.save()) {
    System.out.println("The library has been successfully saved" );
  } else {
    System.out.println("There has been an error in saving \n" );
  }
}
```

The `save` method in `Library` could simply write the `Library` object to a file named 'LibraryData' and return `true` if nothing goes wrong, as shown below.

```
FileOutputStream file = new FileOutputStream("LibraryData");
ObjectOutputStream output = new ObjectOutputStream(file);
output.writeObject(library);
return true;
```

Likewise, we could read the stored data with a method that reverses the above process by opening `LibraryData` and reading the contents into `library`. This simple approach may well suffice for a small 'in-house' system, which is used and maintained by a dedicated programmer, but to have a system that is more suitable for wider usage, some issues need attention.

Maintaining the Singleton Property

The process of retrieving the data has some subtle complications associated with it. The `Library`, `MemberList` and `Catalog` objects are singletons: they cannot have more than one instance. Using the serialization mechanism, *it is now possible to serialize an object and then deserialize it to get a second instance.* For example, see the following pseudocode.

```
Library library = Library.instance();
Serialize library onto a disk file "library1";
Library library2 = Deserialized version of "library1";
Update library (add a member);
Update library2 (delete a book);
```

The first three lines of the pseudo-code are shown pictorially in Fig. 7.19. What has happened is that some user of the `Library` object initially obtained an instance of the `Library` object: essential and valid. In the second line, the user makes a copy of the object on disk: this is also perfectly legal and necessary. What follows in the third step is the problem. The user is now able to deserialize the object and obtain a second copy. The two copies can then diverge via independent updates as in the last two lines.

To understand what the essential problem is, recall that the intent of the singleton pattern is to *ensure that a class has only one instance and provide a global point of access to it.* We now have two mechanisms that can create instances of a class: (*i*) *constructors* and (*ii*) *deserialization.* The first mechanism was controlled by making constructors private and requiring all instantiations to got through the `instance` method. We now need a way of restricting the creation mechanism of deserialization.

Fortunately, due to the manner in which the reading of objects takes place in Java, this is not a complicated task. The default `readObject` method can be overridden to ignore retrieval if a copy already exists in memory. This way, no other class such as `UserInterface` will be able to do direct deserialization.

```
private void readObject(java.io.ObjectInputStream input) {
  try {
    input.defaultReadObject();
    if (library == null) {
```

Fig. 7.19 A pitfall in using
serialization with a singleton

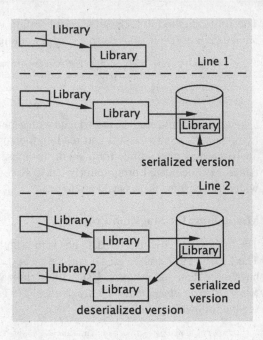

```
      library = (Library) input.readObject();
    } else {
      input.readObject();
    }
  } catch(IOException ioe) {
    ioe.printStackTrace();
  } catch(Exception e) {
    e.printStackTrace();
  }
}
```

If there is no memory-resident copy of the Library object, the retrieve method
reads the disk copy; otherwise, it returns the copy in memory. In case of an unexpected
error, it returns null.

```
public static Library retrieve() {
  try {
    FileInputStream file = new FileInputStream("LibraryData");
    ObjectInputStream input = new ObjectInputStream(file);
    input.readObject();
    return library;
  } catch(IOException ioe) {
    ioe.printStackTrace();
    return null;
  } catch(ClassNotFoundException cnfe) {
    cnfe.printStackTrace();
    return null;
  }
}
```

As discussed earlier, when we read (or write) a `Library` object, the `Catalog` and `MemberList` objects are automatically read (or written). However, since these are singletons, we will need to implement `readObject` for these classes in an analogous manner.

Dealing with Static Fields in Non-singletons

The above modifications take care of preserving the singleton classes, but the static fields in non-singletons pose a different challenge. Since the static field `idCounter` in `Member` stores the value that is used to generate the ID for each new member, this value must be saved along with the library. Since static fields are not serialized, this value will have to be explicitly written in the `writeObject` method of `Member`. The flip-side to this is that we will store a separate copy with each object, and as a result whenever a `Member` object is read, we are assigning a new value to `idCounter`, which makes our implementation very unstable. One simple solution to this is to circumvent the problem by encapsulating the static field as a separate class. The singleton `MemberIdServer`, shown below, holds the `idCounter` and also increments it each time `getId` is invoked.

```
class MemberIdServer implements Serializable {
  private  int idCounter;
  private static MemberIdServer server;
  private MemberIdServer() {
    idCounter = 1;
  }
  public static MemberIdServer instance() {
    if (server == null) {
      return (server = new MemberIdServer());
    } else {
      return server;
    }
  }
  public int getId() {
    return idCounter++;
  }
  // other code not shown
}
```

The methods for `readObject` and `writeObject` are defined as before to throw exceptions if the instance exists. Note that unlike the other objects which can all be reached directly or indirectly from references stored in `Library`, the instance of `MemberIdServer` does not have a stored reference in any other object. This raises the issue how this object will be serialized. The approach we adopt is to (de)serialize it in the file along with the the `library` object. The UI invokes the `save` method, which writes the instances of `Library` and `MemberIdServer` to the file `LibraryData`.

```
public static boolean save() {
  try {
    FileOutputStream file = new FileOutputStream("LibraryData");
    ObjectOutputStream output = new ObjectOutputStream(file);
    output.writeObject(library);
```

```
        output.writeObject(MemberIdServer.instance());
        return true;
    } catch(IOException ioe) {
        ioe.printStackTrace();
        return false;
    }
}
```

The `retrieve` method reads the instance of `Library` and then invokes the
`retrieve` method of `MemberIdServer`. These are defined as `static` methods since no instance of the singleton can exist if it has to be retrieved. The
method in `Library` is shown below; the method in `MemberIdServer` invokes
`readObject` on the input stream after the library has been deserialized.

```
public static Library retrieve() {
    try {
        FileInputStream file = new FileInputStream("LibraryData");
        ObjectInputStream input = new ObjectInputStream(file);
        input.readObject();
        MemberIdServer.retrieve(input);
        return library;
    } catch(IOException ioe) {
        ioe.printStackTrace();
        return null;
    } catch(ClassNotFoundException cnfe) {
        cnfe.printStackTrace();
        return null;
    }
}
```

7.3 Discussion and Further Reading

Converting the model into a working design is by far the most complex part of the
software design process. Although there are only a few principles of good object-
oriented design that the designer should be aware of, the manner in which these should
be applied in a given situation can be quite challenging to a beginner. Indeed, the only
way these can be mastered is through repeated application and critical examination
of the designs produced. It is also extremely useful to study peer-reviewed designs
of software systems that have been published in sources of repute, and discussing
design issues with more experienced colleagues. In this chapter we have attempted
to capture some of this complexity through an example, and also tried to raise and
deal with the questions that trouble the typical beginner.

The sequence of topics so far suggests that the design would progress linearly
from analysis to design to implementation. In reality, what usually happens is more
like an iterative process. In the analysis phase, some classes and methods may get
left out; worse yet, we may not even have spelled out all the functional requirements.
These shortcomings could show up at various points along the way, and we may have
to loop through this process (or a part of this process) more than once until we have
an acceptable design. It is also instructive to remember that we are not by any means

prescribing a definitive method that is to be used at all times, or even coming up with the perfect design for our simple library system. As stated before, our goal is to provide a condensed, but complete, overview of the object-oriented design process through an example. At the end of the previous chapter three student projects were presented. To maximise benefit, the reader is encouraged to apply the concepts to one or more of these projects as he/she reads through the material. From our experience, we have seen that students find this practice very beneficial.

7.3.1 Conceptual, Software and Implementation Classes

Finding the classes is a critical step in the object-oriented methodology. In the course of the analysis–design–implementation process, the idea of what constitutes a class goes through some subtle shifts.

In the analysis phase, we found the **conceptual** classes. These correspond to real-world concepts or things, and present us with a conceptual or essential perspective. These are derived from and used to satisfy the system requirements at a conceptual level. At this level, for instance, we can identify a piece of information that needs to be recognised as an entity and make it a class; we can talk of an association between classes without any thought to how this will be realised.

As we go further into the design process and construct the sequence diagrams, we need to deal with the issue of these conceptual classes will be manifested in the software, i.e., we are now dealing with **software** classes. These can be implemented with typical programming languages, and we need to identify methods and parameters that will be involved. We have to finalise which entities will be individual classes, which ones will be merged, and how associations will be captured.

The last step is the **implementation** class, which is a class created using a specific programming language such as Java or C++. This step nails down all the remaining details: identification and implementation of helper methods, the nitty-gritty of using software libraries, names of fields and variables, etc.

The process of going from conceptual to implementation classes is a progression from an abstract system to a concrete one and, as we have seen, classes may be added or removed at each step. For instance, `Transaction` and `MemberIdServer` were added as software and implementation class respectively, whereas the conceptual class `Borrows` was dropped.

7.3.2 Building a Commercially Acceptable System

The reader having familiarity with software systems may be left with the feeling that our example is too much of a 'toy' system, and our assumptions are too simplistic. This criticism is not unjustified, but should be tempered by the fact that our objective has been to present an example that can give the learner a 'big-picture' of the entire design process, without letting the complexity overwhelm the beginner.

Non-functional Requirements

A realistic system would have several non-functional requirements. Giving a fair treatment to these is beyond the scope of the book. Some issues like portability are automatically resolved since Java is interpreted and is thus platform independent. Response time (run-time performance) is a sticking point for object-oriented applications. We can examine this in a context where design choice affects performance; this is addressed briefly in a later case-study.

Functional Requirements

It can be argued that for a system to be accepted commercially, it must provide a sufficiently large set of services, and if our design methodologies are not adequate to handle that complexity, then they are of questionable value. We would like to point out the following:

- *Additional features can be easily added*: Some of these will be added in the next chapter. Our decision to exclude several such features has been made based on pedagogical considerations.
- *Allowing for variability among kinds of books/members*: This variability is typically incorporated by using inheritance. To explain the basic design process, inheritance is not essential. However using inheritance in design requires an understanding of several related issues, and we shall in fact present these issues and extend our library system in Chap. 9.
- *Having a more sophisticated interface*: Once again, we might want a system that allows members to login and perform operations through a GUI. This would only involve the interface and not the business logic. In Chap. 10, we shall see how a GUI can be modeled as a multi-panel interactive system, and how such features can be incorporated.
- *Allowing remote access*: Now-a-days, most systems of this kind allow remote access to the server. Chapter 12 looks how such features can be introduced through the use of distributed objects.

It should be noted that in practice several of the non-functional requirements would actually be provided by a database. What we have done with the use case model, the sequence diagrams and the class diagrams is in fact an object-oriented schema, which can be used to create an application that runs on an object-oriented database system. Such a system would not only address issues of performance and portability but also take care of issues like persistence, which can be done more efficiently using relations rather than reading and writing the objects. Details of this are beyond the scope of this text.

7.3.3 The Facade Pattern

Earlier on, we discussed our preference for keeping the interface away from the complexity of the business logic implementation. This was done by having a `Library` class that provided a set of methods for the interface and thus served as a single point of entry to and exit from the business logic module. In the language of design patterns, what we created is known as a **facade**.

The structure of the facade is shown in Fig. 7.20. The primary motivation behind using a facade is to reduce the complexity by minimising communication and dependencies between a subsystem and its clients (Fig. 7.21). The facade not only shields the client from the complexity but also enables loose coupling between the subsystem and its clients. Facades are not typically designed to prevent the client from accessing the components within the subsystem.

Perhaps the most ubiquitous example of the use of facade is in designing the interface to an operating system. The system provides various menus through which users may invoke the standard operations of the operating system, thus shielding the user from its complexity. The interface does not prevent users from writing a script to customise operations, which gives them access to the components of the system. Common software packages also employ facades; a compiler is a good example. While the user may have direct access to components like the lexical analyser and the parser, the complexity of the system can be avoided by directly invoking the commands to compile a file.

Using a Facade

Where do we employ this? A situation in which we have:

1. A system with several individual classes, each with its own set of public methods.
2. An external entity interacting with the system requires knowledge of the public methods of several classes.

Fig. 7.20 Structure diagram for facade

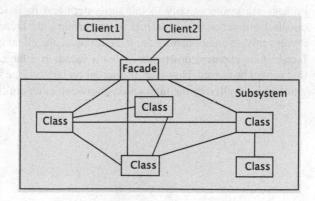

Fig. 7.21 Interactions with a
subsystem without a facade

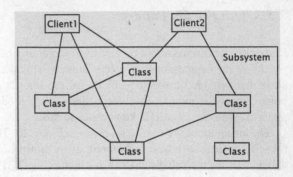

What problem are we facing? A lot of the details of the system have to be
revealed to the external entity, which hurts modularity and abstraction. Coupling becomes tight, since a change to any one class in the system requires
changes to all entities that interact with the system.

How have we solved it? Facade acts as a single class that:

1. Provides a single point of entry through which external entities can interact
   with the system without hurting abstraction.
2. Adapts to changes in individual classes in a manner such that external
   entities are unaffected, as long as the functionality of the system remains
   unchanged.

How have we employed it? The Library class acts as a facade through which the
user interface communicates with the system. Library is aware of all the other
classes and the methods that they provide. The methods in Library employ the
functionality provided by the other classes to complete the tasks required of
the system.

A facade enables the subsystem to have private/protected components. Such components are available only to the subsystem and its descendants, which prevents
clients from accessing these just to get around the facade. When operations that
involve private components have to be invoked, the client is forced to go through the
facade. One apparent downside is that a facade is a largely 'custom-written' class
that cannot be reused. However, the actual coding is quite simple, and the advantage
gained by simplifying the interactions between other entities is worth this effort.

7.3.4 Implementing Singletons

Implementing a singleton correctly is not a trivial matter. In Chap. 5 we overcame the difficulties with creating a singleton hierarchy. In this chapter we have dealt with the issue of serialization. These solutions are very language specific and a careful study of the language features is needed when moving from the software classes to the implementation classes.

There do not appear to be any 'standard mechanisms' in the literature for handling implementation issues. Most languages provide a general collection of features that can be adapted for a variety of purposes. We have used the implementation of `readObject` and `writeObject` in Java to ensure that our purpose is served. Java also provides other methods like `readResolve` and `writeReplace` to override the effects of serialization and deserialization. The `Externalisable` interface can be employed when the serialization has to be fully customised.

7.3.5 Further Reading

The book by Meyer [1] devotes an entire chapter to the problem of class design and makes valuable reading. As we discussed earlier in the book, the notion of design patterns captures the idea that many design situations are similar in nature and a knowledge of the solution to these problems can make a designer more productive. The reader is encouraged to read the book by Gamma et al. [2] to get an exposure to the common design patterns. There are hundreds of other lesser patterns and a catalog of these can be found in [3, 4].

For a sophisticated introduction to the Unified Modeling Language, refer to [5]. The more enthusiastic reader is referred to the Object Management Group's UML Specification available online via www.omg.org.

To understand how an object-oriented schema fits in with a database, we refer the reader to [6].

Projects

1. Complete the designs for the case-study exercises from the previous chapter.

7.4 Exercises

1. Consider a situation where a library wants to add a feature that enables the librarian to print out a list of all the books that have been checked out at a given point in time. Construct a sequence diagram for this use case.
2. Explain the rationale for separating the user interface from the business logic.

3. Suppose the due-date for a book depends not only on the date the book is issued but also on factors such as member type (assume that there are multiple types of membership), number of books already issued to the member and any fines owed by the member. Which class should then be assigned the responsibility to compute the due date and why?

4. (Discussion) There is fairly tight coupling in our system between the Book, Member and Hold classes. Code in Book could inadvertently modify the fields of a Member object. One way to handle this is to replace the Member reference with just the member's ID. What changes would we have to make in the rest of the classes to accommodate this? What are the pros and cons of such an approach?

5. Continuing with the previous question, the Hold object stores references to the Book and Member objects. This may not be necessary. What specific information does Book (Member) require from Hold? Define an interface that contains the relevant methods to retrieve this information. What are the pros and cons of an implementation where Hold implements these interfaces over the design presented in this chapter?

6. (Keeping mutables safe) Suggest a simple scheme for creating a new class SafeMember that would allow us to export a reference to a Member. The classes outside the system should be unaware of this additional class, and access the reference like a reference to a Member object. However, the reference would not allow the integrity of the data to be compromised.

7. Without modifying any of the classes other than Library, write a method in Library that deletes all invalid holds for all members.

References

1. B. Meyer, *Object-Oriented Software Construction* (Prentice Hall, New York, 1997)
2. E. Gamma, R. Helm, R. Johnson, J. Vlissides, *Design Patterns: Elements of Reusable Object-Oriented Software* (Addison-Wesley, Reading, 1994)
3. L. Rising, *The Pattern Almanac* (Addison-Wesley, Boston, 2000)
4. J.M. Vlissides, J.O. Coplien, N.L. Kerth, *Pattern Languages of Program Design 2 (Software Patterns Series)* (Addison-Wesley, Reading, 1999)
5. M. Fowler, K. Scott, *UML Distilled* (Addison-Wesley Longman, Reading, 1997)
6. A. Chaudhri, R. Zicari, *Succeeding with Object Databases: A Practical Look at Today's Implementations with Java and XML* (Wiley, New York, 2000)

Chapter 8
How 'Object-Oriented' Is Our Design?

8.1 Introduction

In the course of the last two chapters, we have seen that the design process involves making several choices. This is quite typical of any engineering design, and should come as no surprise. For instance, when a bridge is designed, an engineer is starting with an architect's plan and is making choices about the kind of materials needed. While doing this, the engineer is typically guided by well-formulated design rules.

Given the multitude of choices that we face during the object-oriented design process, it is only natural to ask if there is a set of rules that can help us make the correct decisions. More specifically, we would like some way of answering two questions a designer often grapples with:

1. *Have I made the right decision in assigning responsibilities?*
and
2. *In case I make a mistake, how can I detect it early and correct it?*

In this chapter we demonstrate via examples how an awareness of a concept known as **refactoring** can help answer the above questions. Refactoring is defined simply as the process of improving the internal structure (design and code) of a piece of software without altering the module's external behavior. The process may be applied to a system in production, or we can use this process just as effectively during development. Practitioners have developed a set of rules that can be used systematically to refactor code. Some of these rules serve as means for detecting where modifications are needed, and it is not surprising that they can often be turned into guidelines for good software practice. The rules are relatively simple and the changes we make are usually small, so it is usually the case that not much goes wrong while refactoring. Familiarity with these rules can help a beginner make decisions about how to assign responsibilities, when to introduce inheritance, etc.

It should be noted that there is a vast amount of knowledge on the subject of refactoring, and our treatment of it in this book merely scratches the surface. Nonetheless, it is useful to see this as an integral part of the object-oriented design process.

© Universities Press (India) Private Ltd. 2015
B. Dathan and S. Ramnath, *Object-Oriented Analysis, Design and Implementation*,
Undergraduate Topics in Computer Science, DOI 10.1007/978-3-319-24280-4_8

8.2 A First Example of Refactoring

Our first example illustrates how the two refactoring rules, EXTRACT METHOD and
MOVE METHOD, are applied during system development. To serve as the platform
for using these rules, we impose some new requirements to the library system we
designed and implemented in Chap. 7. After constructing an initial design and implementing the code, we refine the solution using refactoring rules.

In Sect. 8.2.1 we describe the new requirements and come up with an implementation. Refactoring is done in Sect. 8.2.2.

8.2.1 A Library that Charges Fines: Initial Solution

Consider the situation where the library decides to cut down on truancy by imposing
fines. When an overdue book is returned, the librarian would like to know the amount
of fine and send out a notice to the user regarding the fine payable. The system
should therefore compute the fines and display the relevant information. The resulting
changes in the business process are captured in the use case in Table 8.1.

Table 8.1 *Use-case* Book Return with Fines

Actions performed by the actor	Responses from the system
1. The member arrives at the return counter with a set of books and gives the clerk the books	
2. The clerk issues a request to return books	
	3. The system asks for the identifier of the book
4. The clerk enters the book identifier	
	5. If the identifier is valid, the system marks that the book has been returned and informs the clerk if there is a hold placed on the book; otherwise (that is, in case of an invalid id), it notifies the clerk that the identifier is not valid. If there is a fine involved, the system computes the amount of fine using *Rule 5* and adds it to the user's account and information about the member is displayed. It then asks if the clerk wants to process the return of another book
6. If there is a hold on the book, the clerk sets it aside. He/she then informs the system if there are more books to be returned	
	7. If the answer is in the affirmative, the system goes to Step 3. Otherwise, it exits

This use case for Book Return with Fines is similar to what we had earlier, with one addition—the amount of fine owed is computed whenever a book is returned. Obviously, the Member class needs to be changed to track the amount of fine owed. Also, notice that the use case does not say anything about actually collecting fines from a member and updating the corresponding Member object after the fine is paid. These are left as exercises.

We have the following formula for computing the fine:

Rule 5 *New books (less than a year old) are charged $0.25 for the first day and $0.10 for every subsequent day. Older books are charged $0.15 cents for the first day and $0.05 for every subsequent day. If a book has a hold on it, the amount of fine is doubled.*

Before we construct the modified sequence diagram, we have to decide where the amount of fine owed will be computed. There are three possible options: Library, Book, and Member. We can make a case for each option: Book would be appropriate since it is the return of the book that incurs a fine; Member is where the fine is stored and is therefore the place it could be computed; since both Book and Member are involved in this, Library is perhaps the best place to do the computation. We decide (somewhat arbitrarily) that Library is the place where the fine is computed. The new sequence diagram for returning books is shown in Fig. 8.1.

The returnBook method in Library must now check if a fine is involved: if so, it computes the fine and updates the corresponding Member object by calling the Member's addFine method, so that the fine is accumulated. The books title is also passed so that a transaction can be created to keep a record of the fine.

The returnBook method returns a code that indicates if a fine was involved, so that the interface can alert the library clerk. For this purpose, two new return codes are introduced:

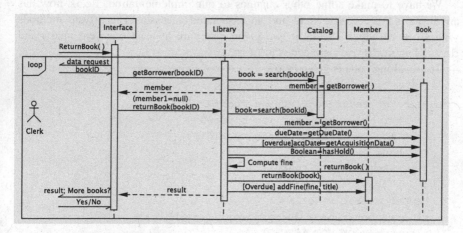

Fig. 8.1 Returning a book and checking for fines

- BOOK_HAS_FINE, which is returned when the book has a fine, but no holds.
- BOOK_HAS_HOLD_FINE, which is returned when the book has both a fine and at least one hold.

The assumption is that the code in the user interface will take appropriate action to notify the clerk in the above circumstances.

A somewhat knotty problem concerns the display of member information, as required in Step 5 of the use case, when there is a fine involved. Since the returnBook method in Library simply returns an integer value to UserInterface, the latter does not have the necessary information to display. We have a couple of options:

- **Option 1** Modify the returnBook method to return more information. The information could be sent as an object with multiple fields, or simply as a string with all the data concatenated.
- **Option 2** Allow the user interface to manage the output by providing additional query operations. These operations would require adding more methods to the Library class.

Implementing the first option requires that we either create a new class to send the result or assemble a string that will have to be parsed in the interface. Neither of these is a good idea since both result in additional coupling between the UI and the back end. On the other hand, adding another query is a very natural thing to do, since our back end is in fact a database. In our situation, we need a new method that returns the borrower of a given book. This query can be invoked by UserInterface at the start of the process, so that it has all the necessary information. This is truly a natural extension of the code development process since the query could conceivably be used in multiple situations, not just when a book is returned. For instance, the library may want to know who the borrower of a book is because its due date has been well past.

We have to make some other changes to our implementation. Book now has an acquisitionDate field and an associated accessor. The private methods yearApart (which checks if two given dates are at least one year apart) and daysElapsedSince are added to Library.

The resulting code is given below.

```
public int returnBook(String bookId) {
  // search for book and its borrower
  Book book = catalog.search(bookId);
  if (book == null) {
    return(BOOK_NOT_FOUND);
  }
  Member member = null;
  if ((member = book.getBorrower()) == null) {
    return(BOOK_NOT_ISSUED);
  }
```

```
    //compute fines
    double fine = 0.0;
    Calendar dueDate = book.getDueDate();
    if (System.currentTimeMillis() > dueDate.getTimeInMillis()) {
      Calendar acquisitionDate = book.getAcquisitionDate();
      if (yearApart(acquisitionDate, dueDate)) {
        fine = 0.15 + 0.05 * daysElapsedSince(dueDate);
      } else {
        fine = 0.25 + 0.1 * daysElapsedSince(dueDate);
      }
      if (book.hasHold()) {
        fine *= 2;
      }
    }
    // final steps
    if (!(member.returnBook(book))) {
      return(OPERATION_FAILED);
    }
    if (fine > 0.0) {
      member.addFine(fine, book.getTitle());
      if (book.hasHold()) {
        return(BOOK_HAS_HOLD_FINE);
      } else {
        return(BOOK_HAS_FINE);
      }
    }
    if (book.hasHold()) {
      return(BOOK_HAS_HOLD);
    }
    return(OPERATION_COMPLETED);
  }
  private boolean yearApart(Calendar date1, Calendar date2) {
    return ((date2.getTimeInMillis() - date1.getTimeInMillis())
                                       / 86400000) > 365;
  }
  private int daysElapsedSince(Calendar date) {
    return (int) ((System.currentTimeMillis() - date.getTimeIn
      Millis())
                                       / 86400000);
  }
```

From the formula for computing fines, we see that we need to compare the due date and the current date and a fine is imposed if the latter is later than the former. To see how to determine which of these two dates is larger, notice the two lines after the comment //compute fines. The static method

`System.currentTimeMillis()` gives the number of milliseconds elapsed since January 1, 1970 and `dueDate.getTimeInMillis()` is the number of milliseconds elapsed since January 1, 1970 for the book's due date. A simple comparison then affords the result.

The method `yearApart()` is used to check if the book's due date is a year or more than its acquisition date. Invoking the method `getTimeInMillis` on the two dates does the trick.

After the fine is computed, the corresponding `Member` object is updated by calling the `addFine` method, so the fine is accumulated. The book's title is also passed, so a transaction can be created to keep a record of the fine.

8.2.2 Refactoring the Solution

Having come up with an initial design and its implementation, we must carefully consider the two questions we said we must ask of the solution: whether the responsibilities have been properly assigned and if mistakes have been made, how to detect and correct them.

We begin with making some observations about the new method:

- It is bigger than before.
- It has more detail.

The second observation is particularly alarming. One of the broad goals we have in object-oriented design is to make each method simple so that unit testing is facilitated. Sometimes longer methods are unavoidable; but excessive amount of detail is usually a more serious indicator that we are making a mistake. Let us first revisit the whole algorithm for returning a book. Here are the steps:

1. Get the reference to the book.
2. Get the reference to the member.
3. Get the due date.
4. Get the acquisition date.
5. Compute fines.
6. Record that the member has returned the book.
7. Add fines to member.
8. Check if there is a hold.
9. Return a result. (If there is a hold, fine, etc.)

Each of these steps except 5 is an application of a single method, which is computed on some object, viz., `catalog`, `book`, or `member`. In the code corresponding to Step 5, we see that we are dealing with a lot of detail about how the fine is being computed. Modular design principles suggest that such details be abstracted out.

The above observation leads us to our first refactoring rule, Extract Method. Considerations involved in applying this rule and the steps for carrying it out are detailed in Fig. 8.2.

EXTRACT METHOD RULE

If you have a code fragment that can be grouped together, turn the fragment into a method and assign it a name that explains the purpose of the method.

It is easy to recognise these fragments from the comments added by the programmer. These comments, which typically take the form of a verb phrase, also suggest how the extracted method should be named. If a code fragment does not appear to have a simple name, it is often unlikely to be a good candidate for extraction into a method. Another indicator is the number of local variables that are modified; if the code fragment modifies only one variable, this strengthens the case for extraction. If a large number of variables are modified, the code fragment should probably be left in place.

The steps involved in applying this rule are as follows.

- Identify a code fragment and copy it into a method named for the intention of that code fragment.

- In the extracted code, locate the references to variables local to the original method and pass these as parameters to the new method.

- For all temporary variables that are used in the fragment, declare corresponding variables in the new method.

- Determine the local variable that is modified by the extracted code and set its type as the return type of the new method.

- Replace the code fragment in the original code with a call to the new method and store the value returned in the local variable identified in the previous step.

Fig. 8.2 Extract method

Note that the fragment that we want extracted is preceded by the comment 'compute fines'. This suggests how the extracted method should be named. We now have the following version of the method.

```
public int returnBook(String bookId) {
  // search for book and its borrower (not shown)

  fine = computeFine(book);

  // final steps not shown
}


public double computeFine(Book book) {
  double fine = 0.0;
  Calendar dueDate = book.getDueDate();
  if (System.currentTimeMillis() > dueDate.getTimeInMillis()) {
```

```
      Calendar acquisitionDate = book.getAcquisitionDate();
      if (yearApart(acquisitionDate, dueDate)) {
        fine = 0.15 + 0.05 * (daysElapsedSince(dueDate) - 1);
      } else {
        fine = 0.25 + 0.1 * (daysElapsedSince(dueDate) -1);
      }
      if (book.hasHold()) {
        fine *= 2;
      }
    }
    return fine;
}
```

The method `returnBook` looks much cleaner now. All it is doing is getting the relevant information by applying appropriate methods and then compiling all the results.

Let us take a closer look at the method that we have extracted. The logic employed by `computeFine` involves examining the fields of `Book` and making decisions based on the values stored in these fields. To get these values, the method repeatedly invokes the accessor methods of book. One of the rules of good object-oriented design is called the Law of Inversion, which says that

> If your routines exchange too many data, put your routines in your data.

What this means is that our focus should be more on the data and less on the process. In a process-oriented design, we do not think adversely about importing all the data elements into the function that implements the process. In a data-centered approach, the parts of the process that are close to one data element are encapsulated as methods and placed into the class corresponding to that data element. The computation for the encapsulated part of the process is then carried out by calling the method on the data element.

The above design principle leads us to the next refactoring rule, MOVE METHOD. The `computeFine` method is moved from `Library` to `Book` using the principles set forth in Fig. 8.3.

After applying the MOVE METHOD rule, have the following code:

```
public int returnBook(String bookId) {
  // search for book and its borrower (not shown)

  fine = book.computeFine();

  // final steps not shown
}
```

MOVE METHOD RULE

If we have a method that is using more features of another class than the class on which it is defined, then the method needs to be moved to the class whose features it is using the most.

This rule is a manifestation of the process of assigning responsibilities to the appropriate class and is perhaps the most frequently applied rule in refactoring. When a method uses too many features of another class, we have a situation where the classes are either collaborating too much or are too tightly coupled. It is not always the case that such a problem will be resolved by moving a method. Sometimes, other patterns may have to be applied that allows objects to communicate without getting too entangled in each other's methods. The simplest and most obvious situation is when a method accesses several fields of another class and almost all its computation is done on these fields.

The steps involved in applying this rule are as follows:

- Make a list of all features used by the method in question.

- Identify the *target* class for the move, i.e, the class whose features are most frequently employed in the computation.

- Examine other features that are not in the most frequently used class and decide if those features need to be moved to the target class as well.

- It could happen that the features from the source that are being moved to the target are being used by other methods in the source. The possibility that these methods also need to be moved should be taken into consideration. It is sometimes easier to move a set of methods and fields instead of a single method.

- Declare the method(s) and field(s) in the target class, and move the code to the new method. Make the necessary adjustments so that the code works in the target class. This would involve changing the names of the features being used.

- Change the code in the source class to reflect the movement of the fields and methods.

As is evident from this description, moving a collection of methods and fields can affect several methods of the source class. Care must be taken to ensure that the new code reflects the changes. When this rule is applied in the presence of inheritance, we have to exercise an additional caveat: *If super-classes and sub-classes of the source class have also declared the method, then the method cannot be moved unless the polymorphism can also be expressed in the target class.*

Fig. 8.3 Move method

The computeFine method in Book is as follows:

```
public double computeFine() {
  double fine = 0.0;
  if (System.currentTimeMillis() > dueDate.getTimeInMillis()) {
    if (yearApart(acquisitionDate, dueDate)) {
      fine = 0.15 + 0.05 * (daysElapsedSince(dueDate) - 1);
    } else {
      fine = 0.25 + 0.1 * (daysElapsedSince(dueDate) -1 );
    }
    if (hasHold()) {
      fine *= 2;
    }
  }
  return fine;
}
private boolean yearApart(Calendar date1, Calendar date2) {
  return ((date2.getTimeInMillis() - date1.getTimeInMillis())
  / 86400000)
                          > 365;
}
private int daysElapsedSince(Calendar date) {
  return (int) ((System.currentTimeMillis()
                - date.getTimeInMillis()) / 86400000);
}
```

Note that we have moved the methods yearApart and daysElapsedSince as well to Book. This process has helped resolve our dilemma about where the fine should be computed. In the initial stages of design, we need not go through the entire process of refactoring to correct our errors. Nonetheless, beginners may often find themselves in a quandary as to where the responsibilities for a certain task should be placed. The exercise of refactoring code helps to formalise some of the basic principles of object-oriented design so that such errors can be caught early in the design process and suitably corrected.

8.3 A Second Look at RemoveBooks

Now that we have an idea of the kinds of issues that we have to watch out for, let us take a second look at the code that we have written to find suitable candidates for refactoring. The sequence diagram for Remove Books looks interesting, since it bears some resemblance to Return Books. Once again, we begin by describing the overall algorithm being followed.

1. Get the reference to the book object from `Catalog`.
2. Check if the book can be removed. We cannot remove a book if it has holds or if it is checked out.
3. If the book is not removable, return the appropriate error code.
4. If the book is removable, remove the reference to the book from `Catalog` and return the appropriate code.
5. We reach this step only if there was a problem removing the book from the catalog. In this case, return an error code.

The second step is the one that is not being carried out by a single method call and, therefore, is our focus for further investigation. Here is the code, with some comments inserted.

```
public int removeBook(String bookId) {
  // Step 1: Get reference to book.
  Book book = catalog.search(bookId);
  if (book == null) {
    return(BOOK_NOT_FOUND);
  }

  // Step 2: Check if book is removable
  if (book.hasHold()) {
    return(BOOK_HAS_HOLD);
  }
  if (book.getBorrower() != null) {
    return(BOOK_ISSUED);
  }

  // Step 3: Attempt the actual removal.
  if (catalog.removeBook(bookId)) {
    return (OPERATION_COMPLETED);
  }

  // Step 4: This error should not happen.
  return (OPERATION_FAILED);
}
```

In Step 2, we have a situation similar to the previous example in that the information stored in `Book` is being used to make a decision in `Library`, with the difference that in this case, we see very little computation being carried out. Our decision, however, should not be based on this fact alone (in a more complicated example, we could have several other reasons for not deleting a book, viz., we may have some 'rare books' that should not be removed, etc.), but should consider where the responsibility for this computation is best assigned. The repeated access to the fields of book suggests that this computation be moved out. As before, we can apply the EXTRACT METHOD and

MOVE METHOD rules in succession. We have the following situation after applying
EXTRACT METHOD:

```
public int removeBook(String bookId) {
  // Step 1: Same as before
  // Step 2: Check if book is removable

  int returnCode = checkRemovability(book);
  if (returnCode != OPERATION_COMPLETED) {
    return returnCode;
  }

  // Remaining steps same as before
}
private int checkRemovability(Book book) {
  if (book.hasHold()) {
    return (BOOK_HAS_HOLD);
  }
  if (book.getBorrower() != null) {
    return (BOOK_ISSUED);
  }
  return OPERATION_COMPLETED;
}
```

Since `checkRemovability` uses attributes of `Book`, it appears that we must
apply the MOVE METHOD rule. After moving this method to `Book` we get the
following end product.

```
public int removeBook(String bookId) {
  // Step 1: Same as before

  // Step 2: Check if book is removable
  int returnCode = book.checkRemovability();
  if (returnCode != OPERATION_COMPLETED) {
    return returnCode;
  }

  // Remaining steps same as before
}
```

In Book we have to add the new method, taking care to change "book" to "this."
The constants belong to Library, so they need to be qualified.

```
public int checkRemovability() {
  if (hasHold()) {
    return (Library.BOOK_HAS_HOLD);
  }
  if (borrowedBy != null) {
    return (Library.BOOK_ISSUED);
  }
  return Library.OPERATION_COMPLETED;
}
```

Let us now pause and take stock of what we have accomplished. We started with one
method in Library with two conditional statements that invoked methods from
Book. We now have a new version that uses named constants that are defined in
Library. This increases the coupling between Book and Library. The benefit
provided by these changes is questionable, and on the flip-side, we have added to
the complexity of our code. In such a situation it is perhaps better not to modify the
original code.

It is important to note here that the control flow in the extracted code for Return
Book has a single point of entry and a single point of exit, which makes it well-suited
for applying the refactoring rules. The multiple exit points in the extracted code of
Remove Book prevent us from reaping significant gains by refactoring.

8.4 Using Generics to Refactor Duplicated Code

As a means to reduce system complexity and development and maintenance effort, it
is important to look for opportunities where the number of classes in a system is kept
as small as possible, subject, of course, to good object-oriented design principles.
Prospects for merging two or more classes arise if they have similar functionality, although they may differ in relatively minor aspects. In the library system, for instance,
MemberList and Catalog are strikingly similar in what they do; of course, there
are some differences: one stores books and the other is a collection of members,
and Catalog has a method to remove books, but no such functionality exists in
MemberList.

In this section, we show how generics may be used in situations such as the above
to factor out some of the commonalities in a manner that most of the complexity is
located in one module. As an example of the use of generics, we develop a generic
class called ItemList, which can be used to store books or members.

8.4.1 A Closer Look at the Collection Classes

We somehow need to tell the system that ItemList should be capable of storing either books or members. For this, the type of element to be stored in the ItemList object is passed as a parameter to the class name itself as given in the following class declaration.

```
public class ItemList<T> implements Serializable {
// generic code
}
```

The reader may recall from Chap. 3 that the idea is that T, a parameter to the class name, stands for an arbitrary type and objects of that type will be stored in the collection.

To implement the methods of this generic collection class, we utilise the logic used in corresponding methods of Catalog. (As we noted before, Catalog is slightly more general than MemberList because the former contains a method to remove items from the collection.)

We need to modify the places where references to specific types occur with generic type names. Specifically, we need to replace the data definition such as

```
private List books = new LinkedList();
```

with

```
private List<T> elements = new LinkedList<T>();
```

Next, we focus on search. Here is the code from Catalog:

```
public Book search(String bookId) {
for (Iterator iterator = books.iterator();iterator.hasNext();){
    Book book = (Book) iterator.next();
    if (book.getId().equals(bookId)) {
      return book;
    }
  }
  return null;
}
```

There are two problems with the code.

1. In each iteration, the id value of an object in the catalog is checked against the given book id. This constitutes fairly tight coupling between Book and Catalog; the parameter to search is of type String, so we build into Catalog the

information that id is of type `String`. The iterator's return type is cast as a `Book`. It also assumes the existence of a method called `getId()`. If we want to use generics and factor out the common code, this coupling has to be eliminated.

2. In the code, note that two books are considered equal (i.e., identical) if their id fields are equal. If the coupling between `Catalog` and `Book` is to be removed, the decision as to which field(s) should be used in the comparison should be made by `Book`, and not left for the collection class. This suggests that the code for deciding how to match the incoming object against the `Book` object must be extracted and moved to `Book`.

A Caveat on Using the Equals Method

We have seen that the responsibility for checking whether a specific book's id is equal to that of some given id should be delegated to the `Book` class itself. At first sight it would appear that we can use the `equals` method to carry out this task. However, a careful look at the definition of this method as described in the Java documentation reveals that this method is unsuitable for use in the present context. Carefully read the following, which is taken from the Java online documentation.

```
The equals method implements an equivalence relation on
non-null object references:
```

- It is reflexive: for any non-null reference value x, x.equals(x) should return true.
- It is symmetric: for any non-null reference values x and y, x.equals(y) should return true if and only if y.equals(x) returns true.

Suppose that we write the equals method in `Book` as below.

```
public boolean equals(Object object) {
   String id = (String) object;
   return (this.id.equals(id));
}
```

As we demonstrate below, the relation implemented by the method is asymmetric. Clearly, there is an implication that the `equals` method expects a `String` object. The `equals` method of the `String` class, however, will not produce the same result when a `Book` object is passed as its parameter. Trace the following piece of code:

```
String id = "id1";
Book book1 = new Book("title1", "author1", id);
System.out.println(book1.equals(id)); // call 1
System.out.println(id.equals(book1)); // call 2
```

Although invocation of the `equals` method on `book1` (commented as `call 1`) results in a `true` output, calling the method on the corresponding `String` object (commented as `call 2`) returns value `false`.

In other words, the `equals` method as implemented above will not result in an equivalence relation. We should, therefore, refrain ourselves from using that method as the vehicle for comparison. Failure to do so could ultimately result in subtle bugs that are likely to be quite difficult to catch: imagine the plight of a programmer who trusts that the above implementation of `equals` follows the requirements set forth in the Java documentation and codes as in `call 2` above!

A Different Approach

To rectify the situation, we implement a method called `matches` in `Book`, which does not impose the equivalence relation requirement. To start with, we implement the code as shown next:

```
public boolean matches(String bookId) {
  return this.id.equals(bookId);
}
```

The `search` method in `Catalog` is modified as follows:

```
public Book search(String value) {
  for (Book element: elements) {
    if (element.matches(value)) {
      return element;
    }
  }
  return null;
}
```

Next, we eliminate type dependence. For this, we replace the type name `Book` with the generic type `T`. (Recall that `T` is the parameter to the class.)

```
public T search(String value) {
  for (T element: elements) {
    if (element.matches(value)) {
      return element;
    }
  }
  return null;
}
```

This change begs the question: *What if* id *were to be of a type other than* String? This additional type dependence is eliminated by introducing a second generic parameter. The class ItemList is now defined as:

```
public class ItemList<T, K> implements Serializable {
  // generic code
}
```

K represents the type of key on which the container matches items. The search is now written as:

```
public T search(K value) {
  for (T element: elements) {
    if (element.matches(value)) {
      return element;
    }
  }
  return null;
}
```

Similar modifications can be made to the other methods. The changes are fairly straightforward.

```
public boolean removeItem(K value) {
  T element = search(value);
  if (element == null) {
    return false;
  } else {
    return elements.remove(element);
  }
}
public boolean insertItem(T item) {
  elements.add(item);
  return true;
}
public Iterator<T> getItems() {
  return elements.iterator();
}
```

While this solution is satisfactory for our limited case, in a more general situation one may wish to use ItemList to create other collection classes. If we were to replace T by some user-defined class C, the code would fail to compile if the method matches was not defined for class C. In other words, to create instantiations of ItemList, we require that T satisfy a specific property, i.e., have a method named matches. This property is named Matchable and is extracted as an interface that T must implement.

```
public interface Matchable<K> {
  public boolean matches(K other);
}
```

The Book and Member classes are modified as below.

```
public class Member implements Serializable, Matchable<String>
{  // fields and other methods
  public boolean matches(String id) {
    return this.id.equals(id);
  }
}
```

```
public class Book implements Serializable, Matchable<String> {
  // fields and other methods
  public boolean matches(String id) {
    return this.id.equals(id);
  }
}
```

Finally, ItemList is defined as:

```
public class ItemList<T extends Matchable<K>, K> implements
  Serializable {
  // generic code
}
```

8.4.2 Instantiating Catalog and MemberList

With the code developed so far, we can create a new catalog as below.

```
ItemList<Book, String> catalog = new ItemList<Book, String>();
```

A similar code can be used to create a collection for members.

However, from the viewpoint of robustness, this approach is unsatisfactory. There can be multiple catalogs and member lists because the constructor can be invoked from the outside. In other words, the class is not a singleton.

Ideally, we would like to put within ItemList<T, K> a static method that returns an ItemList<T, K> object with the correct parameter. The code should look like the following.

```
private static ItemList<T, K> itemList;
private ItemList() {
}
public static ItemList<T,K> instance() {
  if (itemList == null) {
    itemList = new ItemList<T,K>();
  }
  return itemList;;
}
```

Unfortunately, the above code is not legal. Because of the way Java implements generics, the type name T is *erased* from the class definition at compilation time and is not available during execution. Therefore, there can be no useful checks against the type name T. (It would appear that the implementation details are driving the rules of the language, and not vice-versa!)

Catalog is now declared as an extension of ItemList<Book, String>.

```
public class Catalog extends ItemList<Book, String> {
}
```

Now, every public and protected method of ItemList<T extends Matchable<K>, K> is inherited by Catalog.

MemberList is coded in a similar fashion.

We now have two choices for naming the methods of Catalog and MemberList:

1. We could create methods such as removeBook and insertBook inside Catalog and similarly-named methods in MemberList. Thus, instead of having methods with names such as removeItem and insertItem, we end up with the old method names: removeBook, insertBook, etc.

   ```
   public boolean removeBook(String value) {
     return super.removeItem(value);
   }
   public boolean insertBook(Book item) {
     return super.insertItem(item);
   }
   public Iterator<Book> getItems() {
     return super.getItems();
   }
   ```

   This means that Catalog is a *class adapter*, i.e., it is a subclass of ItemList<T extends Matchable<K>, K> and implements a different interface by suitably calling the methods of the superclass.
2. We simply live with the new names insertItem and removeItem, and then modify the Library class to adjust to these changes.

While refactoring a module or a set of modules within a system, it is clearly preferable to ensure that the changes do not require modifications in the rest of the system. In our case, if we choose Option 2, `Library` needs to be updated, which would mean that we should choose Option 1. The number of places in `Library` that refers to these methods is small, so a case could be made for Option 2. In general that is not advisable, however, because there could be many modules with numerous locations that could be affected.

Making `Catalog` a singleton is not hard. See the following code.

```
private static Catalog catalog;
private Catalog() throws Exception {
}
public static Catalog instance() {
  try {
    if (catalog == null) {
      return catalog = new Catalog();
    }
  } catch(Exception e) {
    return null;
  }
  return catalog;
}
```

8.5 Discussion and Further Reading

In this chapter our main focus was to show the importance of being aware of the refactoring rules and how these can in fact lead us to making good choices in the way we assign responsibilities. In practice, being faithful to the refactoring process also results in software that is easier to maintain and understand.

The book by Fowler [1] is the reference for much of the material in this chapter. Among other things, the book emphasises the importance of the role that refactoring can play in keeping a system from falling into decay. While the benefits of refactoring are many, there are also a few caveats one should follow to avoid going overboard, and there are also situations and systems whose characteristics make refactoring difficult. The reader would be well advised to engage in a deeper study of this process before attempting a wider application.

Fowler points out that refactoring, when added to the design process, has the capacity to present us with an alternative to the conventional 'up-front' design which views the development of the design as a blueprint and considers coding to be just a process of going through the mechanics of implementation. While this up-front approach is certainly the one recommended by most textbooks, the process can be tempered by refactoring. Instead of getting the design down to the last detail and then coding it, we work with a loosely defined design, start the coding and 'firm-up' (and correct) the design with some refactoring as we go through the implementation process. This process may be better description of what happens in practice and has the added advantage of giving the designers some flexibility in the choices that they make.

8.6 Exercises

1. Critically examine the design decisions that you have made in the three student projects at the end of Chap. 7 in the light of the information and ideas contained in this chapter. What changes would you like to make?
2. What changes do you need to make to the Member class to track the amount of fine owed?
3. Try to implement ItemList<T extends Matchable<K>, K> as a singleton. What are the difficulties you encounter?
4. Suppose that we do not specify Matchable as a generic interface. What changes will you make? What drawbacks do you foresee?
5. Compile the source files for the classes given for the generic implementation. Make modifications so that all compiler warning messages disappear.
6. In Chap. 7, we pointed out that using 'magic numbers' is poor programming practice, and we replaced them with named constants. This is listed in the literature as a standard refactoring rule [1], *Replace magic number with symbolic constant*, which involves the following steps:

    (a) Declare a constant and set it to the value of the magic number.
    (b) Find all occurrences of the magic number.
    (c) See if magic number matches the usage of the constant; if yes, replace the magic number by the constant.
    (d) Compile and test; code should work exactly as before.

    It has been noted that using named constants does not solve all problems since these can still be interpreted as numbers. A much safer approach in Java is to use the enum construct.
    Develop a refactoring process to replace named constants with enums and apply this to refactor the code developed for the Library so that the result codes returned by Library are all contained in a single enum named LibraryResults. (Hint: this will involve finding references to these named constants in all situations, which include variable declarations and return types of methods.)
7. Modify the library system so that it actually collects the fine owed by a user at the time he/she checks out books.

Reference

1. M. Fowler, *Refactoring: Improving the Design of Existing Code* (Addison-Wesley, New York, 1999)

Part III
Advanced Concepts
in Object-Oriented Design

Chapter 9
Exploring Inheritance

9.1 Introduction

In this chapter we look more deeply at the topic of inheritance, the basic concepts of which were covered in Chap. 3. Inheritance can be done in two ways: by subclassing existing classes and by implementing interfaces. The major goal of inheritance is reuse, but the two approaches achieve this goal in different ways.

We begin this chapter by exploring the idea of subclassing. Using inheritance effectively is not always a straightforward exercise. We show several examples that illustrate distinct circumstances where this approach can be taken.

Like most tools, subclassing must be done with care, or we may end up with an unstable system. In Sect. 9.3 we present some of the considerations while subclassing and an alternative to this approach. An elegant test for deciding whether subclassing is appropriate in a given context is enunciated in the Liskov substitution principle (LSP), which we study in this context.

Section 9.4 discusses the technique of implementing interfaces, with particular reference to Java. While many cases that use this approach are straightforward enough, one does encounter some tricky situations.

Section 9.5 revisits the case-study for the library system and enhances it to include multiple kinds of items. A 'process-oriented' enhancement is presented and critiqued in Sect. 9.6 before presenting an object-oriented solution incorporating inheritance.

Introducing inheritance and replacing a single class with a hierarchy could complicate some issues such as exception handling and functionality enhancement. These are addressed in Sect. 9.7.

Some object-oriented languages permit a class to subclass multiple classes. While this can be useful in some situations, the technique is also quite complicated. The approach and its pros and cons are covered in Sect. 9.8, followed by discussion and suggestions for further reading.

© Universities Press (India) Private Ltd. 2015

B. Dathan and S. Ramnath, *Object-Oriented Analysis, Design and Implementation*,
Undergraduate Topics in Computer Science, DOI 10.1007/978-3-319-24280-4_9

9.2 Applications of Inheritance

This section presents varied applications of inheritance illustrating the different circumstances in which this powerful technique can be used. Although the programming language rules concerning inheritance are not overly complicated as long as multiple inheritance is not involved, the design process can sometimes be tricky. A great deal of insight into how the system would evolve is essential for clean and effective use of inheritance.

9.2.1 Restricting Behaviours and Properties

One circumstance in which inheritance can be applied is when a class has characteristics that are a restriction of the characteristics of some other class. Suppose we have two classes, Rectangle and Square, to represent rectangles and squares. Every square is a rectangle in which length is equal to breadth, i.e., *the property that length be equal to breadth restricts the number of rectangles that qualify to be classified as squares.* Thus, Square is obtained from Rectangle by restricting a property; note that we are not attaching any more functionality to squares than rectangles.

As a second example, suppose that we create a graphical user interface with many types of widgets, including labels. Suppose we have the requirement that the text in all labels be coloured blue. In this case, it is convenient to have a subclass that simply sets the colour to blue. The subclass of JLabel is given below.

```
import java.awt.colour;
import javax.swing.JLabel;
public class SpecialLabel extends JLabel {
  public SpecialLabel(String text) {
    super(text);
    setForeground(colour.blue);
  }
}
```

In this case, the behaviour of SpecialLabel is restricted in that it always displays a blue foreground.

Although the above examples make perfect sense from an abstract view point, the reader should note that a well-established principle of inheritance shows that inheritance might not be justified. Please see Sects. 9.3.4 and 9.9 and Exercise 6.

9.2.2 Abstract Superclass

Sometimes the only purpose of having a superclass is to extract the common attributes and methods of potential subclasses, thus maximising reuse. No objects of the superclass itself are allowed, thus necessitating that the superclass be abstract. In such

Fig. 9.1 Partitioning a set of objects

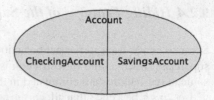

cases we have a set of **subclasses that partition the universe** of objects in the superclass.

As an example, consider accounts in a bank. An account is a general concept, and, perhaps, in some bank, all accounts are checking accounts or savings accounts. The bank allows only opening of checking or savings accounts. Therefore, Account is a class that helps us build software more quickly by providing some of the functionality that is common to all types of accounts. The partitioning is indicated in the Venn diagram in Fig. 9.1, which shows that the set of all accounts is partitioned into savings and checking accounts.

9.2.3 Adding Features

In Sect. 9.2.1, we have seen that sometimes classes are extended to restrict the behaviour of the superclass. Somewhat quite opposite to this, we may extend an ancestor class, by adding new features, to get the descendant. Consider a class named DataStream that serves as a reader of data. Imagine a situation where we need a class that has the added property of 'reReadability,' i.e., reading some input again. To achieve this, we add new functionality, viz., the ability of 'unreading' so that a character read from the stream can be pushed back. This is shown in Fig. 9.2. Another example of this would be a class for 'Moving Vehicle' that can be defined by extending an existing 'Vehicle' and adding the attribute 'speed.'

Fig. 9.2 Adding more features

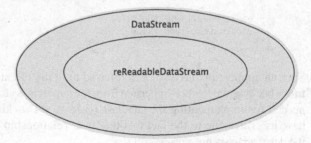

9.2.4 *Hiding Features of the Superclass*

Sometimes we want to restrict behaviour by suppressing some functionality of the
superclass. Such a kind of restriction is discussed in the following example, where
some of the features are eliminated in the subclass.

Let List be a class that allows the creation of a list in which objects can be added
anywhere: in the front, at the tail, or at any position in-between. It is easy to get a
class Queue that allows adding only at the tail and removing from the front. All other
add and remove methods, which allow adding at or removing from other positions,
should be disallowed. This can be accomplished in C++ via private[1] inheritance, as
shown below:

```
#include <iostream.h>
#include <stdlib.h>

class List {
  private:
    // data structures
  public:
    List() {
      // initialize data structures
    }
    bool add(int index, int value) {
    // code to add at the specified position and return true or false
    }
    bool add(int value) {
    // code to add at the end and return true or false
    }
    int remove(int index) {
    // code to delete the object at the specified position and
    // return true or false
    }
    int remove() {
    // code to delete the object at the front and return true or false
    }
};
class Queue: private List {
  public:
    int dequeue() {
      return List::remove();
    }
    bool enqueue(int value) {
      return List::add(value);
    }
};
```

Such an application has also been referred to in the literature as **Structural Inheritance** because the features inherited from the superclass (List) provide the structure
needed for implementing the subclass (Queue). This kind of an application does
have its critics due to the fact that the 'is-a' relationship between the ancestor and
the descendant is not preserved.

---

[1]In private inheritance, all the non-private superclass attributes become private attributes of the
subclass.

9.2.5 Combining Structural and Type Inheritance

We can also have situations where two kinds of inheritance are applied to define a class that suits our application. The most common of such situation is one where one superclass provides the necessary **structure** and another one, usually an interface, defines the **function**. A *binary search tree*, for instance, can be seen as a class that extends *binary tree* (structure inheritance) and implements the `OrderedList` interface (which defines the function of the binary search tree). The `OrderedList` operations are *implemented* using the methods provided by the class representing the binary tree, giving the name **implementation inheritance** to this usage.

9.3 Inheritance: Some Limitations and Caveats

Although it facilitates reuse, inheritance by subclassing is not always the best strategy to construct new classes even if there is justification for doing so on the surface. Among the reasons:

1. Subclassing could result in deep hierarchies, which usually makes it quite difficult to understand the code.
2. In systems that do not support multiple inheritance, subclassing is not always feasible.
3. It may be necessary to hide selected features of the superclass. For example, if we extend the class `java.util.LinkedList` to implement a queue, all of the methods of the superclass will be exposed, which may compromise integrity. Facilities such as the `renames` clause in the language Eiffel facilitate this. Explicitly hiding a superclass's field/method is also possible in C++.
4. Combining inheritance with genericity may result in complications due to implementation issues with a particular language. As we saw in Chap. 8, the erasure property employed by Java results in some inconsistencies when inheritance and genericity are combined.
5. The derived class's type may not be a true subtype of the superclass's type.

We elaborate on each of the above aspects in the following subsections.

9.3.1 Deep Hierarchies

When subclassing, we obviously add one more to the length of the hierarchy. The fields and methods available for use in the derived class include all of the inherited fields and methods and the ones added to the class itself. For example, the class `JFormattedTextField` in the package `javax.swing` has a hierarchy of depth 7, assuming that `java.lang.Object` is at depth 1. Table in Fig. 9.3 shows how the number of fields and methods increase for this specific hierarchy.

Class name	Number of Fields	Number of Methods
java.awt.Component	186	291
java.awt.Container	230	417
javax.swing.JComponent	376	594
javax.swing.text.JTextComponent	440	698
javax.swing.JTextField	479	729
javax.swing.JFormattedTextField	513	757

Fig. 9.3 Complexity increase with hierarchy depth

It is a challenging task to remember the interactions between the methods. Clearly, it is advisable to keep the hierarchy to a reasonable depth.

9.3.2 Lack of Multiple Inheritance

In certain situations, it may be desirable to create a subclass from multiple classes. However, some languages such as Java allow subclassing of at most one class. In such circumstances, we cannot limit ourselves to subclassing, but adopt other approaches in conjunction with it, or abandon subclassing altogether. We discuss this issue in Sect. 9.4.

9.3.3 Changes in the Superclass

While it is not desirable to change the set of methods supported by a class, such changes are sometimes inevitable. (As an example, in the Java class system the class `java.awt.Component` added the public method `setEnabled(boolean)` in JDK 1.1.) Imagine an application system A_1, some classes of which extend a set of classes from some other system A_2. Suppose that A_2 is modified to include a number of useful features. To exploit these enhancements, assume that the corresponding subclasses of A_1 use the new versions.

Although A_1 can now exploit all of the new functionality incorporated into the classes of A_2, there are potential problems as well. To see one possible problem, consider the two classes B and D given below, where D extends B.

```
public class B {
  public void m1() {
  }
}

public class D extends B {
  public void m2() {
  }
}
```

Suppose that the following method is now added to B

```
public int m2() {
  return 1;
}
```

Now class D is illegal because method m2's return type is inconsistent with that of the correspondingly-named method in B.

9.3.4 Typing Issues: The Liskov Substitution Principle

One of the rules that is implicit in the use of inheritance is the *Liskov substitution principle (LSP)* which is stated as follows:

Subclasses should be substitutable for their baseclasses.

The concept seems rather obvious, and at first glance, one wonders what the fuss is all about. After all, this is the essence of the *is-a* relationship of inheritance. To see its significance, let us first quote Liskov.

> If for each object O_1 of type S there is an object O_2 of type T such that for all programs P defined in terms of T, the behaviour of P is unchanged when O_1 is substituted for O_2 then S is a subtype of T.

The subtleties involved in the definition can be brought out through the following example.

A package provides a class SolidRectangle that creates a solid (i.e., all the pixels in the rectangle are filled), axis-parallel (or *isothetic*) rectangle. Each SolidRectangle object is defined by two points, which are the ends of one of the diagonals.

Let us define an *upper triangle* of a solid rectangle as the triangle formed by the end-points of one of the diagonals and the corner of the rectangle 'above' the diagonal. See Fig. 9.4, where the upper triangle is shown shaded. The two rectangles on the left have the diagonal connect the top-left and bottom-right corners of the rectangle. Therefore, the upper triangle comprises the top-left, bottom-right and top-right corners of the rectangle. Similarly, in other two cases, the top-left, bottom-left, and top-right corners constitute the upper triangle. The reader can verify that when corner1.y > corner2.y (see the top row of Fig. 9.4), the third point is formed using *corner2.x* and *corner1.y*; otherwise, the third point is formed using *corner1.x* and *corner2.y*.

Partial code for the class is shown below. The getUpperTriangle method returns the Triangle object corresponding to the upper triangle formed using the diagonal connecting corner1 and corner2.

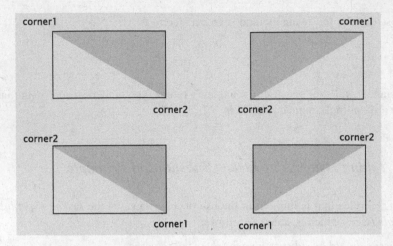

Fig. 9.4 Upper triangle (*shaded*) of a `SolidRectangle`

```
class SolidRectangle {
  private Point corner1;
  private Point corner2;
  public SolidRectangle(Point point1, Point point2) {
    corner1 = point1;
    corner2 = point2;
  }
  public void setCorner1(Point point) {
    corner1 = point;
  }
  public void setCorner2(Point point) {
    corner2 = point;
  }
  public Triangle getUpperTriangle() {
    Point point;
    if ((corner1.x == corner2.x) || (corner1.y == corner2.y)) {
      return null; // degenerate case
    } else {
      if (corner1.y > corner2.y) {
        point = new Point(corner2.x, corner1.y);
      } else {
        point = new Point(corner1.x, corner2.y);
        return (new Triangle(corner1, corner2, point));
      }
    }
  }
}
```

In some situations, it could conceivably be convenient to have a separate class for dealing with an individual pixel, which is just a 1 × 1 rectangle. This suggests that we could simply extend `SolidRectangle` to accommodate this.

```
class Pixel extends SolidRectangle {
  public Pixel(Point point) {
    super(point, point);
  }
}
```

Note that the set of `Pixel` objects is just a subset of the `SolidRectangle` object with the restriction `corner1 = corner2`. Accordingly, the methods for setting these corners should be redefined in the subclass so that this invariant property is preserved.

```
public void setCorner1(Point point) {
  super.setCorner1(point);
  super.setCorner2(point);
}
public void setCorner2(Point point) {
  super.setCorner1(point);
  super.setCorner2(point);
}
```

The `getUpperTriangle` method does not pose any problem for our `Pixel` class, since it will always return `null`. Our troubles start with existing client classes, whose methods have been using the methods of `SolidRectangle`. Consider the following method in a client class that takes as its input parameter a `SolidRectangle` object.

```
public void clientMethod(SolidRectangle rectangle, Point point) {
  Triangle triangle1;
  //... some code
  rectangle.setCorner1(new point(1, 1));
  rectangle.setCorner2(new point(4, 4));
  triangle1 = rectangle.getUpperTriangle();
  if (triangle1.contains(p)) {
    //... some code
  }
}
```

This code was written by a client using `SolidRectangle`, but unaware of `Pixel`. Since the two corners are set to two distinct points, `triangle1` will not be null, and things will be fine. Now if this method is invoked and a reference to a `Pixel` object is passed as the actual parameter, both the corners will end up being assigned the same point, `triangle1` will be `null`, and we end up with a `NullPointerException`. Note that there is no simple fix; we may just have to find such code in all the methods of the client classes, and either check for null pointers or check the type of the objects stored in the `SolidRectangle` references at runtime.

At every step of the this process our choices seemed logical, but we ended up with an undesirable state of affairs. So it is natural to ask: *what went wrong?* The answer lies in a precise definition the *is-a* relationship: *A pixel object 'is-a' SolidRectangle object if and only if the behaviour of Pixel objects conforms to the behaviour of SolidRectangle objects in* **all** *situations.* The above example shows that the behaviour of `getUpperTriangle` does not exhibit such conformance when invoked in conjunction with the `setCorner` methods. One could argue, perhaps, that the method `getUpperTriangle` is itself poorly designed, but that is really not a choice that we can make now. It is important to keep in mind that we are inheriting from the existing class `SolidRectangle` and we must accept all its methods. To cast this in terms of the formal statement of the LSP, when we substitute `Pixel` for `SolidRectangle` the behaviour of any program should remain unchanged. What we have shown here is that for the program `clientMethod`, the behaviour changes when such a substitution is made.

The caveat here for the programmer extending a class is therefore that *one must check all behaviours of the class being extended, even in situations where a subset relationship exists between the corresponding 'real-world' entities.*

9.3.5 Addressing the Limitations

The object-oriented approaches to circumvent these limitations are founded on two thumb rules:

- Inherit from abstract types rather than concrete classes.
- Favour composition over inheritance.

In most situations where we have to use inheritance effectively, some combination of these two thumb rules comes in handy. A simple illustrative example is described below.

Consider a situation where a concrete class C1 exists and we want to create a descendant C2. We could do this by having C2 extend C1, but such a solution would suffer from the problems listed earlier. A better approach would be to define an abstract type C which is implemented by C1. Now C2 can be defined as another concrete class that extends C. In order to reuse the earlier implementation, we have two strategies available. One strategy is to define C as an abstract class, factor out the parts of the implementation that are likely to be used and place these in C. Each of C1 and C2 then put in the details specific to their types. A second strategy would be to define C2 as a class that implements C and *adapts* the implementation provided by C1.

9.4 Type Inheritance

So far, we have discussed cases where a class subclassed another to inherit its properties and behaviours. But reuse need not be realised simply via subclassing. It can also be achieved by inheriting behaviour.

To see how this can be achieved, assume that we have a class C that performs some useful function f on all objects of type T. Then, a class D that wishes to utilise this functionality can do so by acquiring the type T. In Java parlance, for example, T might be an interface that class D implements.

9.4.1 A Simple Example

To make these ideas more concrete, let us look at an example. In the `java.util` package, there is a class called `sort` that as the name implies, sorts objects of type `Comparable`. Here is the essential declaration of that method.

```
static T    sort(List<T> list)
```

where T must be of type `Comparable`.

`Comparable` is an interface with just one method `compareTo`, which has the following signature.

```
int compareTo(T object)
```

Instances of any class that implements the above interface acquire the ability to be sorted using the `sort` method of `Collections`.

Suppose that we have a class `City` that stores the name, state, and population of cities. To make objects of type `City` comparable, we need to have it implement the `Comparable` interface. Each `City` object maintains a reference to the corresponding `State`. So the `compareTo` method of the former employs the `compareTo` method of the latter to complete its work. Here is the code.

```
public class City implements Comparable {
    private String name;
    private State state;
    private int population;
    public City(String name, State state, int population) {
        this.name = name;
        this.state = state;
        this.population = population;
    }
    public int compareTo(Object object) {
        City city = (City) object;
        int result = 0;
        if ((result = name.compareTo(city.name)) == 0) {
            return state.compareTo(city.state);
        }
        return result;
    }
    public boolean equals(City city) {
        return compareTo(city) == 0;
    }
}
```

The class `State` must also be `Comparable` as shown below.

```
public class State implements Comparable {
    private String name;
    public int compareTo(Object other) {
        State state = (State) other;
        return name.compareTo(state.name);
    }
    // other fields and methods
}
```

Inheriting a property is not always as simple as the above example suggests, and Java has two other interfaces, viz., `Cloneable` and `Runnable`, which exemplify some of the subtleties.

9.4.2 The Cloneable Interface

The property of self-replication comes in handy when we are dealing with objects. Due to the complex interconnections, sending out a reference to the original copy of just one object can result in compromising the integrity of the entire system. As we have seen in our case-study with the library system, a `Member` object can store references to several `Book` objects, each of which could have several references to `Hold` objects. Since each `Hold` object has a reference to a member, one could potentially access (or modify) the information about all the members through a single reference. This problem can be avoided by not sending a reference to the original object, but a reference to a carefully constructed clone.

Implementing such a solution is somewhat more complicated than it appears at first. A naive implementation strategy would be to simply do a bit-wise copy (sometimes called a 'shallow' copy) of all the fields of the user object. If we were to attempt this, consider the problem of making a copy of the holds placed by the user. The `Member` object has a field `booksOnHold` that holds a reference to the collection of holds. A bit-wise copy would simply create another reference to this collection. As a result, the method accessing the clone now has a reference to the original `Hold` objects. Creating a copy therefore requires some knowledge about the object being copied, and this knowledge is available only within the object being copied. As an example, the class `Member` must decide how members are copied. Since `Member` includes a collection of `Hold` objects, that collection must be cloned when its `Member` object is cloned. The rule is that every object should decide for itself how it will be cloned, so that the collection should be able to clone itself and provide the rule for its own cloning.

To add to the difficulty, in general, any given object that holds references to other objects has to rely on those objects to create clones of themselves. If some of those objects cannot be cloned, then the given object must have the ability to decide how the situation is to be handled. Accordingly, the mechanism provided by the language to impart the cloneability property to a class must be versatile enough to accommodate all the desirable possibilities.

The `Object` class comes with a protected `clone` method that does the simple bit-wise copy that we describe above. The `Cloneable` interface in Java imparts the property of cloneability to a class. This interface is empty, and a class may choose not to implement this interface, but may nonetheless have to override the `clone` method in `Object` to ensure that things are done correctly. Finally, we have a `CloneNotSupportedException`, which is thrown to signal that a class's `clone` method should not be invoked. The `clone` method in `Object` is declared to throw this exception, thus allowing all subclasses to throw the exception as well.

Any given class can have one of four possible attitudes toward cloning:

1. *Support clone*   In this case the class implements the `Cloneable` interface and declares its `clone` method to throw no exceptions. The author of such a class must ensure that all its contents are `cloneable`.
2. *Conditionally support clone*   This situation arises when a class implements `Cloneable`, but cannot guarantee that its contents can be cloned. In this case the `clone` method will throw the `CloneNotSupportedException` if some of its contents are not `Cloneable`.
3. *Not publicly support clone, but allow subclasses to support clone*   Such a class does not implement `Cloneable`, but may override the default implementation of `clone` to ensure that it works correctly. This would enable its subclasses to invoke `super.clone()` if the subclasses choose to support clone.
4. *Forbid clone*   In this case, the class does not implement `Cloneable` and provides a clone method that always throws the `CloneNotSupported` `Exception`.

As a first example, let us see how to implement the `Cloneable` interface for the `City` and `State` classes given earlier. The clone in `City` requires the following header.

```
public class City implements Comparable, Cloneable {
```

The `clone` method itself is given below. One thing to note is that the immutable classes do not need to be cloned if our only purpose is to protect the original copy. Any attempt to change an immutable object by modifying the clone will not change the original, even though we have a shallow copy. For instance, if an object is simply a collection of `String` objects, a bit-wise copy will create another object that holds references to the same `String` objects as the original. Attempting to modify a `String` creates a new `String` object and therefore the original object is always preserved.

After calling the `clone` method of the superclass, the `state` field is cloned by calling the `clone` method of the `State` class.

```
public Object clone() {
  City copy = null;
  try {
    super.clone();
    copy.state = (State) state.clone();
  } catch(CloneNotSupportedException cnse) {
    return null;
  }
  return copy;
}
```

The `clone` method of the `State` object is straightforward and we omit giving its code. The reader will notice that shallow cloning works just fine.

As a second example, consider cloning a `Member` object in the library system. To clone a user, the following changes are made to the code:

```
class Member implements Cloneable {
  // other fields and methods
  public Object clone() throws CloneNotSupportedException {
    Member member = (Member) super.clone();
    member.booksBorrowed = new LinkedList();
    member.booksOnHold = new LinkedList();
    member.transactions = new LinkedList();
    for (ListIterator iterator = booksBorrowed.listIterator();
                       iterator.hasNext(); ) {
      member.booksBorrowed.add((Book)((Book) iterator.next()).clone());
    }
    for (ListIterator iterator = booksOnHold.listIterator();
                       iterator.hasNext(); ) {
      member.booksOnHold.add((Hold)((Hold) iterator.next()).clone());
    }
    for (ListIterator iterator = transactions.listIterator();
                       iterator.hasNext(); ) {
      member.transactions.add((Transaction)
              ((Transaction)iterator.next()).clone());
    }
    return member;
  }
}
```

Since the clone method for the class `LinkedList` provides only a shallow copy, it is necessary that we create new instances of `LinkedList` for `booksBorrowed`, `booksOnHold` and `transactions`, clone each item in the original versions of these lists and insert them into the clone.

`Member` is now conditionally supporting clone. The classes `Book`, `Hold` and `Transaction` will also have to support clone if we have to successfully clone `Member`. Although this code appears correct (and does in fact do the cloning correctly) it contains a serious flaw: *invoking the clone method could result in infinite recursion*. This is because the `Hold` object stores a reference to the member who placed the hold! The size of the cloned object also poses a problem: *since the* `Hold` *object also stores a reference to* `Book`, *which in turn stores a reference to the borrower, we could potentially clone all the information in the library*. A simple resolution to these problems could be that the `clone` methods in `Book` and `Hold` do not clone the `Member` fields and also set the `Member` references on cloned copies to `null`.

```
class Hold implements Cloneable {
  // other fields and methods
  public Object clone() throws cloneNotSupportedException {
    Hold hold  = (Hold) super.clone();
    hold.member = null;
    hold.book = (Book) book.clone();
    hold.date = (Calendar) date.clone();
    return hold;
  }
}
```

In this situation we see that cloning is serving a purpose beyond that of preserving the original copy. In general, cloning is a non-trivial exercise and we need to be aware

Fig. 9.5 Cloning in the general case: an example

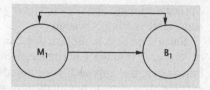

of all the possible complications that can arise when properties like cloneability are inherited by a class.

For an approach that prevents infinite recursion, we could proceed as discussed in the following example. Our approach employs a list of all objects that we have started cloning and the corresponding clone's reference. As we start the cloning process, the list is empty. Suppose we have the situation where member M_1 has borrowed a single book B_1 and we begin the cloning process with M_1 (see Fig. 9.5). It is easy to verify that with no safeguards in place, the cloning will result in infinite recursion. Before cloning the fields of M_1, we add an entry corresponding to M_1 into the list and store the clone's reference. In the process of cloning M_1, we encounter the reference to B_1. Before we clone B_1, we create an entry for it and store the reference to B_1's clone. While cloning the fields of B_1, we encounter M_1 and observe from the list that that we have already started cloning M_1, which means that it should not be cloned again (to prevent infinite recursion). We obtain M_1's clone's reference from the list and store it in B_1's clone.

9.4.3 The Runnable Interface

Software systems often have to employ runtime structures called *concurrent sequential processes (CSPs)*. A simple example of a CSP can be found in the implementation of a bank account. The customer (owner of the account) could be using an ATM to withdraw cash at the same time when a transaction for depositing a check is being processed. Both these actions represent concurrent processes which are accessing a piece of shared data (the account information). In this situation it is vital to ensure that both processes do not try to simultaneously modify the `balance` field in the account; in such a simultaneous access, depending on the order in which the methods for deposit and withdrawal are executed, we could end up with an error.

Java provides a class called `Thread` that can be used for implementing CSPs. In our example, we would have a separate thread for every process that accesses the account object; that is, if a withdrawal and deposit were to be simultaneously carried out, there would be a thread for the withdrawal process and another thread for the deposit. We can then employ *Mutual Exclusion* on the account object, which will ensure that the account is not simultaneously accessed by the two processes. Threads also enable the programmer to implement other operations like suspending a process, making a process sleep for a specified amount of time, prioritise processes, and enable sharing of resources.

Since `Thread` is a class, we can create a new class that has all the features of `Thread` through inheritance. However, since Java does not support multiple inheritance, this approach does not allow the user to create a class that extends an existing class and also has all the properties of `Thread`. This restriction is overcome by providing the `Runnable` interface as a part of the language. This interface allows the programmer to create a class that has all the properties of `Thread`. The following example illustrates the use of this interface to create a simple 'clock' that prints 'tic' and 'toc' at regular intervals.

```java
public class Clock implements Runnable {
  Thread thread = new Thread(this);
  String sound = "tic";
  public void run() {
    try {
      while (true) {
        System.out.println(sound);
        sound = "toc";
        Thread.sleep(1000);
        System.out.println(sound);
        sound = "tic";
        Thread.sleep(1000);
      }
    } catch (InterruptedException ie) {
    }
  }
  public Clock() {
    thread.start();
  }
  public static void main (String[] args) {
    new Clock();
  }
}
```

The `run` method contains an infinite loop that alternately prints the words 'tic' and 'toc' with a 1000 ms delay between consecutive words. This process continues until interrupted by the user.

The `Runnable` interface requires that `Clock` implement the `run` method. Inside `Clock` we create a `Thread`, storing this reference in `thread`. A reference to the `Clock` object is passed to `thread`. (The parameter being supplied here is required to be of type `Runnable`.) The `start` method of `Thread` is invoked in the `Clock` constructor, and this method in turn invokes the `run` method of the `Clock` object. In this interface, a `Thread` object is encapsulated along with the class to provide 'thread-like' properties to objects of the class. In essence, what we have done here is to *achieve the benefits of inheritance using* **object composition.**

Object Composition and Inheritance are the two most common mechanisms for reuse in object-oriented design. In both these mechanisms, the implementation of the new class is defined in terms of the functionality of the existing classes. In case of inheritance, since the internal details of the ancestor class are often visible to the descendant, the resulting scenario is referred to as 'white-box reuse'. On the other hand, object composition requires that the component classes have well-defined interfaces so that they can be used as 'black-boxes'.

Object composition has the obvious advantage of keeping the inheritance hierarchies small, thus reducing the complexity of the system. Also, properties that are not naturally tied to one another are kept separate, so that each class is kept encapsulated and focused on one task. A less obvious advantage is that composition allows us to define the object dynamically at run-time. In the above example, `Clock` has been defined *statically*, since `Thread` will always hold a reference to a `Thread` object. The following example shows how composition can be used to define an object *dynamically*.

```
public class Catalog {
    private List catalogList;
    public Catalog (List list) {
        catalogList = list;
        //other constructor code
    }
    // other fields and methods
}
```

In this case, any object belonging to any class that satisfies the `List` interface can be sent in as a parameter to the constructor. For instance, we could do the following:

```
catalog = new Catalog(new ArrayList());
```

This would create a catalog that uses an `ArrayList` to store the collection of books. Note that such a dynamic definition is possible because `Catalog` is defined by composition; if it had been defined as an extension of, say, `LinkedList`, this would not be possible.

9.5 Making Enhancements to the Library Class

We are now ready to move ahead with the process of employing inheritance and creating hierarchies in our design. Consider a more sophisticated version of the `Library` system that we created in the last chapter. With the advent of technology, our clients now wish to expand their collection to include non-print media. Thus we now have books on tape, CDs, and DVDs in addition to printed books. Also, the library wants to include some periodicals, which are to be handled differently from the other books. For instance, recent periodicals cannot be checked out. For books on tape, CDs and DVDs, we wish to keep track of the duration.

9.5.1 A First Attempt

As a first step in developing our new design, let us ask ourselves the question: *How do these new requirements change the design of our system?* or in more concrete terms, *What new classes/methods need to be added?* and *How do the interactions between the existing classes change?* To answer these, let us examine how the requirements have changed the way in which the business processes are carried out. Consider the use case for issuing a book. The operations needed are the same: viz., *check issuability, compute a due-date and record the transaction.* We could handle these simply by making changes in the methods of the existing Book class.

To simplify the discussion, we restrict ourselves to two types of items that the library lends: books and periodicals. Even with this simplification, we need a mechanism to find out what item (i.e., a book or a periodical) we are dealing with when we process these transactions. One approach could be to add a field bookType to the class Book, which would tell us what kind of a book it is. We would make changes in the method that computes the due-date by switching on the field bookType. Periodicals that are less than three months old are not issuable; otherwise, they can be borrowed for a week. Another difference is that periodicals have no authors.

Let us re-write Book with these enhancements. New fields are added to hold the bookType and dateAcquired and we also declare constants to designate the type of the book.

```
private String title;
private String author;
private String id;
private Member borrowedBy;
private List holds = new LinkedList();
private Calendar dueDate;
private int bookType;
private Calendar dateAcquired;
public static final int BOOK = 1;
public static final int PERIODICAL = 2;
```

Since periodicals and books store different values, we need two constructors. To create a periodical, we use the constructor with two parameters because periodicals have no author parameter.

```
public Book(String title, String author, String id) {
  this.title = title;
  this.author = author;
  this.id = id;
  this.type = BOOK;
}
public Book(String title, String id) {
  this.title = title;
  this.id = id;
  this.type = PERIODICAL;
  this.dateAcquired = new GregorianCalendar();
  this.dateAcquired.setTimeInMillis(System.currentTimeMillis());
}
```

The user interface should allow the user to specify what kind of item is being added to the library. This will require a conditional that will not ask for an author if the item being added is a periodical.

```
public void addBooks() {
  Book result;
  do {
```

```
      String title = getToken("Enter   title");
      String bookID = getToken("Enter id");
      if (yesOrNo("Is this a  book?")) {
        String author = getToken("Enter author");
        result = library.addBook(title, author, bookID);
      } else {
        result = library.addPeriodical(title, bookID);
      }
      if (result != null) {
        System.out.println(result);
      } else {
        System.out.println("Book could not be added");
      }
      if (!yesOrNo("Add more books?")) {
        break;
      }
    } while (true);
  }
```

The method in the UI invokes a different method of `Library` in each case. Accordingly, `Library` provides two methods, one to add periodicals and one to add books.

```
public Book addBook(String title, String author, String id) {
  Book book = new Book(title, author, id);
  if (catalog.insertBook(book)) {
    return (book);
  }
  return null;
}

//new method added for periodical
public Book addPeriodical(String title,  String id) {
  Book book = new Book(title,  id);
  if (catalog.insertBook(book)) {
    return (book);
  }
  return null;
}
```

Let us examine some other methods in `Book`. The process of issuing a book is different from that of a periodical, and that is reflected in the new `issue` method. The `cutoffDate` is computed and compared against `dateAcquired` to decide if the periodical can be issued.

```
public boolean issue(Member member) {
  borrowedBy = member;
  dueDate = new GregorianCalendar();
  dueDate.setTimeInMillis(System.currentTimeMillis());
  switch (bookType) {
    case PERIODICAL:
      Calendar cutoffDate = new GregorianCalendar();
      cutoffDate.setTimeInMillis(System.currentTimeMillis());
      cutoffDate.add(Calendar.MONTH, -3);
      if (cutoffDate.after(dateAcquired)) {
        dueDate.add(Calendar.WEEK_OF_MONTH, 1);
      } else {
        return false;
      }
```

```
        break;
    default:
        dueDate.add(Calendar.MONTH, 1);
        break;
    }
    return true;
}
```

The `getAuthor` and `toString` methods also differ because of the absence of a specific author for periodicals.

```
public String getAuthor() {
    if (bookType == PERIODICAL) {
        return "";
    }
    return author;
}

public String toString() {
    if (bookType == BOOK) {
        return "title " + title + " author " + author + " id " + id
            + " borrowed by " + borrowedBy;
    } else {
        return "title " + title + " id " + id + " borrowed by " +
            borrowedBy + " Acquired  on " + dateAcquired.getTime().toString();
    }
}
```

Likewise, all methods that have different behaviour for books and periodicals will be modified, and this behaviour will be decided based on the value stored in `bookType`. The above enhancement is exactly how a procedural design would be modified. The process varies slightly for each type of data, and this variation is accounted for within the same procedural unit by switching on the kind of data.

9.5.2 Drawbacks of the Above Approach

Before embarking on a critique of such an implementation, it is useful to keep in mind the perspective from which we are approaching the issue. We have two fundamental goals:

- The system should be easy to build and test.
- The system should be adaptable.

It is clear from what we are doing that such an approach involves storing more of the complexity of the system in one class (i.e., `Book`) and its methods. This makes the system difficult to build and test. From the point of view of building, the programmer has to deal with increased complexity of the processes. Examples of this can be seen in the methods like `issue` and `getAuthor`, where the programmer has to be aware of two cases and two possible outcomes that are predicated on the properties of the two kinds of items. Testing adds another dimension of complexity. If we have two categories of objects, each of whose methods handle five different cases, we have a total of ten outcomes to test when we combine them into a single class. As we pack more requirements into a single class, we increase the probability of human error. Another kind of problem is the combinatorial explosion that happens when program segments use a lot of branch statements. Consider, for instance a method with two switch statements, one following the other, each of which has five possible cases. We now have a total of twenty-five possible computational paths when this method executes. This complexity deters the programmer from putting in the assertions needed to catch all exceptional behaviours. As the science of software reliability progresses, it is becoming increasingly clear to researchers that, at least in critical systems, some form of formal verification will be needed. Our focus should therefore be to produce simpler methods.

A second set of problems arise when we apply the adaptability requirement. Changes to business processes, as we well know, are inevitable. In our system these changes can take two forms: (i) *the procedures for performing library operations may change* and (ii) *we may add new categories of items to the library.* The kind of structure that we have above hurts our ability to modify the code in both these situations. When a procedure changes, say we have some new rules for issuing books, we want to ensure that in re-writing the `issue` method we are not messing up the procedure for the periodicals. This also means that when testing the system after the changes, we have to test the system for both books and periodicals. A similar situation develops when we add new categories of items. The existing methods are changed to accommodate one more case, and once again we need the assurance of system behaviour for the new items added as well as the ones that were already in place.

An important (some would argue the most important) guiding tenet of object-oriented design can be summed up in what is referred to as the *open-closed principle (OCP)*:

A module must be open for extension but closed for implementation.

Extension is the process by which new features are added to existing software, and *implementation* is the process that converts an abstract design into concrete code. What this statement implies is that our classes and modules must be written in such a manner that they can be extended, i.e., new features can be added without re-opening the completed implementation, i.e., without the need for modification of the existing code.

It is obvious that OCP is highly desirable, but a deeper understanding is needed when we apply it. Adding new features to software often requires changes to an existing class. Consider, for example, the feature for charging fines that we added in Chap. 8: changes to `Book` and `Member` were inevitable. In such a situation, we want to ensure that classes not directly involved in this (`Catalog`, for instance) are not affected. Exactly which classes will be affected depends on how the responsibilities were assigned for each step of the procedures involved (viz., Return Book). This assignment is a non-trivial task, but the propagation of the effects of change can be contained by proper encapsulation. Sometimes, changes can mostly be handled by defining a separate class that incorporates the new features and have only a minimal effect on other classes. This new class, however, needs to be related in some way with the existing classes, *without changing their implementation.* In a world without inheritance, such a feat is impossible to accomplish; inheritance allows us to extend an existing class so that more features can be added to the descendants, even though the ancestor class remains closed. However, *merely applying inheritance will not satisfy OCP;* as we shall see next, a thorough understanding of how the implementation will be reused is essential.

9.6 Improving the Design

In keeping with the above arguments, we once again examine the process that we used to add the new kinds of items. Since this is a chapter on inheritance, it is pretty obvious that we shall employ it in some way, but before we plunge in, a couple of issues deserve our attention.

As we discussed above, some extensions necessarily affect other classes, and so we ask: *What classes must change to accommodate the new kinds of items?* To properly answer this, we must go back to the analysis. The system is allowing users to add new kinds of items to the library, so it is safe to assume that the users are aware of their existence and also expect the system to reciprocate this awareness. All business is transacted through the UI, which is therefore required to know about the new items. It is not immediate from the analysis that any of the other classes need to be aware of this, and we shall therefore postpone this decision to a later point.

In our example, we are introducing new kinds of items to the library and would like to encapsulate the resulting changes to the system using separate classes. In this context, it is useful to ask: *Is there a set of guiding principles that can be employed when we introduce inheritance to incorporate the new items?* Such principles can then be used to guide the design of our inheritance hierarchy. In practice, software designers are often confronted with situations where changes not anticipated during design need to be incorporated. A closely related question, therefore, would be: *Is there a systematic procedure that we can employ when introducing inheritance?* We shall now discuss answers to the above questions as we revisit the process of adding periodicals to the library.

9.6.1 Designing the Hierarchy

As discussed above, we now have two classes, Book and Periodical. The original design did not have the Periodical class and therefore we need to decide how it will be related to Book. Two obvious choices present themselves (see Fig. 9.6):

Fig. 9.6 Two hierarchies for library items

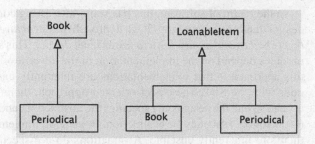

- **Option 1**: *Both classes share a common ancestor.* In this hierarchy we have an ancestor class `LoanableItem` with two descendants, `Book` and `Periodical`. The common ancestor is an abstract class that contains the shared attributes. `Catalog` is defined as a collection of `LoanableItem` and the other classes in the system (`Library`, `Member`, etc.) will be redefined to deal with `Loanable Item` (instead of `Book`).
- **Option 2**: *One class inherits from the other.* Since a `Book` class is already present, `Periodical` simply extends `Book` and overrides the necessary attributes. None of the other classes need to be changed.

When designing a new system, the level of complexity appears to be the same in both options. Option 1 requires an additional class, but has the advantage of treating all the items in a uniform manner. On the other hand, when we are adding features to an existing system like the one we have, Option 1 appears to have several disadvantages. The process of creating the new class `LoanableItem` and modifying all the existing classes can be extremely tedious, whereas the 'quick and dirty' approach of Option 2 has the advantage of speed. Over a long period of time, however, such an approach can be very detrimental to a system.

Any system that needs to be up and running for a long time needs *stability*. Simply put, stability of a system is the amount of work that needs to be put in to disturb the existing equilibrium. If left undisturbed, an unstable system may remain stable for a long time, but with very little effort the equilibrium can be disturbed. Extending the notion to a situation where we have several subsystems within a system, consider something like a house, which has several components: a foundation, a wall structure, a roof, and a dish antenna. The roof depends upon the wall structure, which in turn depends on the foundation. The dish antenna is clearly the least stable of all the parts, and therefore it is very undesirable to depend on it (which may be another reason not to become a TV addict!). On the other hand we want the foundation to be very stable, since all the other components are dependent on it. Since the roof depends on the wall structure, we want to ensure that the wall structure is at least as stable as the roof. To summarise, we want to *depend in the direction of stability*. This rule is often referred to as the **stable dependencies principle (SDP)**. In our case study with the Library, we want to ensure that `LoanableItem` is very stable, since the hierarchy depends on it.

In the realm of software, this has some interesting consequences. A 'procedural design' tends to follow a top-down approach: *the structure starts at the top with high-level choices and points down to lower level details.* This suggests that the high-level modules depend on the implementation in the lower level modules. A problem with this approach is that implementations are inherently unstable, and thus we are at odds with the SDP. The object-oriented approach, therefore turns this dependency around so that the design only specifies the abstraction, and the actual implementation ('concretion') satisfies the abstraction. In general, implementations are concrete and therefore inherently unstable. Abstractions do not specify details and thus remain flexible, which makes them more stable when changes have to be incorporated. Thus we can state the following simple thumb rule:

Depend upon abstractions; avoid depending upon concrete implementations.

The design choice that we shall make is therefore to have an abstract class LoanableItem on which all the concrete implementations depend. The inheritance structure is translated into code as follows:

```
public abstract class LoanableItem implements Matchable<String> {
  // code common to all types of items that the library lends
}
public class Book extends LoanableItem {
  // code specific to books
}
public class Periodical extends LoanableItem {
  // code specific to periodicals
}
```

In the process of filling in the details for these classes, we will decide how these items are created and added to the collection, what attributes are placed in each class, and how the common code is factored out.

Changes to Other Classes

The main purpose of creating such a hierarchy is to protect all the client classes from changes that occur within the hierarchy. The client classes would now depend on the stable abstraction provided by LoanableItem and be completely unaware of the structure below it. All the code in Library will now invoke methods through references of type LoanableItem and Catalog is defined as a collection of LoanableItem. It follows then that the abstract class must also implement the Matchable interface, as shown in the code above.

9.6.2 Invoking the Constructors

Let us examine the process for adding new items to the library collection. Since the UI knows about the different kinds of items, the method for adding items can query the user about the kind of item, collect the necessary parameters and invoke the method in Library. In our earlier implementation we had separate methods

for books and periodicals; this makes the implementation unstable since adding new
kinds of items requires adding methods to `Library`. Let us say we can do this with
a single method, `addLoanableItem`. The code in the UI would be something
like this:

```
private static final int BOOK = 1;        // declaring the constants
private static final int PERIODICAL = 2;
public void addLoanableItems() {
  LoanableItem result;
  do {
    String typeString = getToken("Enter type: "
                                 + BOOK + " for books\n"
                                 + PERIODICAL + " for periodicals\n");
    int type = Integer.parseInt(typeString);
    String title = getToken("Enter title");
    String author = null;
    if (type == BOOK) {
      author = getToken("Enter author");
    }
    String id = getToken("Enter id");
    result = library.addLoanableItem(type, title, author, id);
    if (result != null) {
      System.out.println(result);
    } else {
      System.out.println("Item could not be added");
    }
    if (!yesOrNo("Add more Items?")) {
      break;
    }
  } while (true);
}
```

The method in `Library` must now decide what kind of item to create. This would
imply that we have a conditional in `addLoanableItem` that switches on `type`.
We no longer have to add methods to `Library` if new kinds of items are desired,
but we still need to edit our method to add more clauses to the conditional, which
means we cannot reuse the `Library` class directly.

   Before proposing solutions, let us take another look at why an inheritance hierarchy is a good idea. We wanted to avoid too much complexity in one class and
its methods, so we tried to get rid of conditionals that switched on the type of item
by creating a separate subclass for each type, with a common abstract superclass.
When invoking the methods on items from this hierarchy, we only refer to the type
of the abstract superclass and let dynamic binding take care of the rest. Effectively,
we have moved the complexity of the conditional out of the application code and
into the interpreter. Dynamic binding works because the system keeps track of the
actual concrete subclass of the object even though the reference is stored in a variable declared to have the type of the superclass. When we are invoking constructors,
we are yet to create the object; so we cannot rely on dynamic binding to make the
choice for us. What this implies is that *the conditionals in the constructor invocation
cannot be eliminated.* In other words, conditionals that switch on the input cannot be
eliminated using dynamic binding, unlike conditionals that switch on stored values.

(In a sense, creating new objects is like getting new input, and conditionals on the input are essential for any non-trivial program.) The consequence of all this for our design is that the class that chooses the appropriate constructor will undergo a change. Our goal is to protect `Library` from these changes, and some brainstorming gives us three possibilities:

- **Option 1** One possibility is to extend `Library` and redefine `addLoanable Item` whenever new types of items are added.
- **Option 2** A second option is to move the constructor logic into the abstract super-class `LoanableItem`.
- **Option 3** Third, we could develop a new class that takes care of creating the items.

Things to Remember When Creating an Inheritance Hierarchy

Do not rush in too soon. Remember that inheritance is a relationship between well-understood abstractions and the hierarchy usually emerges 'naturally' in our process. This takes time, except in situations where our data has a pre-existing taxonomy. This implies that we have a *clear data abstraction in mind before constructing the hierarchy*.

Allow for future expansion. Keep in mind that we cannot guess how our system might be used; the best way to plan for that is to be generous when allowing for variations. The rules for this are

- *Define methods to be as general as possible at each level of an inheritance hierarchy.* When writing methods, avoid details that are too specifically tailored for the current set of subclasses; the methods should abstract out common functionality so that subclasses can invoke the superclass method to perform some of the task.
- *Be generous in defining data types and storage to avoid difficult changes later on.* For example, you might consider using a variable of type `double` even though your current data may only require a `float` variable.

Make sure the construction is secure. Since we do not know how our system will be used, it is imperative that we do not allow any legal usage to compromise its integrity.

- *Choose the right access modifiers for your attributes* Applying the optimal access levels to members of a class hierarchy makes the hierarchy easier to maintain by allowing you to control how such members will be used. Declare class members with access modifiers that provide the least amount of access feasible.

- *Only expose items that are needed by derived classes*   Keeping fields `private` helps descendants and clients by reducing naming conflicts and protects them from using items that may need to be changed at a later stage. Members that are only needed by descendants should be marked as `protected`. This ensures that only the derived classes are dependent on these members, which makes it easier to update these members during development.
- *The functionality provided by the methods of the base class should not depend on features that can be overridden*   Make sure that base class methods do not depend on features that can be changed by inheriting classes.

The first choice is easily dismissed; when we extend `Library`, all the classes that depend on it must change. `Library` is a facade and we can therefore expect several other modules to depend on it, which implies that the stability of this module is critical. The other two options share a common underlying principle of designing for change:

> To protect the stability of a module, move the aspects that are likely to change to a different module.

Option 2 suggests that we move this to the class `LoanableItem`. This might seem like a logical assignment of responsibilities, since the constructor invocation is in some way related to the inheritance hierarchy. A closer scrutiny reveals, however, that this would essentially defeat the purpose of introducing inheritance. The abstract superclass is designed to be a *stable abstraction*, that protects the client classes from changes in the hierarchy. It follows that `LoanableItem` should be designed to be unaware of the structure of the hierarchy that lies under it. This leaves us with Option 3, requiring that we create a new module to encapsulate the changes that occur to the logic for invoking constructors. Not surprisingly, this is in fact the standard approach for dealing with this commonly occurring problem.

Implementing a Simple Factory

A **Factory** is typically employed when we want to make a system independent of how its products are created, composed, and represented. In this case, we would like to make the `Library` independent of the process of creating the items. The factory provides a method that can be invoked for creating a new object and thus encapsulates the logic for invocation of constructors. The code for `LoanableItemFactory` is shown below.

```
public class LoanableItemFactory {
   private static final int BOOK = 1;
   private static final int PERIODICAL = 2;
   private static LoanableItemFactory lFactory;
   private LoanableItemFactory() {
   }
```

```
public static LoanableItemFactory instance() {
  if (lFactory == null) {
    return (lFactory = new LoanableItemFactory());
  } else {
    return lFactory;
  }
}
public LoanableItem createLoanableItem(int type, String title,
                                       String author, String id) {
  switch (type) {
    case BOOK:
      return new Book(title, author, id);
    case PERIODICAL:
      return new Periodical(title, id);
    default:
      return null;
  }
}
}
```

The above code defines `LoanableItemFactory` as a singleton that creates objects of type `LoanableItem`. The method `addLoanableItem` in `Library` is modified as follows:

```
public LoanableItem addLoanableItem(int type, String title,
                                    String author, String id) {
  LoanableItemFactory factory =  LoanableItemFactory.instance();
  LoanableItem item = factory.createLoanableItem(type, title,
                                                 author, id);
  if (item != null) {
    if (catalog.insertLoanableItem(item)) {
      return item;
    }
  }
  return null;
}
```

9.6.3 Distributing the Responsibilities

Next we turn to the task of distributing the attributes and the responsibilities across the hierarchy. This is perhaps the most difficult part of designing the hierarchy and requires considerable experience on part of the software designers. It is useful to keep in mind that we are implementing in a manner that allows the classes in the business logic subsystem to be unaware of the structure of the hierarchy itself. This means that any method that is invoked by code in these classes must be a method of `LoanableItem`. We may also have to store the fields and assign access modifiers based on these considerations. With all this in mind, we start with the following minimum set of attributes for our abstract class.

```
public abstract class LoanableItem implements Serializable,
                                        Matchable<String> {
  private String title;
  private String id;
  protected Member borrowedBy;
  protected Calendar dueDate;
  public boolean matches(String other) {
    return (this.id.equals(id));
  }
  public String getTitle() {
    return title;
  }
  public String getId() {
    return id;
  }
  public Member getBorrower() {
    return borrowedBy;
  }
  public String getDueDate() {
    return (dueDate.getTime().toString());
  }
  // other fields and methods
}
```

The fields `title` and `id` are to be immutable and are therefore defined as `private`. The other fields have been declared `protected` so that they may be accessed by the descendants.

Consider a method like `getAuthor`. Periodicals do not have an author, which suggests that the method can be treated as a specialisation for `Book` and left out of the abstract class. However, it is conceivable that a class may wish to invoke the `getAuthor` on some item without knowing its type. In a situation where we are refactoring to replace `Book` with `LoanableItem`, we may have a client class with a method that has a parameter of type `Book`. We would like this code to behave correctly after refactoring, and so it is desirable that the method be included in `LoanableItem`. On the other hand, it is important that a client class does not assign an author for a periodical. In our case this is easily solved since we do not have a method for setting the `author` field; otherwise, we would have to define a default empty method, `setAuthor`, in the abstract class.

We expect that the methods for processing holds will be similar for all items; these are therefore fully implemented in the abstract class to facilitate reuse. We would like to allow descendants to override them as necessary, which means that the list `holds` has to be a protected attribute. All these additions to `LoanableItem` are shown below.

```
protected List holds = new LinkedList();
protected String author;
public String getAuthor() {
  return "";
}
public Iterator getHolds() {
  return holds.iterator();
}
public void placeHold(Hold hold) {
```

```
      holds.add(hold);
   }
   public void removeHold(String memberId) {
      for (ListIterator iterator = holds.listIterator();
                         iterator.hasNext(); ) {
        Hold hold = (Hold) iterator.next();
        String id = hold.getMember().getId();
        if (id.equals(memberId)) {
           iterator.remove();
        }
      }
   }
   public Hold getNextHold() {
      for (ListIterator iterator = holds.listIterator();
                         iterator.hasNext(); ) {
        Hold hold = (Hold) iterator.next();
        iterator.remove();
        if (hold.isValid()) {
           return hold;
        }
      }
      return null;
   }
   public boolean hasHold(){
      ListIterator iterator = holds.listIterator();
      if (iterator.hasNext()) {
         return true;
      }
      return false;
   }
```

9.6.4 Factoring Responsibilities Across the Hierarchy

The attributes listed above are the ones we selected for the common ancestor. As noted
earlier, descendants can override these as needed. Next we examine the responsibilities that are handled in a shared manner between the ancestor and the descendants.
Typically, these methods have some common code that can be factored out and placed
in the common ancestor and other code specific to each type that is implemented in
the descendants.

The first one we examine is the constructor. This is relatively simple in Java,
since a constructor for any subclass must first invoke the superclass constructor.
The constructor for LoanableItem is protected and stores the values of the
common fields title and id.

```
protected LoanableItem(String title, String id) {
   this.title = title;
   this.id = id;
}
```

The constructor for Book has to set the value for author.

```
public Book(String title, String author, String id) {
  super(title, id);
  this.author = author;
}
```

The constructor for `Periodical` needs to store the date of acquisition, and a private field is defined for that. The date itself can be generated using the system clock.

```
private Calendar dateAcquired;
public Periodical(String title, String id) {
  super(title, id);
  this.dateAcquired = new GregorianCalendar();
  dateAcquired.setTimeInMillis(System.currentTimeMillis());
}
```

Next we consider methods like `toString`. Part of this responsibility can be handled by the superclass methods, and the subclass methods simply append the additional information. In the code shown below, the method `LoanableItem` concatenates the fields `title`, `id`, and `borrowedBy`.

```
public String toString() {
  return " title " + title + " id " + id + " borrowed by " + borrowedBy;
}
```

Both subclasses append their types to the string returned by the superclass method. In addition, `Book` appends the `author` field, and `Periodical` appends `date Acquired`.

```
public String toString() {
  return "Book " + " author " + author + super.toString();
}
```

```
public String toString() {
  return "Periodical " + super.toString() + "\n  Acquired On "
         + dateAcquired.getTime().toString();
}
```

Some methods can have more involved cooperation across the hierarchy. Let us examine the method for issuing an item, which involves checking issuability, assigning the item to a `Member` object, and generating and storing the due date. Both checking of issuability and generation of due date involve rules specific to the items. The only common activity is that of assigning the item to a `Member`, which can be factored out. In Java, the process of due date generation can be simplified if we assign the current date as due date (Step 1) and then add the period of loan (Step 2). Step 1 can also be factored out, giving us the following `issue` method for `LoanableItem`.

```
public boolean issue(Member member){
  if (borrowedBy != null) {
    return false;
  }
  dueDate = new GregorianCalendar();
  dueDate.setTimeInMillis(System.currentTimeMillis());
  borrowedBy = member;
  return true;
}
```

Book does not have any additional rules for issuability, so it simply invokes the superclass method and adds the loan period, i.e., one month, if the superclass method returns true.

```
public boolean issue(Member member) {
  if (super.issue(member)) {
    dueDate.add(Calendar.MONTH, 1); //add loan period
    return true;
  } else {
    return false;
  }
}
```

The method in Periodical must first ensure that the periodical is at least three months old before it invokes the superclass method. The loan period of one week is added if everything checks out.

```
public boolean issue(Member member) {
  Calendar cutoffDate = new GregorianCalendar();
  cutoffDate.setTimeInMillis(System.currentTimeMillis());
  cutoffDate.add(Calendar.MONTH, -3);
  if (cutoffDate.after(dateAcquired)) {
    if (super.issue(member)){
      dueDate.add(Calendar.WEEK_OF_MONTH, 1);
      return true;
    }
  }
  return false;
}
```

9.7 Consequences of Introducing Inheritance

From our discussion so far, it should be fairly clear that inheritance provides a lot of benefits to the software development process. In an earlier section, we have discussed some caveats to be followed. In addition to these, inheritance introduces some other problems because of our attempt to ensure that changes that occur within the hierarchy do not affect classes outside the hierarchy. One example of this that we have encountered is the problem of invoking constructors, which we solved with the use of a *factory*. The other solutions follow a similar pattern, in that they create some external structure that in some way parallels the structure in the hierarchy. A couple of such situations are dealt with here.

Introducing an Inheritance Hierarchy Through Refactoring

We sometimes encounter situations in legacy systems where an inheritance hierarchy has to be introduced in order to clean up the existing code. One has to be especially careful when attempting such an exercise since the dependencies involved can be quite complex. A well-designed, systematic procedure can significantly reduce the chances of errors. The following steps can serve as a guide.

Replace Conditional with Polymorphism

If you have a conditional that chooses different behaviour depending on some feature of the object, move each leg of the conditional to an overriding method in a (possibly newly defined) subclass and make the original method abstract.

The steps involved in applying this rule are as follows:

- Identify a conditional statement in a method that changes its behaviour based on the value stored in a particular field. In a large class, it is quite likely that there will be several methods where variation in behaviour is obtained by switching on the same field.
- If the conditional statement is part of a larger method, the conditional may have to be extracted using the EXTRACT METHOD rule (Chap. 8). If such extraction is not easily done, the class may have to be re-examined more closely.
- Define an inheritance hierarchy where the subclasses reflect the variations in the field on which we are switching.
- Create a subclass method that overrides the conditional statement method. Copy one leg of the conditional into each of the subclass methods. and adjust the code so that it fits.
- Remove the conditional from the superclass method and make it abstract. If appropriate, remove the field on which the switching was done.

Note that once the switching is removed, we may no longer need the field to track the variation in the type of the object.

9.7.1 Exception Handling

The following is the standard rule for throwing exceptions when we employ inheritance:

> A subclass method that overrides a method of a superclass may not throw an exception that is not thrown by the superclass method.

This may seem puzzling at first glance—after all a subclass can add new features—but a closer look reveals that this rule is really a consequence of the LSP (see exercises). Of course, such a violation could never be achieved in Java since it can be detected statically at compile time.

There are several situations, however, where we would like to create a subclass and obtain more specific information in the case of exceptional behaviour. As an example, consider a class that processes a stream of data.

```
public class StreamProcessor {
  // fields and constructors not shown
  public void processStream() throws IOException {
  // code not shown
  }
  // other methods not shown
}
```

The method processStream() opens a stream and does some elementary processing of the data and creates an output file. In the course of writing the data, exceptions may arise, which cause the method to throw IOException. A subclass is expected to override this method.

Now consider a subclass of the above, FileProcessor, which uses data from a file. Since a file is a specific kind of data stream, this would be a valid use of inheritance. An exceptional situation arises when the file does not exist, and it is advantageous for users of the subclass to clearly know the reason for the exception.

The subclass with the overriding method is given below.

```
public class FileProcessor {
  String fileName;
  // other fields and constructors not shown
  public void process() throws NoSuchFileException, IOException {
    BufferedReader reader = new BufferedReader(new FileReader(fileName));
    // process the file
  }
  // other methods not shown
}
```

For reasons described earlier, the above code will not compile. The way to get around this is to create an **exception hierarchy**.

```
class NoSuchFileException extends IOException {
  // fields and methods as needed
}
```

Now our client class can be written to deal with the NoSuchFileException as needed and can also ignore the classification by writing a handler for just the IOException.

9.7.2 Adding New Functionality to a Hierarchy

Replacing a class with a hierarchy can pose additional problems when new functionality has to be added. Consider a situation where a client (end user) wants a list of books in the library printed in a certain format. The client chooses the format, and therefore it may have considerable variation. Since the system output is not fully specified at the beginning, this would have to be handled differently from the other features like adding members or checking out books. Such a feature is typically provided by asking the user to encapsulate the format as an object or a process, which can then be invoked from within `Library`. In a situation where we have only one `Book` class, `Library` may accomplish this with a method like the one shown below.

```
public void bookReport(BookFormat format) {
  for (ListIterator iterator = catalog.listIterator(); iterator.hasNext();){
    Book book = (Book) iterator.next();
    format.print(book);
  }
}
```

Essentially, the `print` method in `BookFormat` specifies a printing strategy. `BookFormat` itself is defined as an interface.

```
public interface BookFormat {
  public void print(Book book);
}
```

Each client that wishes to use this feature must first define a class that implements `BookFormat`. The class can be configured with several other attributes that decide the output stream and the `print` method can print the details of the book in the required format. The method in `Library` invokes the `print` method once for each book.

A solution like the one above suffers from two drawbacks:

1. The structure is tailored too specifically for one kind of operation. In our case, this is for printing the books. A client may instead want an operation that checks which books are issued on a particular day. The method `bookReport` suggests that it can only be used for generating reports.
2. The structure is tailored only for one class and cannot accommodate a hierarchy like `LoanableItem`. In case of a hierarchy, we would like to specify different operations for each subclass. In the solution above, the type of parameter to `print` is fixed as `Book`. We could change that to `LoanableItem`, but the method to be called will not be determined dynamically, which would cause the system to treat books and periodicals identically and is therefore not satisfactory.

The standard solution for dealing with this is to use the **visitor pattern.** The intent of this pattern is *to represent an operation to be performed on the elements of an object structure, and is employed to define a new operation without changing the classes of the elements on which it operates.*

In the situation above, we have a new `print` operation to be performed on the items in the `Catalog` object, which are all of type `LoanableItem`; we would like `Library` to provide a functionality that allows the user to apply the `print` operation to all the items in the `catalog` without exposing `Library` to the details of the hierarchy. Note that if we had separate catalogs for each kind of item, this discussion would be moot. However, if we defined `Library` to have separate collections for each kind of item, we have a design where the facade is not protected from changes to the specifications. This would result in the kind of instability that we are trying to avoid.

The solution for this once again follows the principle of *encapsulating change*. We create a separate structure that accommodates the changes and shields the classes that must be kept stable. This is similar to what we did with `LoanableItemFactory`, but we have an additional complication here. Our solution will require `Library` to provide some method like `bookReport`, which must invoke the correct `print` method without knowing what kind of item we are dealing with. In the method presented earlier, we knew that all items were of type `Book` and we could safely perform the cast. With the hierarchy, all we know is that the object returned by the iterator is of type `LoanableItem`. We therefore need some additional machinery to ensure that the correct method is invoked. This differs from the situation where we were invoking constructors, since in that case the kind of item to be created was explicitly specified in `type`.

The solution we develop with the visitor pattern has three components:

- *A **visitor interface** that encapsulates the variability in the object structure.* In our example the variability in the kinds of items stored in `Catalog` is exactly the variability in the `LoanableItem` hierarchy. Our interface, aptly named `LoanableItemVisitor`, therefore parallels the hierarchy by defining a method for each for kind of item.
- *An **accept** method in each visitee.* In our example, the visitees are the concrete classes in the hierarchy. Each of these must have a method with the signature
  `public void accept(LoanableItemVisitor)`
- *A concrete client class for the required functionality that implements the visitor interface.* In our example with `print`, `BookFormat` would be replaced with this concrete client that implements `LoanableItemVisitor`.

The code for the interface is shown below. Note that we provide a method with a parameter of type `LoanableItem` even though no such concrete item can be created. This is to ensure that we have a 'catch-all' that will take care of extreme situations where we have added new items to the hierarchy but not updated the visitor interface.

```
public interface LoanableItemVisitor {
  public void visit(LoanableItem loanableItem);
  public void visit(Book book);
  public void visit(Periodical periodical);
}
```

Every concrete class has an `accept` method as shown below.

```
public void accept(LoanableItemVisitor visitor) {
  visitor.visit(this);
}
```

The concrete class `ItemFormat` takes the place of `BookFormat` and looks something like this.

```
class ItemFormat implements LoanableItemVisitor {
  public void visit (Book book) {
    // code to print a book
  }
  public void visit (Periodical periodical) {
    // code to print a periodical
  }
  public void visit (LoanableItem item){
    System.out.println("Unspecified item");
  }
}
```

The UI provides some method that will allow the user to incorporate this functionality. In our case, we want to provide the functionality to print items, and the client is required to specify the details in `ItemFormat`, as shown above. The method in UI simply invokes the method in `Library`, as shown below:

```
public void printItems() {
  library.processItems(new ItemFormat());
}
```

The advantage of having an interface is that we can write a single method in `Library` which takes care of all such visitors that perform some operation on the items in the catalog. As shown below, we can define any number of operations to be done on the items in the catalog by invoking the `processItems` method.

```
public void processItems(LoanableItemVisitor visitor) {
  for (Iterator iterator = catalog.getLoanableItems();
                       iterator.hasNext();) {
    LoanableItem item = (LoanableItem) iterator.next();
    item.accept(visitor);
  }
}
```

The method `processItems` invokes the `accept` on each item in the `Catalog` object, passing as a parameter the concrete object that implements `Loanable ItemVisitor`, viz., the instance of `ItemFormat` that was created in user interface. As we have seen above, the `accept` method invokes the `visit` method on the visitor passing itself as a parameter. The most appropriate signature is matched to decide which method is to be invoked, i.e., when we invoke `visit` from `Book`, the system will invoke the method `visit(Book)` in the `ItemFormat` object. The two step process (called 'double-dispatch') thus obviates the need to know the class of each catalog item in `processItems`. These details are illustrated in Fig. 9.7.

To ensure that this approach provides the correct response for each item in the hierarchy, note that the `LoanableItemVisitor` interface must be updated whenever a new kind of item is added. However, we would like to ensure that the system does not crash in the event that this update is overlooked or if we choose to retain the old interface. Consider for example, that another kind of item, say DVD, has been added and we have a new class `VideoItem` that extends `LoanableItem`; we

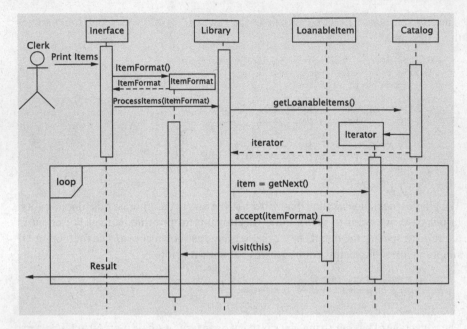

Fig. 9.7 Control flow for the visitor pattern

could be in a situation where the `catalog` contains instances of `VideoItem`, but `LoanableItemVisitor` has not been updated. In this case, the method `visit(LoanableItem)` gets invoked. This may result in a less than ideal system response, since a `VideoItem` object would be treated as a `LoanableItem`, but the system will continue to run and other harmful consequences (such as loss of data in case of a crash) will be avoided. If the `visit` method with the `LoanableItem` parameter did not exist, we would get a run-time error.

9.8 Multiple Inheritance

So far, we have seen situations where a class inherits from only one other class. The term **Multiple Inheritance** is used to describe the ability of a class to subclass multiple classes. Let us consider two examples.

1. A mobile home serves as a home, but could also be driven from location to location. Therefore, it has properties of both a home (it will have bedrooms, kitchen, etc.) and a car (the unit has an engine and can be driven like a car). If we have classes `Car` and `Home`, then the class `MobileHome` can be constructed by utilising the implementations of both of these existing classes.

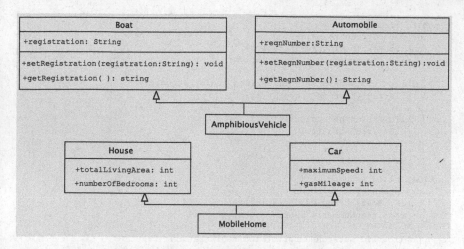

Fig. 9.8 Examples of multiple inheritance

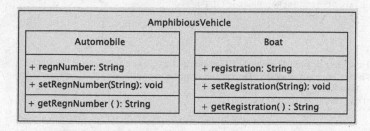

Fig. 9.9 Conceptual view of an AmphibiousVehicle

2. An amphibious vehicle can run on both land and water. It will, therefore, have properties of both an automobile and a boat. With classes `Automobile` and `Boat` available, we can create a class that subclasses both.

Figure 9.8, illustrates these examples using UML diagrams.

In all these examples, the descendant inherits properties from both the ancestors. A `Mobilehome` inherits features such as `maximumSpeed` and `gasMileage` from `Car` and features like `totalLivingArea` and `numberOfBedrooms` from `House`. Programming languages typically allow for multiple inheritance by allowing a class to extend more than one class. This ability does pose some new challenges as we shall see later in this section.

Since the class `AmphibiousVehicle` extends `Automobile` and `Boat`, an instance of an `AmphibiousVehicle` can be viewed as containing both an instance of `Boat` and an instance of `Automobile` (Fig. 9.9).

Consider the following code[2]:

---

[2]Since Java does not support multiple inheritance in this form, this code does not conform to Java syntax.

```
public class Boat {
   private String registration;
   public Boat(String registration) {
     this.registration = registration;
   }
   public void setRegistration(String registration) {
     this.registration = registration;
   }
   public String getRegistration() {
     return registration;
   }
}

public class Automobile {
   private String regnNumber;
   public Boat(String registration) {
      this.regnNumber = registration;
   }
   public void setRegnNumber(String registration) {
     this.regnNumber = registration;
   }
   public String getRegnNumber() {
     return regnNumber;
   }
}

public class AmphibiousVehicle extends Boat, Automobile {
   public AmphibiousVehicle(String registration) {
      Boat(registration);
      Automobile(registration);
   }
}
```

Both Automobile and Boat have a field to store the registration number and AmphibiousVehicle inherits the field from both these classes, as shown in Fig. 9.9. Since these different names essentially capture the same attribute, we have some ambiguity. Consider the following situation:

```
Automobile automobile;
Boat boat;
AmphibiousVehicle vehicle;
```

An AmphibiousVehicle object can be stored in an Automobile reference or a Boat reference.

```
vehicle =  new AmphibiousVehicle("001");
automobile = vehicle;
boat = vehicle;
```

There appear to be several ways in which the registration number of this object can be accessed: vehicle.registration, vehicle.regnNumber, auto mobile.regnNumber or boat.registration. This multiplicity of field names can make the code hard to read. In addition, we now have a possible poly-morphic assignment of the kind:

```
boat = (AmphibiousVehicle) automobile;
```

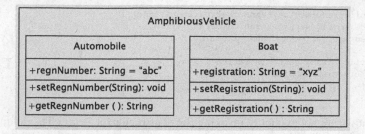

Fig. 9.10 AmphibiousVehicle showing assignments

This would not be possible under single inheritance, since `Car` and `Boat` belong to different hierarchies.

In creating such a hierarchy, it is therefore important to keep the semantics of the attributes in mind. The public methods present a more serious problem. Consider the code

```
vehicle.setRegistration("xyz");
// some code
vehicle.setRegnNumber("abc");
```

This results in the situation shown in Fig. 9.10.

The entities `vehicle.registration` and `vehicle.regnNumber` will now contain different values, causing inconsistencies.

9.8.1 Mechanisms for Resolving Conflicts

Any language that provides a mechanism for multiple inheritance must also provide means for resolving these conflicts. For the example above, let us assume that the designer chooses to store the registration of the `AmphibiousVehicle` in the `Automobile` object, but would like to use the method names `setRegistration` and `getRegistration`. The methods `setRegnNumber` and `getRegnNumber` inherited from `automobile` must now be 'un-inherited' so that there is no ambiguity. One option is to declare the unwanted methods and fields as `abstract` in the descendant class. The class `AmphibiousVehicle` would now be something like this[3]:

```
public class AmphibiousVehicle extends Boat, Automobile {
  public AmphibiousVehicle(String string) {
    Automobile(string);
  }
  public abstract setRegnNumber(String string);
```

---

[3] We would like to remind the reader that the Java-like code we have given below is not valid in the Java language.

```
      public abstract getRegnNumber(String string);
      public void setRegistration(String string) {
        Automobile.setRegnNumber(string);
      }
      public String getRegistration() {
        return Automobile.getRegnNumber();
      }
    }
```

Note that we are not explicitly invoking the constructor for `Boat`. The default constructor is invoked and consequently, there is no copy of the registration being stored in the `Boat` object. The methods `setRegistration` and `getRegistration` have been suitably redefined to access the fields of the `Automobile` object.

9.8.2 Repeated Inheritance

Since multiple inheritance could generate a hierarchy that is not a simple tree, we can end up with a situation where a descendant can be reached from an ancestor by following two different paths, giving rise to what is referred to as the *'diamond of repeated inheritance'* (Fig. 9.11). Such a structure results when we have a class `Vehicle` which serves as an ancestor for both `Automobile` and `Boat`.

```
    public class Vehicle {
      private String registration;
      public Vehicle(String string) {
        registration = string;
      }
      public void setRegistration(String string) {
        registration = string;
      }
      public string getRegistration() {
        return registration;
      }
    }

    public class Automobile extends Vehicle {
      private int maximumSpeed;
      public Automobile(String string, int speed) {
```

Fig. 9.11 Diamond of repeated inheritance

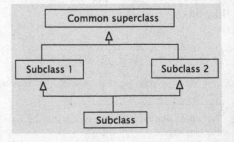

```
        Vehicle(string);
        maximumSpeed = speed;
    }
}

public class Boat extends Vehicle {
    private int maximumKnots;
    public Boat(String string, int knots) {
        Vehicle(string);
        maximumKnots = knots;
    }
}

class AmphibiousVehicle extends Boat, Automobile {
    public AmphibiousVehicle(String string, int speed, int knots) {
        Boat(string, knots);
        Automobile(string, speed);
    }
}
```

This is a more serious problem than what we faced when a field was duplicated. The constructor for AmphibiousVehicle must invoke constructors Automobile and Boat, both of which invoke the constructor for Vehicle. As a result, we have a situation where there are two copies of registration. Note that the registration information is actually being stored in a private field of Vehicle and the only way to access it is through the methods of Vehicle. If the accessor or modifier of AmphibiousVehicle is invoked, it is not clear which copy is being modified. The author of AmphibiousVehicle has to be aware of these issues and should override these methods to ensure that both copies are updated.

When we are dealing with large hierarchies, it is not always possible for the author of the subclass (such as AmphibiousVehicle) to detect the problem. In such a situation, the programming language must ensure that the repeated ancestor is not created twice. C++, for instance, uses the following solution: *The inheritance relationship between* Vehicle *and its immediate descendants should be declared as* **virtual** *(or 'shareable')*. This means that the space occupied by the two Vehicle objects must be shared and as a result the compiler flags an error when the constructor is invoked twice. The constructor in AmphibiousVehicle is then required to explicitly invoke all three constructors. In our 'java-like' syntax, the constructor for AmphibiousVehicle is as follows:

```
public AmphibiousVehicle(String string, int speed, int knots) {
    Vehicle(string);
    Boat(string, knots);
    Automobile(string, speed);
}
```

When the Vehicle constructor is invoked, a Vehicle object is created, and the same space is shared by the Automobile and Boat objects. Since only one copy of the Vehicle attributes is maintained, we have no inconsistency.

When the calls to constructors propagate up the hierarchy, calls to 'virtual ancestors' are ignored. In our example, when the constructor for Boat (or Automobile) is invoked, the call to the Vehicle constructor is ignored because Boat (or

Automobile) is defined a *virtual* descendant of Vehicle and the Vehicle object has already been created. Since the inheritance hierarchy is statically determined, such an approach is feasible.

The above code suffers from two problems:

1. It requires that AmphibiousVehicle be cognizant of the entire hierarchy. If that class's constructor misses any one of the superclass constructor calls and the corresponding class does not have a default constructor, the compiler flags an error.

   On the other hand, if any default constructors exist, the code may end up being buggy. For instance, the code

   ```
   public AmphibiousVehicle(String string, int speed, int knots) {
     Boat(string, knots);
     Automobile(string, speed);
   }
   ```

   would not generate any compiler errors if Vehicle had a default constructor. In this situation, the registration field in Vehicle will be initialised to the default value instead of the specified parameter, string.

2. This approach is not general enough since it cannot work in situations where there is an existing hierarchy and the inheritances are not virtual.

In the example with the AmphibiousVehicle we saw that repeated inheritance can cause a constructor to be invoked twice. We were able to resolve the consistency problem by redefining the methods and attributes. However in situations where invoking the constructor has a more 'visible' effect, this could pose a more serious problem. Consider the following example where Window has two descendants—MenuWindow, which is a window with a menu, and BorderWindow, which is a window with a border. The fourth class, MenuAndBorderWindow, completes the diamond by inheriting from both MenuWindow and BorderWindow.

Consider a situation where we have a method display for displaying the Window. The display method in BorderWindow first invokes the ancestor's display method (which displays the window) and then invokes its own method that displays the border. Likewise, the display method in MenuWindow first invokes the ancestor's display method (which displays the window) and then invokes its own method that displays the menu. How should we deal with the display method of MenuAndBorderWindow? If we invoke the display methods of both the immediate superclasses, we end up in a situation where the window will be displayed twice.

```
public class MenuAndBorderWindow extends MenuWindow, BorderWindow {
// fields and other methods not shown
  public void display() {
    MenuWindow.display();
    BorderWindow.display();
  }
}

public class MenuWindow extends Window {
```

```
// fields and other methods not shown
  public void display() {
    Window.display();
    // code for displaying menu goes here
  }
}

public class BorderWindow extends Window {
// fields and other methods not shown
  public void display() {
    Window.display();
    // code for displaying border goes here
  }
}
```

In general, there is no simple solution to such problems. The software designer has to be aware of these issues and exercise the necessary caution. The above problem, for instance, could be resolved by having MenuAndBorderWindow inherit from all three superclasses. Its display would then first invoke the method in Window and then invoke methods from MenuWindow and BorderWindow that display the menu and the border respectively. (We are assuming here that we can invoke the methods for displaying these; this would be another example of a situation where the protected access mode would come in handy.)

```
public class MenuAndBorderWindow extends MenuWindow, BorderWindow, Window {
  // fields and other methods not shown
  public void display() {
    Window.display();
    BorderWindow.showBorder();
    MenuWindow.showMenu();
  }
}

public class MenuWindow extends Window {
  // fields and other methods not shown
  public void display() {
    Window.display();
    this.showMenu();
  }
  protected void showMenu() {
    // code for displaying the menu
  }
}

public class BorderWindow extends Window {
  // fields and other methods not shown
  public void display() {
    Window.display();
    this.showBorder();
  }
  protected void showBorder() {
    // code for displaying the border
  }
}
```

9.8.3 *Multiple Inheritance in Java*

Java does not support real multiple inheritance in the sense that a class can inherit an implementation from one other class only. To deal with the situation where a class has to inherit attributes from more than one class, the only option is to create the class as a subclass of one of the classes and implement the rest. For example, assume that we would like to create a class C that ideally extends classes C1 and C2 which implement interfaces I1 and I2 respectively. Then, the code for C would be

```
public class C extends C1 implements I1, I2 {
  // code
}
```

Since an interface can be viewed as a type, a class that extends another class and implements an interface can be viewed as a sub-type of both the ancestor class and the interface. This gives the flavour of multiple inheritance to the language. In the above example, objects of type C are also of type I2.

9.9 Discussion and Further Reading

This chapter has explored the uses of inheritance, how to introduce it, and what are some of the consequences of inheritance. Software systems are usually complex, and it is always a difficult task to characterise them completely. Inheritance poses an added challenge since it allows an existing system to change. Attempts have been made by researchers to define taxonomies to understand both the nature of inheritance and to identify changes in the object-oriented systems [1, 2].

The question of when and how to introduce inheritance can be a tricky question. Beginners often tend to follow the lead of textbook examples and introduce inheritance upon finding common fields between classes. This is not only wasteful, but can also lead to problems. Inheritance is a relationship between well-understood abstractions, and should be introduced only when a need for it can be clearly justified based on the principles of object-oriented design. Exceptions are made to this rule only when the classes are being used to model categories of objects in the natural world and there already exists a well-defined taxonomy of these categories.

The *open-closed principle* is perhaps the most applicable design rule to justify introducing inheritance. Note that there is no inherent contradiction in this principle, since the words 'open' and 'closed' apply to different objectives. The modules should be open for further extension, and closed for clients that are depending on it. The client modules are thus assured that any changes introduced into the system later will not necessitate any modifications. It is important to remember here that a class should not be closed too soon. A class must represent a *coherent data abstraction*, i.e., provide a coherent set of services to potential clients. Closing a class too soon and then frequently extending it because the data abstraction was incompletely defined should be construed as an abuse of inheritance.

Our case-study with the library system can also be viewed as an exercise in designing a schema for an object-oriented database. Use of inheritance can be tricky when we create a database. We need to ensure, for instance, that inheritance conflicts (which can arise with multiple inheritance and overriding) are avoided. In addition to these correctness issues, compactness of the schema is also a consideration [3, 4]. Object-oriented databases are commonly mapped to relational databases for efficient storage, and mapping objects to relations can be tricky when inheritance is involved [5].

The *Liskov substitution principle* is a compact reminder of the most basic invariant an inheritance relationship must satisfy. Barbara Liskov's original article appeared as a joint paper with J. Wing in 1994, but the principle was re-formulated more succinctly [6] as follows:

Let q(x) be a property provable about objects x of type T. Then q(y) should be true for objects y of type S, where S is a subtype of T.

Thus, Liskov and Wing's notion of 'subtype' is based on the notion of substitutability; that is, if S is a subtype of T, then objects of type T in a program may be replaced with objects of type S without altering any of the desirable properties of that program (e.g., correctness).

In most situations where the LSP is violated, we find that an ad-hoc relationship has been introduced to use existing code. In our example in this chapter, the fact the relationship between SolidRectangle and Pixel was an ad-hoc one and not a well-designed inheritance structure is underscored by the fact that the only way to fix the problem is to modify clientMethod. This means that the original modules (i.e., SolidRectangle) that were considered closed have been in some way re-opened by introducing inheritance. Thus we have indirectly violated OCP.

As an example of another, perhaps more surprising, example of LSP violation, the reader should look at Exercise 6.

To fix the bugs created by LSP violations, the only option we have is to check every piece of client code and put in conditionals that employ run-time type identification or use exception handlers. This is clearly not feasible. LSP violations are effective reminders of two of the design principles introduced in this chapter, viz., *favour composition over inheritance* and *depend upon abstractions*. If the class Pixel had been implemented by *adapting* SolidRectangle, we would not face any problem with client methods. Our implementation also violates the dependency rule, since SolidRectangle is a concrete implementation.

9.9.1 Design Patterns that Facilitate Inheritance

In this chapter we have introduced two patterns: *factory* and *visitor*. Factories are *creational patterns* that are generally employed for creating objects without specifying the exact class of object. There are some variations on this, and what we have discussed here is perhaps the simplest form in which it can be used. The **factory method** pattern is employed in situations where we have two independent hierarchies, and the concrete classes in the first hierarchy create objects belonging to classes in the second hierarchy. However, the exact kind of object of the second hierarchy to be created is determined using the input provided at run-time. In such a situation, the logic for invocation of the constructor is encapsulated in a separate method in the abstract superclass of the first hierarchy. The **abstract factory** pattern is used in situations where we have several parallel concrete hierarchies, and the system has to be configurable with any one of them. For instance, we could have a hierarchy of *paint objects* for generating paint objects of several colours. The same colours are used for several situations, viz., interior, exterior, furniture, etc. However, the paint object that must be used has a different implementation for each situation. In such a case, we would have an `AbstractcolourFactory` that would have descendants like `InteriorcolourFactory`, `ExteriorcolourFactory`, etc. The `AbstractcolourFactory` would specify the methods (e.g., `makeRed Paint()`) for creating abstract paint objects, and the concrete descendants would implement these methods to provide concrete paint objects for the given situation (the `makeRedPaint` method in `ExteriorcolourFactory` would create `ExteriorRedPaint`). The client class could then be adapted for any painting situation (interior, furniture, etc.) by configuring it with the appropriate concrete factory. The methods in the chosen factory would then be used to generate the concrete paint objects needed for the situation.

The visitor pattern can be used for any general collection of objects, not necessarily constituting a hierarchy. All that we need is that there should be a matching signature for the class of every object in the collection. The `Object` class can be used as a 'catch-all' to prevent run-time errors. Using this pattern increases the cost of execution due to the additional method call. That can be prevented if the language provided the feature of 'double dispatch,' i.e., the parameter type and the concrete class are both matched when invoking dynamic binding. This feature was provided in smalltalk, but has not found favour with other language designers due to the high cost of method calls.

9.9.2 Performance of Object-Oriented Systems

An issue that is often raised with object-oriented systems is that of poor run-time performance. There are several reasons for this and solutions have been proposed; it would be beyond the scope of this text to go into these in any detail. In the context of inheritance, however, we shall look into one of these issues: **the overhead caused by dynamic binding**.

When we subclass the conditional behaviour by introducing an inheritance hierarchy, we rely on dynamic binding to ensure that the correct version of the method is called. This decision has to be made at run-time, as opposed to method calls whose target can be statically determined during compilation. Normally, with every variable in the system, some sort of type information will be stored. In an object-oriented system, due to polymorphism, the actual type of the object whose reference we store in the given variable can change dynamically. The standard way to implement dynamic binding is to have a table of method addresses for each class. Whenever a method is invoked on a variable, the type of object the variable refers to is looked up. The actual type of the reference is used to select the appropriate table, and the method name is used to index the table to determine the address of the method to be invoked. Thus, dynamic binding introduces some additional overhead for every method invocation.

Projects

1. Implement the classes `Account`, `CheckingAccount` and `Savings Account` we outlined in Sect. 9.2.2.
2. Consider the classes `DataStream` and `ReReadableDataStream` in Sect. 9.2.3. Show how to implement the two classes. Remember that `ReReadableDataStream` must work regardless of the source from which `DataStream` reads.
3. Implement the `Cloneable` interface for the `Book`, `Member`, and `Hold` classes without having to set any fields to the `null` value.

9.10 Exercises

1. Extend the `LoanableItem` hierarchy to create new classes for CDs, DVDs and books on tape. CDs and DVDs have several common characteristics. Would it be appropriate for these two classes to inherit from a common superclass? Why?
2. As mentioned in the chapter, a subclass method that overrides a method of a superclass may throw subclasses of exceptions that are thrown by the superclass method, but it cannot throw exceptions that are not thrown by the overridden method. Why?
3. A university registration system has a class `Student` that tracks student information. When a student's GPA falls below a certain level, he/she is placed on academic probation. Would you model this by creating a subclass `WeakStudent` that extends `Student`?
4. Keeping in mind that a circle is a special kind of ellipse in which the two foci coincide, create a scenario in which an LSP violation can occur when a class `Ellipse` is extended to define `Circle`.
5. In Chap. 7, we defined some methods of `Library` to return error codes, whereas others return references to objects. In a more sophisticated system, it is often necessary to return an object that contains both the result code and other information that the UI can display upon request. Define a class `Result` and a hierarchy of subclasses that will take care of this for all the methods in `Library`.
6. Consider the following classes and explain whether LSP is violated in the `main` method.

```
class Rectangle {
  private int width;
  private int height;
  public Rectangle(int width, int height) {
    this.width = width;
    this.height = height;
  }
  public void setHeight(int height) {
    this.height = height;
  }
  public void setWidth(int width) {
    this.width = width;
  }
  public int getHeight() {
    return height;
  }
  public int getWidth() {
    return width;
  }
}
public class Square extends Rectangle {
  public Square(int side) {
    super(side, side);
  }
  public void setWidth(int side) {
    super.setWidth(side);
    super.setHeight(side);
  }
  public void setHeight(int side) {
    super.setWidth(side);
    super.setHeight(side);
  }
  public static void main(String[] s) {
    Rectangle r = new Rectangle(10, 10);
    r.setWidth(5);
    r.setHeight(6);
    if (r.getWidth() * r.getHeight() != 30) {
        System.out.println("Error");
    }
  }
}
```

7. (Case-studies) Examine the projects presented at the end of Chap. 6 and identify
   possible situations where we could get variability in the behaviour of an object.
   Which variabilities will you model using inheritance? Defend your choices based
   on object-oriented design principles.

References

1. B.M.P. Clarke, P. Gibson, Using a taxonomy tool to identify changes in object-oriented software,
   in *7th European Conference on Software Maintenance and Reengineering*, Benevento, Italy,
   26–28 March 2003
2. X. Girod, Conception par objects—MECANO: une methode et un environnement de construction d'application par objects. Ph.D. thesis, University of Joseph Fourier Grenoble I, Grenoble,
   June 1991

3. A. Formica, H.D. Gröger, M. Missikoff, Object-oriented database schema analysis and inheritance processing: a graph-theoretic approach. Data Knowl. Eng. **24**(2), 157–181 (1997)
4. A. Formica, H.D. Gröger, M. Missikoff, An efficient method for checking objectoriented database schema correctness. ACM Trans. Database Syst. **23**(3), 334–369 (1998)
5. S.W. Ambler, *Building Object Applications that Work* (Cambridge University Press, Cambridge, 1998)
6. B.H. Liskov, J.M. Wing, Behavioural subtyping using invariants and constraints, in *Formal Methods for Distributed Processing: A Survey of Object-Oriented Approaches*, ed. by H. Brown, J. Derick (Cambridge University press, Cambridge, 2001), pp. 254–280

Chapter 10
Modelling with Finite State Machines

10.1 Introduction

Our discussion thus far of the object-oriented software construction process has focused on the use case model. While this is a comprehensive technique that finds widespread application, it is inadequate for handling situations where the operations cannot be modeled by end-to-end use cases. This is typically the case with dynamic systems that respond to external input in real-time.

In this chapter, we present two case-studies of systems where the use case model does not suffice. The first of these is a controller for a microwave. (This analysis could be extended to most devices that interact with external entities.) The behavior of the microwave in response to a user's action depends on what state the microwave is in. For instance, if a cook/start button is pressed, the microwave does not always fire up. The case study starts by presenting a model for dealing with this kind of conditional behavior, and then goes on to discuss issues arising in the design and implementation of such systems.

Another commonly occurring situation is the creation of Graphical User Interfaces (GUI), which are used by applications to interact with a user. The program that implements the GUI typically presents different screens at different stages of the interaction. What screen gets displayed depends on the kind of input the application is requesting at that instant. While the underlying application itself may be designed using the use case model, the GUI is modeled as a system that changes its 'appearance' in response to the interaction. It turns out that a similar model is useful for analysing such systems.

10.2 A Simple Example

The use of software to control the behaviour of systems is well known. Such systems can comprise several hardware components, each of which may be turned on or off using embedded software. The system as a whole has to behave in a prescribed

B. Dathan and S. Ramnath, *Object-Oriented Analysis, Design and Implementation*,
Undergraduate Topics in Computer Science, DOI 10.1007/978-3-319-24280-4_10

manner, turning components on or off depending on the input and the other environmental variables. The following is a simple example of such a system.

Problem Consider a simple microwave oven whose behaviour is governed by the following rules:

- The microwave has a door, a light, a power-tube, a button, a timer, and a display.
- When the oven is not in use and the door is closed, the light and the power-tube are turned off and the display is blank.
- When the door is open, the light stays on.
- If the button is pushed when the door is closed and the oven is not operating, then the oven is activated for one minute. When the oven is activated, the light and the power-tube are turned on.
- If the button is pushed when the oven is operating, one minute is added to the timer.
- When the oven is operating, the display shows the number of seconds of cooking time remaining.
- If the door is opened when the oven is operating, the power-tube is turned off.
- When the cooking time is completed, the power-tube and light are turned off.
- Pushing the button when the door is open has no effect.

If we attempt to model this system with use cases, we run into some difficulties. Consider the following set of scenarios:

Scenario 1
open door → place food in oven → close door → push button → wait for cooking to finish → open door → remove food → close door

Scenario 2
open door → place food in oven → close door → push button → wait for cooking to finish → open door → remove food and stir → place food in oven → close door → push button → wait for cooking to finish → open door → remove food → close door

Scenario 3
open door → place food in oven → close door → push button → wait for 30 s → open door → remove food and stir → place food in oven → close door → push button → wait for 45 s → open door → remove food → close door → stir food → open door → place food in oven → push button → wait for cooking to finish → open door → remove food → close door

Clearly, there is no set of standard 'business processes' that can characterise the manner in which an actor interacts with system. What we observe instead is that we are dealing with a continual sequence of events and the manner in which these events are processed depends on the state in which system is. The system may also change state in response to these events. What this suggests is that in order to model the system behaviour accurately, we should treat this as a **finite state machine (FSM)**.

10.3 Finite State Modelling

Formally, an FSM is defined by a set of states, a set of input symbols and a set of transitions. Each transition is defined by a 4-tuple (s_i, s_f, I, O), where s_i is the initial state, s_f is the final state, I is the input that triggers the transition, and O is the associated output, if any. Two different formulations for FSMs can be found in the literature on automata theory. These are the *Mealy machine* and the *Moore machine*. In a Mealy machine, the output depends on the event and the current state; a Moore machine is a simplification in which the output depends only on the state. The two are equivalent as far as their power is concerned, i.e., any system that can be defined in one kind of machine can also be defined in the other, but the number of states and the transitions vary. We shall use a Mealy machine for modelling our FSM.

Returning to our microwave oven, we now try to identify the states in the FSM that would model the behaviour of the microwave oven. An initial examination yields the following possible states:

1. Microwave is idle and the door is closed.
2. Microwave is idle and the door is open.
3. Microwave is in operation.
4. Microwave is interrupted by the door being opened.
5. Microwave has completed cooking.

These states are found by looking at the process of cooking, and viewing each step of the cooking process as a separate state. We have the following events that cause the microwave to change state:

- door is opened
- door is closed
- button is pushed
- clock ticks
- timer runs out

The first three are external events that are the result of the actions of an external user. The last two are internal events triggered by the operation of the microwave.

We can now construct the table in Fig. 10.1, which describes all the actions that correspond to each (*state, event*) pair. The rows in the first column list the possible states of the microwave, while the columns in the first row show the possible external events. An example will make clear how to use this table. With the microwave in the Cooking state (see row 4, column 1) if the door is opened (row 1, column 2), the cell formed by row 4 and column 2 shows that the microwave enters the Interrupted state.

The information in Fig. 10.1 is given using the UML state transition diagram in Fig. 10.2. Each rectangle with rounded corners corresponds to a microwave state. The directed arcs tell what the new microwave state will be when a certain event occurs in a given state. For instance, if the microwave is in the Idle; DoorClosed state (the rectangle at the top-left part of the diagram), one of the arcs leading from the rectangle shows that if the cook button is pressed, the microwave enters the Cooking state.

	Open door	Close door	Press cook	Clock ticks	Timer runs out
Idle; Door closed	Idle; Door open	Idle; Door closed	Cooking	Idle; Door closed	Idle; Door closed
Idle; Door open	Idle; Door open	Idle; Door closed	Idle; Door open	Idle; Door open	Idle; Door open
Cooking	Interrupted	Cooking	Cooking	Cooking	Idle; Door closed
Interrupted	Idle; Door open	Idle; Door closed	Idle; Door open	Idle; Door open	Idle; Door open
Completed	Idle; Door open	Idle; Door closed	Cooking	Idle; Door closed	Idle; Door closed

Fig. 10.1 Transition table for the microwave

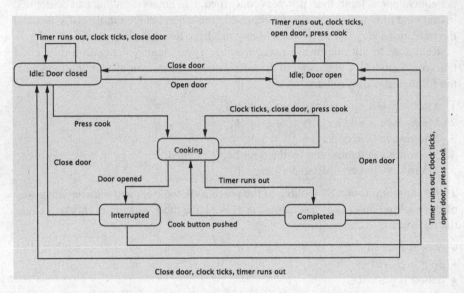

Fig. 10.2 State transition diagram for the microwave oven

One observation we make here is that the behaviour of our finite state machine is identical in the states Idle; Door Closed and Completed. This tells that we do not need separate states to distinguish the behaviour of the system when it is idle with door closed from the behaviour when it has completed cooking. Likewise, states Idle; Door Open and Interrupted are indistinguishable; we can therefore combine these two states into a single state Door Open, and merge states Idle; Door Closed and Completed into a single state, Door Closed. In effect, we have simply dropped states Interrupted and Completed from our model. The reduced FSM is described by Fig. 10.3.

	Open door	Close door	Press cook	Clock ticks	Timer runs out
Door closed	Door open	Door closed	Cooking	Door closed	Door closed
Door open	Door open	Door closed	Door open	Door open	Door open
Cooking	Door open	Cooking	Cooking	Cooking	Door closed

Fig. 10.3 Minimised transition table for the microwave oven

In general, it is important to find an FSM with a small number of states and there are exact algorithms for state minimisation.[1] Usually, fewer states imply a simpler system that is easier to maintain, but in some situations, it may be helpful to add a few redundant states to improve the readability of the design as a whole.

10.4 A First Solution to the Microwave Problem

10.4.1 Completing the Analysis

Having created a model, the next step in our analysis is to identify the conceptual classes. As we did in Chaps. 6 and 7, we start by constructing the list of nouns: Microwave, Powertube, Light, Display, Door, CookButton, etc. The Display and CookButton will be part of the user interface (GUI). Since this is only a 'software simulation', we cannot have a real Powertube or Light, and so we simply have to model these by displaying some message on the GUI. (To make it more realistic,

---

Use-Case Modelling Versus Finite State Modelling

One question that we need to address is: *under what conditions should we use FSMs, and under what conditions do we employ use cases?*

To help answer this question, let us examine how the library system designed in the previous chapters changes with each transaction. At the start of each use case (i.e., transaction), some pre-conditions hold. The final output of the transaction depends on the pre-conditions that were true at the start of the transaction. The state of the system defines (and is defined by) which pre-conditions are true. These pre-conditions, in turn, are determined by the values held by all of the objects in the system. Whenever a transaction is completed, as when a book is issued, the state changes because several objects, including the Book and the Member object, get updated. (Note that this notion of state is somewhat different from the states of the FSM.) Each transaction has one 'most-common' outcome (which we call the *main flow*) and other secondary outcomes, and the set of pre-conditions that hold decides the outcome of the

---

[1]The reader is referred to any text on *digital logic design* or *automata theory*.

transaction. If one were to model such a system by listing all the states and how we can switch between them via transactions, we would have a very complex structure with an unmanageable and possibly unbounded set of states because one could imagine books and members being added and deleted and updated throughout the life of the library system. On the other hand, the set of interactions that an actor can have with the library system is bounded. This indicates that we should prefer the simple functional specification provided by a use case model.

Contrast this situation with the microwave example. Here we have a possibly unbounded number of ways in which the actor can interact with the system. However, from the specifications it is clear that we are only interested in how the system reacts to a given input (sometimes referred to as 'reactive' systems). The nature of the reaction depends on the state the system is in (the word 'state' being used to describe a behavioural response). Also, we typically have only a small set of states in which the system could be at any point, and a clear set of transitions between them which are triggered by events. This indicates that use case modelling is inappropriate and that using an FSM to model the system behaviour would be the best choice.

one could imagine that a system has software drivers to manipulate these devices, and these drivers are being invoked from the controller.) Likewise, the opening and closing of the door is simulated by some GUI component(s). This leaves us with a class for the Microwave, and one for the GUI. The noun 'timer' suggests that we need some mechanism to monitor the passage of time. The microwave can keep track of the time remaining with a field, but will have to be informed about the events that mark each unit of time. This can be done by a `Clock` that generates ticks at regular (viz., one second) intervals.

1. **Microwave** This has the responsibility of keeping track of what state the oven is in, and for turning the power-tube and light on/off. The oven must listen to the following events: *Opening/closing of the door, pushing of the button, and the timer running out*.
2. **GUI display** As described above, the GUI has components for user input, and will display some information to simulate operation. This suggests the following four displays:

   (a) One of the displays tells us whether the unit is cooking or not cooking.
   (b) A second display informs us whether the door is open or closed.
   (c) The third display shows the time remaining for cooking. If the microwave is idle, the display shows 0.
   (d) The fourth display gives the status of the light: whether it is on or off.

3. **Clock** This is a class that generates a clock tick event at regular intervals.

10.4.2 Designing the System

The first step in the design is to identify the software classes. This is an easy task here since the conceptual classes themselves seem to serve our purpose well. The next step is to figure out how the software classes will distribute the responsibilities to achieve the behaviour specified in the model. In our case, this amounts to specifying how the events will be processed. We have two kinds of events:

- *User inputs*: these are recognised by the GUI.
- *Clock Ticks*: these originate in `Clock`.

To describe the manner in which the entities of the system handle these, we shall use sequence diagrams. Figure 10.4 shows how the system handles the user input corresponding to the opening of the door. The diagram suggests that we have a separate method in the `Microwave` class for each kind of event that occurs in the GUI. When the display is updated, we shall assume that the actor can see the result of the action.

The sequence diagram for the other inputs from the user look similar. In each case, `Microwave` does some processing and updates the display. There are several methods to update the different aspects of the display and the appropriate ones will be invoked with the necessary parameters.

Figure 10.5 describes how the system handles a clock tick. Note that unlike the sequence diagrams we have seen earlier, this interaction is not initiated by the actor.

The sequence diagrams for the other events are similar and give us enough information to specify the responsibilities of individual classes. `Microwave` is a singleton class with methods to process the external events (door opening, clock tick, etc.) To mimic the FSM, we keep a variable `currentState` that keeps track of the state the microwave is in. We also need a variable that keeps track of the time remaining for cooking. The class diagram is shown in Fig. 10.6.

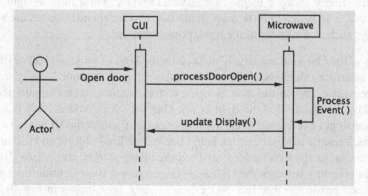

Fig. 10.4 Sequence diagram for door opening

Fig. 10.5 Sequence diagram for processing a clock tick

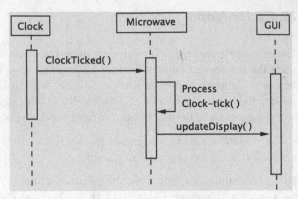

Fig. 10.6 Microwave class diagram

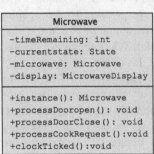

Although a text-based interface is impractical, any number of graphical interfaces are possible. As shown in the sequence diagram for opening the door, the display class must provide methods of two kinds:

- Methods that process the input provided by the user.
- Methods that can be invoked by `Microwave` to display output. The sequence diagram simply shows a method `updateDisplay`, but a little thought would show that it is better to have a set of methods to independently set the several displays such as the status of the light, powertube, etc.

Methods of the first kind are largely defined by the kind of look and feel desired for the user interface. Methods of the second kind represent the functionality required by `Microwave`. When the door is opened, for instance, `Microwave` requests the display to indicate that the light is on. One way we could do this is to have `Microwave` get a reference to the appropriate object within the UI and set it; such an approach results in `Microwave` being tied to one kind of look and feel and any attempt to change the look and feel will require changes to `Microwave`. To avoid such tight coupling between the GUI and `Microwave`, the essential functionality is abstracted out in the interface `MicrowaveDisplay` shown in Fig. 10.7. The method `setMicrowave` configures the display with an instance of `Microwave`. All the other methods are provided to display to the user the current status of the system.

Fig. 10.7 Microwave
display interface

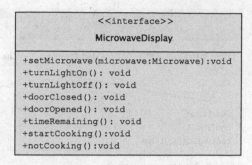

```
                    <<interface>>
                   MicrowaveDisplay

+setMicrowave(microwave:Microwave):void
+turnLightOn(): void
+turnLightOff(): void
+doorClosed(): void
+doorOpened(): void
+timeRemaining(): void
+startCooking():void
+notCooking():void
```

Fig. 10.8 Clock

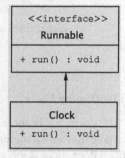

```
      <<interface>>
        Runnable

  + run() : void


         Clock

  + run() : void
```

The class GUIDisplay implements this interface.

The Clock class has to initiate an event at regular intervals, so we model it as a thread. As shown in Fig. 10.8, it implements the Runnable interface.

10.4.3 The Implementation Classes

We are now ready to work out the implementation details. The Clock class is the simplest and is therefore a good place to start. In its constructor, the Clock object gets hold of the reference to the Microwave, which is a singleton. The run method is an infinite loop waking up every second and invokes the clockTicked method on Microwave. The code is given below.

```
public class Clock implements Runnable {
  private static Microwave microwave;
  public Clock() {
    microwave = Microwave.instance();
    new Thread(this).start();
  }
  public void run() {
    try {
      while (true) {
        Thread.sleep(1000);
        microwave.clockTicked();
      }
```

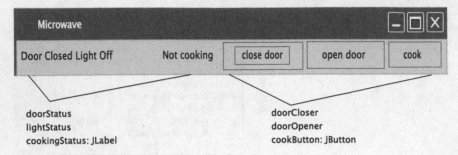

Fig. 10.9 Microwave interface

```
    } catch(InterruptedException ie) {
    }
  }
}
```

The Display Class

GUIDisplay is the concrete class that implements MicrowaveDisplay. To handle user input, it creates a JFrame with a JButton for each kind of operation: open door, close door, and cook.

When run, the program displays the interface given in Fig. 10.9. It has JLabel fields for displaying the status.

```
public class GUIDisplay extends JFrame
    implements ActionListener, MicrowaveDisplay {
  private Microwave microwave;
  private JButton doorCloser = new JButton("close door");
  private JButton doorOpener = new JButton("open door");
  private JButton cookButton = new JButton("cook");
  private JLabel doorStatus = new JLabel("Door Closed");
  private JLabel timerValue = new JLabel("            ");
  private JLabel lightStatus = new JLabel("Light Off");
  private JLabel cookingStatus = new JLabel("Not cooking");
  // other fields and methods
}
```

The constructor lays out all the widgets and sets the GUIDisplay object to be the ActionListener for all the JButton objects.

```
public GUIDisplay() {
  super("Microwave");
  addWindowListener(new WindowAdapter() {
    public void windowClosing(WindowEvent event) {
      System.exit(0);
    }
  });
  getContentPane().setLayout(new FlowLayout());
  getContentPane().add(doorStatus);
  getContentPane().add(lightStatus);
  getContentPane().add(timerValue);
  getContentPane().add(cookingStatus);
  getContentPane().add(doorCloser);
  getContentPane().add(doorOpener);
```

```
      getContentPane().add(cookButton);
      doorCloser.addActionListener(this);
      doorOpener.addActionListener(this);
      cookButton.addActionListener(this);
      pack();
      setVisible(true);
   }
```

The `actionPerformed` method checks the source of the `ActionEvent` and invokes the appropriate method of `Microwave`.

```
   public void actionPerformed(ActionEvent event) {
      if (event.getSource().equals(doorCloser)) {
         microwave.processDoorClose();
      } else if (event.getSource().equals(doorOpener)) {
         microwave.processDoorOpen();
      } else if (event.getSource().equals(cookButton)) {
         microwave.processCookRequest();
      }
   }
```

It is tempting to make `Microwave` the listener for the button clicks, and skip the above step. Note that this would make `Microwave` tightly coupled to the `GUIDisplay` and is therefore undesirable. Finally, we need methods to update the values in the `JLabel` objects that display the system status. This is accomplished by implementing the methods in the `MicrowaveDisplay` interface. As an example, the code for `turnLightOn` is shown below.

```
   public void turnLightOn() {
      lightStatus.setText("Light On");
   }
```

The Microwave Class

Now we discuss the more involved class, `Microwave`. The class maintains the variables for keeping track of the remaining cooking time and the current state. A concrete class that implements `MicrowaveDisplay`, viz. `GUIDisplay`, is instantiated and a reference to it is stored.

```
   public enum States {DOOR_CLOSED_STATE, DOOR_OPENED_STATE, COOKING_STATE};
   private int timeRemaining;
   private States currentState;
   private static Microwave instance;
   private MicrowaveDisplay display;

   private Microwave() {
      currentState = States.DOOR_CLOSED_STATE;
      timeRemaining = 0;
      display = new GUIDisplay();
      display.setMicrowave(this);
      display.timeRemaining(timeRemaining);
      display.turnLightOff(); display.doorClosed();
      display.notCooking();
   }
```

```
public static Microwave instance() {
  if (instance == null) {
    return instance = new Microwave();
  }
  return instance;
}
```

Next we look at the code for processing each of the events. When the clock ticks, `Microwave` needs to take action only if it is in the COOKING_STATE; this action involves decrementing the remaining time, updating the display, and if the timer has run out, switching to the DOOR_CLOSED_STATE. In case of this switch, the display needs to be updated once again. This code is shown below.

```
public void clockTicked(){
  if (currentState == States.COOKING_STATE){
    timeRemaining--;
    display.timeRemaining(timeRemaining);
    if (timeRemaining == 0) {
      currentState = States.DOOR_CLOSED_STATE;
      display.notCooking();
      display.turnLightOff();
    }
  }
}
```

The methods for processing the other events follow a similar pattern. In each case, `Microwave` checks the current state and takes the appropriate action. If the action results in a change of state, some transitional work also needs to be done. As a second example, consider the `processCookRequest` method. The cooking request is processed only if the system is in the COOKING_STATE or the DOOR_CLOSED_STATE. In case of the latter, `currentState` is first changed to COOKING_STATE and the necessary transitional operations are performed. In case of the former, 60 s are added to the time remaining and the display is updated.

```
public void processCookRequest() {
  if (currentState == States.DOOR_CLOSED_STATE) {
    currentState = States.COOKING_STATE;
    display.startCooking();
    display.turnLightOn();
    timeRemaining = 60;
    display.timeRemaining(timeRemaining);
  } else if (currentState == States.COOKING_STATE) {
    timeRemaining += 60;
    display.timeRemaining(timeRemaining);
  }
}
```

The methods for processing the opening and closing of the door are similar and we leave those as an exercise. The `Microwave` class also has the `main` method that gets the show going; this is done by instantiating `Clock`.

```
public static void main(String[] args) {
  new Clock();
}
```

10.4.4 A Critique of the Above Design

The above solution is our first attempt at solving this problem. We have correctly analysed the problem and proposed an 'object-oriented' solution. Our next task is to critically examine our solution to see how well it conforms to the principles of good object-oriented design. With this end in mind, we present two flaws in the above design. As it turns out, these flaws can be corrected by recognising and applying appropriate design patterns.

Extreme Complexity in `Microwave`

`Microwave` has been designed as a large class that takes care of handling all states and events. Although the methods in our class do not seem too complex, it is easy to see that in a larger system, things could easily get out of hand. In previous chapters we have seen that complexity is caused y having a large number of conditionals in our methods. In `Microwave`, each method that processes an event has conditionals that switch on the value stored in `currentState`. In the previous chapter, we created an inheritance hierarchy to subclass the variant behaviour, and succeeded in reducing the complexity of the individual methods and also in facilitating reuse. The question that arises therefore is: *Can we avoid the conditionals that switch on* `currentState` *by subclassing?* The answer is not quite obvious here, since we are dealing with a *dynamic* situation, i.e., the value of `currentState` changes with time, unlike the field `bookType` in the previous chapter which was finalised in the constructor. As it turns out, such a subclassing is indeed possible, but some additional machinery is needed to manage the changes in the value of `currentState`. All of this is handled by using the **state pattern**.

Communication Between Objects

In our design, objects are communicating in two contexts:

1. Events specific to the operation of the microwave, for example, the clicking of the Close Door button.
2. Events of a more general nature that could find relevance in any application. The only such event is the ticking of the clock; this is clearly something that would be relevant in any time-dependent operation.

In both these cases the `Microwave` object is the interested listener. The application specific events are being caught in the GUI and sent to `Microwave` by invoking the appropriate method. There is some coupling involved here, but since the GUI has been developed specifically for this application, this is not a serious concern. The bigger concern is with the fact that this hurts *reuse*. As the system operates, one should expect that changes will be needed and these will require new kinds of events to be added. In our current solution, this will require adding new methods to `Microwave`.

Consider now the more general events, which, in our example, are limited to clock ticks. We have written a class, `Clock`, that is specifically tailored for `Microwave`.

Since the clock serves the same purpose in any application, we would like to have a general Clock class that can be instantiated wherever it is needed.

In both these cases above, what we see is that our system employs a form of communication where the entire responsibility for the communication rests with the sender, which is not desirable. In the first case, it appears to be less harmful, but as we shall see, reuse is facilitated when the responsibility is moved to the listener. In the second case, moving the responsibility to the listener helps us to define a class that can be used across several applications. In general, designs like the one we have make it the responsibility of the event *generator* to get hold of all the listeners and explicitly maintain a reference to each one of them. When the event occurs, every listener must be notified. This is a poor assignment of responsibilities for three reasons.

1. The event generator has to keep track of all the different classes of objects that are interested in listening, and the various ways in which they have to be notified. This makes the sender vulnerable to changes in the listener classes. Instead, we should have one standard format that all listeners must adhere to.
2. Responsibility for registering interest rests with the sender. This implies that when interested listeners are joining the system, the sender must somehow detect them and add them. Instead, if the listeners had this responsibility, they could simply invoke the appropriate method on the sender.
3. The set of listeners cannot change dynamically. We would like to have the flexibility that a listener object can shut off all incoming messages from a particular sender. (This would be preferable to a situation where the listener hears all messages but does not act on those from some sources.) Such a change in listener preference cannot be detected by the sender alone. If the listeners could register and de-register themselves, this would be easily accomplished.

The above drawbacks point to the fact that in a situation where the responsibility rests with the sender, we have **tightly coupled communication**. There are two standard solution frameworks for loosely coupled communication: the **observer pattern** and **event-driven communications**. We shall explore both of these in the context of our system; the observer pattern will be used for listening to clock ticks, and events will be used to transmit external events in the GUI.

10.5 Using the State Pattern

Using the state pattern is closely connected to the idea of modelling with FSMs. All these situations therefore have the following characteristic elements:

1. A collection of states, with each state being defined by distinct behaviour.
2. A set of external inputs to which the system must respond.
3. A **context** in which the FSM operates.

The necessity of the first two is obvious. The third one must exist simply because the states are ephemeral and we need some 'temporal glue' that provides continuity to the system. In addition, the context also serves as a facade for the entire system. In our example, the context does not serve any purpose beyond that; in general the context may be a class that plays a much broader role and the FSM may be used to model only a small portion of the system responsibilities. The context must therefore have the following attributes:

1. A field to track the current state of the FSM.
2. Provide a mechanism to record the change of state.

These two attributes are essential. In addition, the context may provide other attributes depending on the particular details of our implementation. These include, but are not limited to, the following:

1. Provide a mechanism to effect state transitions.
2. Provide methods for entities outside the system to communicate with the FSM.
3. Keep track of external entities that may need to be notified in response to internal changes.

10.5.1 Creating the State Hierarchy

In the solution given in Sect. 10.4, the `Microwave` class had a variable `current State` on which the behaviour was conditionally executed. This is reminiscent of the use of `bookType` in the library system in Chap. 9. Since the design in that case was improved by replacing conditionals with subclasses, we should expect to do something similar here as well with an abstract superclass subclassed by several concrete ones. The natural thing here would be to have an abstract superclass that denotes the microwave state and one concrete subclass for each of the possible actual states.

There is, however, an important difference. The library system would have numerous `LoanableItem` objects, each of which would assume the type of one of the subclasses. In the microwave, however, there is just a single microwave and rather than belong to one of the state subclasses, the microwave actually moves from state to state. As a consequence, it is more appropriate to divide the `Microwave` class into two:

1. A part that deals with state information. This forms a hierarchy formed with an abstract superclass to denote the general idea of a microwave state and one subclass for each of the actual states. This structure is shown in Fig. 10.10.
2. A second part, which deals with the contextual information. We could view the original `Microwave` class now as simply holding the contextual information required for the operation of the FSM. It is therefore aptly renamed `MicrowaveContext`.

Transitioning between states Transitioning to a new state is an operation that involves the knowledge of the other states. Before we decide how to implement

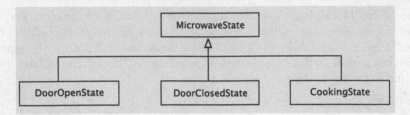

Fig. 10.10   MicrowaveState hierarchy

this, it is important that we examine how the information about the states and transitions is stored. We have seen that the FSM can be represented either by a transition table or in a pictorial fashion with boxes showing the states and arrows showing the transition between them. These two representations correspond roughly to the two standard methods for storing directed graphs: **adjacency matrices** and **adjacency lists**. In an adjacency matrix, we have a centralised storage structure. Each vertex has an associated index, and we use these indices to access the vertices and determine the connectivity between vertices. In an adjacency list, we have a more distributed storage: each vertex contains a list of the vertices which are its immediate neighbours. These two representations lead to two possible implementations for handling transitions between states.

Using the matrix representation

In this approach we first associate an index with each state. It is a common convention to use the index 0 for the initial state, so we assign the index 0 to the closed door state, index 1 to the open door state and 2 to the cooking state. To keep track of this mapping, we create an array; thus the context has an array of `MicrowaveState` named `state` such that `state[0]` would store a reference to the Door Closed state, `state[1]` would store a reference to the Door Open state, and so on. Some applications may designate an error state to handle unexpected conditions; in our case we might use the index 3 if we wished to do that.

Next, we work on the transitions. We know from the state transition table (Fig. 10.3) that transitions may occur only when one of the events occurs. We may assign numeric values 0, 1, 2, 3, and 4 to Open Door, Close Door, Press Cook, Clock Ticks, and Timer Runs Out respectively. Thus, the transition table can be represented as below.

1	0	2	0	0
1	0	1	1	1
1	2	2	2	0

The table is interpreted as follows. The rows correspond to transitions from a given state and the columns represent transitions when a certain input event occurs. For example, entries in the first row (indexed 0) correspond to transitions from the Door

Closed state. Similarly, entries in the first column (indexed 0) show the transitions when the Open Door event occurs. We can interpret the other rows and columns in a similar way. For example, the entry at (2, 4) holds the index of the state that system transitions to when the Timer Runs Out event occurs in the Cooking state.

The Java code for setting up the table would be

```
int[][] transitions = {{1, 0 , 2 , 0 , 0},
                       {1, 0 , 1 , 1 , 1},
                       {1 , 2 , 2 , 2 , 0}};
```

The variable `currentState` now stores an `int`, which is the index of the current state. When a state wants to relinquish control, it invokes the `changeCurrent State` method on the context, passing the index of the needed transition. The code for `changeCurrentState` would be something like this:

```
public void changeCurrentState(int next) {
  currentState = transitions[currentState][next];
  state[currentState].run();
}
```

The parameter `next` would be a number that represents one of the five events and hence would be between 0 and 4.

The method determines the index of the next state by looking up the transition table. The reference to the actual state object is determined by indexing into the array `state` and the `run` method is invoked on the new state.

Note that we are dealing with both *external* and *internal* events. The events Open Door, Close Door, Press Cook and Clock Ticks are external to the FSM, and correspond to real-world events that occur in other subsystems, viz., the GUI and the Clock. The event Timer Runs Out occurs when `timeRemaining` drops to zero; since `timeRemaining` is tracked only inside the FSM, this event is detected internally. This does not pose any difficulty as far as our implementation is concerned. All that is needed is that the state that detects the internal event (Cooking state, in our case) generates the appropriate index (4, in our case) and uses this index as the argument when invoking `changeCurrentState`.

Using the List Representation

In this representation, each state directly provides a reference to the next state when it has to relinquish control. Each concrete state is implemented as a singleton, and therefore the `instance` method can be used for that purpose. The context, of course needs to be informed of the change of state, and this is done once again using the `changeCurrentState` method.

```
public void changeCurrentState(MicrowaveState state) {
  currentState = state;
  currentState.run();
}
```

The context stores a reference to the current state and invokes the `run` method as before.

Both approaches have been referred to in the literature and have their pros and cons. In the matrix approach, each state can be written independently of the others. The `run` method sets up the state with the help of the context, and we have methods for processing all the necessary events. This coding occurs in the driver routine, and is used to populate the transition table. This has the advantage that the code for a state does not have to be modified unless we want to change its behaviour. The transitions can be changed and new states can be linked to existing ones in the driver routine itself. This allows a kind of reuse where we can create a library of states for a particular application domain and use these repeatedly for several applications.

In the list approach, each state is aware of all the other states and therefore the author of each state is required to be aware of how it connects to the FSM. This approach has the advantage of simplicity in that the additional work of decoding all the exit conditions and 'assembling' the FSM is not required. In situations where an FSM is being used to model something specific like, say, an algorithm for a communication protocol, it is unlikely that a library of states can be reused across the domain. In that case it may be beneficial to use the list approach and embed the transition information within each state. *We shall implement the transitions for our case-study using the list approach.*

State classes We now elaborate on the state classes. The abstract class, `Microwave State`, contains methods to handle the various events; its class diagram is shown in Fig. 10.11. The meanings of most of the methods should be obvious. When the microwave changes state, some variables may need to be initialised and the output may have to be changed. It is convenient to have all of these actions executed in a method, which we term `run`.

Next, we develop the class diagrams for the individual states. While in the DoorOpen state, the microwave does not respond to anything other than the door closing. Therefore, in the class diagram for `DoorOpenState` (Fig. 10.12), we show the methods `processDoorClose` and `run`. Similar interpretations can be made for `DoorClosedState` and `CookingState`, which are respectively shown in Figs. 10.13 and 10.14.

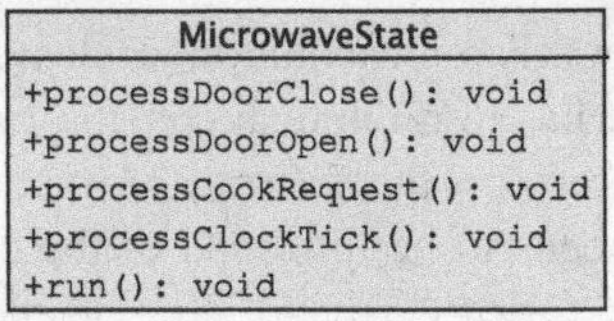

Fig. 10.11 Class diagram for MicrowaveState

MicrowaveState
+processDoorClose(): void
+processDoorOpen(): void
+processCookRequest(): void
+processClockTick(): void
+run(): void

Fig. 10.12 Class diagram for DoorOpenState

DoorOpenState
+processDoorClose(): void
+run() : void

Fig. 10.13 Class diagram
for DoorClosedState

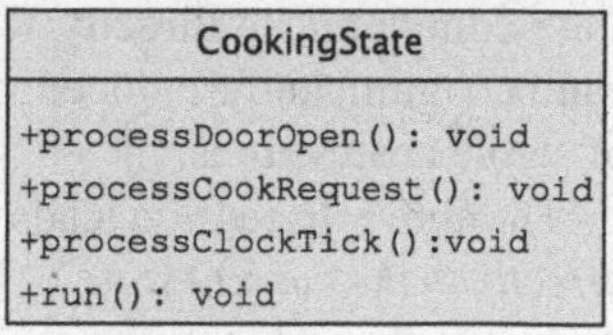

DoorClosedState
+processDoorOpen(): void
+processCookRequest(): void
+run(): void

Fig. 10.14 Class diagram
for CookingState

CookingState
+processDoorOpen(): void
+processCookRequest(): void
+processClockTick():void
+run(): void

Microwave context In the design of the `MicrowaveContext` class, we must address the question of how the concrete state classes perform the necessary computations. Some of the actions may be purely local to the state, and these can be handled in an obvious way. There are two kinds of actions that have an effect outside the state: (i) *actions that require a change of state,* and (ii) *actions that require making changes to an entity outside the FSM.*

Changing the state is handled using one of the mechanisms described previously. (We chose the adjacency list approach.)

In a typical FSM, each state has some impact on the environment in which it is operating. In our case, these are actions that change the display. For instance, when the cook button is pressed while in the cooking state, the number of second remaining should be increased by 60. The question here is how to implement the communication from the cooking state to the display object. It should be no surprise that we have more than one option for handling these.

- **Option 1** *All communication goes through the context.*
- **Option 2** *Each state communicates independently with the external entities.*

If we choose the first option, we have a context that truly behaves like a *facade*, i.e., all communication into and out of the system goes through the context. This is appropriate in situations where we want the entire FSM subsystem to be a unit that can inter-operate with several environments. For instance, we may decide that we are no longer having a simple display to show what is going on, but want to manipulate device drivers that actually turn the light and powertube on and off. Such a change could be accomplished by changing just the context; if we had chosen the second option, every state would have to be changed to communicate with the new external environment. Note that Option 1 requires that the context provide methods for communication that can be invoked by the states. This would result in an additional overhead of a method call, but such a call can be easily *inlined* to reduce the runtime cost.

In the second option, each state must keep track of the concrete entities that it wishes to communicate with and has to be tailored to that interface. This clearly makes the state dependent on these interfaces and thus introduces some additional coupling.

This seems to suggest that Option 1 is always preferable, which would not be correct for the following reason. Consider a situation where each state has some distinct kinds of external entities which it communicates with; *if all the communication went through the context, the context would have to provide methods for each kind of entity, making it a very unwieldy class.* In such a situation it is preferable that each state communicate directly with its external clients. The coupling that may result can be significantly reduced if all the external entities were to be implementations of stable abstractions.

The above discussion leads to a natural question: *Can incoming communication go directly to the current state?* This is clearly a tricky question, since the external entity does not know what the current state is, and revealing such information would clearly lead to a lot of unwanted coupling. As it turns out, these questions are related and we shall examine all of this in Sect. 10.6 when we deal with the issue of communication. For now, we shall make the choice that *all communication goes through the context.* What this implies is that the context has methods for updating the display, which are invoked from the concrete states.

The class diagram for `MicrowaveContext` is shown in Fig. 10.15. In our design all communication between the states and the UI goes through the context. It is convenient to have in the context a method `getDisplay` to provide the reference to the display object, which can be used by the the `MicrowaveState` objects as needed to update the interface. The current state can be changed by executing the method `changeCurrentState`.

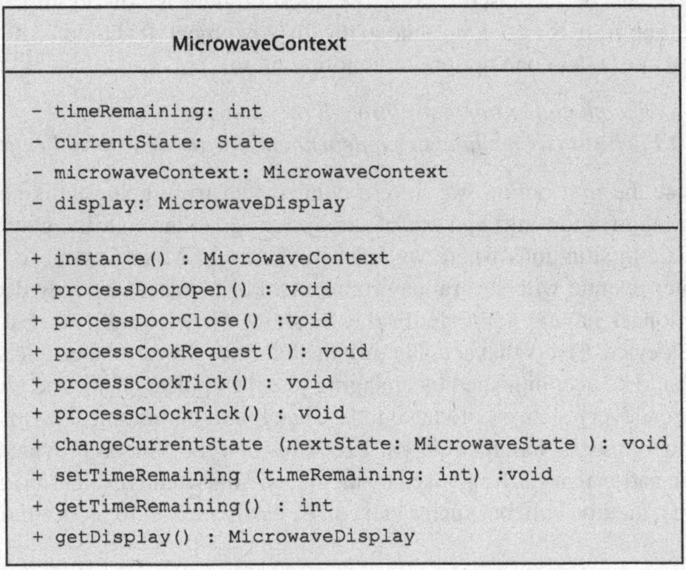

MicrowaveContext
- timeRemaining: int - currentState: State - microwaveContext: MicrowaveContext - display: MicrowaveDisplay
+ instance() : MicrowaveContext + processDoorOpen() : void + processDoorClose() :void + processCookRequest( ): void + processCookTick() : void + processClockTick() : void + changeCurrentState (nextState: MicrowaveState): void + setTimeRemaining (timeRemaining: int) :void + getTimeRemaining() : int + getDisplay() : MicrowaveDisplay

Fig. 10.15 Class diagram for MicrowaveContext

10.5.2 *Implementation*

MicrowaveState has default methods for processing each of the events, and the concrete state classes are supposed to override these to specify the processing required.

```
public abstract class MicrowaveState {
  protected static MicrowaveContext context;
  protected static MicrowaveDisplay display;
  protected MicrowaveState() {
    context = MicrowaveContext.instance();
    display = context.getDisplay();
  }
  public abstract void run();
  public  void processDoorClose() {
  }
  public  void processDoorOpen() {
  }
  public  void processCookRequest() {
  }
  public  void processClockTick() {
  }
}
```

The run method is abstract and is invoked on a state whenever control has to be transferred to that state. Each state must therefore define the run method in an appropriate manner. For instance, when the cooking state is entered, the housekeeping needed is that the light must be turned on, the timer set to 60, and powertube turned on. These details are shown below.

```
public  void run() {
  display.turnLightOn();
  context.setTimeRemaining(60);
  display.startCooking();
  display.displayTimeRemaining(context.getTimeRemaining());
}
```

The default methods are overridden as needed. The method processClockTick in CookingState, for instance, would look something like this:

```
public  void processClockTick() {
  context.setTimeRemaining(context.getTimeRemaining() - 1);
  display.displayTimeRemaining(context.getTimeRemaining());
  if (context.getTimeRemaining() == 0) {
    display.notCooking();
    display.turnLightOff();
    context.changeCurrentState(DoorClosedState.instance());
  }
}
```

The MicrowaveContext class holds a reference to the current state and processes the events by simply passing on the request to the current state. The code for the method processCookRequest now looks like this:

```
public void processCookRequest() {
  currentState.processCookRequest();
}
```

The variable `currentState` is of type `MicrowaveState` and dynamic binding ensures that correct method is invoked. Note that we no longer have a conditional to check what kind of state we are in. Note that some states (e.g., Door Open) are required to ignore this event; for this reason the default method in the abstract class is implemented to do nothing.

Implementing the concrete states Each of these extends `MicrowaveState` and is a singleton. Here are the first two lines of the code for the `CookingState` class.

```
public class CookingState extends MicrowaveState {
  private static CookingState instance;
```

Each state class overrides only a subset of the methods of `MicrowaveState`. The code for handling the external events is essentially the same as what we had in the corresponding methods of `Microwave` in the previous version: the conditional on `currentState` is now absent. Clock ticks are handled in `CookingState` as shown below:

```
public void processClockTick() {
  context.setTimeRemaining(context.getTimeRemaining() - 1);
  display.displayTimeRemaining(context.getTimeRemaining());
  if (context.getTimeRemaining() == 0) {
    context.changeCurrentState(DoorClosedState.instance());
  }
}
```

In this version, we shall leave the `Clock` class largely unchanged. The minor, obvious change is that rather than send signals to the `Microwave` object, `Clock` has to notify the instance of `MicrowaveContext`.

10.6 Improving Communication Between Objects

As we discussed earlier, we have two problems with communication in our earlier design. The first of these involves external entities like `Clock`. In our example, this was tightly coupled to the implementation for `Microwave`, and we shall investigate loosening this coupling using the *Observer* pattern. Next we look at how our system can be made more flexible by taking an *event-based approach* to processing user input.

10.6.1 Loosely Coupled Communication

Loosely coupled communication must have three properties:

1. The listener is responsible for registering interest.
2. All interested listeners share some common interface so that the sender need not distinguish between listeners.

3. The sender has a mechanism for maintaining a collection of the interested listeners.

The **observer pattern** gives us a mechanism that makes this possible. There are two categories of players in the observer pattern:

1. The **observable**, which is usually a single object, and
2. The **observers**, of which there may be several. It is the responsibility of the observable to provide a method by which the observer can register interest. Once this interest has been registered, it is the responsibility of the observable to notify all observers of any changes/events that occur. In order to accomplish this without causing tight coupling, every observer must have a method with a signature that has been agreed upon. Java provides such a mechanism as a part of the language.

Every `Observable` object maintains a list of 'interested observers.' The class `Observable` has the following categories of methods:

1. In the first category, we have methods for maintaining the list of observers. The method `addObserver(Observer observer)` adds the given observer to this list. There are two ways of deleting observers. A single observer can be deleted by using the method `deleteObserver(Observer observer)`, and all of the observers can be deleted by calling the method `deleteObservers()`.
2. The second set of methods support the notification of the observers of 'noteworthy' events occurring within the `Observable` object. Every `Observable` object maintains a flag, 'object changed', to remember whether the object has changed since the last notification to the observers. To notify observers, it is necessary to first call the method `setChanged()` to indicate that a change has occurred. This sets the 'object changed' flag to `true`. After setting the flag, the `Observable` can notify all of the observers in one of two ways: by calling `notifyObservers()` or calling `notifyObservers(Object arg)`. In the latter version of the `notifyObservers` method, `arg` is the object that contains the message to be delivered. Every time `notifyObservers` is invoked, the 'object changed' flag is cleared; that is why we need to call the `setChanged` method whenever a 'noteworthy' change/event occurs. (Repeated invocations of the `notifyObservers` method will not have any effect until the 'object changed' flag is set again.)
3. The third group comprises miscellaneous methods such as `countObservers()` that gets the number of observers of the `Observable` object.

Every class that wishes to be an observer implements the `Observer` interface. The `Observer` interface has the method `update` with the following signature:

```
public abstract void update(Observable object, Object arg);
```

When `notifyObservers` is invoked in the `Observable` object, the `update` method is invoked once for each item in the list of 'interested observers'. The `update` method allows the `Observable` object to send a reference to itself along with a message to the observer.

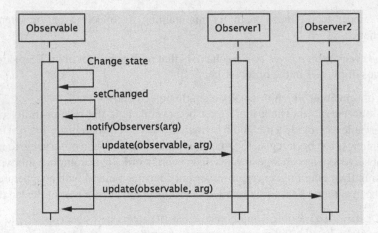

Fig. 10.16 Sequence diagram in a system with one observable and two observers

The interaction between and Observable and two Observer objects is depicted in the sequence diagram in Fig. 10.16. The picture shows an event occurring in the Observable, which calls the setChanged and the notifyObservers methods. In response to the notifyObservers method call, the Observable object calls the update methods of the two observers supplying them with its identity and information about the event(arg).

While utilising the observer pattern in Java, the programmer should be aware of two aspects.

1. In general, a single observer should not be registered more than once with the same Observable object. The Observable object will call the update method of the observer as many times as the number of registrations. The problem could creep into applications where observers are supposed to be deleted and then put back in.
2. The update method of the observer is executed by the Observable thread. This means that the processing of the update method in the observers occurs sequentially. If one of these methods ends up waiting, say for a message, the Observable object will be stuck! Also, the designer must ensure that no matter in what order the update methods get executed, the system will function correctly.

10.7 Redesign Using the Observer Pattern

We now re-implement the microwave system to have the Clock extend Observable and MicrowaveContext implement Observer. Since the Clock object does not maintain a reference to the context anymore, Microwave

Context need not be a singleton. On the other hand, Clock is implemented as a singleton because it can serve as a general class for a variety of applications. This allows the listener (observer) to get hold of the event generator (observable) and register its interest. The modified Clock class is as follows:

```
public class Clock extends Observable implements Runnable {
  private Thread thread = new Thread(this);
  private static Clock instance;
  public enum Events {CLOCK_TICKED_EVENT};
  private Clock(){
    thread.start();
  }
  public static Clock instance() {
    if (instance == null) {
      instance = new Clock();
    }
    return instance;
  }
  public void run(){
    try{
      while (true) {
        Thread.sleep(1000);
        setChanged();
        notifyObservers(Events.CLOCK_TICKED_EVENT);
      }
    } catch (InterruptedException ie) {
    }
  }
}
```

MicrowaveContext implements the Observer interface and the method ClockTicked is replaced by the method update.

```
public class MicrowaveContext implements Observer {
  public void update(Observable source, Object event) {
    // code to process clock tick
  }
  // other attributes as before
}
```

10.7.1 Communication with the User

As we discussed earlier, implementing the communication mechanism requires us to make a decision about the path of the messages. We had decided that all communication would go through the context. We shall now proceed with that assumption and try to improve the reusability of our system.

As it stands, we have provided a separate method in MicrowaveContext for each kind of event. We have a situation where adding new kinds of events would require changing the implementation of the context. The simplest way of avoiding this is to have a single method, say processEvent, and pass the event as a parameter.

This means that all the events should belong to a common type, which can be created using the enum Event, as shown below:

```
public class MicrowaveSupport {
  public static enum Events {DOOR_CLOSED_EVENT, DOOR_OPENED_EVENT,
                             COOKING_REQUESTED_EVENT};
}
```

The class MicrowaveSupport is defined to hold all the events. Note that what we have done is to *encapsulate the variability in a separate class* so that new events can be added without changing the context. The processEvent method in the context simply passes the event on to the current state.

```
public void handleEvent(Object arg) {
  currentState.handle(arg);
}
```

The Observer Pattern

Where do we employ this? An abstraction has several parts, which have to be encapsulated separately, but there is a need to maintain communication between them.

What problem are we facing? Communicating with an object essentially requires that some method of the object be invoked. This implies that the object initiating the communication has to know which method of the recipient(s) is to be invoked. If the sender must keep track of the methods of all recipients, we get tight coupling between the various parts of the abstraction.

How have we solved it? We place the responsibility for communication on the receiver instead of the sender. The sender (also known as the Subject or the Observable) has a method that allows recipients (Observers) to register their interest with the sender. All the recipients of the message implement a common method (or an interface) for receiving messages. When there is a need for communication, the sender invokes the common method on all the receivers that have registered their interest with the sender.

Note that the context does not distinguish between the events anymore. Accordingly, the abstract class MicrowaveState has just a single abstract method handle which must be overridden by each concrete state. The code for the class CookingState is shown below. (It assumes that MicrowaveContext is still a singleton.)

```
public void handle(Object event) {
  if (event.equals(MicrowaveSupport.Events.COOKING_REQUESTED_EVENT)) {
    processCookRequest();
  } else if (event.equals(MicrowaveSupport.Events.DOOR_OPENED_EVENT)) {
    processDoorOpen();
  } else if (event.equals(Clock.Events.CLOCK_TICKED_EVENT)) {
    processClockTick();
  }
}
```

Note that we now have conditionals to distinguish between the events. This is because all the events are travelling along the same path and we have no means of distinguishing them. A similar situation occurs when we have a class that acts as an observer for several observable classes. The advantage to using the enum is the simplicity of implementation when compared with the other options; the disadvantage is that we combine the complexity of several methods into one, requiring switching on the type of event. This complexity is not a big concern when we have a simple system and each state handles only a small number of events, but can be a problem when there are several events to be handled and these originate from divers entities. As one would expect, we have alternate solutions for this that involve creating a separate event hierarchy. We shall examine these options later in this chapter.

10.7.2 The Improved Design

Before proceeding further, let us summarise the changes we have made to the earlier design by examining each class.

The GUIDisplay This class has remained largely unchanged. The only difference is that instead of invoking different methods for processing each event, we now invoke the same method processEvent with different parameters. This code is shown below:

```
public void actionPerformed(ActionEvent event) {
  if (event.getSource().equals(frame.doorCloser)) {
    MicrowaveContext.instance().handleEvent(
        MicrowaveSupport.Events.DOOR_CLOSED_EVENT);
  } else if (event.getSource().equals(frame.doorOpener)) {
    MicrowaveContext.instance().handleEvent(
        MicrowaveSupport.Events.DOOR_OPENED_EVENT);
  } else if (event.getSource().equals(frame.cookButton)) {
    MicrowaveContext.instance().handleEvent(
        MicrowaveSupport.Events.COOKING_REQUESTED_EVENT);
  }
}
```

Clock This class now extends Observable and is not tailored for this particular application, i.e., when a clock tick happens, it simply notifies all the observers.

MicrowaveContext The class was set up as an Observer of Clock. The variability in the events was encapsulated, and a single method, processEvent, was defined in MicrowaveContext to receive all events. A separate hierarchy, viz., MicrowaveState, was created and all the details of processing of events in the different states was delegated to this hierarchy. A class diagram showing all these details is presented in Fig. 10.17.

The manner in which events are handled changes in conformance with the new implementation. The sequence diagram for handling a cooking request event when the microwave is in the DoorClosedState is shown in Fig. 10.18.

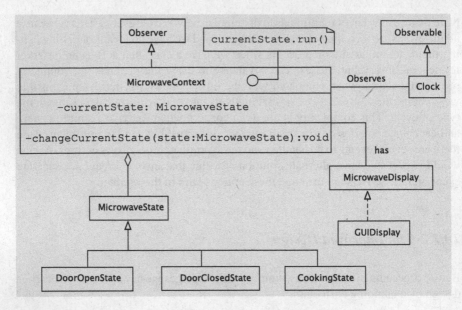

Fig. 10.17 Class diagram for the microwave oven

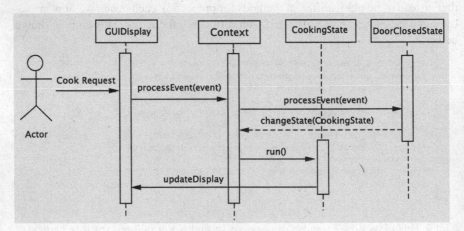

Fig. 10.18 Sequence diagram for cooking request event

10.8 Eliminating the Conditionals

In the design presented above, the `handle` method in each state handles the events. This conditional switches on the kind of event, which in turn is decided by external input. To eliminate these conditionals from the states, it is obvious that our implementation should ensure that each event is delivered to the states in a unique way. Since the events are passed on through method invocations, this would mean having a unique method invocation for each event. However, the context cannot distinguish between these events for reasons discussed earlier, and this implies that we can no longer insist that all communication go through the context. The problem we are faced with is that of ensuring that only the current (i.e., active) state processes the event. We have two broad approaches for ensuring this.

1. *Take the context out of the picture completely i.e., each state takes full responsibility for performing exactly as the system requires.* This approach would use something like the event handling system provided by Java, which behaves very much like a customised observer pattern. We have an event source and an event listener interface which correspond respectively to the observable and the observer. The listener classes must implement the event listener interface and register themselves with the source object; when the event occurs, the method in the event listener interface is invoked on all the registered listeners. If we use this approach for our microwave oven, we will have a different event listener method for each event. For the reasons mentioned earlier, these cannot be implemented by the context. Each state therefore implements the needed event listener interfaces and also takes responsibility for registering and de-registering itself with the event sources.
2. *Use the context as a 'switchboard' that connects the event with the current state.* This would clearly have to be done without knowing the type of the concrete event or the concrete state, thus requiring some form of double dispatch. We create a hierarchy of events and a parallel hierarchy of listener interfaces. Each state implements the necessary interfaces as before. Since the concrete `MicrowaveState` object that is currently active changes constantly, we need to use a two-step process in which the source communicates the event to the context, which then invokes a method on the event object passing the current state as a parameter. The method in the event then invokes the method in the listener interface.

10.8.1 Using the Java Event Mechanism

In this approach, the current state object receives notifications directly from the source of the event, without going through the context. For each type of event, there is a separate 'manager' object that takes on the responsibility of delivering the events to the appropriate state. For example, consider a click on the door close button. The display object informs the `DoorCloseManager` object, which notifies all the listeners.

The Java event mechanism involves creating classes for the events and their sources and interfaces that the listeners will implement. Let us go through each of this, making the necessary modifications to our microwave system.

The Event Classes

We create a class for each event, by extending `EventObject`. The code for the `DoorCloseEvent` is shown below.

```
public class DoorCloseEvent extends EventObject {
  public DoorCloseEvent(Object source) {
    super(source);
  }
}
```

The only work here is to define the constructor. The source of the event is stored in the superclass object.

The Event Source
In our system, the events will be generated in response to button clicks. We can designate GUIDisplay as the source. It is customary that responsibilities of the source include providing mechanisms for registering and de-registering listeners and also notifying them when an event occurs. Doing this for all the microwave events in the GUI, however, causes unnecessary entanglement of responsibilities. Instead, we create a separate class DoorCloseManager, which handles all the other responsibilities. This class is created by extending JComponent so that we can inherit some of the functionality for managing the events.

```
public class DoorCloseManager extends JComponent {
  private EventListenerList listenerList;
```

```
private static DoorCloseManager instance;
private DoorCloseManager() {
  listenerList = new EventListenerList();
}
public static DoorCloseManager instance() {
  if (instance == null) {
    return instance = new DoorCloseManager();
  }
  return instance;
}
public void addDoorCloseListener(DoorCloseListener listener) {
  listenerList.add(DoorCloseListener.class, listener);
}
public void removeDoorCloseListener(DoorCloseListener listener) {
  listenerList.remove(DoorCloseListener.class, listener);
}
public void processEvent(DoorCloseEvent event) {
  EventListener[] listeners
    = listenerList.getListeners(DoorCloseListener.class);
  for (int index = 0; index < listeners.length; index++) {
    ((DoorCloseListener) listeners[i]).doorClosed(event);
  }
}
}
```

This class is defined as a singleton, so that the concrete states can access it and register themselves. The event constructors are invoked when the button clicks are detected in the GUI, as shown below.

```
public void actionPerformed(ActionEvent event) {
  if (event.getSource().equals(doorCloser)) {
    DoorCloseManager.instance().processEvent(new DoorCloseEvent(this));
  }
  // code for handling other events
}
```

The GUIDisplay object is stored as the source, which enables us to track the actual source, if needed for an exception. The code above invokes the processEvent method of the DoorCloseManager which then notifies all the listeners.

The Event Listeners

All event listeners must implement the corresponding listener interface. All these interfaces are defined to extend EventListener so that the methods in JComponent can be reused.

```
public interface DoorCloseListener extends EventListener {
  public void doorClosed(DoorCloseEvent event);
}
```

Each concrete state implements the required listeners and does the necessary house-keeping. Note that this includes registering as a listener within the run method, and de-registering before the changeCurrentState method is invoked.

```
public class DoorOpenState extends MicrowaveState
                           implements DoorCloseListener {
  // other fields and methods
```

```
public  void run() {
  display.stopCooking();
  display.openDoor();
  display.turnLightOn();
  display.displayTimeRemaining(context.getTimeRemaining());
  DoorCloseManager.instance().addDoorCloseListener(this);
}
public void doorClosed(DoorCloseEvent event){
  DoorCloseManager.instance().removeDoorCloseListener(this);
  context.changeCurrentState(DoorClosedState.instance());
}
}
```

10.8.2 Using the Context As a 'Switchboard'

Sometimes, we may have to deal with situations where the communication has to go
through a facade. In such an FSM, we cannot use the Java event structure unless the
context participates in the process and is aware of all kinds of events in the system,
which may not be desirable. As it turns out, we can construct a solution where the
context has a single `handleEvent` method and each individual state takes care of
implementing the listener methods it is interested in. This can be accomplished by
adding some machinery to the event classes and paying the price of an additional
method call. Such a system consists of the following elements.

1. **An event hierarchy** We have an abstract class `MicrowaveEvent`, which is
   extended by the concrete event classes `DoorOpenEvent`, `DoorCloseEvent`,
   etc. This is shown in Fig. 10.19.
2. **A listener interface hierarchy** The hierarchy parallels the event hierarchy and
   is shown in Fig. 10.20. We have a general interface for `MicrowaveEvent`
   `Listener` which corresponds to the abstract event, extended by specific interfaces for each concrete event. We need the general interface, since the abstract
   class `MicrowaveState` has to be a listener but cannot implement any of the
   specific interfaces.

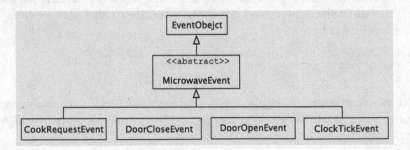

Fig. 10.19 Event hierarchy for the microwave oven

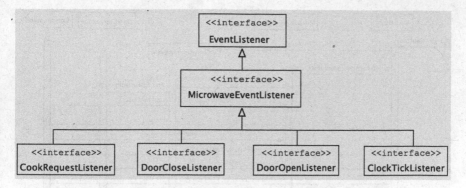

Fig. 10.20 Listener hierarchy for the microwave oven

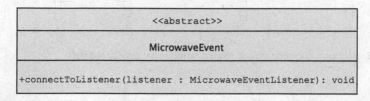

Fig. 10.21 MicrowaveEvent class diagram

3. **A method for the event to accept the listener** The abstract event has an abstract method `connectToListener` (Fig. 10.21), which the concrete events must implement. This method will be invoked by the context (or any 'switchboard') when it receives an event, and passes as a parameter the object that should be notified of the event.
4. **A method to send the listener to the event** This method resides in the 'switchboard'.
5. **The concrete listeners** Finally, we have the concrete classes that implement the specific listener interfaces, which in our example are the concrete states.

To demonstrate how the classes and interfaces will be used to eliminate conditionals, we examine the sequence diagram in Fig. 10.22, which shows what happens when we press the 'Cook' button while the current state is DoorClosedState. The sequence of actions is as follows:

1. The user clicks the 'Cook' button. This generates an instance of `ActionEvent` and control goes to the `actionPerformed` method of `GUIDisplay`.
2. The `actionPerformed` method notes that the event is a cook request, so it creates an instance of `CookRequestEvent`. It then sends the event as parameter to the `handleEvent` method of `MicrowaveContext`.
3. In the `handleEvent` method of `MicrowaveContext`, the parameter is used to call `connectToListener`. This is another polymorphic call. This ends up calling the `connectToListener` method of `CookRequestEvent`.

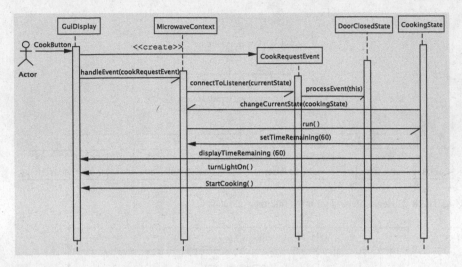

Fig. 10.22 Sequence diagram for cook request while in the DoorClosed state

4. The `connectToListener` receives the current state as parameter, which it uses to call the `processEvent` method of `DoorClosedState` (which is the current state) with `CookRequestEvent` as parameter.
5. The `processEvent` method changes the current state, which in turn modifies the display.

10.8.3 Implementation

The `MicrowaveEvent` class is abstract and extends `java.util.Event Object`. The `connectToListener` method is critical for making the switchboard function correctly.

```
import java.util.*;
public abstract class MicrowaveEvent extends EventObject {
  public MicrowaveEvent(Object object) {
    super(object);
  }
  public abstract void connectToListener(MicrowaveEventListener listener);
}
```

Each concrete event implements `connectToListener` and must invoke the appropriate method in the listener interface. However, *the parameter is explicitly known to implement only the general interface; we therefore cast the object to the specific listener interface and then invoke the method.* Since this cast may fail, the method is declared to throw the `ClasscastException`. The implementation of `connectToListener` for `CookRequestEvent` is shown below. Since not all states need to handle the event, we might want to suppress message displays if a `ClassCastException` object is thrown.

Note that the `connectToListener` method needs to verify during execution that `listener` belongs to the class `CookRequestListener`. This verification is automatically done through downcasting and is therefore an application of RTTI.

```
public class CookRequestEvent extends MicrowaveEvent {
  public CookRequestEvent(MicrowaveDisplay display) {
    super(display);
  }
  public void connectToListener(MicrowaveEventListener listener) {
    try {
      ((CookRequestListener) listener).processEvent(this);
    } catch (ClassCastException cce) {
    // message
    }
  }
}
```

The code for `MicrowaveEventListener` and one of its subinterfaces, `CookRequestListener`, are shown below.

```
public interface MicrowaveEventListener {
  public void processEvent(MicrowaveEvent event);
}
public interface CookRequestListener extends MicrowaveEventListener {
  public void processEvent(CookRequestEvent event);
}
```

The `handleEvent` method in the context casts `currentState` as a listener before it is passed; since the declared type of this variable is the abstract class `MicrowaveState`, such a cast would not be possible if we did not have the general listener interface.

The code has to reside in a `try` block for obvious reasons; to facilitate debugging, we add the `logException` method to the state classes.

```
public void handleEvent(MicrowaveEvent event) {
  try {
    event.connectToListener((MicrowaveEventListener) currentState);
  } catch (ClassCastException cce) {
    currentState.logException(cce);
  }
}
```

Partial code for the `CookingState` is shown below. Note that we no longer need to register or de-register and need to implement methods only for the events that this state is interested in.

```
import java.util.*;
public class CookingState extends MicrowaveState implements
        DoorOpenListener, CookRequestListener, ClockTickListener {
  // code for making the class a singleton
  public void run(){
    context.setTimeRemaining(60);
    display.displayTimeRemaining(context.getTimeRemaining());
```

```
      display.turnLightOn();
      display.startCooking();
    }
    public void processEvent(DoorOpenEvent event) {
      context.changeCurrentState(DoorOpenState.instance());
    }
    public void processEvent(CookRequestEvent event) {
      context.setTimeRemaining(context.getTimeRemaining() + 60);
      display.displayTimeRemaining(context.getTimeRemaining());
    }
    // other methods
  }
```

Before closing the subject, we should see some alternatives to downcasting when implementing the `connectToListener` method in the event classes. We could use the `instanceof` method to ensure that the listener indeed implements the appropriate interface. This approach is likely to execute faster since the overhead associated with the exception is avoided, but does not report situations where unexpected state–event combinations show up at runtime. Another alternative would be to have all states implement all listener interfaces, making methods to handle events that are not of interest to it no-ops; this would, however, mean that all states would have to be changed when new events are added, thus hurting reuse.

Eliminating Conditionals in `GUIDisplay`

As it stands, we still have conditionals in the `GUIDisplay` class. While a general approach to eliminating conditionals in the user interface might be tedious if not impossible, it turns out that we can eliminate them completely in `GUIDisplay`. The approach could be used to reduce the number of conditionals in user interface classes in general. The idea involves creating a separate class for each type of button. All such button classes extend some common functionality given in the class `GUIButton`.

```
import javax.swing.*;
public abstract class GUIButton extends JButton {
  public GUIButton(String string) {
    super(string);
  }
  public abstract void inform(MicrowaveContext context,
                             MicrowaveDisplay display);
}
```

The button for issuing the cook request is an instance of `CookButton` coded as below.

```
public class CookButton extends GUIButton {
  public CookButton(String string) {
    super(string);
  }
  public void inform(MicrowaveContext context, MicrowaveDisplay source) {
    context.handleEvent(new CookRequestEvent(source));
  }
}
```

Finally, the code in `GUIDisplay` simply calls the *inform* method on the source of the event.

```
public void actionPerformed(ActionEvent event) {
  ((GUIButton) event.getSource()).inform(MicrowaveContext.instance(),
    this);
}
```

10.9 Designing GUI Programs Using the State Pattern

Let us consider the execution of a typical GUI program. Initially, the program displays
a window and waits for an input from the user such as a click on a button or selection
of an item in a list box. The program processes this request and displays another
screen, waiting, once again, for an input from the user.

When the program has displayed a window, we can view that as the current 'state'
of the program. The event caused by user's actions such as button clicks and list
selections, is the input to the state. Based on the state and the current input, the
program takes some actions and makes a transition to another state, which displays
yet another window.

Of course, a GUI program may not always wait for a user input when it displays
a window. As an example, assume that the program presents a snapshot of a file
system. The user may invoke a command to copy a set of files perhaps by dragging
some icons or by doing a 'copy and paste'. The program may choose to display a
simple window (a message box) with some message like 'copying in progress'. This
window may not have any widgets for human use. The window disappears when
copying is finished.

In the above case, the display of the message box represents the copying state of
the program. The state's input is a notification from some copying code that copying
has been completed.

10.9.1 Design of a GUI System for the Library

We briefly describe our approach to GUI design by building a GUI for the library system. The interface is more or less equivalent to the text-based interface we developed
in Chap. 7.

Obviously, we need one screen for displaying the main menu, a screen for allowing
the addition of books, yet another one for adding a member, and so on. Each of these
screens corresponds to a state of the program.

Since there are too many states to be conveniently presented in a single diagram,
we present our design in smaller parts.

The main menu and add books We have a state, MainMenu, for displaying the
main menu. This has a number of buttons, each of which selects an operation on the
library. When the 'Add Book' button is clicked, the system goes to the AddBook
state. Since we anticipate that we will get a number of books to be added, we will

provide two buttons here: one to add a book and the other to signal that the screen can be dismissed. The state transition diagram is shown in Fig. 10.23.

Add member When we click the 'Add Member' button on the main menu, the system goes to AddMember, displaying a window to let the user input member details. After entering, the user may click the 'OK' button to enter the data into the library. The system displays the result in a new window (a new state), ShowResult, from which control goes to MainMenu when the user clicks the 'OK' button.

In AddMember, the user may also choose the 'Cancel' option to abandon the operation.

The details are shown in Fig. 10.24.

Issue books The state transition diagram is given in Fig. 10.25. As the reader may expect, the system goes to IssueBooks when the user clicks 'Issue Books' on the main menu. In this state, the user may enter the member id and click 'OK' or click 'Cancel' to return to the main menu. If a valid member id is entered, the system moves to the GetBookId state, which lets the user enter a book id. After entering each id, the user may click the 'OK' button to enter one more book id. Clicking 'Done' takes the system back to the MainMenu state.

Fig. 10.23 Main menu and add books

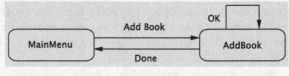

Fig. 10.24 Main menu and add member

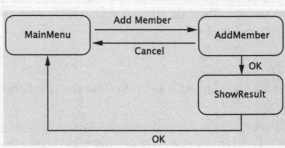

Fig. 10.25 Main menu and issue books

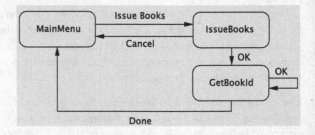

Return books and remove books The state transition diagrams for both cases are similar. After the appropriate choice ('Return Books' and 'Remove Books') is made from the main menu, the state is changed to either ReturnBooks or RemoveBooks. In each of these states, the user can enter a book id and click 'OK' or press 'Done' to return to the main menu. The state transition diagram is shown in Fig. 10.26.

Place hold and remove hold These two also have similar state transition diagrams and are shown in Figs. 10.27 and 10.28. We assume that explanations for the previous cases should provide enough clues to understand these cases.

Print transactions The flow of control is depicted in Fig. 10.29. Since a member may have had many transactions on a given date, the result is shown in a state called ShowLongResult.

Process holds The state transition is similar to 'Add Books' and is given in Fig. 10.30. We leave the implementation of *Renew Books* as an exercise.

Fig. 10.26 Remove books and return books

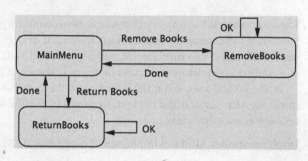

Fig. 10.27 Place hold

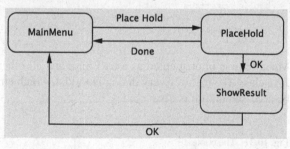

Fig. 10.28 Remove hold

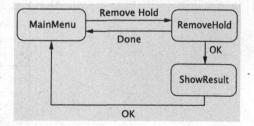

Fig. 10.29 Print transactions

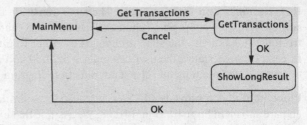

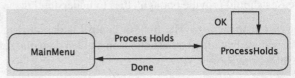

Fig. 10.30 Process holds

10.9.2 The Context

The system needs to transfer information between some pairs of states. For example, the member id entered in IssueBooks is to be used in GetBookId, and the transactions from GetTransactions must be given to ShowLongResult. This is achieved by means of a context, a singleton. The class diagram is shown in Fig. 10.31.

In the IssueBooks state, the user enters the member id clicks 'OK'. The state stores the member id in the context, retrieved by GetBookId. Similar transfers occur between some other pairs of states.

Implementation All states implement the interface UIState, which is given below.

```
public interface UIState {
  public void handle(Object event);
  public void run();
}
```

MainMenu is implemented as a JFrame and all other states are extensions of the Java class JDialog. Every dialog is modal, which ensures that main menu cannot be accessed until it is dismissed.

Fig. 10.31 The context

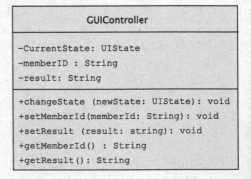

10.10 Discussion and Further Reading

10.10.1 Implementing the State Pattern

The state pattern can be implemented in different ways, and the particular implementation that we choose depends on the role played by the context and the kind of relationship we have between the states. At one end of the spectrum we have an implementation where the context is nothing but a repository for shared information. This is the approach recommended in [1]. When a state has completed all of its actions, it passes control to the next state along with a reference to the context object. We have two choices as to how this can be realised. One approach is to create a new instance of a state whenever a state terminates. Another approach is where each state is a singleton and the current state invokes `instance` to obtain a reference to the next state. In such an implementation, there is some coupling between the individual states and requires that each state be fully responsible for listening and responding to external events.

At the other end of the spectrum, we have a situation where each state is completely unaware of the existence of other states. This is accomplished by the current state terminating with a call to the context, which looks up a transition table to decide what the next state should be [2]. The context in this implementation provides methods to add states and transitions, which populate the transition table. These methods are accessed through a driver routine, thus allowing the context to be reused in other applications. Such an approach is particularly suitable for designing multi-panel interactive systems, such as the GUI for the library [3]. The approach that we have taken in the design of the microwave system lies somewhere in the middle of this range. The context stores the current state and also serves as a facade, but has nothing to do with the transition table.

10.10.2 Features of the State Pattern

The examples in the chapter should be illustrative enough that the following salient aspects of the state pattern can be appreciated.

1. An application can be in one of many states, and its behaviour depends on the state it is in. In our example, the microwave object can be in one of three possible states: Cooking, Door Open, and Door Closed.
2. We create one class per state. We may choose to put their common functionality in an abstract superclass or make all of these states implement a common interface, so that they all conform to some common type.
3. One instance of each state class is created. In the case of the microwave oven, the three classes corresponding to the three states are all singletons. This way, unnecessary object creation and deletion are avoided.

4. There is a context that orchestrates the whole show. This object remembers the current state and any shared data.
5. Exactly one state is active at any given time. The context delegates the input event to the state that is currently active and therefore only the active state responds to events.
6. When an event that requires a change of state occurs, we determine the next state, which then becomes active. For example, this transfer of control occurs for the microwave application by having each state determine the next state and then calling the `changeCurrentState` method of the context.
   The mechanism for deciding the next state can be done in one of two ways.

   (a) One approach would be to have a centralised controller that uses the matrix (see Sect. 10.5.1) to decide what the next state is. In this technique, after responding to an event, the state can return the input event to the controller, which can use the current state and the input event to determine the next state.
   (b) The second approach is to have the current state determine the next state. We used this approach in our Microwave example.

The advantages of using the pattern are:

1. There is no longer a need to switch on the state in order to decide what action needs to be taken. Instead, we polymorphically choose a method to be executed.
2. New states can be added and old states reused without changing the implementation. For example, in the microwave example, we can resume cooking after an interruption by simply having a new version of the class `CookingState`. (The reader is encouraged to make this modification.)
3. The code is more cohesive. Each state contains code relevant to it and nothing else. Only events that are of interest in this state are processed.

10.10.3 Consequences of Observer

The simplicity of the observer pattern belies the power it conceals. In essence, we have allowed an arbitrary object to be registered as a listener, and the observable invokes a method (viz. `update`) provided by the observer. Likewise, an object can become a listener to an arbitrary number of classes. As one should expect, such power brings along a lot of caveats and consequences.

For a start, we have the problem of memory leaks. In a system that provides automatic garbage collection, objects for which no references are maintained can be cleaned up during garbage collection. If an observable stores a reference to an object, it is tricky to decide when the object is no longer needed and some explicit mechanism may be needed to signal the end of *an object's* lifetime. Next we have the problem of the order in which observers are notified. The pattern itself does not specify any order and if any temporal ordering is desired, explicit mechanisms such as introduction of intermediaries may be needed [4].

Since any arbitrary object can become a listener, we may end up in situations where an update method invoked by the observable has unsafe code, say for instance, an unhandled exception or a delay. The standard approach to avoid this is for the observable to have every observer on a separate thread. This solution in turn leads to other caveats for programmers, such as not registering listeners from within constructors and not adding new listeners when existing ones are being notified [5].

A class that listens to several observables can end up with an `update` method that is quite complex. The order in which an observer deals with notifications from observables can change the result of the computation. Two such problems, viz., *cyclic dependencies* and *update causality* are discussed in [6].

Computation involving threads has its own share of pitfalls, and these have to be understood in the context of the observer pattern. Several questions arise, such as, *How do you handle simultaneous notifications on multiple threads? What about modifying the listener list from one thread while notifications are in progress on another?* and *What happens when the notification is sent from one thread to an object that is being used by a second thread?* These and other issues are discussed in [7].

10.10.4 Recognising and Processing External Events

The entire process for receiving and processing input involves the following steps: (i) *providing a mechanism for input on the UI;* (ii) *listening to user actions on the input mechanism;* (iii) *generating appropriate internal events;* (iv) *processing the events.*

In our implementation, steps (i) through (iii) are performed in the UI and (iv) in the back-end. It is tempting to carry out (ii) through (iv) in the back-end, since it appears to make the process more efficient. However, from the point of view of reuse, that approach makes for a poor system and efficiency issues can be handled in other ways. Generally speaking, the UI is responsible for the 'look and feel' and the back-end handles the processing. Reuse is most benefited if the back-end is 'UI-agnostic', and that would be impossible if step (ii) is to be done in the back-end. A UI may provide a user with multiple mechanisms for the same operation (using a menu, a key sequence, etc.) and the back-end should be able to handle all these uniformly. It is therefore desirable that steps (i) to (iii) be completed in the UI. The secondary question then arises as to which object in the UI should implement `actionListener`. This is addressed in one of the exercises.

Next we deal with the issue of communicating the event to the back-end. At first glance, the observer pattern seems suitable for this, but a closer examination tells us that this may lead to a situation where the observer must use a conditional to distinguish between several observables. It is therefore preferable to use one of other mechanisms discussed in the chapter.

10.10.5 Handling the Events

We have discussed three mechanisms for dealing with events in this chapter. Creating an enum is the simplest, but does not allow us pass on any information along with the event and requires the use of conditionals. The standard event handling mechanism provided by Java requires that we have an event source that can register listeners that implement a custom interface and notify them when the event occurs. This requires the listener object to take full responsibility for ensuring that the connection is made. A third approach is to use a form of double dispatch where the source is aware of a switchboard that can connect the event to the listener. This approach can be generalised to other situations by having the event classes extend EventObject and the listener interfaces extend EventListener. The trade-off here is that we have an additional method call, but the listener does not have to do any extra housekeeping.

Events can be classified as **low-level** events, which represent window-system occurrences or low-level input, and **semantic** events which include all other events. A button click is a semantic event which is defined to occur when the mouse is pressed and released over the button's display. We could therefore achieve the same functionality by tracking the mouse movement and mouse clicks, which are low-level events. In general, it is preferable to listen for semantic events since there may be alternative mechanisms (such as key sequences) that can activate a button.

In addition to the features presented in the chapter, Java provides some other features for custom events. Notable among these is the facility for directly manipulating the system event queue. This can be useful in situations where events have to be added, removed, or bypassed, and also in situations where update of graphical components is involved. Although it is not particularly useful for the kind of systems we have presented here, we shall go through the basic steps of this process using our microwave as an example.

To be placed in the queue, the event must extent AWTEvent instead of Event Object as we did earlier. To define a subclass of AWTEvent, we need to give an unused *event ID number* to the superclass. These details are shown for the CookRequestEvent below. (The choice of 1111 is arbitrary.)

```
class CookRequestEvent extends AWTEvent {
  public CookRequestEvent(CookRequestManager manager) {
    super(manager, COOK_REQUEST_EVENT);
  }
  public static final int COOK_REQUEST_EVENT =
                     AWTEvent.RESERVED_ID_MAX + 1111;
}
```

Next, we need a way to actually post the event on the event queue. This is done in the actionPerformed method. Note that the source is cited as the CookRequestManager instance. This is because the system automatically calls the processEvent method of the source to dispatch the events, unlike the earlier case where processEvent was explicitly called from actionPerformed.

```
public void actionPerformed(ActionEvent event) {
  EventQueue queue = Toolkit.getDefaultToolkit().getSystemEventQueue();
  if (event.getSource().equals(cookButton)) {
    queue.postEvent(new CookRequestEvent
                      (CookRequestManager.instance()));
  }
  // code to process other events
}
```

Finally, we have the code for dispatching the events. The method `processEvent` must ensure that it has the right kind of event before it notifies the listeners.

```
public class CookRequestManager extends JComponent {
  // other fields and attributes
  public void processEvent(AWTEvent event) {
    if (event instanceof CookRequestEvent) {
      CookRequestEvent cookRequestEvent = (CookRequestEvent) event;
      EventListener[] listeners
            = listenerList.getListeners(CookRequestListener.class);
      for (int index = 0; index < listeners.length; index++) {
        ((CookRequestListener)listeners[index]).cookingRequested
                                        (cookRequestEvent);
      }
    } else {
      super.processEvent(event);
    }
  }
}
```

Projects

1. **Creating a controller for a digital camera** A digital camera has several possible modes of operation. Each mode has its own interface, and the user can switch between modes. One mode, for instance, is the *Viewing* mode, in which stored pictures can be viewed, deleted, etc. In the *Setting* mode other parameters such as the kind of pictures to be taken, can be modified.

   - Study models of digital cameras on the market and define a set of requirements for the UI.
   - Design a software controller that meets these specifications.

   Note that in such a system, both the view and the behaviour will change when the state changes. Also, in a typical camera, the control buttons remain the same regardless of the mode of operation, but the effect of activating them changes. How will you model such functionality?

2. **A user interface for a warehouse management system** In Chap. 6, a case-study for a warehouse database was presented. Create a complete GUI for such a system.

   - The UI has an initial login panel that allows the user to log in. The user could be a *client*, a *salesclerk* or a *manager*. Each type of user has a different set of access privileges. This will involve having some kind of password protection and can be accomplished using a separate subsystem that tracks the registered users and their passwords. The GUI will directly communicate with this system.

- When a user logs in, the appropriate menu is revealed. A salesclerk, for instance, performs operations like processing purchase orders from clients, receiving shipments, etc. However, a salesclerk can become a particular client and do those operations too. The salesclerk menu should provide an option like 'become a client'. Likewise, a manager can become a salesclerk.
- The GUI should have a 'back' button to go back to a previous state.
- Each menu panel should have a 'logout' option.

When a salesclerk becomes a client, this will require that we go through a panel that collects the particular client's ID. When the logout option is chosen, the state should go back to the salesclerk menu, whereas if the user was a client, the user will be logged out. Can this state be shared by the client and the salesclerk? How will you accomplish this? If the final choice of next state depends on stored information, where should this information be stored and in which class should the next state be computed? How is this impacted by the manner in which we are implementing the state pattern?

3. Implement a simple CD player. The player has the following buttons:

   (a) Insert/Eject: If a CD is inside the player, pressing this button causes the CD to be stopped and ejected. Otherwise, a CD is inserted and played.
   (b) Play: causes the player to resume playing a CD (if a CD is inside) from the position it was paused or from the beginning. If there is no CD, pressing this button has no effect.
   (c) Stop: causes the player to pause playing/fast-forwarding/rewinding, so pressing the Play button later causes the player to resume from this position. If this button is pressed when the player is paused, the CD is stopped, so a further push of the Play button plays the CD from the start. If there is no CD, pressing this button has no effect.
   (d) Fast Forward: If a CD is inside, the player plays the CD forward at double speed. Pressing this button while fast forwarding causes the player to resume playing again. If there is no CD, pressing this button has no effect.
   (e) Rewind: If a CD is inside, the player plays the CD backward at double speed. Pressing this button while rewinding causes the player to resume playing again. If there is no CD, pressing this button has no effect.

   All CDs play for exactly one hour. When the player reaches the end of the CD while playing or fast-forwarding, it stops (so it reverts to the start). The user interface must be a GUI with the above five buttons and two displays: one showing the number of minutes and seconds elapsed if playing a CD and the other showing the state: like 'playing', 'paused', etc.

4. A room has the following options for climate-control: blow a fan, use an air-conditioner, employ a heater, or do nothing. A temperature regulator for the room operates can be set in one of four different modes to choose the desired option. (Imagine a slider control that can be set to one of the four positions.)

(a) Do nothing: None of the three devices (fan, air-conditioner, and heater) is active.
(b) Fan: The fan blows for ten minutes and then stays inactive for another ten minutes; the cycle repeats.
(c) Air-conditioner: The air-conditioner immediately turns on. If the room temperature is too high, it operates the air-conditioner until the room temperature hits the set temperature.
(d) Heater: The heater immediately turns on. If the room is too cold, it operates the heater until the room temperature hits the set temperature.

Apart from the four manual controls, assume that the regulator gets three other signals: room is too hot, room is too cold, and the temperature is just right.

Develop the state transition table and diagram. Implement the system.

10.11 Exercises

1. Modify the microwave implementation so that each button is an `actionListener` and performs the necessary actions when the button is clicked. How does this impact the overall complexity of the system?
2. Modify the implementation of the microwave controller so that individual states register with event sources. What changes will have to be made to the state classes? How will the states access the object with which they have to register/de-register themselves?
3. Modify the UI for the microwave so that the buttons OpenDoor and CloseDoor are replaced by a single `JSlider`. Discuss the simplicity/difficulty of effecting such a change for all the event processing options discussed in the chapter.
4. In the implementation of the state pattern for the microwave, the context keeps track of the current state, but the next state is decided by the current state. Suggest at least two other implementations of the state pattern for the microwave. Compare and contrast all three implementations in the context of performance, simplicity of design and ease of reuse.
5. Draw sequence diagrams to document the flow of control for the microwave system for each of the following cases:

   (a) When the Java event framework is used.
   (b) When the context is used as a switchboard.

6. Modify the design of the microwave system to add each of the following requirements:

   (a) An 'extend cooking' button is added to the display; if this button is pressed when cooking is in progress, 30 s are added to the cooking time.
   (b) The system has a 'clear' button that sets the remaining cooking time to zero. The system also stores the remaining time if the cooking is interrupted by

the opening of the door. When the system enters the cooking state again, this stored value is used as the cooking time; however, if the clear button has been pressed in the meantime, it runs for 60 s.

(c) The system displays an 'error' message if an inappropriate action is performed. For instance, if the cook button is pressed when the door is open, the message 'Please close the door' is displayed.

7. In the GUI implementation of the library system, draw the state transition diagram for renewing books and write the corresponding code.

8. Rewrite the code for the `connectToListener` method using the alternative approaches discussed in the text.

References

1. E. Gamma, R. Helm, R. Johnson, J. Vlissides, *Design Patterns: Elements of Reusable Object-Oriented Software* (Addison-Wesley, Boston, 1994)
2. T. Cargill, *C++ Programming Style* (Addison-Wesley Professional, Reading, 1992)
3. B. Meyer, *Object-Oriented Software Construction* (Prentice Hall, Upper Saddle River, 1997)
4. Unknown, The observer pattern. Core Java technologies. Technical tips. http://java.sun.com/developer/JDCTechTips/, January 2006
5. B. Goetz, Java theory and practice: be a good (event) listener. guidelines for writing and supporting event listeners. http://www.ibm.com/developerworks/, July 2005
6. D. Gruntz, Java design: on the observer pattern. Technical report, University of Applied Sciences, Aargau (2004)
7. A. Holub, Programming java threads in the real world, part 6: the observer pattern and mysteries of the awteventmulticaster. http://www.javaworld.com/javaworld/jw-03-1999/jw-03-toolbox.html, March 1999

Chapter 11
Interactive Systems and the MVC Architecture

11.1 Introduction

So far we have seen examples and case-studies involving relatively simple software systems. This simplicity enabled us to use a fairly general step-by-step approach, viz., specify the requirements, model the behaviour, find the classes, assign responsibilities, capture class interactions, and so on. In larger systems, such an approach may not lead to an efficient design and it would be wise to rely on the experience of software designers who have worked on the problem and devised strategies to tackle the problem. This is somewhat akin to planning our strategy for a game of chess. A chess game has three stages—an opening, a middle game and an endgame. While we are opening, the field is undisturbed and there are an immense number of possibilities; toward the end there are few pieces and fewer options. If we are in an endgame situation, we can solve the problem using a fairly direct approach using first principles; to decide how to open is a much more complicated operation and requires knowledge of 'standard openings'. These standard openings have been developed and have evolved along with the game, and provide a framework for the player. Likewise, when we have a complex problem, we need a framework or structure within which to operate. For the problem of creating software systems, such a structure is provided by choosing a **software architecture**.

In this chapter, we start by describing a well-known software architecture (sometimes referred to as an **architectural pattern**) called the **Model–View–Controller** or **MVC** pattern. Next we design a small interactive system using such an architecture, look at some problems that arise in this context and explore solutions for these problems using design patterns. Finally, we discuss pattern-based solutions in software development and some other frequently employed architectural patterns.

© Universities Press (India) Private Ltd. 2015
B. Dathan and S. Ramnath, *Object-Oriented Analysis, Design and Implementation*,
Undergraduate Topics in Computer Science, DOI 10.1007/978-3-319-24280-4_11

11.2 The MVC Architectural Pattern

The model view controller is a relatively old pattern that was originally introduced in the Smalltalk programming language. As one might suspect, the pattern divides the application into three subsystems: model, view, and controller. The architecture is shown in Fig. 11.1. The pattern separates the application object or the data, which is termed the Model, from the manner in which it is rendered to the end-user (View) and from the way in which the end-user manipulates it (Controller). In contrast to a system where all of these three functionalities are lumped together (resulting in a low degree of cohesion), the MVC pattern helps produce highly cohesive modules with a low degree of coupling. This facilitates greater flexibility and reuse. MVC also provides a powerful way to organise systems that support multiple presentations of the same information.

  The model, which is a relatively passive object, stores the data. Any object can play the role of model. The view renders the model into a specified format, typically something that is suitable for interaction with the end user. For instance, if the model stores information about bank accounts, a certain view may display only the number of accounts and the total of the account balances. The controller captures user input and when necessary, issues method calls on the model to modify the stored data. When the model changes, the view responds by appropriately modifying the display.

  In a typical application, the model changes only when user input causes the controller to inform the model of the changes. The view must be notified when the model changes. Instance variables in the controller refer to the model and the view. Moreover, the view must communicate with the model, so it has an instance variable that points to the model object. Both the controller and the view communicate with the user through the UI. This means that some components of the UI are used by the controller to receive input; others are used by the view to appropriately display the model and some can serve both purposes (e.g., a panel can display a figure and also accept points as input through mouseclicks). It is important to distinguish the UI from the rest of the system: beginners often mistake the UI for the view. This is easy error to make for two reasons. In most systems, due to the nature of the desired look and feel and the technologies available, there is a single window in which the entire

Fig. 11.1 The model–view–controller architecture

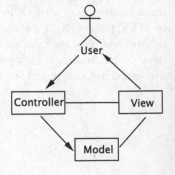

application is housed. This means ,that there has to be a common subsystem that provides the functionality needed both for the view and the user interface. The other source of potential confusion is that the UI presents to the user an image of how the system looks, and this can be mistakenly construed as the view. This interface must include components that are in fact part of the controller (e.g., buttons for giving commands). When we talk of MVC in the abstract sense, we are dealing with the architecture of the system that lies behind the UI; both the view and the controller are subsystems at the same level of abstraction that employ components of the UI to accomplish their tasks. From a practical standpoint, however, we have a situation where the view and the UI are contained in a common subsystem. *For the purpose of designing our system, we shall refer to this common subsystem as the view.* The view subsystem is therefore responsible for all the look and feel issues, whether they arise from a human–computer interaction perspective (e.g., kinds of buttons being used) or from issues relating to how we render the model. Figure 11.2 shows how we might present the MVC architecture while accounting for these practical considerations.

User-generated events may cause a controller to change the model, or view, or both. For example, suppose that the model stored the text that is being edited by the end-user. When the user deletes or adds text, the controller captures the changes and notifies the model. The view, which observes the model, then refreshes its display, with the result that the end-user sees the changes he/she made to the data. In this case, user-input caused a change to both the model and the view.

On the other hand, consider a user scrolling the data. Since no changes are made to the data itself, the model does not change and need not be notified. But the view now needs to display previously-hidden data, which makes it necessary for the view to contact the model and retrieve information.

More than one view–controller pair may be associated with a model. Whenever user input causes one of the controllers to notify changes to the model, all associated views are automatically updated.

It could also be the case that the model is changed not via one of the controllers, but through some other mechanism. In this case, the model must notify all associated views of the changes.

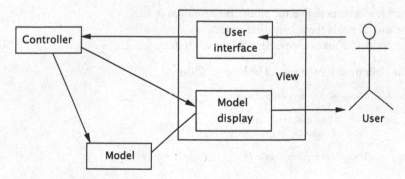

Fig. 11.2 An alternate view of the the MVC architecture

The view–model relationship is that of a subject–observer. The model, as the subject, maintains references to all of the views that are interested in observing it. Whenever an action that changes the model occurs, the model automatically notifies all of these views. The views then refresh their displays. *The guiding principle here is that each view is a faithful rendering of the model.*

11.2.1 Examples

Suppose that in the library system we have a GUI screen using which users can place holds on books. Another GUI screen allows a library staff member to add copies of books. Suppose that a user views the number of copies, number of holds on a book and is about to place a hold on the book. At the same time, a library staff member views the book record and adds a copy. Information from the same model (book) is now displayed in different formats in the two screens.

A second example is that of a mail sever. A user logs into the server and looks at the messages in the mailbox. In a second window, the user logs in again to the same mail server and composes a message. The two screens form two separate views of the same model.

Suppose that we have a graph-plot of pairs of (x, y) values. The collection of data points constitutes the model. The graph-viewing software provides the user with several output formats—bar graphs, line graphs, pie charts, etc. When the user changes formats, the view changes without any change to the model.

11.2.2 Implementation

As with any software architecture, the designer needs to have a clear idea about how the responsibilities are to be shared between the subsystems. This task can be simplified if the role of each subsystem is clearly defined.

- The view is responsible for all the presentation issues.
- The model holds the application object.
- The controller takes care of the response strategy.

The definition for the model will be as follows:

```
public class Model extends Observable {
  // code
  public void changeData() {
    // code to update data
    setChanged();
    notifyObservers(changeInfo);
  }
}
```

Each of the views is an `Observer` and implements the `update` method.

```
public class View implements Observer {
  // code
  public void update(Observable model, Object data) {
    // refresh view using data
  }
}
```

If a view is no longer interested in the model, it can be deleted from the list of observers.

Since the controllers react to user input, they may send messages directly to the views asking them to refresh their displays.

For each feature, we start with a detailed list of specifications, stated clearly enough so that they can be classified as belonging to one of the three categories. In general, there is always an initiation step for each operation; the manner in which the user is to be shown the feature and the manner in which it is invoked are part of the presentation. What the system should do when the request is made is a part of the response strategy, and the controller manages this part of the show. This strategy may involve interacting with the user in tandem with making changes to the application object. What is needed from the user is part of the response strategy, but how the system communicates with the user is a presentation issue. Changes to the application object are made by invoking the methods of model. As the application object is modified, the display needs to be modified to reflect the changes. Modifying the display is again a matter for presentation.

Clearly, there is a lot of entanglement here between the three parts, and it is a challenge to keep everything separate. The controller invokes the methods provided by the model so that the separation is relatively easy to implement. There can be confusion around drawing a line between the responsibilities of the view and the controller for reasons explained earlier. Likewise, keeping the business logic away from the display (or model–view separation) can be tricky in situations where there is a close relationship between the stored data and the methods for rendering it. As we design and implement a case-study in the following pages, we make decisions as various situations arise. Although the philosophy behind this architecture is easily stated, the details are best explained by example.

This means that it is not always possible to have a clean division of the components such that some components are designated for data input and the rest are for data display. Therefore, it is quite difficult to decide which components belong to the controller and which ones are part of the view. Surely, the view has to display data and, in general, some of its components end up as mechanisms for user input.

The approach we use to resolve this is to create a UI with functionality to serve the purpose of both the view and the controller. Display components will be available to the view, which invokes the appropriate display commands. Components which capture events generated by user inputs are configured to pass on the message to the appropriate subsystem; note that events for some operations (like scrolling) are handled by the view, whereas others (like add, delete) are sent to the controller.

11.2.3 Benefits of the MVC Pattern

1. Cohesive modules: Instead of putting unrelated code (display and data) in the same module, we separate the functionality so that each module is cohesive.
2. Flexibility: The model is unaware of the exact nature of the view or controller it is working with. It is simply an observable. This adds flexibility.
3. Low coupling: Modularity of the design improves the chances that components can be swapped in and out as the user or programmer desires. This also promotes parallel development, easier debugging, and maintenance.
4. Adaptable modules: Components can be changed with less interference to the rest of the system.
5. Distributed systems: Since the modules are separated, it is possible that the three subsystems are geographically separated.

11.3 Analysing a Simple Drawing Program

We now apply the MVC architectural pattern to the process of designing a simple program that allows us to create and label figures. The purpose behind this exercise is twofold:

- *To demonstrate how to design with an architecture in mind* Designing with an architecture in mind requires that we start with a high-level decomposition of responsibilities across the subsystems. The subsystems are specified by the architecture. The designer gets to decide which classes to create for each subsystem, but the the responsibilities associated with these classes must be consistent with the purpose of the subsystem.
- *To understand how the MVC architecture is employed* We shall follow the architecture somewhat *strictly*, i.e., we will try to have three clearly delineated subsystems for Model, View, and Controller. Later on, we will explore and discuss variations on this theme.

As always, our design begins with the process of collecting requirements.

11.3.1 Specifying the Requirements

Our initial wish-list calls for software that can do the following.

1. Draw lines and circles.
2. Place labels at various points on the figure; the labels are strings. A separate command allows the user to select the font and font size.
3. Save the completed figure to a file. We can open a file containing a figure and edit it.
4. Backtrack our drawing process by undoing recent operations.

Compared to the kinds of drawing programs we have on the market, this looks too trivial! Nonetheless, it is sufficient to show how the responsibilities can be divided so that the MVC pattern can be applied. What we shall also see, later on, is how new features can be added without disrupting the existing classes.

In order to attain this functionality, the software will interact with the user. We need to specify exactly how this interaction will take place. It should, of course, be user-friendly, fast, etc., but as in earlier examples, these non-functional requirements will not be the focus of our attention. Without more ado, let us adopt the following 'look and feel:'

- The software will have a simple frame with a display panel on which the figure will be displayed, and a command panel containing the buttons. There will be buttons for each operation, which are labeled like Draw Line, Draw Circle, Add Label, etc. The system will listen to mouse-clicks which will be employed by the user to specify points on the display panel.
- The display panel will have a cross-hair cursor for specifying points and a_ (underscore) for showing the character insertion point for labels. The default cursor will be an arrow.
- The cursor changes when an operation is selected from the command menu. When an operation is completed, the cursor goes back to the default state.
- To draw a line, the user will specify the end points of the line with mouse-clicks. To draw a circle, the user will specify two diametrically opposite points on the perimeter. For convenient reference, the center of each circle will be marked with a black square. To create a label, the starting point will be specified by a mouse-click.

11.3.2 Defining the Use Cases

We can now write the detailed use cases for each operation. The first one, for drawing a line, is shown in Table 11.1.

Table 11.1 Use-case table for Drawing a line

Actions performed by the actor	Responses from the system
1. The user clicks on the Draw Line button in the command panel	
	2. The system changes the cursor to a cross-hair
3. The user clicks first on one end point and then on the other end point of the line to be drawn	
	4. The system adds a line segment with the two specified end points to the figure being created. The cursor changes to the default

Table 11.2 Use-case table for Adding a Label

Actions performed by the actor	Responses from the system
1. The user clicks on the Add Label button in the command panel	
	2. The system changes the cursor to a cross-hair cursor
3. The user clicks at the left end point of the intended label	
	4. The system places a_ at the clicked location
	5. The system waits for the user response
5. The user types a character or clicks the mouse at another location	
	6. If the character is not a carriage return the system displays the typed character followed by a_, and the user continues with Step 5; in case of a mouse-click, it goes to Step 4; otherwise it goes to the default state

The use case for drawing a circle can be done analogously.

To give the system better usability, we allow for multiple labels to be added with the same command. To start the process of adding labels, the user clicks on the command button. This is followed by a mouse-click on the drawing panel, following which the user types in the desired label. After typing in a label, a user can either click on another point to create another label, or type a carriage return, which returns the system to the default state. These details are spelled out in the use case in Table 11.2.

The system will ignore almost all non-printable characters. The exceptions are the Enter (terminate the operation) and Backspace (delete the most-recently entered character) keys. A label may contain zero or more characters.

We also have use cases for operations that do not change the displayed object. An example of this would be when the user changes the font, shown in Table 11.3.

The requirements call for the ability to save the drawing and open and edit the saved drawings. The use cases for saving, closing and opening files are left as exercises. In order to allow for editing we need at least the following two basic operations: *selection* and *deletion*. The use case Select an Item is detailed in Table 11.4.

There are some details here that need to be fleshed out in later stages. We have not specified how the system would indicate the change to the *selection mode*. We could do this by changing the cursor or altering the display in some other way. This use case requires that the display should indicate which items have been selected. This can be done by drawing these items in a different colour.

It is possible that the user's click does not fall on any item; in that case, the system simply ignores the mouseclick and returns to the default mode.

Table 11.3 Use-case table for Change Font

Actions performed by the actor	Responses from the system
1. The user clicks on the Change Font button in the command panel	
	2. The system displays a list of all the fonts available
3. The user clicks on the desired font	
	4. The system changes to the specified font and displays a message to that effect

Table 11.4 Use-case table for Select an Item

Actions performed by the actor	Responses from the system
1. The user clicks on the Select button in the command panel	
	2. The system changes the display to the *selection mode*
3. The user clicks the mouse on the drawing	
	4. If the click falls on an item, the system adds the item to its collection of selected items and updates the display to reflect the addition. The system returns the display to the default mode

Deletion will be done by having a button in the GUI that the user can click; whenever this button is clicked, all the selected items are deleted. The use case for this is left as an exercise.

The reader would note that this system is restrictive in many ways. This has been done for simplicity and will not in any way detract from the design experience. In fact, it will highlight the extendability of the design when we extend the functionality with very little disturbance to the existing code.

11.4 Designing the System

The process of designing this system is somewhat different from our earlier case studies owing to the fact that we have selected an architecture. Our architecture specifies three principal subsystems, viz., the Model, the View and the Controller. We have a broad idea of what roles each of these play, and our first step is to define these roles in the context of our problem. As we do this, we look at the individual use cases and decide how the responsibilities are divided across the three subsystems. Once this is taken care of, we look into the details of designing each of the subsystems.

11.4.1 Defining the Model

Our next step is to define what kind of an object we are creating. This is relatively simple for our problem; we keep a collection of line, circle, and label objects. Each line is represented by the end points, and each circle is represented by the X-coordinates of the leftmost and rightmost points and the Y-coordinates of the top and bottom points on the perimeter (see Fig. 11.3).

For a label, the model stores the coordinate's starting position, the text, and the style and size of the characters in the string. The collection is accessed by the view when the figure is to be rendered on the screen. The model also provides mechanisms to access and modify its collection objects. These would be methods like `addItem(Item)`, `getItems()`, etc.

11.4.2 Defining the Controller

The controller is the subsystem that orchestrates the whole show and the definition of its role is thus critical. When the user attempts to execute an operation, the input is received by the view. The view then communicates this to the controller. This communication can be effected by invoking the public methods of the controller. Let us examine in detail the various implementation steps for the processes described in the use cases.

Drawing a Line

1. The user starts by clicking the Draw line button, and in response, the system changes the cursor. Clearly, changing the cursor should be a responsibility of the view, since that is where we define the look and feel. This would imply that the view system (or some part thereof) listen to the button click. The click indicates that the user has initiated an operation that would change the model. Since such operations have to be orchestrated through the controller, it is appropriate that the

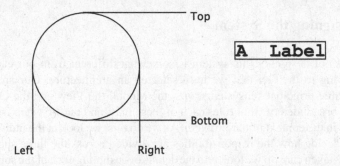

Fig. 11.3 Representing a circle and a label

controller be informed. The controller creates a line object (with both endpoints unspecified).

2. The user clicks on the display panel to indicate the first end point of the line. We now need to designate a listener for the mouse clicks. This listener will extract the coordinates from the event and take the necessary action. Both the view and the controller are aware of the fact that a line drawing operation has been initiated. The question then is, which of these subsystems should be responding to the mouse-click? Having the controller listen directly to the mouse-clicks seems to be more efficient, since that will reduce the number of method invocations. However there are several reasons why this is not a good choice. First, the methods/interfaces (e.g., `MouseListener` in Java) to be implemented depend on the manner in which the view is being implemented. This means that the *controller is not independent of the view*, thus hurting reuse. A second reason is that we can have multiple ways to input the points. For instance, when trying to draw a precise figure, a user may prefer to specify the points as coordinates through some kind of dialog, instead of clicking the mouse. *These accommodations are part of the look and feel, and do not belong in the controller.* Finally, we have the problem of *reading and interpreting the input.* In our particular situation, this manifests itself as the process of mapping device coordinates to the image coordinates. Most of the graphical display tools available nowadays use a coordinate system where the origin corresponds to the top-left corner of the display rectangle, with X coordinates increasing from left to right and Y coordinates increasing from top to bottom (also known as *device coordinates*). Programs that generate and use graphics often prefer the standard Cartesian coordinate system. Thus we might have a situation where the model is being created with Cartesian coordinates, whereas mouse clicks and graphical output must use device coordinates and points have to be mapped from one system to the other. The conversion of Cartesian coordinates to device coordinates is best done in the view since it knows and is responsible for the *nature and format of the output* (points specified as device coordinates). The reverse operation of converting device coordinates of input points to Cartesian coordinates must also, therefore, be done by the view, which means that the view must capture the input. Therefore, although a performance penalty is incurred, we favour the implementation where the mouse-click is listened to in the view. The view then communicates these coordinates to the controller, after performing any transformation or mapping that may be needed. At this point we need to decide how the system would behave during the period between the clicks. For instance, should the point for the first click be highlighted in any way? Since the use case does not specify anything, we can ignore this issue for the time being, i.e., no change happens until both end points are clicked.

3. The user clicks on the second point. Once again, the view listens to the click and communicates this to the controller. On receiving these coordinates, the controller recognises that the line drawing is complete and updates the line object.

4. Finally, the model notifies the view that it has changed. The view then redraws the display panel to show the modified figure.

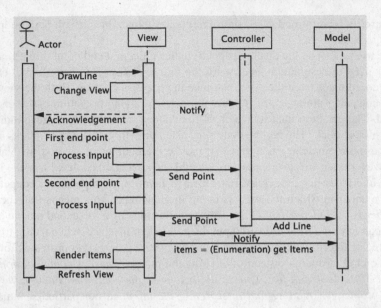

Fig. 11.4 Sequence of operations for drawing a line

This sequence of operations across the three subsystems can be captured by a high-level sequence diagram as shown in Fig. 11.4. Note that unlike the sequence diagrams in earlier chapters, this does not spell out all the classes involved or the names of the methods invoked.

Drawing a Circle

The actions for drawing a circle are similar. However, we now have some additional processing to be done, i.e., the given points on the diameter must be converted to the the four integer values, as explained in Fig. 11.3. Note that this requires a mapping to convert the input to the form required by the model. This can be performed in the controller, since these representations are equivalent.

Adding a Label

This operation is somewhat different due to the fact that the amount of data is not fixed. The steps are as follows:

1. The user starts by clicking the Add Label button. In response, the system changes the mouse-cursor, which, as before is the responsibility of the view.
2. The user clicks the mouse, and the system acknowledges the receipt of the mouse click by placing a_ at the location. This would result in changing what the drawing looks like. As decided earlier, we will maintain the property that the view is a faithful rendering of the model. The view therefore notifies the controller that the operation has been initiated, and the controller modifies the model. One issue

that we have to resolve is that of assigning the appropriate size and style to the characters in the label. To implement this, we have to address the following:

- *Which subsystem 'remembers' the current style and size?* Since the user cannot be expected to specify the size and style with each character, these have to be stored somewhere. For our situation, we shall assume that these are stored in the view and passed on to the controller when the label construction operation is initiated.
- *When do the changes to size and style take effect?* To simplify our system, we assume that these will take effect for the next label that is created. What this means is that the style and size have to be uniform for any given label, and if a change is made to any of these while we are in the process of creating a label, these changes will not take immediate effect.

3. The user types in a character. Once again, the view listens to and gets the input from the keyboard, which is communicated to the controller. Once again the controller changes the model, which notifies the view.
4. The user clicks the mouse or enters a carriage-return. This is appropriately interpreted by the view. In both cases, the view informs the controller that the addition of the label is complete. In case of a mouse click, the controller is also notified that a new operation for adding a label has been initiated.

This sequence of steps is explained in Fig. 11.5. *Note that the view interprets the keystrokes: as per our specifications ordinary text is passed on directly to the controller, control characters are ignored, carriage-return is translated into a command, etc. All this is part of the way in which the system interacts with the user, and therefore belongs to the view.*

Dealing with the Environmental Variables

Most interactive systems need to remember the values of certain parameters to make the system user-friendly. For instance, a word-processing system remembers the size and font of the characters so that the user does not have to specify these with every operation. We refer to these parameters as **environmental** variables. In our example, for creating a label, we choose to store these in the view, and this has some consequences for the behaviour of the system.

Consider a document creation system that has Times-Roman as the default font. When the system starts up, the font parameter stores the value 'Times-Roman'. If the user selects a different font, say Helvetica, then this parameter is changed and any following text input is displayed in Helvetica. The font parameter could be stored in the model or in the view. If we store this in the model, then the font information does not have to be sent by the view to the controller, along with the text. In addition, this would result in storing the font parameter when the figure is saved to a file.

Now consider what happens when the file is retrieved at some later time. The font parameter would be set to Helvetica, and this font would apply to all the text input. On the other hand, if the font type is stored in the view, storing and retrieving would set the font back to Times-Roman (the default). Clearly, this is a choice that has to be made when the behaviour of the system is being decided.

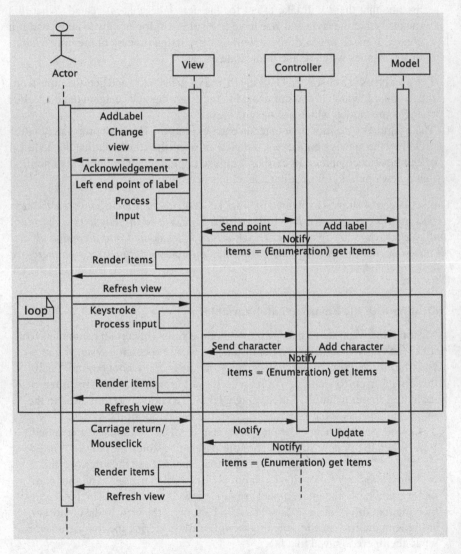

Fig. 11.5 Sequence of operations for adding a label

Sharing Responsibilities Between the View and the Controller

When we employ the MVC architecture, there is often a gray area between the responsibilities of the controller and those of the view, particularly for the kind of software discussed in this case-study. Issues that fall in this area can be confusing to the beginner, particularly since widely varying opinions have been expressed. Some of these issues have come up in this section and need clarification.

Accepting user input In our approach above, all user input is received by the view. Indeed, the view is the only mechanism through which the user can interact and the view parses all the input that comes in. The idea here is that the system as a whole be 'UI agnostic', i.e., the design of the system does not depend on how the UI has been implemented.

Consider the situation where the user gives a command. This is done by a button click. It is tempting to let the controller, or one of its components, listen to the click and take action. However, this creates problems if the UI is changed so that the same commands can instead be given by keystrokes. In such a situation, a change in the UI, or even in the look and feel, can force changes in the controller. In addition, there could be situations where the same operation can be initiated in multiple ways. If the controller has to accommodate all of these, it adds to the complexity of the controller and causes tight coupling.

Once an operation has been initiated, we have the issue of accepting the data. Once again, while some designers have argued that the data be received in the controller, this approach is fraught with problems. The data could be in one of several formats. For instance, a UI designer might want to accommodate for users to type in coordinate locations instead of clicking with the mouse. (This could be important for drawing precise geometric figures.) Having the controller deal with multiple formats is not desirable. A second, more serious issue is that when the data needs some 'correction' to adjust for the display. For instance, consider a situation where the figure is being drawn with *Cartesian coordinates* due to the nature of the application. The mouse-click specifies the value in coordinates with reference to the object that is being used for the display (in Java, this would be the `JPanel`, or a `JScrollPane`), which will have to be mapped to the Cartesian values. Doing this mapping in the controller would mean exposing the controller to all the details of the components used by the view. The important thing to keep in mind is that the view is providing the user with several input mechanisms, and therefore should be responsible for receiving and interpreting the data. *The task of accepting and standardising user input is therefore the responsibility of the view.*

Processing and Storing the input Once the standardised data is available, it is incorporated into the model. All data is received in conjunction with some operation, and hence the details of how the data is to be used to change the model are part of the operation. This activity is independent of the UI, implying that this would be the responsibility of the controller.

11.4.3 Selection and Deletion

The software allows us to delete lines, circles, or labels by selecting the item and then invoking the `delete` operation. These shall be treated as independent operations since selection can also serve other purposes. Also, we can invoke selection repeatedly so that multiple items can be selected at any given time.

When an item is selected, it is displayed in red, as opposed to black. The selection is done by clicking with the arrow (default) cursor. Lines are selected by clicking on one end point, circles are selected by clicking on the center, and labels are selected by clicking on the label.

The steps involved in implementing this are as follows:

1. The user gives the command through a button click. This is followed by a mouse click to specify the item. Both of these are detected in the view and communicated to the controller.
2. In order to decide what action the controller must take, we need to figure out how the system will keep track of the selected items. Since the view is responsible for how these will be displayed (in red, for instance) the view must be able to recognise these as selected when updating the display. Since the view gets the items from the model, it would seem appropriate that the model have a mechanism to flag the selected items. This can be done by having a tag field for each item, or simply by moving the selected items to a separate container. We shall use the latter.
3. The next step is to iterate through the (unselected) items in the model to find the item (if any) that contains the point. Since the model is to be used strictly as a repository for the data, the task of iterating through the items is done in the controller, which then invokes the methods of the model to mark the item as selected.
4. Model notifies view, which renders the unselected items in the default colour (black) and the selected items in red. View gets an enumeration of the two lists separately and uses the appropriate colour for each. Note that model only stores a separate list of the selected items. It is the view that decides how the two lists are to be rendered.

Deletion is a simpler operation. The button click is heard in the view and passed on to the controller, which simply requests the model to delete all selected items.

11.4.4 Saving and Retrieving the Drawing

The use cases for the processes of saving and retrieving are simply described: *the user requests a save/retrieve operation, the system asks for a file name which the user provides and the system completes the task.* This activity can be partitioned between our subsystems as follows:

1. The view receives the initial request from the user and then prompts the user to input a file name.
2. The view then invokes the appropriate method of the controller, passing the file name as a parameter.
3. The controller first takes care of any clean-up operation that may be required. For instance, if our specifications require that all items be unselected before the drawing is saved, or some default values of environment variables be restored, this must be done at the stage. The controller then invokes the appropriate method in the model, passing the file name as a parameter.
4. The model serializes the relevant objects to the specified file.

This completes the first step of distributing the responsibilities across the three subsystems. Note that unlike the earlier case studies, we did not look for classes and methods and try to create a class interaction diagram right away. This would be fairly typical when we are designing a larger software system with some advance notice about the kind of architecture being employed. As we progress through the details, we might also realise that our partitioning of responsibilities across the subsystems may have to shift a little due to other considerations. This is not unusual, since the architecture only gives us broad guidelines, and not a detailed design.

11.5 Design of the Subsystems

The next step of the process is to design the individual subsystems. In this stage, the classes and their responsibilities are identified and we get a more detailed picture of how the required functionality is to be achieved. Since the model should remain independent of the 'look-and-feel' of the system and should remain stable, it is appropriate that we design it first.

11.5.1 Design of the Model Subsystem

Consider the basic structure of the model and the items stored therein. From Sect. 11.3, we know that the model should have methods for supporting the following operations:

1. Adding an item
2. Removing an item
3. Marking an item as selected
4. Unselecting an item
5. Getting an enumeration of selected items
6. Getting an enumeration of unselected items
7. Deleting selected items
8. Saving the drawing
9. Retrieving the drawing

Based on the above list, it is straightforward to identify the methods. The class diagram is shown in Fig. 11.6. The class Item represents a shape such as line or label and enables uniform treatment of all shapes within a drawing.

Since the methods, getItems() and getSelectedItems() return an enumeration of a set of items, we need polymorphic containers in the model. The view uses these methods to get the objects from the model as an enumeration of the items

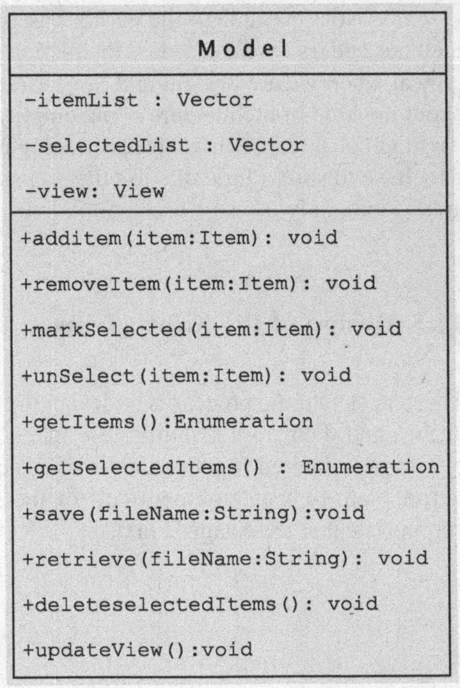

Fig. 11.6 Class diagram for model

Model
-itemList : Vector
-selectedList : Vector
-view: View
+additem(item:Item): void
+removeItem(item:Item): void
+markSelected(item:Item): void
+unSelect(item:Item): void
+getItems():Enumeration
+getSelectedItems() : Enumeration
+save(fileName:String):void
+retrieve(fileName:String): void
+deleteselectedItems(): void
+updateView():void

stored and draws each one on the display panel. The model must also keep track of the view, so it needs a field for that purpose.

The method `updateView` is used by the controller to alert the model that the display must be refreshed. It is also invoked by methods within the model whenever the model realises that its data has changed. This method invokes a method in the view to refresh the display.

11.5.2 Design of Item and Its Subclasses

Clearly, `Item` will have several subclasses, one for each shape. Each subclass will store attributes that are relevant to the corresponding shape.

Rendering the items A tricky issue regarding the design is how the items should be rendered. Rendering is the process by which the data stored in the model is displayed by the view. Regardless of how we implement this, the actual details of how the drawing is done are dependent on the following two parameters:

- *The technology and tools that are used in creating the UI* For instance, we are using the Java's Swing package, which means that our drawing panel is a `JPanel` and the drawing methods will have to be invoked on the associated `Graphics` object.
- *The item that is stored* If a line is stored by its equation, the code for drawing it would be very different from the line that is stored as two end points.

The technology and tools are known to the author of the view, whereas the structure of the item is known to the author of the items. Since the needed information is in two different classes, we need to decide which class will have the responsibility for implementing the rendering. We have the following options:

Option 1 Let us say that the view is responsible for rendering, i.e., there is code in the view that accesses the fields of each item and then draws them. Since the model is storing these items in a polymorphic container, the view would have to query the type of each item returned by the enumeration in order to choose the appropriate method(s).

Option 2 If the item were responsible, each item would have a `render` method that accesses the fields and draws the item. The problem with this is that the way an object is to be rendered often depends on the tools that we have at our disposal. For instance, consider the problem of rendering a circle: a circle is almost always drawn as a sequence of short line segments. If the only method given in the toolkit is that for drawing lines, the circle will have to be decomposed into straight lines. In addition to the set of tools, there are other specific features that the technology has. Using the Swing package in Java, for instance, implies that all the drawing is done by invoking the methods on the `Graphics` object associated with the drawing panel.

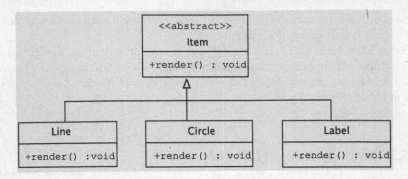

Fig. 11.7 The item class and its subclasses

At this point it appears that we are stuck between two bad choices! However, a closer look at the first option reveals a fairly serious problem: *we are querying each object in the collection to apply the right methods.* This is very much at odds with the object-oriented philosophy, i.e., *the methods should be packed with the data that is being queried.* This really means that the render method for each item should be stored in the item itself, which is in fact the approach of the second option. This simplifies our task somewhat, so we can focus on the task of fixing the shortcomings of the second option.

The structure of the abstract Item class and its subclasses are shown in Fig. 11.7.

Catering to Multiple UI Technologies

Swing is just one package for drawing. Before it was developed, there was (and still is) the AWT (Abstract Windowing Toolkit) package available to Java programmers, and it is conceivable that there may appear some other drawing toolkits. Let us assume that we have available two new toolkits, which are called, for want of better names, HardUI and EasyUI. Essentially, what we want is that each item has to be customised for each kind of UI, which boils down to the task of having a different render method for each UI. One way to accomplish this is to use inheritance.

To adapt the design to take care of the new situation, we have the Circle class implement most of the functionality for circle, except those that depend on the UI technology. We extend Circle to implement the SwingCircle class. Similar extensions are now needed for handling the new technologies, HardUI and EasyUI. Each of the three classes has code to draw a circle using the appropriate UI technology. The idea is shown in Fig. 11.8.

In each case, the render method will decompose the circle into smaller components as needed, and invoke the methods available in the UI to render each component. In addition, each method would have to get any other contextual information. For instance, with the Swing package, the render method would get the graphics object from the view and invoke the drawOval method. The code for this could look something like this:

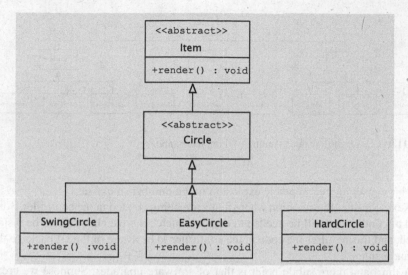

Fig. 11.8 Catering to multiple UI technologies

```
public class SwingCircle extends Circle {
  // circle class for SwingUI
  public void render() {
    Graphics g = (View.getInstance()).getGraphics();
    g.drawOval(/* parameters */);
  }
}
```

The actual parameters for drawOval would depend on any mapping needed, but would be computed using quantities stored in the Circle object. In addition to the Graphics object, we may need several other pieces of information from the context, such as the size of the drawing area, etc. The model could potentially employ several types of items, each of which has a corresponding abstract class.

Clearly, we need abstract classes for implementing the technology-independent parts of lines (Line) and labels (Label). They are extended by classes such as SwingLabel, SwingLine, EasyLabel, etc. This extension adds another six classes. Each abstract class ends up with as many subclasses as the number of UIs that we have to accommodate.

This solution has some drawbacks. The number of classes needed to accommodate such a solution is given by:

Number of types of items × Number of UI packages

As is evident from the pictorial view of the resulting hierarchy (see Fig. 11.9), this causes an unacceptable explosion in the number of classes.

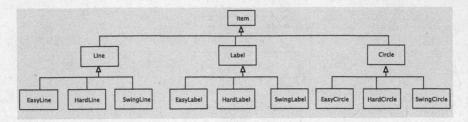

Fig. 11.9 Class explosion due to multiple UI implementations

This causes an unacceptable explosion in the number of classes.

Next, consider the situation where items are being created in the controller. Some kind of conditional will be needed to decide which concrete class should be instantiated, and this requires the code in the controller to be aware of the UI package that we are using.

A third and more subtle point is that of software upgrades. Suppose we create a version of our drawing program that supports the HardUI package and we use that to create a figure. All the items created in the model will belong to the HardUI subclasses, and can be used only with a system where the HardUI package is available. If a later version of the software does not support HardUI (or we move the files to a system that does not support it), we cannot access the old files anymore. If the objects created in the model were independent of the type of UI, this problem could be avoided.

Can all these problems be circumvented? What we have here are two subsystems viz., the model and the view, each of which has its own classification viz., the types of items and the types of UIs. We are creating objects that account for both of these variations. Since the Item subclasses are being created in the model, the types of items are an *internal variation*. On the other hand, the subclasses of Circle, Line, and Label (such as HardCircle) are an *external variation*. The standard approach for this is to factor out the external variations and keep them as a separate hierarchy, and then set up a *bridge* between the two hierarchies. This standard approach is therefore called the **bridge pattern.**

We already have the hierarchy that captures the variation in the items. We need a second hierarchy to capture the variation in the drawing methods, due to the variation in the UIs. The hierarchy of the UIs has an interface UIContext and as many concrete implementations as the number of different UIs we need. Figure 11.10 describes the interaction diagram between the classes and visually represents the bridge between the two hierarchies.

Since the only variation introduced in the items due to the different UIs is the manner in which the items were drawn, this behaviour is captured in the UIContext interface as shown in Fig. 11.11.

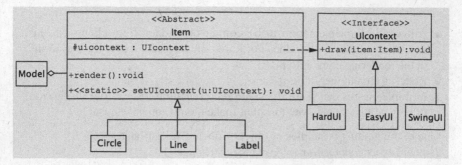

Fig. 11.10 Interaction diagram for the bridge pattern

Fig. 11.11 UIContext
interface

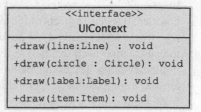

Using the Bridge Pattern

The intent of the bridge pattern is as follows: *Decouple an abstraction from its implementation so that two can vary independently.* In our example, the abstraction is the abstract class `Item`. The `render` method of this abstraction has different implementations for different UIs. Using inheritance to allow for the different implementations has the following drawbacks:

- The abstractions and implementations cannot be modified and reused independently.
- If the variations in the implementation are introduced from two independent sources, keeping them in the same hierarchy could have a multiplicative effect on the number of concrete classes.

The bridge pattern takes care of these problems avoiding a permanent binding between the two. This gives our design the following desirable properties:

- Both abstraction and implementation are independently extensible (UIContext and Items change independently).
- Changes in the implementation do not affect the clients (if the SwingUI is changed, no other class is affected).

- Allows the implementation to be completely hidden from clients (in our case-study, the controller does not know anything about how the variations in the rendering come into play).
- Reduces the number of classes.
- Multiple classes can share the same representation. (Recall our discussion of how going to a new versions can make old documents unusable.)

One of the guiding principles of object-oriented design[1] states:
Favour object composition over class inheritance.

This principle is usually applied in the context that object composition allows us to achieve reuse by assembling existing components and get the needed functionality. The effectiveness of the bridge pattern can also be related back to this idea. If several aspects of the implementation (each of which is represented by some abstract method) of an abstraction have to be varied independently, the abstraction itself can be viewed as a composition of all the aspects of the implementation. The bridge pattern says that in such a case, having the abstract class as a composition of hierarchies that represent each of these aspects of the implementation is a definite improvement over relying entirely on inheritance. The flip side of this pattern, as often happens with applying object oriented principles, is that we lose some performance due to the indirection.

Note that the total number of classes is now reduced to

Number of types of items + Number of UI packages

Since we have only one concrete class for each item, the creation process is simple. Finally, by factoring out the `render` method, we are no longer concerned with what kind of UI is being used to create the figure, or what UI will be used to edit it at a later stage. Our software for the model is thus 'completely' reusable.

As is often the case in the object-oriented design, one price we pay is through a loss of performance. In this case, this is seen in the increased number of method calls. Every time we invoke the `render` method, we have to get the model and the UIContext, in addition to invoking the drawing method.

Reflecting on the design The `UIContext` interface has a separate method for drawing each of the shapes, thereby establishing a one-to-one mapping with the shapes (circle, line, label). In general, such a one-to-one mapping is neither necessary nor realistic. Assume that we want to start supporting a new shape, say `Triangle`, with the obvious semantics, in our drawing program. This is clearly an example of a change that one should expect in a drawing program and, within reason, it should

---

[1] GoF, p. 127

impact as few interfaces and classes as possible. The class `Triangle` can then be written as below.

```
public class Triangle extends Item {
  private Line line1;
  private Line line2;
  private Line line3;
  // Fields, constructor, and other methods
  public  void render() {
    uiContext.draw(line1);
    uiContext.draw(line2);
    uiContext.draw(line3);
  }
}
```

Similarly, we could support arbitrary polygons.

This demonstrates a couple of things. For one, it justifies the use of the bridge pattern in our design. We are varying the `Item` hierarchy while requiring no changes at all to the `UIContext` hierarchy. In addition, it shows that the methods of `UIContext` can be quite 'general purpose' and not tied exclusively to one specific shape.

Suppose we restrict `UIContext` to the following:

```
public interface UIContext {
  public void draw(Point point1, Point point2); // for Line
  public void draw(String string, RenderInformation information);
                                        // for Label
}
```

As the reader might guess, `draw` with the two `Point` parameters renders a line connecting the given points. The other `draw` method draws a sequence of characters with information such as the font and font size specified in an as yet unimplemented class named `RenderInformation`. Clearly, the `Line` class's `render` method can call the first `draw` method of `UIContext` and the label can be drawn by calling the second `draw` method. We do not require any additional functionality, since any shape can be drawn by decomposing it into a large number of lines.[2] Since there is no method to draw a circle, the `Circle` class must repeatedly invoke the first `draw` method to render the circle.

Employing option 1 Assume that rather than assigning the responsibility of drawing an `Item` object to the object itself, we have the view draw all the items. This could be accomplished by having methods such as `draw(Line line)` and `draw(Circle circle)` in the view subsystem. Every view will potentially have a different implementation of these methods. To render the items, a reference to the current view is obtained and the appropriate `draw` method is then called on that object.

While the methods that result from employing Option 1 are essentially the same as we get using the bridge pattern, there is a difference in that the bridge pattern employs a different class for each UI technology whereas Option 1 employs a set of `draw` methods for each view.

---

[2]This is in fact exactly how most curve drawing algorithms are implemented.

11.5.3 Design of the Controller Subsystem

Unlike the view, which by definition could be implemented in multiple ways, we structure the controller so that it is not tied to a specific view and is unique to the drawing program.

The view receives details of a shape (type, location, content, etc.) via mouse clicks and key strokes. As it receives the input, the view communicates that to the controller through method calls. This is accomplished by having the fields for the following purposes.

1. For remembering the model;
2. To store the current line, label, or circle being created. Since we have three shapes, this would mean having three fields.[3]

When the view receives a button click to create a line, it calls the controller method makeLine. To reduce coupling between the controller and the view, we should allow the view to invoke this method at any time: before receiving any points, after receiving the first point, or after receiving both points. For this, the controller has three versions of the makeLine method and keeps track of the number of points independently of the view.

The execution of makeLine causes the line to be part of the model. The view can set the endpoints of the line via the setLinePoint method.

The approach to add a label is similar to the one for adding a line. For a label, remember that by pressing the backspace the user can delete a character, so we provide a method removeCharacter for this purpose.

The controller also supplies a method (selectItem) that the view can call when it receives the command to select an item. The controller searches through the entire list of unselected items and determines if one of them is selected, and if so, it moves the item from the list of unselected items to the list of selected items.

The rest of the methods are for deleting selected items and for storing and retrieving the drawing and are fairly obvious. The class diagram is shown in Fig. 11.12.

To implement the saving and retrieval of files, the only objects to be serialized are the list(s) of the Item objects, which is a straightforward process. However, one of our stated goals is that of allowing a file to be retrievable even if the software has been modified so that we have a different version of the view, or if new features are added. This means that in the new version of the software the concrete UIContext may be different from the one that was used to create the items in the serialized list. One solution to this could be to set uiContext to null in all the objects being stored to disk and then reset these when the objects are read from disc. This solution is inelegant and some what worrisome in that the objects are being modified when saved and retrieved.

This is a reason why we have made Item an abstract class (instead of an interface). This enables us to store UIContext as a static field in this class, along with the

---

[3]We leave the circle implementation as an exercise, so we end up having only two fields in our design.

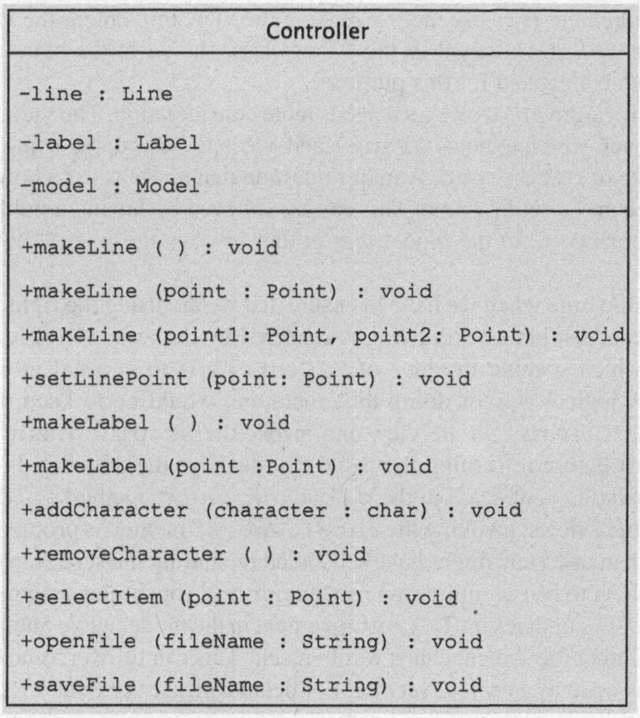

Controller
-line : Line -label : Label -model : Model
+makeLine ( ) : void +makeLine (point : Point) : void +makeLine (point1: Point, point2: Point) : void +setLinePoint (point: Point) : void +makeLabel ( ) : void +makeLabel (point :Point) : void +addCharacter (character : char) : void +removeCharacter ( ) : void +selectItem (point : Point) : void +openFile (fileName : String) : void +saveFile (fileName : String) : void

Fig. 11.12 Controller class diagram

static method `setUIContext` to modify it. The `UIContext` object is thus not a part of the object that is saved. This is consistent with the basic idea of the Bridge pattern, which calls for separation between the items and the manner in which they are rendered.

11.5.4 Design of the View Subsystem

The separation of concerns inherent in the MVC pattern makes the view largely independent of the other subsystems. Nonetheless, its design is affected by the controller and the model in two important ways:

1. Whenever the model changes, the view must refresh the display, for which the view must provide a mechanism.
2. The view employs a specific technology for constructing the UI. The corresponding implementation of `UIContext` must be made available to `Item`.

The first requirement is easily met by making the view implement the `Observer` interface; the `update` method in the `View` class, shown in the class diagram in Fig. 11.13, can be invoked for this purpose.

The issue regarding `UIContext` needs more consideration. The view consists of a drawing panel, which extends `JPanel` and needs to be updated using the appropriate instance of `UIContext`. A major question that arises is as to how and when this variable is to be set in `Item`. This can be achieved by having a public method, say `setUIContext`, in the model that in turn invokes the `setUIContext` on `Item`.

However, the time when we have to ensure that we are using the right instance of `UIContext` is just before a drawing is rendered by the view. Also, it is the view that knows which specific instance of `UIContext` is to be used in conjunction with itself. A logical way of doing this, therefore, would be to keep track of the appropriate `UIContext` in the view and invoke the `setUIContext` method in the model just before refreshing the panel that displays the drawing. In the Swing package, repainting is effected in the `paintComponent` method.

With multiple views, invoking the `setUIContext` method is problematic. Consider: more than one view might have scheduled repainting the screen, which would cause all of them to be executing `paintComponent` (or similar drawing method). If one of the views updates the `UIContext` field in the model while another is in the middle of painting the screen, chaos would result. This can be overcome by viewing the repainting code as a *critical section*. For details, please see Sect. 11.11.5.

Accepting input We have already decided that the user will issue commands by clicking on buttons. In the current implementation, we will assume that coordinate information (endpoints of lines, starting point of labels, etc.) will be specified by

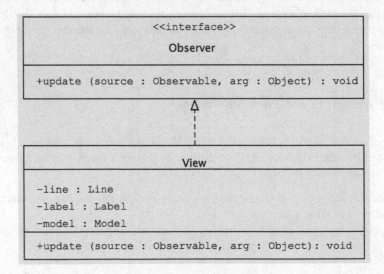

Fig. 11.13 Basic structure of the view class

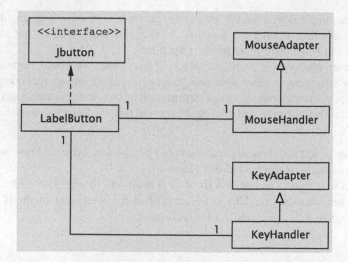

Fig. 11.14 Organisation of the classes to add labels

clicking on the panel. To catch these clicks, we need a class that acts as a mouse listener, which in Java demands the implementation of the MouseListener[4] interface.

Commands to create labels, circles, and lines all require mouse listeners. Since the behaviour of the mouse listener is dependent on the command, we know from previous examples in the book that a truly object-oriented design warrants a separate class for capturing the mouse clicks for each command. Since there is a one-to-one correspondence between the mouse listeners and the drawing commands, we have the following structure:

1. For each drawing command, we create a separate class that extends JButton. For creating labels, for instance, we have a class called LabelButton. Every button is its own listener.
2. For each class in (1) above, we create a mouse listener. These listeners invoke methods in the controller to initiate operations.
3. Each mouse listener (in (2) above) is declared as an inner class of the corresponding button class. This is because the different mouse listeners are independent and need not be known to each other.

The idea is captured in Fig. 11.14. The class MouseHandler extends the Java class MouseAdapter and is responsible for keeping track of mouse movements and clicks and invoking the appropriate controller methods to set up the label. In addition to capturing mouse clicks, the addition of labels requires the capturing of keystrokes. The class KeyHandler accomplishes this task by extending KeyAdapter.

---

[4]The reader is asked to study the documentation on this and other related interfaces and classes.

In another implementation, the view may choose to have other listeners that keep track of events like resising the window, zooming-in, etc. These do not affect the model and can be handled by redrawing the figure.

If the user abandons a particular drawing operation, we could be in a tricky situation where there is more than one MouseHandler object receiving mouse clicks and performing conflicting operations such as one object attempting to create a line and another trying to add a label. To prevent this, we have two mechanisms in place.

1. The KeyAdapter class also implements FocusListener to know when key strokes cease to be directed to this class.
2. The drawing panel ensures that there is at most one listener listening to mouse clicks, key strokes, etc. This is accomplished by overriding methods such as addMouseListener and addKeyListener.

11.6 Getting into the Implementation

11.6.1 Item and Its Subclasses

This class Item is abstract and its implementation is as follows:

```
import java.io.*;
import java.awt.*;
public abstract class Item implements Serializable {
  protected static UIContext uiContext;
  public static void setUIContext(UIContext uiContext) {
    Item.uiContext = uiContext;
  }
  public abstract boolean includes(Point point);

  protected double distance(Point point1, Point point2) {
    double xDifference = point1.getX() - point2.getX();
    double yDifference = point1.getY() - point2.getY();
    return ((double) (Math.sqrt(xDifference * xDifference +
                        yDifference * yDifference)));
  }
  public void render() {
    uiContext.draw(this);
  }
}
```

The UIContext and its significance were discussed earlier in the context of using the bridge pattern. The includes method is used to check if a given point selects the item.

The Line class looks something like this:

```
public class Line extends Item {
  private Point point1;
  private Point point2;
  public Line(Point point1, Point point2) {
```

```
        this.point1 = point1;
        this.point2 = point2;
    }
    public Line(Point point1) {
        this.point1 = point1;
    }
    public Line() {
    }
    public boolean includes(Point point) {
        return ((distance(point, point1 ) < 10.0) || (distance(point, point2)
               < 10.0));
    }
    public void render() {
        uiContext.draw(this);
    }
    // setters and getters for the two points
}
```

The class provides three constructors. A client may thus construct a `Line` object without knowing either endpoint, or by specifying one point, or after gathering both endpoints.

Unlike `HardUI` and `EasyUI`, which are 'imaginary' UI technologies, we can readily construct an implementation of `UIContext` for the Java Swing technology.

```
public class SwingUI implements UIContext {
    private Graphics g;
    // Any other fields to hold context variables
    public void setGraphics(Graphics graphics) {
        g = graphics;
    }
    // any other methods to set context variables
    public void draw(Circle circle) {
        g.drawOval(/* parameters */);
    }
    public void draw(Line line) {
        g.drawLine(/* parameters */);
    }
    public void draw(Label label){
        g.drawString(/* parameters */);
    }
    public void draw(Item item) {
        // error message
    }
}
```

As was the case earlier, `draw` needs information from both the UI and the item. The UI information is obtained within the context object and the item is passed in as a reference. The only difference is that instead of doing all this in the `render` method of `Item`, we invoke the appropriate draw method on the UI object with which the view has been configured.

11.6.2 Implementation of the Model Class

The class maintains `itemList` and `selectedList`, which respectively store the items created but not selected, and the items selected. The constructor initialises these containers.

```
public class Model extends Observable {
  private Vector itemList;
  private Vector selectedList;
  public Model() {
    itemList = new Vector();
    selectedList = new Vector();
  }
  // other methods
}
```

The `setUIContext` method in the model in turn invokes the `setUIContext` on `Item`.

```
public static void setUIContext(UIContext uiContext) {
  Model.uiContext = uiContext;
  Item.setUIContext(uiContext);
}
```

As an `Observable`, the model notifies all of the views when it needs to inform them of changes. We have seen that this approach allows us to change `UIContext` dynamically, and also supports the displaying of multiple views simultaneously, where each view is using a different `UIContext`.

At the moment, we handle the drawing of items (including a possibly 'incomplete' one), especially labels, by having a method `updateView` in the model, which is called by the controller at appropriate moments, for example after each character is read in from the keyboard. The method simply asks that the view be refreshed.

```
public void updateView() {
  setChanged();
  notifyObservers(null);
}
```

The `addItem` method is simple: it just stores the item in `itemList` and redraws the screen.

```
public void addItem(Item item) {
  itemList.add(item);
  updateView();
}
```

The class also provides a method to delete an item.

```
public void removeItem(Item item) {
  itemList.remove(item);
  updateView();
}
```

When an item is selected by the user, the model marks it as selected by transferring the item from `itemList` to `selectedList` as below.

```
public void markSelected(Item item) {
  if (itemList.contains(item)) {
    itemList.remove(item);
    selectedList.add(item);
    updateView();
  }
}
```

Selected items are deleted using the `deleteSelectedItems`.

```
public void deleteSelectedItems() {
  selectedList.removeAllElements();
  updateView();
}
```

The `getItems` method is used by the controller to determine which item is selected. The view uses the same method to render the items.

```
public Enumeration getItems() {
  return itemList.elements();
}
```

11.6.3 Implementation of the Controller Class

The class must keep track of the current shape being created, and this is accomplished by having the following fields within the class.

```
private Line line;
private Label label;
```

When the view receives a button click to create a line, it calls one of the following controller methods. The controller supplies three versions of the `makeLine` method and keeps track of the number of points independently of the view.

```
public void makeLine() {
  makeLine(null, null);
  pointCount = 0;
}
public void makeLine(Point point) {
  makeLine(point, null);
  pointCount = 1;
}
public void makeLine(Point point1, Point point2) {
  line = new Line(point1, point2);
  pointCount = 2;
  model.addItem(line);
}
```

The variables `pointCount` and `model` are both fields within the `Controller` class that respectively keep track of the number of points received and the instance of the `Model` class.

The execution of `makeLine` causes the line to be part of the model. The view can set the endpoints of the line via the following method.

```
public void setLinePoint(Point point) {
  if (++pointCount == 1) {
    line.setPoint1(point);
  } else if (pointCount == 2) {
    pointCount = 0;
    line.setPoint2(point);
  }
  model.updateView();
}
```

After it receives each end-point, the controller calls the model's `updateView` method to inform it that the view should be updated.

The approaches to draw a circle and add a label are similar. For a label, remember that by pressing the backspace the user can delete a character. So we provide a method `removeCharacter` for this purpose.

The following method is called by the view when it receives the command to select an item. The controller searches through the entire list of unselected items and determines if one of them is selected, and if so, it moves the item from the list of unselected items to the list of selected items.

```
public void selectItem(Point point) {
  Enumeration enumeration = model.getItems();
  while (enumeration.hasMoreElements()) {
    Item item = (Item)(enumeration.nextElement());
    if (item.includes(point)) {
      model.markSelected(item);
      break;
    }
  }
}
```

11.6.4 Implementation of the View Class

The view maintains two panels: one for the buttons and the other for drawing the items.

```
public class View extends JFrame implements Observer {
  private JPanel drawingPanel;
  private JPanel buttonPanel;
  // JButton references for buttons such as draw line, delete, etc.
  private class DrawingPanel extends JPanel {
    // code to redraw the drawing and manage the listeners
  }
  public View() {
    // code to create the buttons and panels and put them in the JFrame
  }
  public void update(Observable model, Object dummy) {
    drawingPanel.repaint();
  }
}
```

The code to set up the panels and buttons is quite straightforward, so we do not dwell upon that.

The `DrawingPanel` class overrides the `paintComponent` method, which is called by the system whenever the screen is to be updated. The method displays all unselected items by first obtaining an enumeration of unselected items from the model and calling the `render` method on each. Then it changes the colour to red and draws the selected items.

```
public void paintComponent(Graphics g) {
  model.setUI(NewSwingUI.getInstance());
  super.paintComponent(g);
  (NewSwingUI.getInstance()).setGraphics(g);
  g.setColor(Color.BLUE);
  Enumeration enumeration = model.getItems();
  while (enumeration.hasMoreElements()) {
    ((Item) enumeration.nextElement()).render();
  }
  g.setColor(Color.RED);
  enumeration = model.getSelectedItems();
  while (enumeration.hasMoreElements()) {
    ((Item) enumeration.nextElement()).render();
  }
}
```

The `DrawingPanel` class also overrides the `addMouseListener`, `addKey-Listener`, and `addFocusListener` methods. This is to ensure that there is at most one listener for each type of event on the drawing panel.

```
private MouseListener currentMouseListener;
public void addMouseListener(MouseListener newListener) {
  removeMouseListener(currentMouseListener);
  currentMouseListener = newListener;
  super.addMouseListener(newListener);
}
```

Similarly, we ensure that there is just one listener for events related to the keyboard.

Although the various button classes are alike in many respects, some are more complicated than others. One of the more complicated ones is `LabelButton`, which is responsible for handling label creation requests. Constructors of most button classes get a reference to the view, and the ones that need to access the drawing panel also get a reference to the panel.

```
public class LabelButton extends JButton implements ActionListener {
  protected JPanel drawingPanel;
  protected View view;
  private KeyHandler keyHandler;
  private MouseHandler mouseHandler;
  private Controller controller;
  public LabelButton(Controller controller, View jFrame, JPanel jPanel) {
    super("Label");
    this.controller = controller;
    keyHandler = new KeyHandler();
    addActionListener(this);
    view = jFrame;
    drawingPanel = jPanel;
  }
  public void actionPerformed(ActionEvent event) {
    drawingPanel.addMouseListener(mouseHandler = new MouseHandler());
```

```
    }
    private class MouseHandler extends MouseAdapter {
      // details not shown
    }
    private class KeyHandler extends KeyAdapter implements FocusListener {
      // details not shown
    }
  }
```

When this button is clicked, an instance of MouseHandler is created, and it becomes the sole listener of mouse clicks. MouseHandler overrides the mouseClicked method to determine the starting point of the label. Besides asking the controller to set up a Label object with the given starting point, the code makes the drawing panel receive further button clicks and keyboard events. Also note that the KeyHandler is a FocusListener as well, which lets it know when it longer receives keyboard input.

```
public void mouseClicked(MouseEvent event) {
  view.setCursor(new Cursor(Cursor.TEXT_CURSOR));
  Controller.instance().makeLabel(event.getPoint());
  drawingPanel.requestFocusInWindow();
  drawingPanel.addKeyListener(keyHandler);
  drawingPanel.addFocusListener(keyHandler);
}
```

In its keyTyped method, KeyHandler transmits all printable characters to the Label object via the controller. The keyPressed method distinguishes between the enter and backspace keys. For the former, it stops listening to mouse clicks and keyboard events. If the backspace is pressed, the label is made to delete the last typed character.

```
public void keyTyped(KeyEvent event) {
  char character = event.getKeyChar();
  if (character >= 32 && character <= 126) {
    Controller.instance().addCharacter(event.getKeyChar());
  }
}
public void keyPressed(KeyEvent event) {
  if (event.getKeyCode() == KeyEvent.VK_ENTER) {
    view.setCursor(new Cursor(Cursor.DEFAULT_CURSOR));
    drawingPanel.removeMouseListener(mouseHandler);
    drawingPanel.removeKeyListener(keyHandler);
    drawingPanel.repaint();
  } else if (event.getKeyCode() == KeyEvent.VK_BACK_SPACE) {
    Controller.instance().removeCharacter();
  }
}
```

If the user terminates label creation by clicking on a button, as opposed to hitting the Enter key, the system executes the focusLost method of KeyHandler, which properly ends the command.

```
public void focusLost(FocusEvent event) {
  view.setCursor(new Cursor(Cursor.DEFAULT_CURSOR));
  drawingPanel.removeMouseListener(mouseHandler);
```

```
    drawingPanel.removeKeyListener(keyHandler);
    drawingPanel.repaint();
}
```

Finally, just before it refreshes the screen, the view sets up UIContext within the model appropriately:

```
public void paintComponent(Graphics g) {
  model.setUI(NewSwingUI.getInstance());
  // rest of the code not shown
}
```

11.6.5 The Driver Program

The driver program sets up the model. In our implementation the controller is independent of the UI technology, so it can work with any view. The view itself uses the Swing package and is an observer of the model.

```
public class DrawingProgram {
  public static void main(String[] args){
    Model model = new Model();
    Controller.setModel(model);
    Controller controller = new Controller();
    View.setController(controller);
    View.setModel(model);
    View view = new View();
    model.addObserver(view);
    view.show();
  }
}
```

11.6.6 A Critique of Our Design

The partial design of the view and the model are quite robust. We have examined some of the issues to be taken care of earlier on, and the implementation takes them into consideration. The controller appears to be quite straightforward, and we simply need to add methods to handle all the operations.

Let us see how the design stands up to the task of adding a new operation, say, to draw a polygon.

1. We need to provide a new button which informs the user that the new operation is available. We also should create a mouse handler to handle mouse clicks, etc. These changes are relatively obvious and clearly unavoidable. Even then, note that most of the classes in the view are left unchanged.
2. The model is not affected by adding new types of items, operations or new UIs.
3. The UIContext interface does not have to be necessarily extended when new kinds of items are added. We refer the reader to the discussion in Sect. 11.5.2.

4. The controller should have new methods such as makePolygon and addPoint
   ToPolygon. It is not clear that this change is not a consequence of some basic
   flaw in our design. For instance, it might be possible to replace the methods
   makeLine, makeCircle, etc. by a single method, say makeShape.

Thus one drawback to our approach is that we need to change the controller
class every time new operations are added or even if we change the way things are
implemented. In addition, the controller has all the implementation in one class,
which makes things complicated.

A more tricky problem is that of implementing *undo*. Clearly some kind of a stack
would be needed to remember the operations that have been completed. When an
undo is requested, an element from the top of the stack is popped, and this element
has to be 'decoded' to find out what the last operation was. This would require
some kind of conditional, and the complexity of this method would increase with the
number of different kinds of operations that we implement. In earlier chapters we
have seen how such complexity can be reduced by *replacing conditional logic with
polymorphism*. In the next section we examine a pattern that can help us improve the
design of the controller.

11.7 Implementing the Undo Operation

In the context of implementing the undo operation, a few issues need to be highlighted.

- *Single-level undo versus multiple-level undo* A simple form of undo is when only
  one operation (i.e., the most recent one) can be undone. This is relatively easy,
  since we can afford to simply clone the model before each operation and restore
  the clone to undo.
- *Undo and redo are unlike the other operations* If an undo operation is treated
  the same as any other operation, then two successive undo operations cancel each
  other out, since the second undo reverses the effect of the first undo and is thus
  a redo. The undo (and redo) operations must therefore have a special status as
  meta-operations if several operations must be undone.
- *Not all things are undoable* This can happen for two reasons. Some operations
  like 'print file' are irreversible, and hence undoable. Other operations like 'save to
  disk' may not be worth the trouble to undo, due to the overheads involved.
- *Blocking further undo/redo operations* It is easy to see that uncontrolled undo
  and redo can result in meaningless requests. In general, it is safer to block redo
  whenever a new command is executed. Consider a situation where we have the
  sequence: *Select(a), undo, Select(a), redo*. The redo tries to mark *a* as selected,
  and this could result in an exception depending on how things are implemented. A
  more severe problem arises with *Create Rectangle(r), Colour Rectangle(r, blue),
  undo, Delete(r), redo*. Here, the redo will attempt to colour a rectangle that does
  not exist any more.

- *Solution should be efficient* This constraint rules out naive solutions like saving the model to disk after each operation.

Keeping these issues in mind, a simple scheme for implementing undo could be something like this:

1. Create a stack for storing the history of the operations.
2. For each operation, define a data class that will store the information necessary to undo the operation.
3. Implement code so that whenever any operation is carried out, the relevant information is packed into the associated data object and pushed onto the stack.
4. Implement an undo method in the controller that simply pops the stack, decodes the popped data object and invokes the appropriate method to extract the information and perform the task of undoing the operation.

One obvious approach for implementing this is to define a class StackObject that stores each object with an identifying String.

```
public class StackObject {
   private String name;
   private Object object;
   public StackObject(String string, Object object) {
     name = string;
     this.object = object;
   }
   public String getName() {
     return name;
   }
   public Object getObject() {
     return object;
   }
}
```

Each command has an associated object that stores the data needed to undo it. The class corresponding to the operation of adding a line is shown below.

```
public class LineObject {
   private Line line;
   public Line  getLine() {
     return line;
   }
   public LineObject(Line line) {
     this.line = line;
   }
}
```

When the operation for adding a line is completed, the appropriate StackObject instance is created and pushed onto the stack.

```
public class Controller {
   private Stack history;
   public void makeLine(Point point1, Point point2) {
     Line line = new Line(point1, point2);
     model.addItem(line);
     history.push(new StackObject("line", new LineObject(line)));
```

```
    }
    // other fields and methods
}
```

Decoding is simply a matter of popping the stack reading the `String`.

```
public void undo() {
    StackObject undoObject = history.pop();
    String name = undoObject.getName();
    Object obj = undoObject.getObject();
    if (name.equals("line")) {
        undoLine((LineObject)obj);
    } else if (name.equals("delete")) {
        undoDelete((DeleteObject)obj);
    } else if (name.equals("select")) {
        undoSelect((SelectObject)obj);
    }
    // one else if for each command
}
```

Finally, undoing is simply a matter of retrieving the reference to and removing the line form the model.

```
public class Controller {
    public void undoLine(LineObject object){
        Line line = object.getLine();
        model.removeItem(line);
    }
}
```

There are two obvious drawbacks with this approach:

1. *The long conditional statement in the undo method of the controller.*
2. *The need to rewrite the controller whenever we make changes such as adding or modifying the implementation of an operation.*

The object-oriented approach for dealing with the first drawback is to subclass the behaviour by creating an inheritance hierarchy and *replace conditional logic with polymorphism.* (Recollect that this is accomplished by making the original method abstract and moving each leg of the conditional to an overriding method in the corresponding subclass.)

Let us refactor the code to accomplish this. Before replacing the conditional, however, we see that undo in the controller is mostly working off the data stored in `StackObject` and our first order of business is to extract and move this method.

```
public class Controller {
    private Stack history;
    public void undo() {
        StackObject undoObject = history.pop();
        undoObject.undo(this);
    }
    // other fields and methods
}

public class StackObject {
    public void undo(Controller controller) {
```

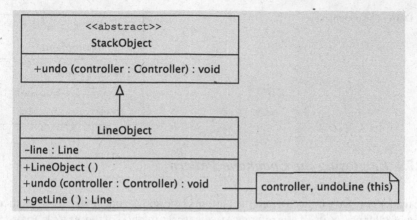

Fig. 11.15 Representing the drawing of a line

```
    String name = getName();
    Object object = getObject();
    if (name.equals("line")) {
      controller.undoLine((LineObject)object);
    } else if (name.equals("delete")) {
      controller.undoDelete((DeleteObject)object);
    } else if (name.equals("select")) {
      controller.undoSelect((SelectObject)object);
    }
  }
  // other fields and methods
}
```

Now our conditional is in `StackObject` and we are ready to subclass this behaviour. Since each kind of data object is associated with an operation, our hierarchy will have a subclass corresponding to each operation. For example, to represent the drawing of a line, we have the class `LineObject` as a subclass of `StackObject` (Fig. 11.15).

This is a lot simpler and cleaner, although we have paid a price by increasing the number of method calls. Note that we no longer 'decode' the stored objects and therefore the name field is not required. The `makeLine` method is simplified, so it just creates a `LineObject` and pushes it onto the stack.

```
  public void makeLine(Point point1, Point point2) {
    Line line = new Line(point1, point2);
    model.addItem(line);
    history.push(new LineObject(line));
  }
```

In the next subsection, we look into creating a fully reusable controller.

Fig. 11.16 The command class

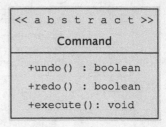

11.7.1 Employing the Command Pattern

The reader may have noticed a familiar pattern in the above code. In its `undo` method, the controller passes itself as a reference to the `undo` method of the `StackObject`. In turn, each subclass of the `StackObject` (e.g., `LineObject`) passes itself as reference when invoking the appropriate undo method of the controller. This is an implementation of *double dispatch* that we used when employing the *visitor* pattern and was wholly appropriate when introducing new functionality into an existing hierarchy. In this context, however, we find that this results in unnecessarily moving a lot of data around. One of the lasting lessons of the object-oriented experience is the supremacy of data over process (The Law of Inversion), which we discussed in Chap. 8, which we can utilise in this problem by using the **command pattern.**

The intent of the command pattern is as follows (see foonote 1):

> Encapsulate a request as an object, thereby letting you parametrise clients with different requests, queue or log requests, and support undoable operations.

We have partially satisfied this intent in our scenario by associating an object with each operation. For instance, whenever we execute an operation to create a line, a `LineObject` is created and pushed onto the stack. What we have failed to recognise so far is that this object need not merely be a repository of associated data but can also encapsulate the routines that need access to this data.

The command pattern provides us with a template to address this. The abstract `Command` class has abstract methods to `execute`, `undo` and `redo`. See Fig. 11.16.

The default `undo` and `redo` methods in `Command` return `false`, and these need to be overridden as needed by the concrete command classes.

The mechanism is best explained via an example, for which we develop a somewhat simplified sequence diagram for the command to add a line (Fig. 11.17).[5]

Adding a line Since every command is represented by a `Command` object, the first order of task when the Draw Line command is issued is to instantiate a `LineCommand` object. We assume that we do this after the user clicks the first endpoint although there is no reason why it could not have been created immediately after receiving the

---

[5]The sequence diagram abstracts out the complexity of the multiple classes associated with the UI into a single class called View.

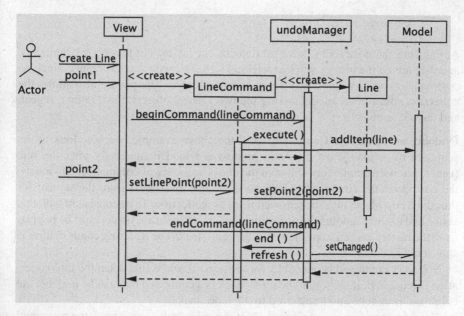

Fig. 11.17 Sequence diagram for adding a line

command. In its constructor, `LineCommand` creates a `Line` object with one of its endpoints specified.

The central idea behind the command pattern is to employ two stacks: one for storing the commands that can be undone (history stack) and the other for maintaining the commands that may be redone (redo stack). The class `UndoManager` maintains these stacks. (We refer to the corresponding object by the term **undo manager**.) The undo manager plays the role of the controller, but we have given it a new name to highlight its main function. We take the approach that as soon after the command object is created, the view informs the undo manager, which is then expected to initiate its bookkeeping operations. Similarly, when the view has received all of the data needed to complete the command, it notifies the `UndoManager` once more. The two methods `beginCommand` and `endCommand` are for these two purposes.

In the course of execution of the `beginCommand` method, the undo manager ensures the the `Line` object gets added to the model. This way, should the view be refreshed, the partial line will be shown on the screen.

When the command is completed and the `endCommand` method is executed, the undo manager pushes the command onto the history stack. This way the latest command is always at the top of this stack. To prevent inconsistencies of the kind we described at the very beginning of this section, we clear the redo stack whenever a new command is issued.

Assume that the user issues the sequence of commands:

> Add Label (Label 1)
> Draw Circle (Circle 1)

Add Label (Label 2)

Draw Line (Line 1)

At this time, there are four Command objects, one for each of the above commands, and they are on the history stack as in Fig. 11.18. The redo stack is empty: since no commands have been undone, there is nothing to redo. The picture also shows the collection object in the model storing the two Label objects, the Circle object, and the Line object.

Undoing an operation Continuing with the above example, we now look at the sequence of actions when the undo request is issued immediately after the line (Line 1) has been completely drawn in the above sequence of commands. Obviously, the user views the command as undone if the line disappears from the screen: for this, the Line object must be removed from the collection. To be consistent with this action and to allow redoing the operation, the LineCommand object must be popped from the history stack and pushed onto the redo stack. The resulting configuration is shown in Fig. 11.19.

Not every command is undoable. So the general rule is that when the undo operation is requested, if the top of the undo stack is a command that can be undone, the command is undone and transferred to the redo stack.

The redo operation is simple enough: if the redo stack is not empty, the command must be re-executed, and the top object in the redo stack must be transferred to

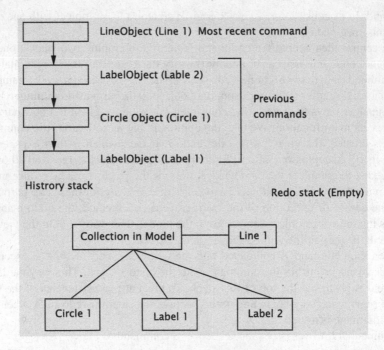

Fig. 11.18 Status of the stacks and the collection in the model

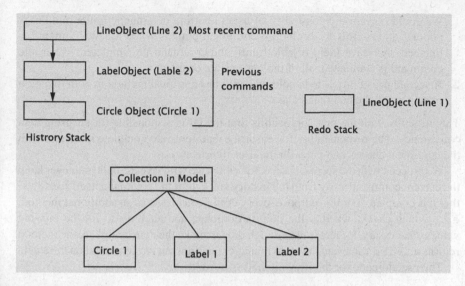

Fig. 11.19 Status of the stacks and the collection in the model after undo

the history stack. The redo involves updating the model: the `redo` method of the `Command` object calls the `execute` method to do the necessary actions. For the `LineCommand` object, this involves adding the line back to the model's collection object.

As we noted earlier, not every command may be undoable, or, at least, is not worth the trouble. If an undoable operation is on the undo stack, the undo cannot proceed beyond that operation although there might be undoable operations underneath it in the stack. To get around this problem, we might choose to not push undoable commands onto the stack. This can be accomplished by making the command itself assume the responsibility for pushing onto the history stack. This can conveniently be done in the class's constructor.

A related issue concerns unfinished commands. We use the term *incomplete command* to refer to a command that has not yet been properly terminated. An *incomplete item* is an item, such as a line or a label, that might not have proper values for every field. We use the term *complete item* to refer to an item for which the user has supplied (or the system has invented) all the input necessary for completely specifying the item. For example, suppose a user clicks the 'Create Line' button and clicks one point. Before clicking a second time to specify the second point, suppose the user clicks the 'Add Label' button. The Create Line command is incomplete. Moreover, the line is also incomplete at this stage, and it is already stored in the model, which now ends up containing incomplete data. One could argue that it was the user's fault, but the program must tolerate such errors and it would be nice if there was a way to fix this problem.

How should this be handled? We can suggest at least two ways:

1. We could prevent the possibility of users aborting commands in the middle. A popular approach is to disable all command buttons when a new command is finished and leave them disabled until the command is completed. When the command is completed, all of the buttons are enabled.
2. A second possibility is to handle this with an additional method in both the undo manager and the command class.

The difficulty with the first approach is that the UI is responsible for ensuring data consistency. The responsibility for ensuring that items are complete must rest with the command classes and not with the user interface.

We proceed with the second choice, for which we will have the undo manager keep the current command away from the history stack until the command itself 'certifies' that it is complete. For this purpose, every command class has an additional method, end, which checks whether the item is complete and attempts to fill the missing values if necessary. If there is not enough data to make the item complete, the method returns a false value and the undo manager does not put the command on the stack.

The pseudo-code for the end method is as follows:

```
public boolean end() {
   if item is incomplete
      attempt to complete using data already received;
      if cannot be completed
         return false;
      end if
   end if
   return true
}
```

The undo manager does not push a new command onto the stack until it is clear that the item is complete.

We now explain the implementation of the above concepts.

11.7.2 Implementation

Subclasses of Command The concrete command classes (such as LineCommand) store the associated data needed to undo and redo these operations. Just as the makeLine method in the previous implementation had three versions, the LineCommand class has three constructors, allowing some flexibility in the design of the view.

The implementation of methods specific to the Command class are shown below. The execute method simply adds the command to the model so the line will be drawn. To undo the command, the Line object is removed from the model's collection. Finally, redo calls execute.

```
public void execute() {
   model.addItem(line);
}
public boolean undo() {
```

```
     model.removeItem(line);
     return true;
   }
   public boolean redo() {
     execute();
     return true;
   }
```

As explained earlier, the class has a method called end, which attempts to complete
an unfinished command. The situation is considered hopeless if both endpoints are
missing, so the object removes the line from the model (undoes the command) and
returns a false value. Otherwise, if the line is incomplete (has at least one endpoint
unspecified), the start and end points are considered the same. The implementation
is:

```
   public boolean end() {
     if (line.getPoint1() == null) {
       undo();
       return false;
     }
     if (line.getPoint2() == null) {
         line.setPoint2(line.getPoint1());
     }
     return true;
   }
```

UndoManager It declares two stacks for keeping track of the undo and redo operations: (history) and (redoStack). The current command is stored in a field
aptly named currentCommand.

```
   public class UndoManager {
     private Stack history;
     private Stack redoStack;
     private Command currentCommand;
   }
```

If the command was not properly terminated, we arrange matters such that
currentCommand will not be null when a new command is issued. Recall that
when a new command is issued, the beginCommand method of the undo manager
is called. If currentCommand is not null at this time, the undo manager attempts
to complete it by calling the command's end method. The beginCommand method
is implemented as below.

```
   public void beginCommand(Command command) {
     if (currentCommand != null) {
       if (currentCommand.end()) {
         history.push(currentCommand);
       }
     }
     currentCommand = command;
     redoStack.clear();
     command.execute();
   }
```

The undo and redo are straightforward operations.

```
public void undo() {
  if (!(history.empty())) {
    Command command = (Command) (history.peek());
    if (command.undo()) {
      history.pop();
      redoStack.push(command);
    }
  }
}

public void redo() {
  if (!(redoStack.empty())) {
    Command command = (Command)(redoStack.peek());
    if (command.redo()) {
      redoStack.pop();
      history.push(command);
    }
  }
}
```

When a command is complete, the view calls the `endCommand` method of the undo manager, which pushes `currentCommand` onto the history stack and sets `currentCommand` to `null`.

```
public void endCommand(Command command) {
  command.end();
  history.push(command);
  currentCommand = null;
  model.updateView();
}
```

Handling the input The view declares one button class for each command (add label, draw line, etc.). The class for handling line drawing is implemented as below.

```
public class LineButton  extends JButton implements ActionListener {
  // fields for view, drawing panel, handlers, etc.
  public LineButton(UndoManager undoManager, View jFrame, JPanel jPanel) {
    // store the parameters and create the mouse listener
  }
  public void actionPerformed(ActionEvent event) {
    // change the cursor
    drawingPanel.addMouseListener(mouseHandler);
  }
  private class MouseHandler extends MouseAdapter {
    public void mouseClicked(MouseEvent event) {
      if (first point) {
        lineCommand = new LineCommand(event.getPoint());
        UndoManager.instance().beginCommand(lineCommand);
        } else if (second point) {
        lineCommand.setLinePoint(event.getPoint());
        drawingPanel.removeMouseListener(this);
        view.setCursor(new Cursor(Cursor.DEFAULT_CURSOR));
        UndoManager.instance().endCommand(lineCommand);
      }
    }
  }
}
```

The above class thus directly creates the appropriate command object when a request comes from a user.

11.8 Drawing Incomplete Items

Recall the terms incomplete item and complete item we introduced in the previous section. There are a couple of reasons why in the drawing program we might wish to distinguish between these two types of items.

1. Incomplete items might be rendered differently from complete items. For instance, for a line, after the first click, the UI could track the mouse movement and draw a line between the first click point and the current mouse location; this line keeps shifting as the user moves the mouse. Likewise, if we were to extend the program to include triangles, which need three clicks, one side may be displayed after two clicks. Labels in construction must show the insertion point for the next character.
2. Some fields in an incomplete item might not have 'proper' values. Consequently, rendering an incomplete item could be more tricky. An incomplete line, for instance, might have one of the endpoints null. In such cases, it is inefficient to use the same render method for both incomplete items and complete items because that method will need to check whether the fields are valid and take appropriate actions to handle these special cases. Since we ensure that there is at most one incomplete item, this is not a sound approach.

We can easily distinguish between incomplete items and complete items by having a field that identifies the type. The render method will behave differently based on this field. The approach would be along the following lines.

```
public class Line {
  private boolean incomplete = true;
  public boolean isIncomplete() {
    return incomplete;
  }
  // other fields and methods
}

public class NewSwingUI implements UIContext {
  // fields and methods
  public void draw(Line line) {
    if (line.isIncomplete()) {
      draw incomplete line;
    } else {
      draw complete line;
    }
  }
}
```

In circumstances such as the above, where we have variant behaviour based on field values, the object-oriented philosophy dictates subclassing, i.e., we treat the incomplete item as a different class of object with its own rendering method. We create classes for incomplete items (such as `IncompleteLabel`) that are subclasses of items (such as `Label`). Since the class `IncompleteLabel` is a subclass of `Label`, the model is unaware of its existence. Once the object is created, the incomplete object can be removed from the model.

The details are as follows.

```
import java.awt.*;
public class IncompleteLabel extends Label {
  public IncompleteLabel(Point point) {
    super(point);
  }
  public void render() {
    // code for rendering IncompleteLabel
  }
  public boolean includes(Point point) {
    return false;
  }
}
```

One problem we face with the above approach is that UIContext must include the method(s) for drawing the incomplete items (draw(IncompleteLabel label), in our example). This suggests that UIContext needs to be modified. However, the manner in which incomplete items are rendered is an issue that largely relates to the look and feel of the system. For instance, UIContext might not have a method draw(IncompleteLine line) and creator of some view (NewSwingUI, for instance) might wish to include that. In general, we would like a solution that allows for a *customised presentation* which may require subclassing the behaviour of some concrete items. This can be accomplished through RTTI. In particular, the situation where the NewSwingUI wants its own method for drawing an incomplete line is implemented as follows:

```
public class NewSwingUI implements UIContext {
  // fields and methods
  public void draw(Line line) {
    if (line instanceof IncompleteLine) {
      this.draw((IncompleteLine) line);
    } else {
      //code to draw Line
    }
  }
}
```

Where Should We Employ RTTI?

The use of RTTI can be puzzling to a beginner. On the one hand its application is actively discouraged; this attitude is fully justified since a novice developer can feel tempted to employ RTTI and resolve problems that really need a more thoughtful approach and a carefully designed hierarchy with appropriate design patterns. On the other hand, there are situations where it is necessary to check the type of an object at run time, as we have seen in Chaps. 5 and 10 and also in the case of the incomplete items in this chapter. In the examples in the earlier chapters, the development of the solution naturally led to the use of RTTI. In Chap. 5, the only way to know the exact type of the class that invoked the constructor was to invoke getClass().getName(). In Chap. 10, we had a situation where the expected behaviour was that the right kind of listener would be passed as a parameter. If the expectation was met, the downcast would succeed; if not, throwing the exception was the right thing to do. In some situations, as with incomplete items in this chapter, it may not be so clear. A simple thumb rule for resolving this conundrum is to examine all the options that are available.

Consider what other choices we have for incorporating incomplete items. One approach would be to define `UIContext` to contain draw methods for all the incomplete items as well. This means that all concrete contexts must implement (dummy, perhaps) draw methods for incomplete items. Apart from the tedium of this and the fact that we are doubling the number of classes in the basic system, we have a solution that does not really allow for flexibility for the view to define the look and feel. We could conceivably have a system with different kinds of incomplete labels, each associated with different processes for label creation. With RTTI, we have a solution that allows for variability in a manner that does not affect other parts of the implementation.

The `LineCommand` object creates an `IncompleteLine` and adds this to the model. This new class is thus known only to the controller and `NewSwingUI`. When the label creation is complete, the `IncompleteLine` object is removed from the model and replaced with a `Line` object. This implementation therefore gives a solution where variability is contained.

Finally, we examine item creation in this new context. Assume that the user clicks on the 'Add Label' button. On the creation of the `LabelCommand` object, an `IncompleteLabel` object is created and stored within the command object. When label is completed, the `end` method of the command object is called, and in this method, a `Label` object is created and data from the incomplete version is copied to it. The `IncompleteLabel` object is deleted from the model and the `Label` object takes its place. The relevant code from `LabelCommand` is shown below.

```
public void end() {
  model.removeItem(label);
  String text = label.getText();
  label = new Label(label.getStartingPoint());
  for (int index = 0; index < text.length(); index++) {
    label.addCharacter(text.charAt(index));
  }
  execute();
}
```

This completes the basic implementation of our simple graphical system. Note that if any new operation has to be added, all we have to do is create new classes that extend `Command` and `Item`, and modify the view to allow the user to invoke the new operation. Modifying the view is simply a matter of defining a new class that extends `JButton` and adding an instance of this class to the button panel. The model, the view and the controller are essentially repositories for the items, buttons, and commands respectively, and thus provide a framework for creating the specified system.

11.9 Adding a New Feature

Most interactive systems that are used to create graphical objects, allow users to define new kinds of objects on the fly. A system for writing sheet music may allow a user to define a sequence of notes as a group. This would enable the user to manipulate these notes as a group, making copies of these as needed. In a system for drawing electrical circuits, a set of components interconnected in a particular way could be clustered together as a 'sub-circuit' that can then be treated as a single unit. In a drawing program like the one we have created, a complex figure may be created as a collection of lines and circles, which may have to be moved around a single unit. In all these cases, the user-friendliness of the system would be considerably improved if a feature is provided to enable such operations.

Let us examine how our system needs to be modified to accommodate this. The process for creating such a 'compound' object would be as follows: *The user would select the items that have to be combined by clicking on them. The system would then highlight the selected items. The user then requests the operation of combing the selected items into a compound object, and the system combines them into one.*

Which Subsystem 'Owns' a Class?

In our original approach to designing this system using the MVC architecture, we were partitioning the responsibilities between the three subsystems. As we looked into the finer details of the implementation, we encountered some problems and found some suitable patterns that could improve our design. The use of these patterns, however apparently 'blurs' some of the clear boundaries.

Consider for instance the bridge pattern. We created the `UIContext` interface within the model to house the `draw` methods of all the items. The model does not have the information, however, to create a concrete instance of `UIContext` and this task is left to the `View` class. `UIContext` and its implementing classes belong to the view subsystem.

The original controller was replaced by a collection of classes including `UndoManager` and the various subclasses of `Command`, so they could be considered belonging to the controller subsystem. The undo manager defines the interface for the command but does not have any information on how each individual command should receive and process input.

The reader should realise that the subsystems are only providing a context within which the details can be fleshed out. The controller is providing a format for the creation of commands and also a system that manages these commands. When a command has to be added, a class is defined and the view is modified to allow for its invocation. Likewise the model provides a template for rendering all the kinds of items, but a complete knowledge of the view is needed to provide a concrete implementation.

From a more practical view, it does not matter much whether we can label a class as belonging to any specific subsystem. What we need to worry about are properties such as modularity, proper assignment of responsibilities, cohesive classes, low coupling between classes, ease of meeting changing requirements, performance, and so on. The MVC paradigm provides the guidelines, and it is up to the designer to make decisions that ensure these properties.

Once a compound object has been created, it can be treated as a any other object. This process can be *iterated,* i.e., a compound object can be combined with other objects (which could themselves be compound or simple objects) to create another compound object. The system also allows the user to 'breakdown' a compound item into its constituent items by first selecting the item(s) to be broken down and then choosing the 'decompose' operation. Note that if a compound item is created by combining two compound items, then decomposing it will give us back the two original compound items. Finally, the system must have the ability to undo and redo these operations.

Since we have to store a collection of items, an obvious approach to implementing this would be to create a new kind of item that maintains a collection of the constituent items. This would be a concrete class and would look like this:

```
public class CompoundItem {
  List items;
  public CompoundItem(/* parameters */) {
    //instantiate lists
  }
  public Enumeration getItems() {
    //returns an enumeration of the objects in Items
  }
  // other fields and methods
}
```

Since `items` consists of both simple items and compound items, it seems logical that all entities stored in `items` are designated as belonging to the class `Object`. The model would also have to be modified so that the container classes would hold collections of type `Object`.

Consider now any class that examines at the collection of items in the model (i.e., a 'client' class). One of these would be the `SelectCommand`. When a `SelectCommand` object gets the coordinates of the mouse click, it iterates through the collection in the model to determine the selected item. If the object is a simple item, it would be cast as an `Item` and the `includes` method would be invoked; if the object is a compound item, it would be cast as a `CompoundItem` and the `getItems` method would be invoked to get an enumeration of the objects that make up the compound item. Clearly, this is not the most desirable state of affairs since the client method is querying the type of the object (which is akin to switching on the fields of the object) to determine what operation is to be performed. Our standard approach in such situations is to create an inheritance hierarchy and use dynamic

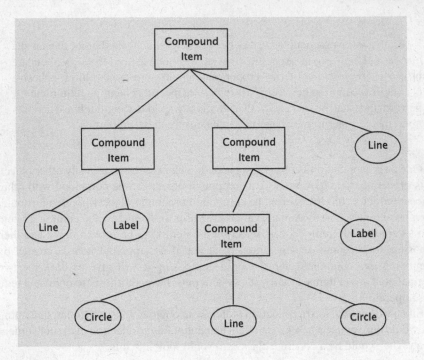

Fig. 11.20 Tree structure formed by compound items

binding. The dilemma here is that we have a two fundamentally different kinds of entities: *a simple item is a single item, whereas a compound item is a collection of items.* The **composite pattern** gives us an elegant solution to this problem.

The intent of the composite pattern is as follows (see footnote 1):

> *Compose objects into tree structures to represent part-whole hierarchies. Composite lets clients treat individual objects and compositions of objects uniformly.*

A compound item is clearly a composition of simple items. Since each compound item could itself consist of other compound items, we have the requisite tree structure (see Fig. 11.20).

The class interaction diagram for the composite pattern is shown in Fig. 11.21. Note that the definition of the compound item is *recursive* and may remind readers of the recursive definition of a tree. Following this diagram, the class CompoundItem is redefined as follows:

```
public class CompoundItem extends Item {
  List items;
  public CompoundItem(/* parameters */){
    //instantiate lists
  }
  public void render(){
    // iterates through items and renders each one.
  }
```

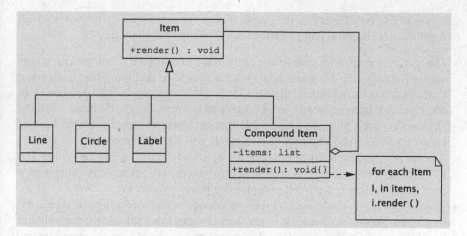

Fig. 11.21 Composite structure of the item hierarchy

```
public boolean includes(Point point) {
   /* iterates through items and invokes includes  on each item.
      Returns true if any of the items returns true and false otherwise. */
}
public void addItem(Item item) {
   // Adds item to items
}
   // other fields and methods
}
```

Modifying the system to allow for creating compound objects is just like any of the operations discussed earlier. The system already has an operation for selecting items. Once that is complete, user chooses the 'create composite' operation. This would require that a new class be defined (extending JButton) and that the view be modified to add this button to the button panel. A new class, CompositeCommand (extending Command) is defined. The execute method of this class removes all the selected items from the Model and adds them to a new CompoundItem object, which is then added to the Model. The view renders a CompoundItem exactly in the same way as it renders any other instance of Item. Note also that the select operation invokes the includes method on CompoundItem exactly as it would on simple items.

11.10 Pattern-Based Solutions

As explained earlier a pattern is a solution template that addresses a recurring problem in specific situations. In a general sense, these could apply to any domain. (A standard opening in chess, for instance, can be looked at as a 'chess pattern'.) In the context of creating software, three kinds of patterns have been identified. At the highest level, we have the **architectural patterns**. These typically partition a system into subsystems and broadly define the role that each subsystem plays and how they all fit together. Architectural patterns have the following characteristics:

- *They have evolved over time* In the early years of software development, it was not very clear to the designers how systems should be laid out. Over time, some kind of categorisation emerged, of the kinds software systems that are needed. In due course, it became clearer as to how these systems and the demands on them change over their lifetime. This enabled practitioners to figure out what kind of layout could alleviate some of the commonly encountered problems.
- *A given pattern is usually applicable for a certain class of software system* The MVC pattern for instance, is well-suited for interactive systems, but might be a poor fit for designing a payroll program that prints paychecks.
- *The need for these is not obvious to the untrained eye* When a designer first encounters a new class of software, it is not very obvious what the architecture should be. One reason for this is that the designer is not aware of how the requirements might change over time, or what kind of modifications are likely to be needed. It is therefore prudent to follow the dictates of the wisdom of past practitioners. This is somewhat different from design patterns, which we are able to 'derive' by applying some of the well-established 'axioms' of object-oriented analysis and design. (In case of our MVC example, we did justify the choice of the architecture, but this was done by demonstrating that it would be easier to add new operations to the system. Such an understanding is usually something that is acquired over the lifetime of a system.)

At the next level, we have the *design patterns*. These solve problems that could appear in many kinds of software systems. Once the principles of object-oriented analysis and design have been established it is easier to derive these. Examples of these can be found throughout this text.

At the lowest level we have the patterns that are called **idioms**. Idioms are the patterns of programming and are usually associated with specific languages. They typically refer to the use of certain syntactic elements of the language. As programmers, we often find ourselves using the same code snippet every time we have to accomplish a certain task. Sometimes, we may save these as 'macros' to be copied and pasted as needed thus enabling us to be more productive in terms of code-generation. Idioms are something like these, but they are usually carefully designed to take the language features (and quirks!) into account to make sure that the code is safe and efficient. The following code, for instance, is commonly used to swap:

```
temp = a;
a = b;
b = temp;
```

In *Perl*,[6] the list assignment syntax allows us to employ a more succinct expression:

```
($a, $b) = ($b, $a);
```

---

[6] A commonly used scripting language.

This would be an example of an idiom for Perl. In addition to safety and efficiency, the familiarity of the code snippet makes the code more readable and reduces the need for comments. Typical Perl programmers might be more comfortable with the second whereas a Java programmer would prefer the first.

Not all idioms are without conflict. There are two possible idioms for an infinite loop:

```
for (;;) {
// some code
}
while (true) {
// some code
}
```

It has been argued that the first one should be preferred for efficiency, since no expression evaluation is involved at the end of each iteration. However, with the availability of optimising compilers and increasing hardware capacity nowadays, some programmers are making a case for the second one based on readability and elegance.

Familiarity with and acceptance of established patterns is clearly a must for success in any domain of activity. Most of our focus in our case studies has therefore been to convince the student of their usefulness by showing how they provide elegant solutions to naturally arising design problems. However, as mentioned earlier, it is much more difficult for a beginner to grasp the significance of architectural patterns in this manner.

11.10.1 Examples of Architectural Patterns

The Repository

This architecture is characterised by the presence of a single data structure called the *central repository*. Subsystems access and modify the data stored in this. An example of such a system could be software used for *managing an airline*. The subsystems in this case could be the ones for managing reservations, scheduling staff, and scheduling aircraft. All of these would access a central data repository that holds information about aircraft, staff, and passengers. These would be inter-related, since a choice of an aircraft could likely influence the choice of staff and be influenced by the volume of passenger traffic. In such systems, the control flow can be dictated by the central repository (changes in the data characteristics could trigger some operations), or from one of the subsystems. Another application of such a system could be for managing a large bank. The account information would have to be centrally located and could be accessed and modified from several peripheral locations. A software development system or a compiler could also employ such an architecture by having a centralised parse-tree or symbol table.

The Client-Server

In such a layout, there is a central subsystem known as a *server* and several smaller subsystems known as *clients* which are typically quite similar. There is a fair amount of independence in the control flow, and each subsystem may be using a different thread. Synchronisation techniques are often employed to manage requests and transmit results.

The world-wide-web is probably the best example of such an architecture. The browsers running on PCs are like clients and the sites they access play the role of servers. The server could also be housing a database and the clients could be processes that are querying and updating the database. A variant/generalisation of this is the **peer-to-peer** architecture where the client/server role of the subsystems are interchangeable. These variants are typically hard to design due to the possibility of deadlocks and a myriad of other problems that can complicate the flow of control.

The Pipe and Filter

The system in this case is made up of *filters*, i.e., subsystems that process data, and *pipes*, which can be used to interconnect the filters. The filters are completely mutually independent and are aware only of the input data that comes through a pipe, i.e., the filter knows the form and content of the data that came in, not how it was generated. This kind of architecture produces a system that is very flexible and can be dynamically reconfigured. In their simplest form, the pipes could all be identical, and each filter could be performing a fixed task on data input stream. An example of this would be that of processing incoming/outgoing data packets over a computer network. Each 'layer' would be like a filter that adds to, subtracts from or modifies the packet and sends it forward.

The Unix operating system is a more sophisticated version of such an architecture, and allows the user to create more complex operations by linking together simpler ones. In its most general form, one could have pipes that 'reformat' the data, so that any sequence of filters could be used.

11.11 Discussion and Further Reading

Software architectures and design patterns bear some similarity in that they both present efficient solutions to commonly occurring problems. The process of learning how to apply these are however very different. It is possible (and perhaps pedagogically preferable) to 'discover' design patterns by critically examining our designs and refactoring them. Such a process does not lend itself well to the task of learning about architectures due to the complexity of the problem we are encountering. The software designer's best bet is to learn about commonly used architectures in the given problem domain and adapt them to the current needs [1].

In this chapter and the previous one, we introduced design patterns by coming up some 'reasonable' design and then critically examining it using our knowledge of the principles of object-oriented analysis and design. This process is not very different from that of refactoring to introduce patterns into existing code. The process for refactoring to introduce patterns has been well-studied and cataloged [2, 3].

11.11.1 Separating the View and the Controller

When studying the MVC architecture, we often hear the phrase 'model–view separation', which refers to the idea that we keep the reality and representation distinct from each other. In our case-study, we have done this by having the model manage a list of items, and leaving all other responsibilities to other subsystems.

The separation between view and controller is less clear. In our implementation, we have chosen to make the knowledge of concrete command classes available to the classes that receive the user request. This makes for a clean implementation, since the request is immediately packed into an object that can be managed by the controller. The literature does mention other of ways of implementing the command pattern, which are based on the notion that the command object must be created in the controller subsystem. One approach that has been suggested is to allow the requests for operations to be received in a class in the controller. This has the drawback that the controller must implement methods (like `ActionListener`) that are really dependent on the view implementation, thus causing tight coupling. Another approach is to capture the request as a string (see [4]), which is then parsed in a command factory to generate the command object. This results in an unnecessary loss of performance.

All of this underscores the fact that the view and controller are not easily and clearly separable in every context. One obvious question that arises is: *Why not move the controller operations into the view?* This has led to a variant of the MVC, called the 'document-view' architecture, where the document holds the Model and the view handles the functions of the controller as well.

11.11.2 The Space Overhead for the Command Pattern

One of the drawbacks of the command pattern is that it places a large demand on the memory resources, which in turn has a serious effect on runtime. Some systems restrict the number of levels of undo and redo to some manageable number to avoid this problem, but this solution may not always be acceptable.

Another approach that has been proposed is that each command be a singleton that keeps its own `history` and `redoStack` objects. No instances of command are created at the time of invocation, but the controller pushes a reference to the singleton command object into its own history stack. The invoked command creates the data object necessary to undo the operation and pushes it into its own `history` stack. This approach is particularly beneficial if we go with a Document–View architecture.

11.11.3 How to Store the Items

The manner in which items are stored in the model can affect the time it takes to render the items and thus affect performance. Consider the problem of rendering a curve that is specified by user as a collection of 'control points'. If the constructor decomposed the curve into a collection of line segments, then the process of rendering would be to simply draw each line segment. On the other hand, if the model stored only the control points, rendering (i.e., the corresponding draw method in the concrete UIContext) would have to compute all the line segments and then draw them. In the first case we are creating a large number of objects and storing these in the model. The rendering could be slowed down because of the large number of objects that have to be accessed. In the second, rendering may be delayed by the amount of computation. In general, memory access involves a much greater overhead than computation, and therefore one would expect the second approach to give better runtime performance.

11.11.4 Exercising Caution When Allowing Undo

Implementing the undo operation can be quite tricky. The process of executing a command could involve the methods of several classes and care must be taken to ensure that these are correctly reversible. A full treatment of this is beyond the scope of this text, but we can highlight a few of these issues.

What Should be Saved to Undo an Operation?

We must keep in mind that what we are undoing is the consequences of the operation on the entire system. Consider the process of undoing the creation of a line. The only input to the operation are the two end points, and elementary mathematics tells us that we do not need any other information to define a line. However, this information is not sufficient for us to undo the effects of this operation. The consequence to the system is that the a line object is added to the model, and what we need to store is a reference to this object. The model also must allow for a specified item to be removed; if this were not possible, the operation of removing a line would not be undoable.

Designing and Implementing with Undo in Mind

The manner in which responsibilities are divided between the model and the controller and the public methods that are implemented can affect the ease of undo operations. Since our Line object is created in the controller, it is easy to store this in the command object and then use the reference to remove the object when undoing. If the model took the end points and invoked the constructor, we would need some additional machinery to implement undo. Likewise, our model has a method to remove a specified item, which is effectively an 'undo' of the operation that adds an item. If the methods invoked by the command object on other subsystems cannot be easily reversed, it may not be feasible to undo the operation.

11.11.5 Synchronising Updates

We have already alluded to the problem that could occur when multiple views concurrently update the UIContext field in the model. This is a well known problem in operating systems and the reader is referred to standard texts in the field [5] for a detailed description.

One possible solution is to use binary semaphores. For this, we first create the following class.

```
public class Synchroniser {
  private boolean drawing;
  public synchronised void beginDrawing() {
    try {
      while (drawing) {
        wait();
      }
    } catch (InterruptedException ie) {
    }
    drawing = true;
  }
  public synchronised void endDrawing() {
    drawing = false;
    notifyAll();
  }
}
```

Assume that the class is made a singleton. When the view is ready to start drawing, which would be at the very beginning of the paintComponent method in our example code, it invokes the beginDrawing method. After completing the drawing, that is, just before leaving the paintComponent method in our case, the view invokes endDrawing. The beginDrawing and endDrawing methods together ensures several desirable properties, including the following: at most one view is painting at any given time and every view gets a chance to paint, eventually.

Another solution employs monitors. Please see Silberschatz [5] for a description.

Projects

1. *Creating a simple spreadsheet.* The sheet will display a simple grid and allow for data and formulae to be entered into the boxes. The following features will be available:

   - Allow for a column to be widened. This will be done by user selecting a column and activating the operation from the menu
   - Automatic evaluation and re-evaluation of formulae
   - Drawing a graph using data from two columns

2. Implement the drawing program described in this chapter using the *Document–View* architecture. Implement each command as a singleton that keeps its own stack. What pros and cons do you see for this approach?
3. Create a simple graphical toy that consists of a circle, triangles and rectangles. All these shapes will be filled, and represent a 2-dimensional ball and 2-dimensional triangular and rectangular blocks. A menu will allow the user to create new blocks, change the colour of an existing shape, move the shapes, increase the size of the ball, rotate the blocks or drop the ball. When the ball is dropped, it will fall vertically and thereafter behave in accordance with the idealised laws of physics, with a coefficient of restitution of 0.5 (half the kinetic energy is lost whenever the ball collides with a block or a boundary). The blocks do not move when hit by the ball. There will be a designated threshold so that when the ball's velocity drops below this threshold, it will be assumed to have stopped.

11.12 Exercises

1. Modify the drawing program so that whenever a delete operation is invoked, a confirmation request is made by the system.
2. During the rendering process, the view invokes the `render()` method on the item, which then invokes the `draw` method on the `UIContext`. Since the concrete UIContext is decided by the view, can we modify the implementation to have the view directly invoke `draw`? What changes would be needed to do this? What are the pros and cons of this approach?
3. Modify the line drawing operation so that multiple lines can be created with one request.
4. Some drawing systems allow for lines of varying thickness. How would such a feature be implemented?
5. Write a formal use case for the decompose operation and implement it.
6. Modify the circle drawing operation so that the first click specifies the centre. After that, a 'circle of variable radius' is drawn such that centre is on the first click and the current cursor position lies on the boundary. When the second point is clicked, a circle is drawn with first mouse click as centre and second mouse click on the circle boundary.
7. A line can be specified by two points or by an equation. Consider a system where an 'origin' can be specified by a mouse click. After this is done, a line is specified by an equation of the form $ax + by + c = 0$ (the input would specify a, b and c). The line specified by this equation is drawn with reference to the current location of the origin. Note that this line would span the entire drawing panel. How would you implement such an operation?
8. Modify the line drawing operation so that the user has an option to cancel the command at any time before it is completed. This would involve adding a 'cancel' operation to our button panel.

9. Add an operation for drawing a triangle that allows for undoing individual mouse clicks. The triangle will be specified by mouse clicks on the three vertices.

10. (Drawing a closed cubic curve.) The B-spline is a popular cubic curve, since it makes it very easy to draw a smooth curve consisting of many segments. Implement this feature as follows: (i) *the user clicks on a succession of points, terminating by clicking on the first point again;* (ii) *after 4 clicks, the first piece of the curve appears;* (iii) *an additional piece is rendered at each subsequent click.* The curve is drawn using the mouse click locations as 'control points'. Four control points are used to generate each section of the curve, with the first four generating the first section, clicks 2, 3, 4 and 5 generating the next section and so on. For any four control points, P_0, P_1, P_2 and P_3, the curve can be generated by the parametric equation:

$$B(t) = \frac{1}{6}(-P_0 + 3P_1 - 3P_2 + P_3)t^3 + \frac{1}{2}(P_0 - 2P_1 + P_2)t^2$$
$$+ \frac{1}{2}(-P_0 + P_2)t + \frac{1}{6}(P_0 + 4P_1 + P_2) \tag{11.1}$$

The parameter t varies between 0 and 1, and is incremented in small steps, with one intermediate curve point being generated at each step. The curve itself is drawn as a series of line segments, each segment connecting the curve points generated by successive increments.

11. Implement the command that allows the user to select the font and font size; the code should also let the user boldface, underline, and italicise labels.

12. Re-implement the view subsystem using the state pattern.

13. Implement the following functionality in the drawing program: the user should be able to select a single figure by clicking the mouse on the figure or select multiple figures by holding the control key while clicking; it should then be possible to move the selected item(s). The operation should be undoable.

14. Implement the ability to draw polygons in the drawing program.

15. In the drawing program, implement the functionality to create rectangles and load images into these rectangles. The command should be undoable.

References

1. F. Buschmann, R. Meunier, H. Rohnert, P. Sommerlad, M. Stal, *Pattern-Oriented Software Architecture: A System of Patterns*, vol. 1 (Wiley, New York, 2001)
2. M. Fowler, *Refactoring: Improving the Design of Existing Code* (Addison-Wesley, Reading, 1999)
3. M. Fowler, K. Scott, *UML Distilled* (Addison-Wesley Longman, Reading, 1997)
4. M. Grand, *Patterns in Java: Catalogue of Reusable Design Patterns Illustrated with UML*, vol. 1 (Wiley, New York, 2002)
5. A. Silberschatz, P.B. Galvin, G. Gagne, *Operating System Concepts* (Wiley, New York, 2006)

Chapter 12
Designing with Distributed Objects

As businesses grow, they often set up operations over large geographic areas that may span multiple states or even countries and often find it desirable to process data at their point of origin or create results at the location where they are needed. As a consequence, businesses usually install multiple computer systems that are interconnected by communication links, and applications run across a network of computers rather than on a single machine. Such systems are called distributed systems.

Distributed processing offers a number of advantages. It is more economical and efficient to process data at the point of origin. Distributed systems make it easier for users to access and share resources. They also offer higher reliability and availability: failure of a single computer does not cripple the system as a whole. It is also more cost effective to add more computing power.

Distributed computing is not without its share of drawbacks. First, the software for implementing them is complex. Although a distributed system is made up of multiple computers, its design must somehow ensure that users, for the most part, are able to view it as a centralised system; it must coordinate actions between a number of possibly heterogeneous computer systems; if data is replicated, the copies must be made mutually consistent. Second, data access may be slow because information may have to be transferred across communication links. Third, securing the data is a challenge. As data is distributed over multiple systems and transported over communication links, care must be taken to guarantee that it is not lost, corrupted, or stolen.

As the final, major topic of the book, we address the process of designing and implementing a distributed, object-oriented application system. We present two approaches to building a such systems. The first mechanism uses *Java Remote Method Invocation (Java RMI)*, which is a piece of software, generally called middleware, that helps mask heterogeneity. The second approach uses the world-wide web itself to access data processed at remote sites.

© Universities Press (India) Private Ltd. 2015
B. Dathan and S. Ramnath, *Object-Oriented Analysis, Design and Implementation*,
Undergraduate Topics in Computer Science, DOI 10.1007/978-3-319-24280-4_12

12.1 Client/Server Systems

Distributed systems can be classified into peer-to-peer systems and client-server systems. In the former, every computer system (or node) in the distributed system runs the same set of algorithms; they are all equals, in some sense. The latter, the client/server approach, is more popular in the commercial world. In client/server systems, there are two types of nodes: clients and servers. A client machine sends requests to one or more servers, which process the requests, and return the results to the client. Many applications can use this model and these days the software at many clients are web browsers.

In this chapter, we look at the implementation of object-oriented systems that use the client/server paradigm. We look at the architecture itself in Sect. 12.1.1.

12.1.1 Basic Architecture of Client/Server Systems

To keep matters simple, we assume that although the client/server systems we build may have multiple clients, they will have just one server. It is not difficult to extend the techniques to multiple servers, so this is not a serious restriction. Figure 12.1 shows a system with one server and three clients. Each client runs a program that provides a user interface, which may or not be a GUI. The server hosts an object-oriented system. Like any other client/server system, clients send requests to the server, these requests are processed by the object-oriented system at the server, and the results are returned. The results are then shown to end-users via the user interface at the clients.

Fig. 12.1 Client/Server systems

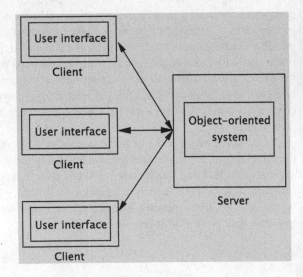

Fig. 12.2 Difficulty in accessing objects in a different JVM

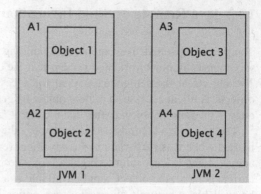

There is a basic difficulty in accessing objects running in a different Java Virtual Machine (JVM). Let us consider two JVMs hosting objects as in Fig. 12.2. A single JVM has an address space part of which is allocated to objects living in it. For example, objects object 1 and object 2 are created in JVM 1 and are allocated at addresses A1 and A2 respectively. Similarly, objects object 3 and object 4 live in JVM 2 and are respectively allocated addresses A3 and A4. Code within Object 2 can access fields and methods in object 1 using address A1 (subject, of course, to access specifiers). However, addresses A3 and A4 that give the addresses of objects object 3 and object 4 in JVM 2 are meaningless within JVM 1. To see this, suppose A1 and A3 are equal. Then, accessing fields using address given by A3 from code within JVM 1 will end up accessing memory locations within object 1.

This difficulty can be handled in one of two ways:

1. By using object-oriented support software: The software solves the problem by the use of proxies that receive method calls on 'remote' objects, ship these calls, and then collect and return the results to the object that invoked the call. The client could have a custom-built piece of software that interacts with the server software. This approach is the basis of Java Remote Method Invocation and is covered in Sect. 12.2.
2. By avoiding direct use of remote objects by using the Hyper Text Transfer Protocol (HTTP). The system sends requests and collects responses via encoded text messages. The object(s) to be used to accomplish the task, the parameters, etc., are all transmitted via these messages. This approach has the client employ an Internet browser, which is, of course, a piece of general purpose software for accessing documents on the world-wide web. In this case, the client software is ignorant of the application structure and communicates to the server via text messages that include HTML code and data. This is the technique used for hosting a system on the Web; it is definitely more popular and we cover it in Sect. 12.3.

12.2 Java Remote Method Invocation

The goal of Java RMI is to support the building of Client/Server systems where the server hosts an object-oriented system that the client can access programmatically. The objects at the server maintained for access by the client are termed **remote objects**. A client accesses a remote object by getting what is called a **remote reference** to the remote object. After that the client may invoke methods of the object.

The basic idea behind RMI is to employ the **proxy** design pattern. This pattern is used when it is inefficient or inconvenient (even impossible, perhaps) to use the actual object. (Please refer to Fig. 12.3 for a description of the proxy pattern.) In the current context, the object is only available at a remote site. If the same object is to be available at multiple client sites, one option is to download a copy of the object to all client sites, but such replication of objects introduces synchronisation issues when the object is to be updated. Instead, the proxy pattern creates a *proxy* object

Using a proxy

Where do we employ this? This pattern is used when it is inefficient or inconvenient (even impossible, perhaps) to create/use an actual object. Perhaps creating an object may be too time consuming, in which case the use of this pattern lets postponement of this creation until the actual object is needed.

Examples of its use include distributed systems in which we need to access objects remotely. Another example would be opening a document that embeds graphical objects that are too time consuming to create.

How have we solved it? In the distributed systems case, the use of a proxy allows us to access the remote object by reference. That way, updates from multiple clients are made directly to the object. In contrast, we may choose to copy the object to the point of use; however, replication always introduces consistency issues that need the employment of expensive protocols.

In the example of documents referring to graphical objects, the proxy creates the actual image object only when so asked by the document object itself. After the image is created, all requests sent to the proxy are directed to the actual image itself.

In both examples, notice that the client always maintains a reference to the proxy, which delegates the responsibility of carrying out the operations to the actual object.

How have we employed it? Java RMI employs proxies to stand in for remote objects. All operations exported to remote sites (remote operations) are implemented by the proxy. Proxies are termed *stubs* in Java RMI. These stubs are created by the RMI compiler.

Fig. 12.3 Using a proxy

Fig. 12.4 Client/Server
systems

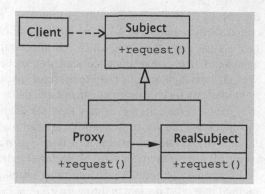

at each client site that accesses the remote object. The proxy object implements all of the remote object's operations that the remote object wants to be available to the client. The set up is shown in Fig. 12.4. When the client calls a remote method, the corresponding method of the proxy object is invoked. The proxy object then assembles a message that contains the remote object's identity, method name, and parameters. This assembly is called **marshalling**. In this process, the method call must be represented with enough information so that the remote site knows the object to be used, the method to be invoked, and the parameters to be supplied. When the message is received by it, the server performs **demarshalling**, whereby the process is reversed. The actual call on the remote method of the remote object is made, and any return value is returned to the client via a message shipped from the server to the proxy object.

The system maintains a separate proxy for remote object. When an object asks for a reference to a remote object, it is handed a reference to the object's proxy instead. Setting up remote object access in RMI, even for a small application, involves a number of steps. In fact, as we shall see, once we learn to set up a simple application system, we will have learned the tools and techniques for creating almost any client/server system using this technology. As we discuss each major concept, we will illustrate it using a running example.

Setting up a remote object system is accomplished by the following steps:

1. Define the functionality that must be made available to clients. This is accomplished by creating **remote interfaces**.
2. Implement the remote interfaces via **remote classes**.
3. Create a server that serves the remote objects.
4. Set up the client.

These are elaborated in the following sections.

12.2.1 Remote Interfaces

The first step in implementing a remote object system is to define the system functionality that will be exported to clients, which implies the creation of a Java interface. In the case of RMI, the functionality exported of a remote object is defined via what is called a *remote interface*. A remote interface is a Java interface that extends the interface `java.rmi.Remote`, which contains no methods and hence simply serves as a marker. Clients are restricted to accessing methods defined in the remote interface. We call such method calls **remote method invocations.**

Remote method invocations can fail due to a number of reasons: the remote object may have crashed, the server may have failed, or the communication link between the client and the server may not be operational, etc. Java RMI encapsulates such failures in the form of an object of type `java.rmi.RemoteException`; as a result, all remote methods must be declared to throw this exception.

In summary, a remote interface must extend `java.rmi.Remote` and every method in it must declare to throw `java.rmi.RemoteException`. These concepts are shown in the following example.

```
import java.rmi.*;
public interface BookInterface extends Remote {
   public String getAuthor() throws RemoteException;
   public String getTitle() throws RemoteException;
   public String getId() throws RemoteException;
}
```

Remote objects implement remote interfaces. They may implement more methods, but clients are restricted to accessing methods declared in the remote interfaces.

12.2.2 *Implementing a Remote Interface*

After the remote interfaces are defined, the next step is to implement them via *remote classes*. Parameters to and return values from a remote method may be of primitive type, of remote type, or of a local type. All arguments to a remote object and all return values from a remote object must be serializable. Thus, in addition to the requirement that remote classes implement remote interfaces, we require that they also implement the `java.io.Serializable` interface. Parameters of non-remote types are passed by copy; they are serialized using the object serialization mechanism, so they too must implement the `Serializable` interface.

Intuitively, remote objects must somehow be capable of being transmitted over networks. A convenient way to accomplish this is to extend the class `java.rmi.server.UnicastRemoteObject`.

Thus, the implementation of `BookInterface` is as below.

```
import java.io.*;
import java.rmi.*;
import java.rmi.server.*;
```

```
public class Book extends UnicastRemoteObject implements
                BookInterface, Serializable {
  private String title;
  private String author;
  private String id;
  public Book(String title1, String author1, String id1)
          throws RemoteException {
    title = title1;
    author = author1;
    id = id1;
  }
  public String getAuthor()  throws RemoteException {
    return author;
  }
  public String getTitle()  throws RemoteException {
    return title;
  }
  public String getId()  throws RemoteException {
    return id;
  }
}
```

Since it is a remote class, Book must be compiled using the RMI compiler by invoking the command rmic as below.

```
rmic Book
```

The compiler produces a file named Book_Stub.class, which acts as a proxy for calls to the methods of BookInterface. When the constructor for the remote class (Book in the above case) is invoked, the constructor for UnicastRemoteObject *exports* the remote object. When an exported remote object is passed as a parameter or returned from a remote method call, the stub for that remote object is passed instead of the object itself. The stub itself contains a reference to the serialized object and implements all of the remote interfaces that the remote object implements. All calls to the remote interface go through the stub to the remote object.

Remote objects are thus passed by reference. This is depicted in Fig. 12.5, where we have a single remote object that is being accessed from two clients. Both clients maintain a reference to a stub object that points to the remote object that has a field named a. Suppose now that Client 1 invokes the method setA with parameter 5. As we have seen earlier, the call goes through the stub to the remote object and gets executed changing the field a to 5. The scheme has the consequence that any changes made to the state of the object by remote method invocations are reflected in the original remote object. If the second client now invokes the method getA, the updated value 5 is returned to it.

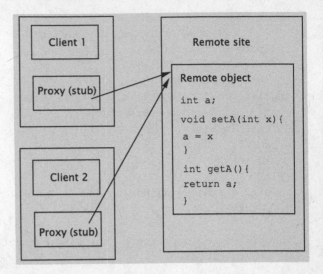

Fig. 12.5 Passing of remote objects as references

In contrast, parameters or return values that are *not* remote objects are passed by value. Thus, any changes to the object's state by the client are reflected only in the client's copy, not in the server's instance. Similarly, if the server updates its instance, the changes are not reflected in the client's copy.

12.2.3 Creating the Server

Before a remote object can be accessed, it must be instantiated and stored in an object registry, so that clients can obtain its reference. Such a registry is provided in the form of the class `java.rmi.Naming`. The method `bind` is used to register an object and has the following signature:

```
public static void bind(String nameInURL, Remote object)
        throws AlreadyBoundException, MalformedURLException,
        RemoteException
```

The first argument takes the form `//host:port/name` and is the URL of the object to be registered; `host` refers to the machine (remote or local) where the registry is located, `port` is the port number on which the registry accepts calls, and `name` is a simple string for distinguishing the object from the other objects in the registry. Both `host` and `port` may be omitted in which case they default to the local host and the port number of 1099, respectively.

The process of creating and binding the name is given below.

```
try {
  <interface-name> object = new <class-name>(parameters);
  Naming.rebind("//localhost:1099/SomeName", object);
} catch (Exception e) {
  System.out.println("Exception " + e);
}
```

The complete code for activating and storing the Book object is shown below.

```
import java.rmi.*;
import java.rmi.server.*;
import java.rmi.registry.Registry;
import java.rmi.registry.LocateRegistry;
import java.rmi.RemoteException;
import java.rmi.server.UnicastRemoteObject;
public class BookServer {
  public static void main(String[] s) {
    String name = "//localhost:1099/" + s[0];
    try {
      BookInterface book = new Book("t1", "a1", "id1");
      Naming.rebind(name, book);
    } catch (Exception e) {
      System.out.println("Exception " + e);
    }
  }
}
```

In the above code, we assume that when the server code is executed, it is provided with the name that should be associated with the Book object.

12.2.4 The Client

A client may get a reference to the remote object it wants to access in one of two ways:

1. It can obtain a reference from the Naming class using the method lookup.
2. It can get a reference as a return value from another method call.

Let us see how the first of these approaches can be accomplished. In the following we assume that an object of type SomeInterface has been entered into the local registry under the name SomeName.

```
SomeInterface object = (SomeInterface) Naming.lookup
                        ("//localhost:1099/SomeName");
```

After the above step, the client can invoke remote methods on the object. In the following code, the getters of the `BookInterface` object are called and displayed.

```
import java.util.*;
import java.rmi.*;
import java.net.*;
import java.text.*;
import java.io.*;
public class BookUser {
  public static void main(String[] s) {
    try {
      String name = "//localhost/" + s[0];
      BookInterface book = (BookInterface) Naming.lookup(name);
      System.out.println(book.getTitle() + " " + book.getAuthor()
                              + " " + book.getId());
    } catch (Exception e) {
      System.out.println("Book RMI exception: " + e.getMessage());
      e.printStackTrace();
    }
  }
}
```

Just as in the case of the server, the client needs to know the name that is bound to the object, so it must be started with that name as the parameter.

12.2.5 Setting up the System

To run the system, create two directories, say `server` and `client`, and copy the files `BookInterface.java`, `Book.java`, and `BookServer.java` into `server` and the file `BookUser.java` into `client`. Then compile the three Java files in `server` and then invoke the command

```
rmic Book
```

while in the `server` directory. This command creates the stub file `Book_Stub.class`. Copy the client program into `client` and compile it.

Run RMI registry and the server program using the following commands (on Windows).

```
start rmiregistry
java -Djava.rmi.server.codebase=file:C:\Server\BookServer
BookServer MyBook
```

The first command starts the registry and the second causes the `Book` instance to be created and registered with the name `MyBook`.

Finally, run the client as below from the `client` directory.

```
java -Djava.rmi.server.codebase=file:C:\Client\BookUser
BookUser MyBook
```

The client code starts, looks up the object with the name `MyBook`, calls the object's
getter methods, and displays the values.

12.3   Implementing an Object-Oriented System on the Web

Without doubt, the world-wide web is the most popular medium for hosting distributed applications. Increasingly, people are using the web to book airline tickets,
purchase a host of consumer goods, make hotel reservations, and so on. The browser
acts as a general purpose client that can interact with any application that talks to it
using the Hyper Text Transfer Protocol (HTTP).

One major characteristic of a web-based application system is that the client (the
browser), being a general-purpose program, typically does no application-related
computation at all. Of course, it is possible to ship a Java applet with a web page and
have the applet do some computation, but this is not hugely popular. All business
logic and data processing take place at the server. Typically, the browser receives web
pages from the server in HTML and displays the contents according to the format,
a number of tags and values for the tags, specified in it. In this sense, the browser
simply acts as a 'dumb' program displaying whatever it gets from the application
and transmitting user data from the client site to the server.

The HTML program shipped from a server to a client often needs to be customised:
the code has to suit the context. For example, when we make a reservation on a
flight, we expect the system to display the details of the flight on which we made the
reservation. This requires that HTML code for the screen be dynamically constructed.
This is done by code at the server.

For server-side processing, there are competing technologies such as Java Server
Pages and Java Servlets, Active Server Pages (ASP), and PHP. In this book we study
Java Servlets.

12.3.1   HTML and Java Servlets

As we have stated earlier, any system that ultimately displays web pages via a browser
has to create HTML code. HTML code displays text, graphics such as images, links
that users can click to move to other web pages, and *forms* for the user to enter data.
We will now describe the essential code for doing these.

An HTML program can be thought of as containing a header, a body, and a trailer. The header contains code like the following:

```
<!DOCTYPE html PUBLIC "-//W3C//DTD HTML 4.01 Transitional//EN">
<html>
<head>
  <meta content="text/html; charset=ISO-8859-1"
  http-equiv="content-type">
  <title>A Web Page</title>
</head>
```

The first four lines are usually written as given for any HTML file. We do not elaborate on these, but observe words such as `html` and `head` that are enclosed between angled brackets (< and >). They are called **tags**. HTML tags usually occur in pairs: start tag that begins an entry and end tag that signals the entry's end. For example, the tag `<head>` begins the header and is ended by `</head>`. The text between the start and end tags is the element content.

In the fifth line we see the tag `title`, which defines the string that is displayed in the title bar. The idea is that the string `A Web Page` will be displayed in the title bar of the browser when this page is displayed.

As a sample body, let us consider the following.

```
<body>
<h1>
     <span style="color: rgb(0, 0, 255);">
     <span style="font-family: lucida bright;">
     <span style="font-style: italic;">
     <span style="font-weight: bold;">
        An Application
     </span>
     </span>
     </span>
     </span>
  </h1>
  </body>
```

The body contains code that determines what gets displayed in the browser's window. Some tags may have attributes, which provide additional information. For example, see the line

```
     <span style="color: rgb(0, 0, 255);">
```

where the tag `span` has its attribute `style` modified, so that the text will be in blue colour: the reader may have guessed that `rgb` stands for the amount of red, green, and blue in the color, whose the values can range from 0 to 255. As the examples suggest, attributes always come in name/value pairs of the form `name="value"`. They are always specified in the start tag of an HTML element.

The body contains code to display the string `An Application` in the font Lucida bright, bolded, italicised, and in blue color.
The last line of the file is

```
</html>
```

Obviously, it ends the HTML file.

Entering and Processing Data

The reader is probably familiar with web pages that allow the user to enter information that the system processes. For example, a search engine provides a field in which we type in some search terms. When an accompanying button is clicked, the system transfers control to the search engine that displays results of the search.

This is accomplished by using what is called a **form** tag in HTML. The complete code that allows us to enter some piece of text in the web page is given below.

```
<!DOCTYPE html PUBLIC "-//W3C//DTD HTML 4.01 Transitional//EN">
<html>
<head>
 <meta content="text/html; charset=ISO-8859-1"
 http-equiv="content-type">
 <title>Sample Form</title>
</head>
<body>
   <form action="/servlet/apackage.ProcessInput" method="post">
     <table>
       <tr>
           <td align="right">Enter Data:</td>
           <td><input type="text" name="userInput"></td>
       </tr>
       <tr>
           <td><input type="submit" value="Process"></td>
       </tr>
     </table>
   </form>
</body>
</html>
```

Let us get a general understanding of the above piece of code. Consider the code that begins with the line

```
<form action="/servlet/apackage.ProcessInput" method="post">
```

The tag `form` begins the specification of a set of elements that allow the user to enter information. The `action` attribute specifies that the information entered by the user is to be processed by a Java class called `ProcessInput.class`, which resides in the package `apackage`.

There are two primary ways in which form data is encoded by the browser: one is GET and the other is POST. GET means that form data is to be encoded into a URL while POST makes data appear within the message itself. See Fig. 12.6 for the considerations in deciding which of these methods should be used.

The tag `<table>` begins the creation of a table. Each row of the table is described using the tag `<tr>`, and the tag `<td>` defines a cell in the table. The line

```
<td><input type="text" name="userInput"></td>
```

GET or POST?

While considering the question of which of the two methods, GET or POST, should be employed to transmit form data, it is helpful to remember that GET inserts the data in the URL itself whereas POST includes the data as part of the message. As a consequence, the URLs created for the POST and GET methods differ in that the latter completely identifies the server resource. This implies that the resource from the URL of the GET method can be used from other web pages to access the same resource, a capability that is not possible with the URL of POST.

A section in the HTTP/1.1 specifications talks about a kind of client/server interactions called **safe interactions**. In a safe interaction, users are not responsible for the result of the interaction, and GET is the appropriate method to use in such situations. To understand the concept of safe interactions, consider a web page (call it page 1) that asks the user to agree to some conditions by checking a box before allowing him/her to download a piece of software from a second page (say, page 2). Suppose that the form data, which includes the checkbox, from page 1 is transmitted using GET. Clearly, the URL completely identifies page 2. This URL can then be used to provide a link, called a deep link, to Page 2 from an unrelated web page (say, page 3), and any use of this link from page 3 is an unsecure way of accessing the resource.

It should be noted, however, that trying to hide the resource location is not a foolproof mechanism: one could look at the source file of the web page to craft a link to the resource.

One of the HTTP usage recommendations is that the GET method should be used only when the form processing is **idempotent**, that is, the result is the same whether the form is processed once or multiple times. This definition, however, should not be taken too literally. Generally speaking, if resubmitting a form does not change the application data stored at the server (even if it changes other entities such as log files), it is appropriate to use GET. In other circumstances, the POST method should be used to transmit form data.

Generally speaking, results from the GET method are cached, but data obtained from POST are not. As a consequence, GET method may execute faster than POST.

Fig. 12.6 Get and post: a brief comparison

thus creates a cell, which is actually an input field where the user can enter data. This is indicated by the `<input>` tag two attributes of which, `type` and `name`, are modified in this example. One attribute is `type`, which specifies what the type of input is: here we have `"text"`, which means plain text. (Some other possibilities such as `"password"`, which makes the entry unreadable on the screen, will be covered later in the chapter.) The second attribute, `name`, must be given a unique value: the value names the input element, somewhat like an identifier.

Next, look at the line

```
<td><input type="submit" value="Process"></td>
```

This line creates a button of type `"submit"`, which when clicked causes the form data to be sent to the server. The button has the label `Process`.

The server-side code `ProcessInput` is an example of a **servlet,** which uses the request-response paradigm. Servlets can process data sent using the HTTP protocol via a form. They can handle multiple requests concurrently. We create a servlet by extending the class `HttpServlet` as below.

```
public class ProcessInput extends HttpServlet {
```

Since we transmitted form data using the POST method, we need to override a method called `doPost`. This method has two parameters, `request` and `response` that respectively encapsulate the data sent by the client and the response to the client.

The header of the `doPost` method is given below.

```
public void doPost(HttpServletRequest request,
                   HttpServletResponse response) throws
                   IOException, ServletException {
```

Data sent by the client through the form is retrieved using the `request` object as below.

```
String input = request.getParameter("userInput");
```

Note that `userInput` corresponds to the name of the field in the form.

After the data is captured and processed, the servlet creates an HTML page using the response object as below.

```
response.setContentType("text/html");
response.getWriter().println("<!DOCTYPE html PUBLIC \"-//W3C//DTD "+
                   "HTML 4.01 Transitional//EN\">");
```

The first line states that the data is HTML and the second line begins the HTML code. The complete code for the servlet is given below.

```
package apackage;
import javax.servlet.*;
import javax.servlet.http.*;
import java.awt.event.*;
import java.util.*;
import java.io.*;
public class ProcessInput extends HttpServlet {
  public void doPost(HttpServletRequest request,
                     HttpServletResponse response) throws IOException,
                     ServletException {
    String input = request.getParameter("userInput");
    response.setContentType("text/html");
    response.getWriter().println("<!DOCTYPE html PUBLIC \"-//W3C//DTD " +
                          "HTML 4.01 Transitional//EN\">");
    response.getWriter().println("<html>");
    response.getWriter().println("<head>");
    response.getWriter().println("<meta content=\"text/html;" +
                          " charset=ISO-8859-1\"" +
                          "http-equiv=\"content-type\">");
    response.getWriter().println("<title>Response to Input</title>");
    response.getWriter().println("</head>");
    response.getWriter().println("<body>");
    response.getWriter().println("You entered " + input);
    response.getWriter().println("</body>");
    response.getWriter().println("</html>");
  }
  public void doGet(HttpServletRequest request,
                    HttpServletResponse response) throws IOException,
                    ServletException {
    doPost(request, response);
  }
}
```

Although we do not use the GET method, we have overridden it, so that in case the form is changed to use the GET method, the system will continue to work.

The architecture for serving web pages is depicted in Fig. 12.7. Assume that an HTML page is displayed on the client's browser. The page includes, among other things, a form that allows the user to enter some data. The client makes some entries in the form's fields and submits them, say, by clicking a button. The data in the form is then transmitted to the server and given to a Java servlet, which processes the data and generates HTML code that is then transmitted to the client's browser, which displays the page.

12.3.2 Deploying the Library System on the World-Wide Web

We now undertake the task of designing and developing a web-based version of the library system. Of course, we cannot do everything exactly as in a real library: in particular, we do not have machines that scan bar codes on books, but we will do as close a job as possible as a real system.

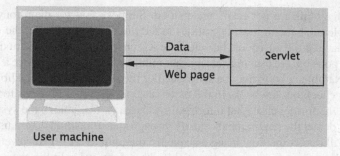

Fig. 12.7 How servlets and HTML cooperate to serve web pages

Developing User Requirements

As in any system, the first task is to determine the system requirements. We will, as has been the case throughout the book, restrict the functionality so that the system's size is manageable.

1. The user must be able to type in a URL in the browser and connect to the library system.
2. Users are classified into two categories: *superusers* and *ordinary members*. Superusers are essentially designated library employees, and ordinary members are the general public who borrow library books. The major difference between the two groups of users is that superusers can execute any command when logged in from a terminal in the library, whereas ordinary members cannot access some 'privileged commands'. In particular, the division is as follows:

    (a) Only superusers can issue the following commands: add a member, add a book, return a book, remove a book, process holds, save data to disk, and retrieve data from disk.
    (b) Ordinary members and superusers may invoke the following commands: issue and renew books, place and remove holds, and print transactions.
    (c) Every user eventually issues the exit command to terminate his/her session.

3. Some commands can be issued from the library only. These include all of the commands that only the superuser has access to and the command to issue books.
4. A superuser cannot issue any commands from outside of the library. They can log in, but the only command choice will be to exit the system.
5. Superusers have special user ids and corresponding password. For regular members, their library member id will be their user id and their phone number will be the password.

Interface requirements It turns out that due to the nature of the graphical user interface, an arbitrarily large number of sequences of interactions are possible between the user and the interface. Employing the use-case model alone to determine the requirements would necessitate the use of too many conditionals, and the resulting sequence diagrams are not easily understood. Suppose that for their convenience, users be able to abandon most operations in the middle; for example, the user may decide to place a hold on a book, but when the screen to enter the book id and duration of the hold pops up, the user may change her mind and decide not to place a hold. For a second example, a book may be self issued or the member may ask a library staff member to check out the book. In the latter case, the member id needs to be input, whereas in the former case, that information is already available to the system.

We thus depict the requirements mostly through state transition diagrams. (A little later, we will depict the flow using a sequence diagram as well.) However, a single transition diagram is too large and unwieldy. Therefore, we split the state transition diagram into a number of smaller ones.

Logging in and the Initial Menu

In Fig. 12.8, we show the process of logging in to the system. When the user types in the URL to access the library system, the log in screen that asks for the user id and password is displayed on the browser. If a valid combination is typed in, an appropriate menu is displayed. What is in the menu depends on whether the user is an ordinary member or a superuser and whether the terminal is in the library or is outside.

1. The Issue Book command is available only if the user logs in from a terminal in the library.
2. Commands to place a hold, remove a hold, print transactions, and renew books are available to members of the library (not superusers) from anywhere.
3. Certain commands are available only to superusers who log in from a library terminal: these are for returning or deleting books, adding members and books, processing holds, and saving data to and retrieving data from disk.

A superuser has to be logged in from a terminal in the library, or the menu will simply contain the command to exit the system. It may seem somewhat strange that

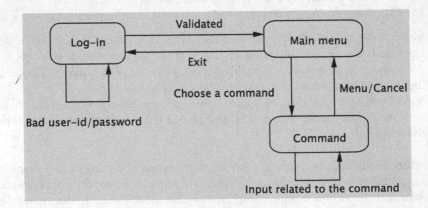

Fig. 12.8 State transition diagram for logging in

a superuser has no access to the library system from outside of the library whereas an ordinary member has several commands at her disposal. But note that it makes not much sense to allow a superuser to issue most of the commands from outside the library: a superuser cannot deal with a library member from the outside, so commands to add members, issue, return, and renew books, place and remove holds and print transactions are not applicable. Also, a superuser cannot be reasonably expected to add or remove books from the outside. One could make a case that a superuser be allowed to process holds and save and retrieve data from the outside, but it is hard to see why a superuser would work from the outside just for issuing these commands.

When the user types in the URL for the library, the system presents a log-in screen for entering the user id and password. If the user types in a bad user id/password combination, the system presents the log in screen again with an error message.

On successful validation, the system displays a menu that contains clickable options. The Command State in Fig. 12.8 denotes the general flow of a command. When a certain command is chosen, we enter a state that represents the command. How the transitions take place within a command obviously depends on what the command is. All screens allow an option to cancel and go back to the main menu. If this option is chosen, the system goes on to display the main menu awaiting the next command.

When the exit command is chosen, the system logs the user out and presents the log in screen again.

Add Book

The flow is shown in Fig. 12.9. When the command to add a book is chosen, the system constructs the initial screen to add a book, which should contain three fields for entering the title, author, and id of the book, and then display it and enter the Add Book state. By clicking on a button, it should be possible for the user to submit these values to system. The system must then call the appropriate method in the Library class to create a Book object and enter it into the catalog. The result of the operation is displayed in the Command Completed state.

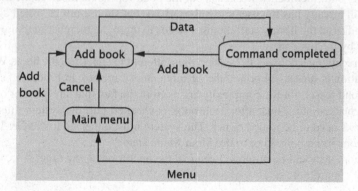

Fig. 12.9 State transition diagram for add book

Fig. 12.10 State transition
diagram for saving data

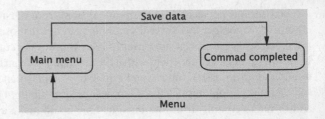

From the Command Completed state, the system must allow the user to add
another book or go back to the menu. In the Add Book state, the user has the option
to cancel the operation and go back to the main menu.

Add Member, Return Book, Remove Book

The requirements are similar to the ones for adding books. We need to accept some
input (member details or book id) from the user, access the `Library` object to
invoke one of its methods, and display the result. So we do not describe them here
nor do we give the corresponding state transition diagrams.

Save Data

When the data is to be written to disk, no further input is required from the user. The
system should carry out the task and print a message about the outcome. The state
transition diagram is given in Fig. 12.10.

Retrieve Data

The requirements are similar to those for saving data.

Issue Book

This is one of the more complicated commands. As shown in the state transition
diagram in Fig. 12.11, a book may be checked out in two different ways: First, a
member is allowed to check it out himself/herself. Second, he/she may give the book
to a library staff member, who checks out the book for the member. In the first case,
the system already has the user's member id, so that should not be asked again. In
the second case, the library staff member needs to input the member id to the system
followed by the book id.

After receiving a book id, the system must attempt to check out the book. Whether
the operation is successful or not, the system enters the Book Id Processed state.

A second reason for the complexity arises from the fact that any number of books
may be checked out. Thus, after each book is checked out, the system must ask if
more books need to be issued or not. The system must either go to the Get Book Id
state for one more book id or to the Main Menu state.

As usual, it should be possible to cancel the operation at any time.

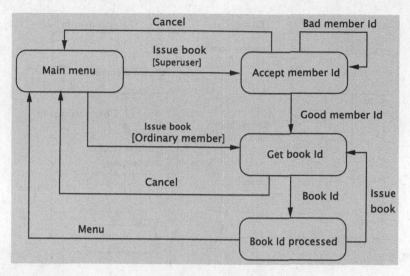

Fig. 12.11 State transition diagram for issuing books

Place Hold, Remove Hold, Print Transactions

The requirements for these are similar to those for issuing a book, so we omit their description.

Renew Books

The system must list the title and due date of all the books loaned to the member. For each book, the system must also present a choice to the user to renew the book. After making the choices, the member clicks a button to send any renew requests to the system. For every book renewal request, the system must display the title, the due date (possibly changed because of renewal), and a message that indicates whether the renewal request was honoured. After viewing the results, the member uses a link on the page to navigate to the main menu.

The state transition diagram is given in Fig. 12.12.

Design and Implementation

To deploy the system on the web, we need the following:

1. Classes associated with the library, which we developed in Chap. 7; you will recall that this includes classes such as `Library`, `Member`, `Book`, `Catalog`, and so on.
2. Permanent data (created by the save command) that stores information about the members, books, who borrowed what, holds, etc.
3. HTML files that support a GUI for displaying information on a browser and collecting data entered by the user. For example, when a book is to be returned, a screen that asks for the book id should pop up on the browser. This screen will

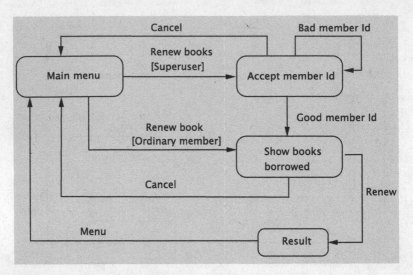

Fig. 12.12   State transition diagram for renewing books

have a prompt to enter the book id, a space for typing in the same, and a button to submit the data to the system.
4. A set of files that interface between the GUI ((3) above) and the objects that actually do the processing ((1) above). Servlets will be used to accomplish this task.

Structuring the files HTML code for delivery to the browser can be generated in one of two ways:

1. Embed the HTML code in the servlets. This has the disadvantage of making the servlets hard to read, but more dynamic code can be produced.
2. Read the HTML files from disk as a string and send the string to the browser. This is less flexible because the code remains static.

We attempt to combine the two approaches so as to utilise the advantages of both approaches without sacrificing either flexibility or cleanliness of code. Almost all HTML code is generated by reading files from disk; where needed, simple changes are applied to these files, so the desired functionality is achieved.

Having made the decision that most of the HTML code will be stored in files, the next question is how to set them up.

1. Create a separate HTML file for every type of page that needs to be displayed. For example, create a file for entering the id of the book to be returned, a second file for displaying the result of returning the book, a third file for inputting the id of the book to be removed, a fourth one for displaying the result of removing the book, etc.

2. Exploit the commonalities between the commands and create a number of HTML code fragments, a subset of which can be assembled to form an HTML file suitable for a specific context.

The first option has the advantage of simplicity. However, the reader can probably guess that the number of HTML files could be a problem. A rough calculation shows that at least 28 files are needed even without considering the intricacies associated with some of the commands such as Issue Book and Renew Book.

Although the second option is more involved because of the need to assemble a big file from several fragments, we find that it presents some advantages over the first. First, it reduces the number of files somewhat. More importantly, however, there is a great deal of duplication in the files in the first approach; duplication brings with it the problem of inconsistency. For example, to change the way the library's name is displayed in the screens, every one of the HTML files will need to be updated! We thus opt for the second choice.

Examples of HTML file fragments To show how this approach works in practice, consider the two commands, one for returning and the other for removing books. In both, the user must be presented with a web page that asks him/her to enter a book id. We have just one file that displays this page. However, the servlet that needs to be invoked will change depending on the context. Therefore, we code the servlet name as below.

```
<form action="GOTO_WITH_BOOKID" method="post">
```

By simply changing the string GOTO_WITH_BOOKID in the servlet, we can use the same HTML file in multiple situations.

A similar approach is taken for accepting member ids.

For every web page, the header should display a title that depends on the context. We maintain just one file for the header. This file has a string TITLE that stands for the title of the web page. Depending on which page is being displayed, TITLE is replaced by an appropriate string, which gets displayed in the title bar.

When a command is completed, we need to display a web page. For most commands, the data to be displayed is small enough that it can be thought of as a simple string. We, therefore, employ just one file, commandCompleted.html, to carry out this task. This file is adapted, however, in two different ways.

1. The result to be displayed will vary on the command as well as whether the operation was successful. To take care of this, the file has a string called RESULT.

```
<h3> RESULT <br></h3>
```

This may be replaced by strings such as Book not found and Member added. Once the file is read into a string, the RESULT string is replaced by the appropriate result of executing the command. The following pseudocode gives the idea.

```
String result;
Member member;
String htmlFile = getFile("commandCompleted.html"):
if ((member = library.addMember(name, address, phone)) == null) {
  htmlFile = htmlFile.replace("TITLE", "Member not Added");
  result = "Member could not be added";
} else {
  htmlFile = htmlFile.replace("TITLE", "Member Added");
  result = member.getName() + " ID: " + member.getId() + " added";
}
htmlFile = htmlFile.replace("RESULT", result);
```

2. To reduce the number of mouse clicks, the user may be given the option to repeat the command whose result is displayed by the commandCompleted.html file. For example, after completing the Add Book command, we need to give an option to issue the command once again so that the user can add another book. Since the code where control should go to depends on the command that was just executed, some adaptation is in order. This is facilitated by having the line

```
<a href="REPLACE_JS">REPLACE_COMMAND</a><br>
```

in the HTML file.

In the case of Add Member, we substitute REPLACE_COMMAND by Add Book, which provides a link that the user can click, and REPLACE_JS by addmemberinitialization, which locates the Java class that is given the control when the link is clicked.

```
htmlFile = htmlFile.replace("REPLACE_J,S", "addmemberinitialization");
htmlFile = htmlFile.replace("REPLACE_COMMAND", "Add Member");
```

How to remember a user Servlets typically deal with multiple users. When a servlet receives data from a browser, it must somehow figure out which user sent the message, what the user's privileges are, etc. Each request from the browser to the server starts a new connection, and once the request is served, the connection is torn down. However, typical web transactions involve multiple request–response pairs. This makes the process of remembering the user associated with a connection somewhat difficult without extra support from the system.

The system provides the necessary support by means of what are known as **sessions**, which are of type HttpSession. When it receives a request from a browser, the servlet may call the method getSession() on the HttpServletRequest object to create a **session object**, or if a session is already associated with the request, to get a reference to it. To check if a session is associated with the request and to optionally create one, a variant of this method getSession(boolean create) may be used. If the value false is passed to this method and the request has no valid HttpSession, this method returns null.

When a user logs in, the system creates a session object as below.

```
HttpSession session = request.getSession();
```

When the user logs out, the session is removed as below.

```
session.invalidate();
```

Requests other than log in requires the user to be logged in. The following code evaluates to true if the user does not have a session: that is, the user has not logged in.

```
request.getSession(false) == null
```

A session object can be used to store information about the session. In the library system, we would like to store the user id, the type of terminal from which the user has logged in, and some additional information related to the user. The methods for this are

1. `void setAttribute(String name, Object value)`
   This command binds `value`, the object given in the second parameter, to the attribute specified in `name`. By setting the second parameter to `null`, the attribute can be removed.

2. `Object getAttribute(String name)`
   The attribute value associated with `name` is returned.

3. `void removeAttribute(String name)`
   This method deletes the specified attribute from this session.

Configuration The server runs with the support of Apache Tomcat, which is a **servlet container**. A servlet container is a program that supports servlet execution. The servlets themselves are registered with the servlet container. URL requests made by a user are converted to specific servlet requests by the servlet container. The servlet container is responsible for initialising the servlets and delivering requests made by the client browser to the appropriate servlet.

The directory structure is as in Fig. 12.13. We store the HTML files in a directory named `Library`, which is a subdirectory of `webapps`, which, in turn, is a subdirectory of the home directory of Tomcat. The servlets are in the package `library`, which is stored in `Library/WEB-INF/classes`. The implementation of the backend classes such as `Member`, `Catalog`, etc. is in the package `basicImplementation`.

Our implementation requires that the user create an environment variable named `LIBRARY-HOME` that has as value the absolute path name of the directory that houses the HTML files.

The deployment descriptor elements are defined in a file called `web.xml`. While this file permits a large number of tags, our use of them is limited to mapping the URLs to servlets. To understand how this is done, first examine the following lines of XML code.

Fig. 12.13 Directory
structure for the servlets

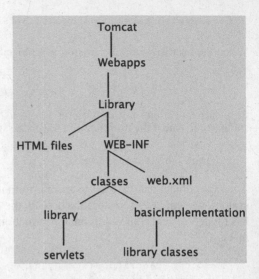

```
<servlet-mapping>
    <servlet-name>LoginServlet</servlet-name>
    <url-pattern>/login</url-pattern>
</servlet-mapping>
```

Thus when we write code such as

```
URL=login
```

in the HTML file, the string login is mapped to the servlet name LoginServlet.

But the servlet name given by the tag <servlet-name> is just a name that is mapped to the fully-qualified class name of the servlet as below.

```
<servlet>
    <servlet-name>LoginServlet</servlet-name>
    <servlet-class>library.Login</servlet-class>
</servlet>
```

In the web.xml file for our application, a servlet such as library. IssueBook Initialization (<servlet-class>) is mapped from the <servlet-name> of IssueBookInitializationServlet, which, in turn, is mapped from the URL pattern of issuebookinitialization, that is, the name of the original servlet in lower-case.

The list of superusers and their passwords is stored in a file named Privileged Users. The IP addresses of all client machines located in the library are listed in a file named IPAddresses. Both files are to be stored in the same directory that has the HTML files.

To run the system, first Tomcat needs to be started and then the library system needs to be accessed from a browser by typing in the URL of the Tomcat home concatenated with /Library. The file index.html in the library directory is then accessed; this file directs the request to the servlet Login.

Structure of servlets in the web-based library system A servlet receives data from a browser through a HttpServletRequest object. This involves parameter names and their values, IP address of the user, and so on. For example, when the form to add book is filled and the Add button is clicked, the servlet's doPost method is invoked. As we have seen earlier, this method has two parameters: a request parameter of type HttpServletRequest and a response parameter of type HttpServletResponse.

Each command is organised as a combination of one to three servlets. They need a number of common utility functions during the course of processing. These methods and doPost and doGet are collected into a class named LibraryServlet. This class has the structure shown in Fig. 12.14.

Most of the methods of LibraryServlet fall into one of five categories:

1. One group contains methods that store information about the user. This information includes the user id, the type of terminal from which the user has logged in, etc. and are stored in attributes associated with the session object. The methods are addAttribute, setAttribute, getAttribute, and deleteAllAttributes.
2. Methods to validate users and help assess access rights. The validateSuper User method checks whether the user is a superuser and validateOrdinary

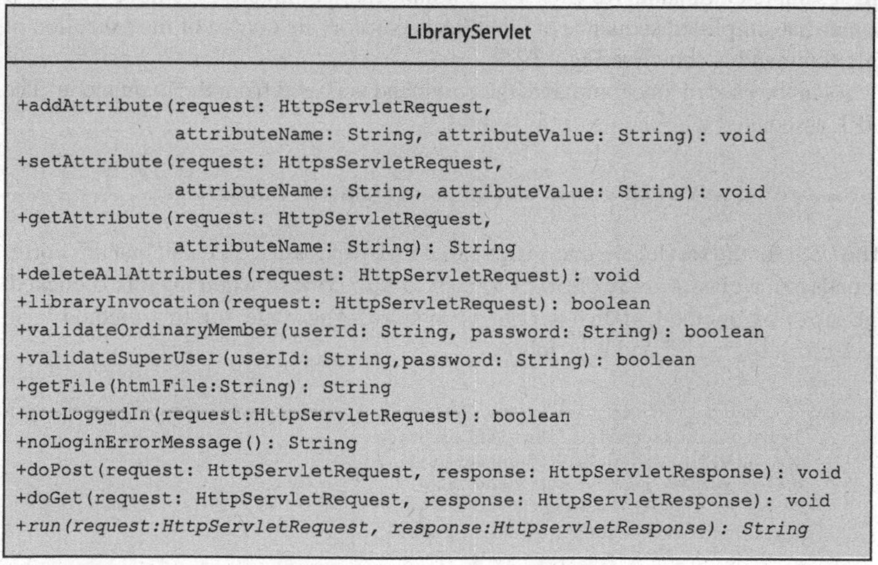

```
                              LibraryServlet

+addAttribute(request: HttpServletRequest,
              attributeName: String, attributeValue: String): void
+setAttribute(request: HttpsServletRequest,
              attributeName: String, attributeValue: String): void
+getAttribute(request: HttpServletRequest,
              attributeName: String): String
+deleteAllAttributes(request: HttpServletRequest): void
+libraryInvocation(request: HttpServletRequest): boolean
+validateOrdinaryMember(userId: String, password: String): boolean
+validateSuperUser(userId: String,password: String): boolean
+getFile(htmlFile:String): String
+notLoggedIn(request:HttpServletRequest): boolean
+noLoginErrorMessage(): String
+doPost(request: HttpServletRequest, response: HttpServletResponse): void
+doGet(request: HttpServletRequest, response: HttpServletResponse): void
+run(request:HttpServletRequest, response:HttpservletResponse): String
```

Fig. 12.14 Class diagram for Library servlet

Member does the same job for ordinary members. The method library Invocation returns true if and only if the user has logged in from a terminal located within the library.
3. The getFile method reads an HTML file and returns its contents as a String object.
4. The fourth group of methods are used for handling users who may have invoked a command without actually logging in. The method notLoggedIn returns true if and only if the user has not currently logged in. The method noLoginError Message returns HTML code that displays an error message when a person who has not logged in attempts to execute a command.
5. The final group of commands deal with processing the request and responding to it. The doGet message calls doPost, which does some minimal processing needed for all commands and then calls the abstract run method, which individual servlets override.

In our design, all servlets inherit from LibraryServlet and will override the run method. Some of these are simple while others are more involved. Except for a couple of servlets that deal with log in, the structure of the run method is as below.

```
if the user has not logged in
    return an html page that displays "Not logged in"
else
    return an html page that is the result of processing the request
```

Execution flow Processing a request sometimes involves simply generating an HTML page, which is quite straightforward. This is best understood by following a sample command. We choose as example, the command to remove a book. A somewhat simplified sequence of what takes place in the course of the execution of this command is shown in Fig. 12.15.

As in the case of any command, the command is issued from the main menu. The URL associated with the text is as below:

```
<a href="removebookinitialization">Remove book</a>
```

The URL for the servlet is removebookinitialization; recall that this corresponds to the class RemoveBookInitialization, so when the link is clicked, the doPost method of that servlet is invoked. The code for this method is in LibraryServlet and is as follows:

```
public void doPost(HttpServletRequest request, HttpServletResponse response)
        throws IOException, ServletException {
    response.setContentType("text/html");
    String page = run(request, response);
    if (!notLoggedIn(request)) {
      setAttribute(request, "page", page);
    }
    response.getWriter().println(page);
}
```

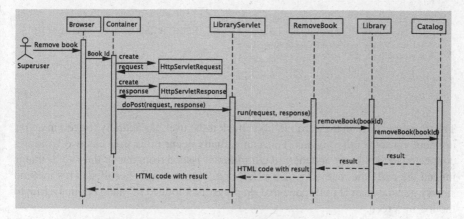

Fig. 12.15 Simplified sequence diagram for removing books

The first line in the method specifies the type of the file for the `response` object: whatever is written to the response object is treated as HTML. The `run` method is invoked, which is implemented within the subclass. This method returns HTML code as a `String` object and is saved in the attribute named `page` of the session. This helps in the following way. The system always remembers the last page displayed. If the user tries to log in from a different window of the browser, that page is redisplayed. It also helps when the user overwrites the current page by visiting some other site and wants to come back to the library system. Finally, the page is written out and gets displayed in the browser.

The check for whether the user has logged in was discussed before and is repeated for convenience.

```
public boolean notLoggedIn(HttpServletRequest request) {
    return request.getSession(false) == null;
}
```

The code for removing a book begins with the servlet `RemoveBook Initialization`, whose `run` method is given below.

```
package library;
import javax.servlet.*;
import javax.servlet.http.*;
public class RemoveBookInitialization extends LibraryServlet {
    public String run(HttpServletRequest request,
                      HttpServletResponse response) {
        if (notLoggedIn(request)) {
            return noLoginErrorMessage();
        }
        String htmlFile = getFile(HEADER);
        htmlFile = htmlFile.replace("TITLE", "Remove Book");
```

```
        htmlFile += getFile(GET_BOOK_ID);
        htmlFile = htmlFile.replace("GOTO_WITH_BOOKID", "removebook");
        htmlFile += getFile(CANCEL);
        htmlFile += getFile(END_PAGE);
        return htmlFile;
    }
}
```

The first three lines in the run method check if the user has actually logged in and is not here via some other means. This can actually occur if the user has two windows connected to the library and the exit command is issued from one of the two. If that is indeed the case, the method noLoginErrorMessage() is called. This method simply generates an HTML page that displays 'Not logged in' and supplies a link to the log in screen.

In the case that the user is actually logged in, the HTML page is assembled. It includes reading four files: one to begin the HTML page and the other to end it. In between, a form to enter the book id and a link to cancel the command are inserted. As a consequence, the browser at the client displays a page that either requires the user to enter the id of a book that should be removed or click on a link to cancel the command and return to the main menu.

The process of ensuring that the user had logged in and using the header file to begin assembling the HTML file is common to all servlets, so we will not explain these actions in further discussion.

The HTML code for entering the book id is given below.

```
<form action="GOTO_WITH_BOOKID" method="post">
<table>
<tr>
  <td align="right">Id:</td>
  <td><input type="text" name="bookId"></td>
</tr>
<td><br><input type="submit" value="Enter Book Id"></td>
</tr>
</table>
</form>
```

In the normal course of action, the user would enter a book id and click the button labelled Enter Book Id. Notice the lines

```
<form action="GOTO_WITH_BOOKID" method="post">
```

in the HTML file and the line

```
htmlFile = htmlFile.replace("GOTO_WITH_BOOKID", "removebook");
```

in the servlet. The place holder GOTO_WITH_BOOKID is replaced by the URL removebook. Therefore, when the user submits the form, the RemoveBook servlet is initiated. The code for this class is given below.

```
package library;
import javax.servlet.*;
import javax.servlet.http.*;
public class RemoveBook extends LibraryServlet {
  public String run(HttpServletRequest request,
                    HttpServletResponse response) {
    if (notLoggedIn(request)) {
      return noLoginErrorMessage();
    }
    String id = request.getParameter("bookId");
    String htmlFile = getFile(HEADER);
    htmlFile += getFile(COMMAND_COMPLETED);
    htmlFile += getFile(END_PAGE);
    String result;
    if ((result = library.removeBook(id)) == null) {
      htmlFile = htmlFile.replace("TITLE", "Book not Removed");
      result = "Book could not be removed";
    } else {
      htmlFile = htmlFile.replace("TITLE", "Book Removed");
    }
    htmlFile = htmlFile.replace("RESULT", result);
    htmlFile = htmlFile.replace("REPLACE_JS", "removebookinitialization");
    htmlFile = htmlFile.replace("REPLACE_COMMAND", "Remove Book");
    return htmlFile;
  }
}
```

The path to the run method is once again via the doPost method in Library Servlet. The id of the book to be removed is retrieved by invoking the command getParameter on the request object. We then start assembling the HTML page to respond to the request. The removeBook method in the Library class is invoked and the result of the command is used to replace the place holder RESULT. The servlet provides two choices at this stage: the user may remove another book or go back to the main menu. The option to go back to the main menu is common to all commands, so it is hard-coded in the HTML file for command completion. However, the command to be repeated depends on what command we are in, so the place holders REPLACE_JS and REPLACE_COMMAND are replaced by the URL of the servlet and an appropriate piece of text that the user can click on.

The code for some other commands (returning a book, adding a book, adding a member, and processing holds) are quite similar and warrants no further explanation. The code for saving and retrieving data are simpler. The implementation for the other commands, issuing a book, placing a hold, removing a hold, and printing transactions are more complicated, but they are all similar. So we next explain the implementation for issuing a book.

Issuing books Issuing books is complicated by the fact that an ordinary member may self-issue a book or may ask a library staff member, a superuser, to issue the book for himself/herself. (See the state transition diagram in Fig. 12.11.) In the former case, we need to skip asking the member's id and in the latter case, the system must present a screen for entering the member id.

Like all other commands, the user clicks on a link to issue books; the HTML file contains the lines

```
<td valign="top" width="160">
<a href="issuebookinitialization">Issue book</a>
<br></td>
```

The click on `Issue book` causes the servlet `IssueBookInitialization` to execute. This servlet checks if the user is a superuser, and if so, a screen to accept the member id is displayed; otherwise, the member to whom the book should be issued is known and a screen to accept a book id is displayed. The code is given below.

```
public class IssueBookInitialization extends LibraryServlet {
    public String run(HttpServletRequest request, HttpServletResponse response) {
      if (notLoggedIn(request)) {
        return noLoginErrorMessage();
      }
      boolean privileged = getAttribute(request, "userType").equals("Privileged");
      String memberId = getAttribute(request, "currentUserId");
      String htmlFile = getFile(HEADER);
      htmlFile = htmlFile.replace("TITLE", "Issue Book");
      if (privileged) {
        htmlFile += getFile(GET_MEMBER_ID);
        htmlFile = htmlFile.replace("GOTO_WITH_MEMBERID", "issuebookgetmemberid");
      } else {
        htmlFile += getFile(GET_BOOK_ID);
        htmlFile = htmlFile.replace("GOTO_WITH_BOOKID", "issuebookgetbookid");
      }
      htmlFile += getFile(CANCEL);
      htmlFile += getFile(END_PAGE);
      return htmlFile;
    }
}
```

We now discuss how we remember the member for whom the book is to be issued. Recall that the session object can store attributes and that commands such as issuing a book and placing a hold are always carried out for a specific member. That member's id is stored in the attribute `currentUserId`. If the session was for an ordinary member, the value for this attribute is the member's id itself. Otherwise, when a superuser is logged in, the value changes depending on the member for whom the command is being carried out; when the command does not involve a member (for example, the superuser is adding books), the value of this attribute is the empty string (" ").

From the above discussion, clearly,

```
String memberId = getAttribute(request, "currentUserId");
```

would be the empty string if the user is a superuser and the logged-in-member's id otherwise.

The servlet `IssueBookGetMemberId` retrieves the id of the member to whom books should be issued:

```
String memberId = request.getParameter("memberId");
```

If the member id is invalid, the HTML file consists of an error message and a form to accept the member id. In this case, note that control will come back to the same servlet.

```
if (!library.searchMembership(memberId)) {
  htmlFile +=  getFile(COMMAND_COMPLETED);
  htmlFile = htmlFile.replace("RESULT", "Could not locate member");
  htmlFile += getFile(GET_MEMBER_ID);
  htmlFile = htmlFile.replace("GOTO_WITH_MEMBERID", "issuebookgetmemberid");
  htmlFile = htmlFile.replace("REPLACE_JS", "");
  htmlFile = htmlFile.replace("REPLACE_COMMAND", "");
}
```

If the member id is valid, it is remembered in the attribute `currentUserId` and a form for capturing the book id is created.

```
setAttribute(request, "currentUserId", memberId);
htmlFile += getFile(GET_BOOK_ID);
htmlFile = htmlFile.replace("GOTO_WITH_BOOKID", "issuebookgetbookid");
htmlFile += getFile(CANCEL);
```

The `IssueBookGetBookId` servlet gets the book id from the form, retrieves the value of the attribute `currentUserId` to get the member id and calls the `issueBook` method of `Library`. The result is then used to replace the string RESULT in the `commandCompleted` HTML file.

```
String bookId = request.getParameter("bookId");
String memberId = getAttribute(request, "currentUserId");
Book book;
String result;
if ((book = library.issueBook(memberId, bookId)) == null) {
  result = "Book could not be issued";
} else {
  result = book.getTitle() + "issued.";
}
htmlFile = htmlFile.replace("RESULT", result);
htmlFile += getFile(GET_BOOK_ID);
htmlFile = htmlFile.replace("GOTO_WITH_BOOKID", "issuebookgetbookid");
```

The result of invoking `issueBook` is stored in the string RESULT as has been the case for other commands. (This part of the HTML code also has the option to return to the main menu.) We then concatenate the HTML file that contains the form to enter a book id, so the user has the option to enter another book id. The system continues executing this servlet until the user decides to go back to the main menu.

Renewing books Book renewal begins in the same manner as book issuing: the member id needs to be accepted if the user is a superuser; otherwise, that step can be bypassed.

To allow renewal, the title and due date all of the books checked out to the user must be displayed. Also, for each book a checkbox needs to be shown, so the user can check it if he/she wants the book to be renewed. The HTML code, stored in the file `renewBook.html`, for this part of the process is given below.

```
<tr>
 <td> TITLE </td>
 <td> DUE_DATE </font> </td>
 <td> <input type="checkbox" name="RENEW" /> </td>
</tr>
```

The type `checkbox` denotes a checkbox control, which the user can click to indicate that a book should be renewed. The three strings, `TITLE`, `DUE_DATE`, and `RENEW` are placeholders for the book title, book id, and the name of the checkbox control. The idea is that the above five lines of code will be replicated as many times as the number of books checked out. The names of the possibly multiple checkboxes need to be different, which is the task of the servlets.

The list of books must be assembled from two servlets: `RenewBooks Initialization` if the user is an ordinary member and `RenewBooksGet MemberId` if the user is a superuser. Since the code to perform this task is a bit lengthy, it is extracted into `LibraryServlet`.

The code, given below, first gets an iterator for the books checked out. The HTML file is built up from the file `renewBook.html` we described earlier. The strings `TITLE` and `DUE_DATE` are respectively replaced by the book's title and due date. A unique name for the checkbox is generated by replacing the string `RENEW` by the concatenation of `renew` and a counter that is incremented once per loop iteration.

Now, for some slightly more complicated task. The `RenewBooks` servlet must somehow discover the book id and other details of the books that are to be renewed. Also, we list the title and due date (possibly changed) of each book to be renewed and a status message that says whether the book was renewed or not. This demands that we remember the details of all the books in the order we displayed them. These are stored in the attributes `bookId`, `title`, and `dueDate`, each concatenated with the value of the counter. Also, the number of books displayed is also stored in the attribute `numberOfBooks`.

```
protected String assembleBooks(HttpServletRequest request, String memberId) {
   int counter = 0;
   String htmlFile = "";
   for (Iterator issuedBooks = library.getBooks(memberId);
             issuedBooks.hasNext(); counter++) {
```

```
      Book book = (Book) (issuedBooks.next());
      htmlFile += getFile(RENEW_BOOKS);
      htmlFile = htmlFile.replace("TITLE", book.getTitle());
      htmlFile = htmlFile.replace("DUE_DATE", book.getDueDate());
      setAttribute(request, "bookId" + counter, book.getId());
      setAttribute(request, "title" + counter, book.getTitle());
      setAttribute(request, "dueDate" + counter, book.getDueDate());
      htmlFile = htmlFile.replace("RENEW", "renew" + counter);
    }
    setAttribute(request, "numberOfBooks", counter + "");
    return htmlFile;
  }
```

As we mentioned above, when the user responds, the servlet `RenewBooks` comes into play. The servlet enters a loop iterating as many times as there are number of books checked out. If the checkbox is clicked, the condition `request.get Parameter("renew" + counter) != null` evaluates to true. The servlet retrieves the book's title from the attribute `bookTitle` and replaces the TITLE in the HTML file `renewedBook.html`. An attempt is made to renew the book using the member id and book id obtained from stored attributes. If the renewal is successful, the string `DUE_DATE` in `renewedBook.html` is replaced by the new due date. Otherwise, the old due date replaces the string.

Notice also that we delete all of the attributes created for the renewal process.

```
String memberId = getAttribute(request, "currentUserId");
int numberOfBooks = Integer.parseInt(getAttribute(request, "numberOfBooks"));
for (int counter = 0; counter < numberOfBooks; counter++) {
  if (request.getParameter("renew" + counter) != null) {
    htmlFile += getFile(RENEWED_BOOKS);
    String bookId = getAttribute(request, "bookId" + counter);
    String title = getAttribute(request, "title" + counter);
    String dueDate = getAttribute(request, "dueDate" + counter);
    htmlFile = htmlFile.replace("TITLE", title);
    Book book = library.renewBook(bookId, memberId);
    if (book != null) {
      htmlFile = htmlFile.replace("RENEWED", "renewed");
      htmlFile = htmlFile.replace("DUE_DATE", book.getDueDate());
    } else {
      htmlFile = htmlFile.replace("RENEWED", "book not renewable");
      htmlFile = htmlFile.replace("DUE_DATE", dueDate);
    }
    request.getSession(false).removeAttribute("bookId" + counter);
    request.getSession(false).removeAttribute("title" + counter);
    request.getSession(false).removeAttribute("dueDate" + counter);
  }
}
request.getSession(false).removeAttribute("numberOfBooks");
```

Logging in and logging out When the class `LibraryServlet` is loaded, it reads the files `PrivilegedUsers` and `IPAddresses` and copies the information to main memory. When a user logs in, we have seen that control goes to the `Login` servlet. It assembles the log in screen for display by the browser.

Assume now that the user types in a user id and password and sends them to the server. The `Index` servlet reads in the user id and password and calls a method named `getMenu` in the class `MenuBuilder`. This class is responsible for checking the validity of the user and returning the appropriate menu. The class `MenuBuilder` itself is not a servlet, so to utilise the methods of `LibraryServlet`, it needs the reference to the `Index` servlet. To call some of these methods, `MenuBuilder` also needs the request object. For uniformity, we also pass the response object, although it is not currently used. The method thus has 5 parameters: a reference to the `Index` servlet, the request and response objects, and the user-id and password.

First, the code checks if the user is a superuser by calling the method `validate SuperUser` of `LibraryServlet`, and if so, the attribute `userType` is given the value `Privileged`. Otherwise, the `LibraryServlet` class's `validate OrdinaryMember` method is called to see if the user is a member of the library; in that case, the `userType` attribute is set as `Ordinary`. Also, note the use of the boolean variables `privileged` and `validated`. In the event of an invalid user-id–password combination, a `null` value is returned to the `Index` servlet, which redisplays the log-in screen with an error message.

```
if (servlet.validateSuperUser(userId, password)) {
  servlet.setAttribute(request, "userType", "Privileged");
  validated = true;
} else if (servlet.validateOrdinaryMember(userId, password)) {
  servlet.setAttribute(request, "userType", "Ordinary");
  privileged = false;
  validated = true;
}
if (!validated) {
  return null;
}
```

With a successful log-in, the method checks whether the terminal used is within the library premises or outside. The attribute `location` reflects this assessment. The `currentUserId` is set to the user's id for ordinary users and to the empty string (`" "`) for privileged users. (We have already seen how this attribute is used to handle commands such as Issue Book.)

```
if (servlet.libraryInvocation(request)) {
  servlet.setAttribute(request, "location", "Library");
  location = LIBRARY;
} else {
  servlet.setAttribute(request, "location", "Outside");
}
servlet.setAttribute(request, "userId", userId);
if (!privileged) {
```

```
      servlet.setAttribute(request, "currentUserId", userId);
    } else {
      servlet.setAttribute(request, "currentUserId", "");
    }
    return getMenu(servlet, privileged, location);
```

The final step is to return the appropriate menu. This is done by the method `getMenu` that has three parameters. The code assembles the HTML page by reading from four different files in addition to the files for beginning and ending the page. These meet the requirements we set forth under 'Developing User Requirements'. If the user has logged in from the library, the Issue Book command is inserted into the menu. For privileged users, commands such as Add and Remove Book are inserted. Ordinary members always get to issue commands such as placing a hold and removing a hold. These commands are also available to superusers who log in from a library terminal. Finally, the exit command is available to all users from anywhere.

```
   private String getMenu(LibraryServlet servlet, boolean privileged,
                                                  boolean location) {
     boolean OUTSIDE = false;
     boolean LIBRARY = true;
     String html = servlet.getFile(LibraryServlet.HEADER);
     if (location == LIBRARY) {
       html += servlet.getFile(LibraryServlet.LIBRARY_COMMANDS);
     }
     if (privileged && location == LIBRARY) {
       html += servlet.getFile(LibraryServlet.PRIVILEGED_COMMANDS);
     }
     if (!privileged || location == LIBRARY) {
       html += servlet.getFile(LibraryServlet.GLOBAL_COMMANDS);
     }
     html += servlet.getFile(LibraryServlet.EXIT_COMMAND);
     html += servlet.getFile(LibraryServlet.END_PAGE);
     return html;
   }
```

There is a third version of the `getMenu` method, which gets invoked when a user goes back to main menu from the middle or at the end of a command. In this case, the user id and password are already known; so the attributes are read from the session object to determine what the menu should be. The menu itself is created using the 3-parameter `getMenu` method (the second version) we just discussed. This third version also sets the attribute `currentUserid` to the empty string (" ") for privileged users. The critical part of the code is given below.

```
  if (!servlet.getAttribute(request, "userType").equals("Privileged")) {
     privileged = false;
  } else {
     servlet.setAttribute(request, "currentUserId", "");
  }
```

```
if (servlet.getAttribute(request, "location").equals("Library")) {
    location = LIBRARY;
}
return getMenu(servlet, privileged, location);
```

12.4 Discussion and Further Reading

RMI provides a level of abstraction much higher than the traditional communication
mechanism in networks, viz. sockets. A socket is an endpoint of a communication
channel to or from which data is transmitted in the network. Sockets are analogous
to phones and a socket allocated on a machine is uniquely associated with a process
running on it. The type of socket associated with a process depends on the transport
layer in use (TCP or UDP, for example). A socket can have an associated port number
using which processes may send messages to it. Socket programming is possible in
many modern programming languages including C and Java. The book by Stevens
[1] is an excellent reference for programming in C in the Unix environment.

The difficulty with the socket model of programming is that it is very different from
the imperative paradigm of programming, which involves procedure calls. Remote
Procedure Call (RPC) [2] provides an improved model that allows programs to issue
a call to a procedure in another address space, which could actually be in a remote
computer on a network. For the most part, this can be done without worrying about the
underlying network. The code that runs on a centralised machine would run without
too much modification on a network as well. RPC is a popular way of implementing
distributed systems using the C programming language. Businesses that have made
use of RPC include Xerox, Sun, and Microsoft. RMI is essentially RPC extended to
the world of object-oriented systems. For a description of RPC, see RFC 707.

The Common Object Request Broker Architecture (CORBA), standardised by the
Object Management Group (OMG), is another approach to distributed object-based
computing. It allows a distributed, heterogeneous collection of objects to interoperate,
and automates many common network programming tasks such as object registration,
location, and activation, error-handling, parameter marshalling and demarshalling,
security control and concurrency control.

Like RMI, the services that a CORBA object provides are defined by its interface.
Again, as in RMI, object references are really of interface types. The Object Request
Broker (ORB) is responsible for delivering requests from a client to a remote object
and to return the results.

The ORB does a little more than just send requests and receive replies. Unlike
RMI, CORBA is language independent (it is also platform independent), and the
ORB plays a crucial role in this. The client may issue the request in a programming
language different from that of the CORBA object to which it issues the request. The
ORB does the necessary translation between programming languages. Language
bindings are defined for all popular programming languages. For a quick overview
of CORBA, refer to [3].

As mentioned in the chapter, the Java Servlet technology is just one of the tools available for creating web-based systems. PHP is a scripting language that usually runs on the server side. It can have HTML code embedded into it and outputs web pages. ASP.NET is another competing scripting technology from Microsoft for building web-based applications. JSP is similar to PHP and ASP, the difference being that we intersperse Java code with HTML code to create dynamic web pages. Other technologies such as Ruby on Rails (RoR) are also available.

The World Wide Web Consortium develops technologies for the utilisation of the web. This includes specifications for HTML and HTTP. The reader is encouraged to take a look at their site at http://www.w3.org/ to get an overview of the work provided by that group.

12.5 Exercises

1. Consider the implementation of the library system using Java RMI with a single server that runs classes such as `Library`, `Catalog`, `Book`, etc., multiple clients, each running an instance of `UserInterface`. Which classes do you need to modify? What other modifications do you need to make? Examine the parameters and return values for the remote method calls and verify that they all conform to RMI requirements.
2. Modify the distributed library system so that a command to list the catalog is available.
3. Consider the solution to Question 2. Incorporate a mechanism by which a user can place holds on books by selecting one or more books from the catalog listing.
4. Learn another technology for implementing web-based systems. A relatively easy exercise would be to learn Java Server Pages (JSP). Re-implement the library system using JSP. What are the advantages of JSP compared to Java servlets?
5. Suppose that instead of allowing no commands (other than exit) to be issued by a superuser from terminals outside the library, we want them to be able to do some telecommuting from outside. Make changes to the web-based system so that the commands to save and retrieve data and the command to process holds can be done by a superuser from anywhere.

References

1. R. Stevens, *UNIX Network Programming* (Prentice Hall, Englewood Cliffs, 1998)
2. A.D. Birrell, B.J. Nelson, Implementing remote procedure calls. ACM Trans. Comput. Syst. **2**(1), 39–59 (1984)
3. O.M. Group. Corba basics. http://www.omg.org/gettingstarted/corbafaq.htm

Chapter 13
The Unified Modelling Language

Throughout this book we have used several kinds of UML diagrams to describe various aspects of the system under consideration. UML is a complex language and it is hard to grasp all the details at the beginning. In this chapter, we re-visit UML to gain a broader perspective that will enable us to use it more effectively. Also, we take a closer look at the UML diagrams that were not dealt with in-depth in the earlier chapters.

The OMG specification states:

> The Unified Modelling Language (UML) is a graphical language for visualizing, specifying, constructing, and documenting the artefacts of a software-intensive system. The UML offers a standard way to write a system's blueprints, including conceptual things such as business processes and system functions as well as concrete things such as programming language statements, database schemas, and reusable software components.

The important point to note here is that UML is a "language" for specifying, and not a method or procedure. The UML is used to define a software system, to detail the artefacts in the system, to document and construct—it is the language that the blueprint is written in. The UML may be used in a variety of ways to support a software development methodology (such as the Rational Unified Process), but in itself it does not specify that methodology or process.

UML can be seen as a mechanism for defining the notation and semantics for several kinds of models (or domains). Although the exact domain under which a particular UML diagram falls can be a matter of discussion, we can roughly categorise the diagrams among the following domains:

1. User Interface Model: Describes the boundary and interaction between the system and users. Corresponds in some respects to a requirements model.
2. Interaction or Communication Model: Describes how objects in the system will interact with each other to get work done.

© Universities Press (India) Private Ltd. 2015
B. Dathan and S. Ramnath, *Object-Oriented Analysis, Design and Implementation*,
Undergraduate Topics in Computer Science, DOI 10.1007/978-3-319-24280-4_13

3. State or Dynamic Model: State charts describe the states or conditions that classes assume over time. Activity graphs describe the workflows the system will implement.
4. Logical or Class Model: Describes the classes and objects that will make up the system.
5. Physical Component Model: Describes the software (and sometimes hardware components) that make up the system.
6. Physical Deployment Model: Describes the physical architecture and the deployment of components on that hardware architecture.

The semantics of these domains are such that each of these domains presents a different view of the system. A system design methodology often uses only a subset of the domains, and exactly which ones are used is usually decided by the people in charge of a project. To make such a decision, it is imperative to know what kind of a model each domain gives us, so that a clear communication occurs between all those involved in the project.

During the various stages of the creation of software, we need different kinds of models. When the system is initially being defined, we rely on the User Interface Model. The UML diagram used for this is the use-case diagram, which shows the interaction between the actors and the various use cases. This was discussed in Chaps. 2 and 6.

The Interaction Model is useful when we want to flesh out the details of the all the required behaviours. The interaction model describes how objects in the system will interact (collaborate) with each other to get work done. In the context of UML, a *collaboration* is a description of a collection of objects that interact to implement some behaviour within a context. Collaboration diagrams are created to represent how these classes collaborate to provide specific behaviours. There are 3 kinds of diagrams that model the collaboration (i.e., interaction and communication) between objects: **sequence diagrams, communication diagrams**, and **timing diagrams**.

Sequence diagrams were dealt with extensively in Chap. 7, where we used them to describe in detail how the software classes would interact to achieve the required functionality for our Library system. We do not address them any further here. **Communication diagrams** are used show the message flow between objects in an application and also imply the basic associations (relationships) between classes. When showing the associations between classes, we could have a *static* description which shows only the classes and the roles played by members of each class. Such a diagram is called a **specification-level communication diagram.** In a *dynamic* description, we show the messages that flow between the instances of the collaborating classes, and hence these are called **instance-level communication diagrams. Timing diagrams** are a type of interaction diagram, where the focus is on timing constraints and are used to explore the behaviours of objects throughout a given period of time. Later in this chapter, communication diagrams and timing diagrams will be used to describe some aspects of the projects discussed in this book.

Statecharts and **activity diagrams** are two ways in which the dynamic model can be captured. Statecharts describe finite state machines that describe the various states of a component of the system; these were dealt with in Chap. 10. Activity diagrams, which represent the flow of control from one activity to another, are discussed next. A more recent addition to the UML family are **interaction overview diagrams**. These focus on the overview of the flow of control of the interactions. They are a variant of the activity diagram, where the nodes are the interactions or interaction occurrences. They are useful to understand how the interaction occurrences come together in defining the system and are therefore a part of the dynamic model of a system.

The logical model and the component models tell us what software entities have to be created. We discussed **class diagrams** in Chap. 7. The additional diagrams for representing these models are **component diagram**, **composite structure diagram**, **package diagram** and the **object diagram**.

Finally, we discuss the **deployment diagram**, which describes the deployment of the components on the hardware.

13.1 Communication Diagrams

As already stated, communication diagrams *(formerly referred to as collaboration diagrams)* are used show the message flow between objects in an application, implying the basic associations (relationships) between classes.

A **specification-level communication diagram** is a *static* description which shows only the classes and the roles played by members of each class, while an **Instance-level Communication Diagram** is a *dynamic* description which shows the messages that flow between the instances of the collaborating classes. (It should be noted that instance-level diagrams are very similar to sequence diagrams and it would be very unusual if a design of a project provides descriptions using both these kinds of diagrams.)

13.1.1 Specification-Level Communication Diagrams

The model that we created in Chap. 6 consisted of a set of use cases. Each use-case represents a scenario and each class has some role to play in the scenario. As an example, consider the scenario of checking out a book to a user. This scenario is used multiple times in the use case Checkout Books. The entities (software classes) that play a role are the MemberList, Catalog, Member and Book. The role to be played by the objects of a class in a particular scenario is called a *ClassifierRole*. Quite often, particularly in less complex systems, the ClassifierRole for a class cannot be distinguished from the class itself. Thus the ClassifierRole for the Book class is Book, the ClassifierRole for the Member class is Member, etc.

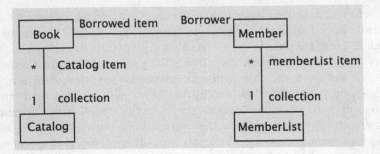

Fig. 13.1 Specification-level diagram for Book Checkout

Within a scenario, the specific role that a class has with respect to another class is called an *AssociationRole*. The association between the two classes is then termed as a *Link*. If two boxes are connected by a link, they form a *collaborating pair*. Each entity in the pair plays a particular role in the link (different from its ClassifierRole); this is the *AssociationRole* of the entity. In Fig. 13.1, there is a link between Book and Catalog. Catalog is merely a collection of Books and so the AssociationRoles are just "collection" and "catalog item" respectively. In the link between Book and Member, the AssociationRoles are "borrowed item" and "borrower" respectively. Thus the class "Book" has the ClassifierRole "Book" with two AssociationRoles, viz., "catalog item" and "borrowed item".

Note that this scenario corresponds to the use-case for checking out books. The diagram explains which classes in the Library subsystem collaborate when a book has to be checked out and defines the nature of the relationship (collaboration) between all pairs of these classes. However, the specification-level diagram does not give us the details of actions taken by each of the objects, i.e., it does not tell us *how* the collaboration occurs.

A second example involving the drawing program from Chap. 11 is shown in Fig. 13.2. This diagram shows how the classes collaborate to create a circle. The GUI transmits the user requests to the `CircleCommand`. The label `/CircleCommand:Command` denotes that `CircleCommand` is an entity of type `Command`. The `CircleCommand` plays the role of the request processor in this association. The `CircleCommand` then acts as a creator to create the `Circle`, which is an entity of type `Item`. Once the Item has come into existence, it has to be drawn. This is shown in the association between the `Circle` and the `UIContext`. In our case, the particular `UIContext` is the `SwingUI`, and this is represented by the label. In the resulting association, the `Circle` is a drawable item and the `UIContext` is a drawing tool. Finally, we have an association between the `UIContext` and the GUI, in which the GUI behaves as the drawing medium.

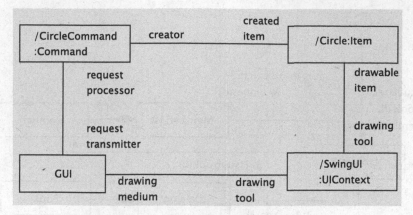

Fig. 13.2 Specification-level diagram for drawing a circle

In our examples, the role played by any participating class (the ClassifierRole) does not change; we can say that the ClassifierRole is synonymous with the class itself. In more complex systems, a class may play multiple ClassifierRoles. In diagrams where two ClassifierRoles are associated with the same class, the Classifier-Roles should be distinct in terms of their requested operations and the values of attributes.

13.1.2 Instance-Level Communication Diagrams

In an instance-level diagram, we show how the instances of the classes collaborate with each other to complete the task. As one would expect, the collaboration takes place by passing messages, i.e., methods of one class being invoked by the other. This in turn implies that the links now have arrows on them; the arrow points from class that invokes the method towards the class whose method is being invoked. The label on each link describes the name of the method, the parameters passed and the result. In addition, we have a unique number next to each message; these numbers indicate the order in which the messages are sent.

Figure 13.3 shows how this would be used to represent the checking out of a book. When the Library receives a request to checkout a book, it first sends a search message to MemberList, which returns a reference to the Member object. Next it sends a search message to Catalog, which returns a reference to the Book object. Next it sends the issueBook message to Member, and finally the issue message to the Book.

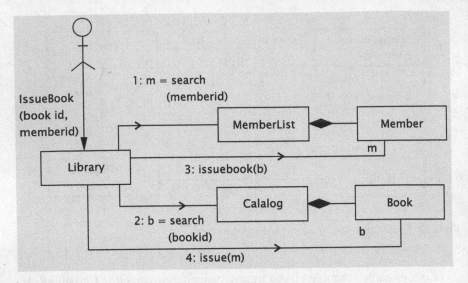

Fig. 13.3 Instance-level diagram for Book Checkout

13.2 Timing Diagrams

UML timing diagrams describe two system characteristics:

- the change in state or value of one or more elements over time
- the interaction between timed events and the time and duration constraints that govern them.

When both the characteristics are juxtaposed we get a picture of how the interaction between the objects is connected to the change in the objects' state. The state change can happen due to external events and trigger interaction with other objects, or the state change may occur due to a message being received from another object. Thus the timing diagram can provide a mechanism for understanding the internal dynamics of the system.

There are two kinds of figures that are used to describe this: the **Value Lifeline** and the **State Lifeline.** The Value Lifeline shows the change in value over time, whereas the State Lifeline shows the change in state.

As a simple example, consider a card-swipe system that provides access through a door. To gain access a user (card-holder) swipes the card. There is a wait period when the system processes the card and then a period when the access is granted. The user is thus in one of three possible states: *Idle, Waiting* and *Has access.* The system can be modelled as being in one of two states: *Idle* and *Activated.* When the card is swiped, the system goes from Idle to the Activated state. When the card is validated, a event is triggered that allows access, and after a short interval a second event is triggered that removes access and the system returns to the Idle state.

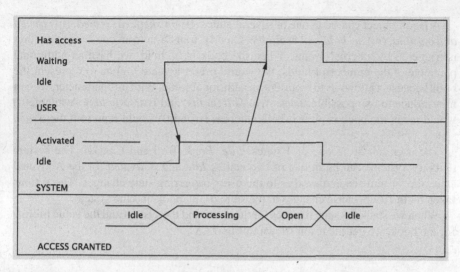

Fig. 13.4 Timing diagram for a card-swipe

All of this can be expressed by stacking the state lifelines for the user and the system as shown in Fig. 13.4. The horizontal segments of these lifelines represent the intervals when the system stays in a particular state and vertical segments denote transitions between states. The third lifeline is a value lifeline which is describing the status of the transaction. Each hexagon corresponds to the system staying in a particular state. The length of the hexagon denotes the length of time the system was in that state; within each hexagon we write the name of the state and any associated values.

In the figure the first event that occurs is that the User swipes the card, and goes from the Idle state to the Waiting state. A message is sent to the System which then enters the Activated state. In this system, we allow for the possibility of a small delay between when the user swipes the card and when the System enters the Activated state; this is indicated by the arrow not being vertical. For the transaction as a whole, however, as soon as the card is swiped, the system enters the Processing state. After some processing, the System sends a message to the user, presumably by unlocking a door, and there is a small associated delay. The transaction enters the Open state only when the User gets the message. After a brief period, we assume that the door will get locked again. At this point both the System and the User become Idle and the transaction is assumed to be complete.

For the Library system (from Chap. 6), consider the following sequence of events:

user1 checks out book; user2 places hold, user3 places hold, user1 returns book, user2 is informed, user2 fails to show up in allotted time, user3 is informed, user3 checks out book.

A Book object can be in one of several states: (i) *on shelf*, (ii) *issued*, (iii) *issued and on-hold*, (iv) *on-hold and available*. Clearly, transition from one state to another is triggered by external events. When the book is on hold, we have an additional parameter—the number of holds. We would prefer a value lifeline to represent the book because it allows us to represent an additional value. With this parameter, we can now reduce to two possible states: *Available(holds)* and *Issued(holds)*. Available(0) would mean the book is on the shelf, whereas Issued(0) would represent the *issued* state.

The user can be in one of 4 states: *Idle, Book, Wait* and *CanGet*. The system (Library system) can be in one of two states: *Idle* and *Activated*. In the Activated state, the system sends messages to the users triggering state changes. The actions taken by the users cause changes in the state of the book and the system.

When we stack the state lifelines for the users and the system and the value lifeline for the book, we get the result shown in Fig. 13.5.

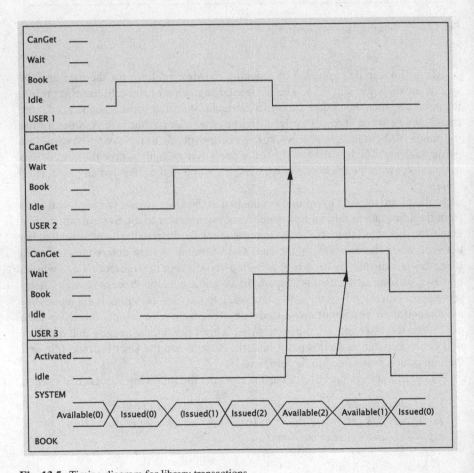

Fig. 13.5 Timing diagram for library transactions

When User1 checks out the book, he/she goes from Idle to Book. When User2 and User3 place holds, they enter the Wait state. The Book object accordingly goes from the Available(0) state to the Issued(2) state as a result of these events. The System remains Idle until the book is returned. At this point Book enters the Available(2) state, and System becomes activated and sends a message to User2. We are assuming some delay in the sending of the message, indicated by the arrow not being vertical. User2 changes state only upon receiving the message. Since User2 does not show up, the System remains Activated and after a while sends a message to User3. If User2 had checked out the book, the System would have gone back to the Idle state and no further messages would have been sent. The System returns to the Idle state concurrently with User3 checking out the book.

This scenario is centred around a Book. A different scenario can be created that is centred around a User. The state of a User can be characterised by the books that they have checked out, the books on which they have placed a hold on and the books that are currently waiting for them at the library. This information will be captured in a value lifeline. Each book on which a hold has been placed is either Issued or Available. If the user checks out the book when it becomes Available, the book gets added to the list of books checked out by the user. If the user does not check out in the allotted time, book is dropped from the list. Constructing such a timing diagram is not of much use since it does not capture the interaction between the entities but merely logs the activities of the User.

For the example of the microwave in Chap. 10, the communication between the GUI, the Microwave and the Clock can be captured in a timing diagram. The Microwave can be in one of 3 states: *Cooking, DoorOpen* and *Idle*. In the GUI, we assume that the cook button is disabled when the door is open; this implies that the GUI can be modeled as being in one of two states: *DoorOpen* and *DoorClosed*. In the DoorOpen state the GUI does send any signals to the Microwave; when the door is closed, a signal is immediately sent to the microwave. (On the other hand, if the cook button is not disabled, we have a model where the GUI is always in the same state and passes all signals to the microwave.) The clock is represented by an alternating sequence of pulses, and a message is sent at the leading edge. Once again, there is a possibility of a small delay in the arrival of the message from the clock, which is indicated by the arrows not being vertical (Fig. 13.6).

The system as a whole is represented using a value lifeline, since this allows us to keep track of the remaining time. *Cook(n)* represents the situation where we have *n* seconds of cooking time left; the `doorClosedIdle` is represented as *Cook(0)*. *DoorOpen* represents the situation where the door is open.

Figure 13.6 shows how these lifelines can be stacked for a small window of time. At the start of the window, the microwave is cooking with two seconds left. The following events occur: *timer runs out, door is opened, door is closed, cook button pressed, door opened after two seconds, door closed.*

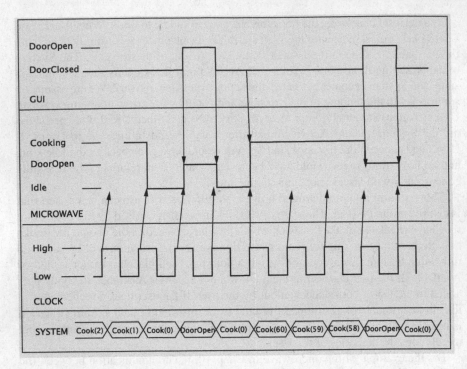

Fig. 13.6   Timing diagram for the microwave

13.3 Activity Diagrams

Activity diagrams show the flow of control from one activity to another. This flow may happen sequentially or concurrently. Each activity is one of the steps in a larger operation; the diagram as a whole describes how the operation is completed.

Figure 13.7 shows an activity diagram for checking out a book from our Library. The activities to be completed are accepting the ID, verifying the ID, accepting the book, checking the issuability of the book, stamping the due date and handing the book to the member. These are the activities listed/implied in the detailed use case for Book Checkout. Note that the sequence diagram for Book Checkout also shows a similar flow of control; *in the case of sequence diagrams, however, the flow of control is from object to object.*

The UML notation also allows us to show concurrent activities using **fork** and **join** operations. Usually, the concurrent activities are performed by different players and it is meaningful to use **swimlanes** to depict these. Each player has a dedicated swimlane as shown in Fig. 13.8. Here we have dropped the branches for invalid ID and unsuccessful checkout to reduce the clutter. The member is expected to wait

Fig. 13.7 Activity diagram
for Book Checkout

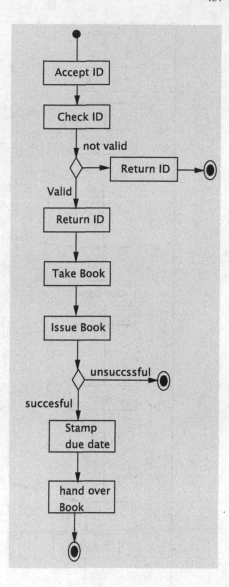

when the clerk verifies the ID and also when the book is being checked out. These can therefore be treated as concurrent activities. The entire process begins with the member presenting the ID and this is followed by a fork operation to denote the concurrent activities of the two players. Likewise, the two players must synchronise again when the verification is complete and this synchronisation is represented by a join.

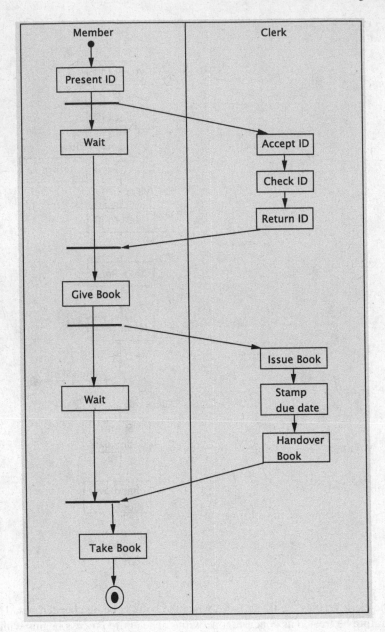

Fig. 13.8 Activity diagram showing swimlanes

13.4 Interaction Overview Diagrams

The interaction overview diagram consists of nodes connected by directed arcs. Each node represents an *interaction occurrence*, which could be represented by a sequence diagram or a communication diagram. Each node has one incoming arc and one outgoing arc. Diamond boxes are used to indicate a branch or a merge; whenever a branch is employed there is an associated Boolean condition.

Consider an extension of our Library case study that allows two additional use cases: *Search for a book by title* that takes a title form the actor and determines if a book with that title is in the catalog, and *Check book availability* that takes a user and a book and determines if the book can be issued to the user at that time. The associated sequence diagrams can be easily constructed and are left as an exercise.

We can now construct an interaction overview diagram that captures a user's attempt to check out a desired book. The details of this are shown in Fig. 13.9. Each of the boxes marked **sd** represent sequence diagrams for the operation named in the

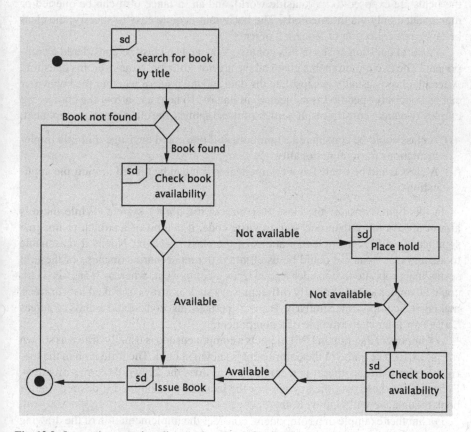

Fig. 13.9 Interaction overview diagram for a Book Checkout

box. (The boxes are sometimes marked **ref** to indicate that it could be any kind of interaction diagram.) If the book is found but not available, a hold is placed and the user waits until the book is available. The wait is represented by a loop, where the user repeatedly checks the book availability.

13.5 Component Diagrams

Simply stated, a component is any module that is a part of a system and has two properties:

1. It encapsulates its state
2. It exhibits behaviour that can be concisely described.

As a simple example of a component, consider the `MemberList` class in the Library system we studied in Chaps. 6 through 9. It obviously encapsulates its state: none of the fields are exposed to the outside world, and an instance of it can be queried or manipulated only via the methods. The behaviour is quite easy to specify: the class behaves as a collection of `Member` objects.

A natural question arises in this context: When can a class be considered a component? The two requirements given above are not sufficient to answer this question. After all, classes usually encapsulate the data and the issue of whether the behaviour can be concisely specified is subjective in nature. To help us narrow the choice, we employ two more constraints. If neither of these applies, the class is not a component.

(i) A class could be considered a component if one could envisage multiple implementations for its functionality.
(ii) A class could be treated as a component is if it can be reused in multiple applications.

In this light, consider the class `Member` in the library system. While there is almost always more than one way to write code, it is a bit of a stretch to imagine significantly different implementations of the class `Member`. Nor is it reasonable to assume that `Member` could be used in a different scenario. Because of these, it seems inappropriate to consider `Member` as a component, whereas `MemberList` could be implemented in clearly different ways such as arrays or linked lists or trees, making it a component. Similarly, `Book` is perhaps just considered a class, whereas `Catalog` is another example of a component.

A component diagram in UML depicts a component and is usually drawn as shown in Fig. 13.10. The name of the component is shown in bold. The little icon in the top-right corner indicates that it is a component as does the keyword «component». Either one of these two, the keyword or the icon, may be omitted if desired. In this book though, we will employ both.

For another example of a component, consider the implementation of the drawing program in Chap. 11. In Sect. 11.5, we considered the issue of catering to multiple

Fig. 13.10 Component
diagram: Example 1

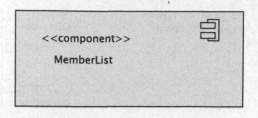

user interface technologies. The idea is that the interface UIContext would capture the variations in the technologies, whereas the hierarchy rooted in Item would
represent the differences between the items. We could have multiple modules, each
implementing the UIContext interface. UIContext is called a **provided interface** of SwingUI. Any implementation of UIContext could be used, depending
on the technology, making SwingUI a component.

Figure 13.11 shows one way of depicting SwingUI as a component. The full
circle connected to the component represents the provided interface. An alternative
representation is given in Fig. 13.12; the diagram shows the class SwingUI as a
component that implements the interface UIContext. The methods implemented
by SwingUI are documented in this representation.

Consider the Clock class in the implementation of the microwave system of
Sect. 10.7. This could be considered a component because it could be used in any
application that requires timed signals spaced one second apart; moreover, it is just

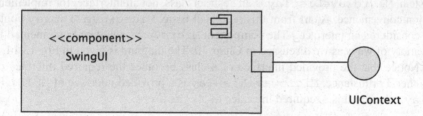

Fig. 13.11 Component diagram: Example 2

Fig. 13.12 Component
diagram: Example 3

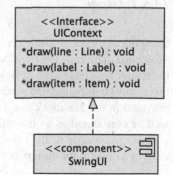

Fig. 13.13 Component
diagram: Example 4

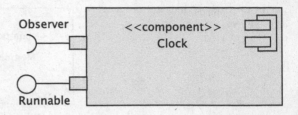

one possible implementation of the interface Runnable. It sends out a signal every second, but one could easily substitute a different implementation that sends signals at a different frequency. The class has two important properties:

1. It implements the Runnable interface, which is a requirement of classes that use the clock. Runnable is a provided interface.
2. It requires that any class that uses it implement the Observer interface. Observer is said to be a **required interface**.

The concepts are depicted in Fig. 13.13. As we discussed earlier, the circle represents the Runnable interface implemented by Clock. The half-circle with the word Observer means that any class that uses Clock must implement the Observer interface.

For a slightly more involved example, consider the microwave system. We could think of it as comprising three components: GUIDisplay, Clock, and Microwave. GUIDisplay implements the functionality of MicrowaveDisplay. (In our system, MicrowaveDisplay is an abstract class, not an interface, for implementation convenience. Apart from this technical issue, MicrowaveDisplay could be considered an interface.) The component Microwave could be implemented in a variety of ways as we discussed in Chap. 10. The diagram is given in Fig. 13.14.

Notice that the provided interface of a class becomes the required interface of another. For instance, MicrowaveDisplay is a provided interface of GUIDisplay, whereas it is a required interface of Microwave.

13.5.1 Usage

Component diagrams show certain aspects of relationships that are not apparent in other class diagrams. The relationship between provided and required interfaces helps the reader understand the design better. It is worthwhile noting that although some types may be implemented as abstract classes instead of interfaces, the functionality provided in the abstract class may be so insignificant that such a class could very well be considered as an interface and shown as such in component diagrams. The ultimate purpose is to help the reader understand the design and the spectrum of choices available for design and implementation.

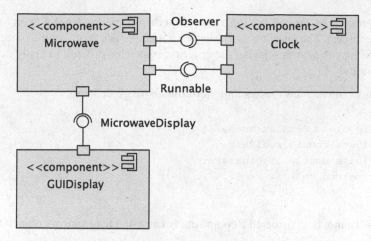

Fig. 13.14 Component diagram: Example 5

13.6 Composite Structure Diagrams

Some classes are complicated enough to warrant a separate form of documentation. For instance, consider a figure such as a rectangle, which is represented by a `Rectangle` object. The object may store four `Line` objects, in addition to other things such as line colour and line type (dashed or continuous, etc.). In such a situation, it is often the case that the `Line` objects are not shared between multiple figures. For example, even if a `Triangle` object exists with one or two lines falling exactly at the same coordinates as the corresponding `Line` objects of a `Rectangle`, there would be separate `Line` objects for the `Triangle` object. In other words, the `Line` objects in the `Rectangle` object are exclusively for the use of the rectangle.

In such a case, we dignify the class by calling it a **composite** and use a composite structure diagram to depict it. While the distinction between a composite and a class may appear fuzzy, the following three rules should help the reader make the determination.

1. The class must have at least one member with a non-primitive type. In this context, it seems appropriate to ignore language-specific definition of primitive types. For example, a language may designate every value as an object; this may include integers, characters, and Booleans. All of these types and strings should be considered primitive types.
2. At least one non-primitive member of the class must be exclusively for the use of the class. When an object is destroyed, either that member should be destroyed as well, or it should be entrusted for the exclusive use of another object.
3. At least one member that satisfies the second criterion should be a "part" of the object. For instance, consider a rectangle; each of the four lines that is an edge of the rectangle is intuitively a "part" of the rectangle object. On the other hand, if we have a player object in a card-playing program store all the cards that have

been played so far, the list itself cannot perhaps be considered a "part" of the player object. The question as to whether a member is a "part" of the object may not be easy to answer, making the criterion somewhat difficult to apply in some situations.

Let us examine a few classes in light of the above guidelines.

```
public class ComplextNumber {
   private double realPart;
   private double imaginaryPart;
   // methods
}
```

The class cannot be considered a composite because the fields are not objects themselves.

Consider the following Java declaration of a Customer class.

```
public class Customer {
   private String name;
   private String address;
   private City city;
   private State state;
   private String phone;
   // methods
}
```

The members, name, address, and phone are primitive types, whereas city and state are not. Therefore, the class meets the first requirement set forth earlier. In general, there will be multiple customers from the same state and even from the same city. Therefore, those two objects are not for the exclusive use of a specific customer. Because of that reason, the class cannot be considered a composite.

Let us look at the Member class of the library system.

```
public class Member implements Serializable {
   private static final long serialVersionUID = 1L;
   private String name;
   private String address;
   private String phone;
   private String id;
   private static final String MEMBER_STRING ="M";
   private List booksBorrowed = new LinkedList();
   private List booksOnHold = new LinkedList();
   private List transactions = new LinkedList();
   // methods
}
```

The three list objects are for the exclusive use of the Member object. Nonetheless, it is difficult to imagine them being part of a member. Hence, it seems appropriate to reject Member as a composite.

Finally, let us consider the following GUI class in the microwave example from Chap. 10.

```
private class SimpleDisplay extends JFrame {
    private JButton doorCloser = new JButton("close door");
    private JButton doorOpener = new JButton("open door");
    private JButton cookButton = new JButton("cook");
    private JLabel doorStatus = new JLabel("Door Closed");
    private JLabel timerValue = new JLabel("             ");
    private JLabel lightStatus = new JLabel("Light Off");
    private JLabel cookingStatus = new JLabel("Not cooking");
    // methods
}
```

The members satisfy all of the three properties. The frame is made up of a number of widgets that live and die with the frame. The members are for the exclusive use of the GUI. It would be appropriate to call this a composite.

A composite may be shown as in Fig. 13.15. The window consists of three buttons and four labels. There are no direct connections between the parts, except that clicking on some buttons may cause certain labels to change their displays and some other buttons to be enabled or disabled.

A more explicit relationship between parts of a composite object is illustrated in Fig. 13.16. We employ a **connector** to indicate a relationship between pairs of Line objects that form the Rectangle object. Lines line1 and line2 share point1, a Point object. Similar interpretations can be made for the other connectors.

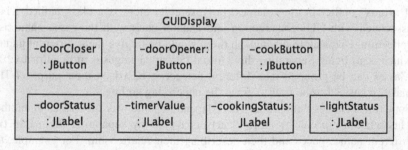

Fig. 13.15 Composite structure diagram: Example 1

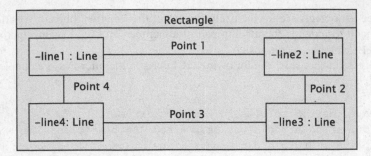

Fig. 13.16 Component structure diagram: Example 2

13.7 Package Diagrams

In many scenarios—not just in computer science—it is necessary to organise large collections. For example, related books are put in the same group in a library or a bookshop. A departmental store has a number of departments each of which hold related items. The utility of such organization is quite apparent.

The situation in computer science, especially in an object-oriented system, is similar. As software becomes more complex, it becomes important to ensure that the modules are properly organised. A **namespace** is an artefact used as a collection of unique names. Entries within two distinct namespaces may have the same name, with the namespace itself used to disambiguate such conflicts.

A **package** is a namespace. It helps developers to develop modules in a non-interfering way. In some situations, it also helps users.

Let us look at a familiar example. Even though the API classes that support the Java language do not form an application system, they are organised into a number of packages. Such an arrangement is beneficial for more than one reason.

1. It avoids conflict in class names. For example, there is a class named `List` associated with GUI construction and another class with the same name as a collection. One way to distinguish them would be to give them different names, which is artificial. Separating them into different packages is more attractive.
2. Classes can be grouped into different categories based on their purpose. This makes it easier for the user to grasp the underlying architecture.
3. Sometimes classes within one group depend in some way on classes in another. This relationship can be more clearly conveyed by separating them into two different name spaces and then describing their relationship. For example, the package `javax.swing` contains components that fire events in the package `javax.swing.event`.

In contrast, when a simple application, say, one with a handful of classes, is being implemented, it is probably not critical to consider a grouping of the classes. For instance, although the library system in Chaps. 6 through 8 was quite illustrative of many design issues, there were only a few classes. All of the functionality was accessible only to the library staff—there were no conflicting class names, etc. There was no real need to organise the modules in any way.

But consider a slightly more advanced library system. In our new system, users of the library system are divided into three categories:

1. Public (who might become members): They can do the following.

    (a) Apply for membership (via a browser). The library staff will have to prepare a card and probably mail it to the member.
    (b) Check out books.
    (c) Display the catalog in various ways.
    (d) Display information about their account.
    (e) Pay fines using a credit card.
    (f) Update personal information (for example, phone number).

2. Library staff who handle request from a person/member for the following:

    (a) Applying for membership
    (b) Check out books
    (c) Queries on library holdings
    (d) Get information about their account
    (e) Pay fines using a credit card
    (f) Update personal information (for example, phone number)

3. System administrators who deal with the installed software and hardware to:

    (a) add, remove, and update information about library staff, give them access privileges, etc.,
    (b) back up and reload data,
    (c) recover the database in case of a crash.

While we are not going to design the system, it is not hard to see that there will be some modules that are of common utility to one or more of the modules related to the above functionality. We would also need a separate GUI system for each of the above classes of users.

The overall organisation of the system can be described by means of a package diagram. In a typical system, there could be a large package containing more packages nested in it. The nested packages themselves may be large containing even more nested packages. A package is represented by a rectangle with a tab. In a large package, the name of the package is written in the tab. An example is shown in Fig. 13.17. A smaller package (see Fig. 13.18) has its name written inside the larger rectangle rather than in the tab.

For the library system, a *possible* package diagram is shown in Fig. 13.19. (We emphasise *possible* because we have not really designed the system here.) The Library package nests several packages: a pair of GUI and functional packages for the members, staff, and administrators.

The member functionality depends on the staff functionality for completing some of the actions. For instance, if a person fills out and submits an application form

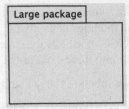

Fig. 13.17 Large package

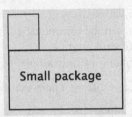

Fig. 13.18 Small package

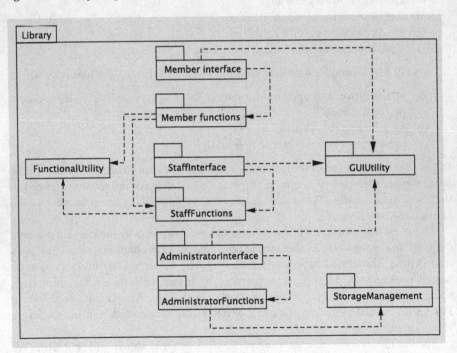

Fig. 13.19 Package diagram

for membership, there must be an invocation of some way for the staff package to generate an identification card; part of the functionality for id card generation may be in the member package.

The relationships between packages are indicated by dashed lines. Since there is some similarity between some of the functionality in the member package and the staff package, it may be appealing to have a common utility package that implements the common needs. For example, the member and staff functionality packages allow credit card payment of fines. The functionality for verifying the card information and actually making the payment would be implemented in the utility package. The class(es) in the member and staff packages that deal with fine payment would make use of this common utility. The utility package could also extract the details of storing and retrieving information from long-term storage. The underlying database may be implemented using the relational model and thus a mapping between the object-oriented model used in the program code and the relational model employed for data storage is inevitable. This could be done by custom software or off-the shelf software, or a combination of the two. The line from the member and staff packages to the utility package represents this dependence of the member and staff packages on the utility package.

The storage package is meant for supporting database backup, reload, and recovery. Much of this may again be a combination of off-the-shelf and custom software. The administrative staff would depend on this software for data maintenance activities.

Note that a dependency line between two packages does not imply a dependency between all pairs of classes in the two packages.

13.8 Object Diagrams

While a class diagram shows the relationships between classes, an object diagram shows a partial or complete view of the objects that exist at a given point in time and the relationships between the objects. An object diagram is more concrete than a class diagram and thus serves as a snapshot of the system, an example that adds to the conceptual understanding of the design. The diagram also serves the designers in identifying the concrete classes.

Obviously, there can be an infinite number of object diagrams, so one must be careful in selecting the proper object diagram to show. The one with a large number of objects would lack clarity and impair understanding; if the number of objects is too small, some of the generalisation that could have been demonstrated may not come through.

A simple example of an object diagram is shown in Fig. 13.20. As in several other examples in this chapter, we draw from the library example. In the system we have two members, whom we refer to as John and Mary. These are two Member objects as shown in the picture. The values of the attributes of the two objects are marked.

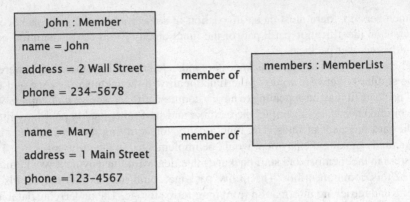

Fig. 13.20 Object diagram: Example 1

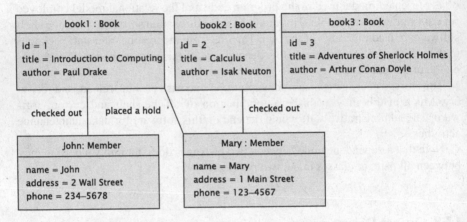

Fig. 13.21 Object diagram: Example 2

The MemberList class has two **links** emanating from it to the two objects. The links imply that MemberList is a collection, storing references to the two Member objects.

A second example is shown in Fig. 13.21. The members are the same as in the previous example. There are three books, two of which are checked out to John and Mary respectively. There are three books, one of which is checked out to John while a second one is borrowed by Mary. Note that we have added labels to the links to explain what the links mean.

13.9 Deployment Diagrams

Although the analysis phase does not specify the hardware or software configuration, it is often the case that the user community will have at least a vague idea of the eventual setup. For example, users may know whether a distributed or centralised configuration is needed. The configuration will be more clearly defined during the design stage, and it is highly desirable to document the eventual configuration. The Deployment Diagram is used for this purpose.

Unlike most of the other UML diagrams, the deployment diagram depicts the configuration of the finished product. It shows the placement of the hardware and software components, called **artefacts**, in the system. An artefact could be a hardware component such as a network router, software such as operating systems, middleware, applications, database tables, and so on.

Let us consider the library system developed in Chap. 7 being extended to a distributed environment. Assume that the distributed system is implemented using Java Remote Method Invocation (RMI). As discussed in Chap. 12, the system consists of the following components:

1. A server that implements the library functions. This consists of the `Library` and other classes such as `Member`, `Catalog`, etc. As explained in Chap. 12, `Library` now provides remote methods that can be invoked from other computer systems via remote object invocations.
2. One or more clients that implement the user interface. An example would be the `UserInterface` class developed in Chap. 7, enhanced for RMI.

In this scenario, we have a server machine that hosts the business logic, which includes `Library`, `MemberList`, `MemberIdServer`, and `Catalog`. In this diagram, we have shown only the singleton instances. Although not depicted, instances of MEMBER, BOOK, and TRANSACTION are also on this machine.

Each clerk station contains an instance of `UserInterface`. There could be many such machines, all of which are connected to the server. The communication is via RMI. The stubs and skeletons associated with RMI are not shown, but are implied by the fact that the interconnection explicitly shows the employment of RMI.

As one can guess, in a deployment diagram we will be showing one box for each artefact (Fig. 13.22). The artefact could be a hardware or software entity. Such a box is called a **node**. Nodes can contain more nodes in them. The node for the clerk

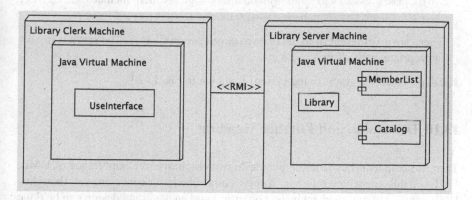

Fig. 13.22 Deployment diagram, Example 1

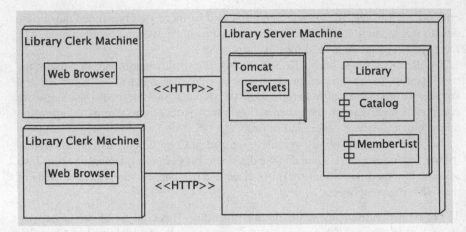

Fig. 13.23 Deployment diagram, Example 2

machine (hardware artefact) contains a node for the Java Virtual Machine (software artefact), which in turn contains the node for `UserInterface`.

A similar interpretation can be made of the server machine as well. Note that `MemberList` and `Catalog` are treated as components and are shown using the corresponding notation.

For a second example, assume that the library is implemented with a web interface. Again, we have done the system development in Chap. 12. The configuration would have two or more machines:

1. Client machines, which could be used by library members or clerks. These machines will run a web browser.
2. A server machine, which consists of the following:

   (a) Tomcat to host the classes for handling requests coming from the user via the browser. These are called servlets.
   (b) Classes associated with the business logic, which includes `Library`, `MemberList`, `MemberIdServer` and `Catalog`.

   These are no different from the classes developed in Chap. 7. The servlets invoke appropriate methods in `Library`.

The deployment diagram for the system is shown in Fig. 13.23.

13.10 Discussion and Further Reading

There is some tendency in some people to overemphasise the importance of UML. UML is a documentation tool, i.e., it serves as a vehicle for conveying our thoughts. UML cannot replace good analysis; however, good analysis and design can be done without using UML.

UML has come in for some criticism, not all of which are undeserved. As the term "unified" suggests, the notation is a compromise on the many prior existing and competing notations for documenting object-oriented systems. People seem to use the notation differently, suggesting confusion, ambiguity, and inconsistency.

The most authentic source on UML is the Object Management Group's web site, http://www.uml.org/. The page http://www.omg.org/gettingstarted/what_is_uml.htm provides an overview. As of the time of writing this document, the latest UML specification was available via http://www.omg.org/spec/UML/2.4.1/Infrastructure/PDF/. We would like to warn the reader that the document makes for pretty hard reading: until the reader gets some significant experience in using the tool, there is little point in delving into this document in any serious fashion. Instead, we recommend the much friendlier work by Rumbaugh, Jacobson, and Booch [1].

A popular tool for UML modelling is IBM Rational Rose. The OMG web site has references to other tools.

The UML also defines extension mechanisms for extending the UML to meet specialised needs. A UML Extension is formally defined as a set of Stereotypes, TaggedValues, Constraints, and Notation icons that collectively extend and tailor the UML for a specific domain or process. An example of this is the Erickson-Penker Business Process Modelling extension. As the Business Process Model typically has a broader and more inclusive range than just the software system being considered, it also allows the analyst to clearly map what is in the scope of the proposed system and what will be implemented in other ways (e.g. a manual process). In addition to symbols for representing a business process, this custom extension allows the user to represent things like the consumable resources needed by a business process, information needed by the process, etc. Further discussion on this is beyond the scope of this book.

Reference

1. R.W. Sebesta, *Concepts of Programming Languages* (Addison-Wesley, Reading, 2007)

Appendix
Java Essentials

A.1 Language Basics

Although Java is an object-oriented language, one could broadly divide its features into two parts:

- The non-object-oriented features.
- The object-oriented features.

However, object-orientedness is built into the language such that it is quite difficult to completely avoid the term 'object' while discussing even simple programs. However, such discussion can be kept to a minimum.

We do not plan to cover every aspect of the Java language—just the features needed to cover the discussions in the book are covered. We also do not propose to do a formal presentation of the syntax.

A.2 A Simple Java Program

Here is the standard example of a Hello World program.

```
public class HelloWorld {
  public static void main(String[] args) {
      System.out.println("Hello, World!");
   }
 }
```

Compilation and execution You can types this up in any text editor. The program *must* be stored in a file named `HelloWorld.java`. It is compiled by typing

```
javac HelloWorld.java
```

As you might have guessed, `javac` is the Java compiler. The compiler reads `HelloWorld.java` and creates a file called `HelloWorld.class`.

© Universities Press (India) Private Ltd. 2015

B. Dathan and S. Ramnath, *Object-Oriented Analysis, Design and Implementation*,
Undergraduate Topics in Computer Science, DOI 10.1007/978-3-319-24280-4

The `HelloWorld.class` file contains what are called "byte codes." Normally, compilers convert a high level language program into a machine language program suitable for execution by the native hardware. In the case of Java, though, the byte codes in the compiler output are instructions for the Java Virtual Machine (JVM), not for the hardware. Java programs run on JVM and not directly on the hardware.

To execute the program, type

```
java HelloWorld
```

The program prints the single line

```
Hello, World!
```

Anatomy of the program It is not hard to guess that the message `Hello, World!` is printed by the line

```
System.out.println("Hello, World!");
```

in the program.

It is virtually impossible to write any interesting Java program without using classes and objects. So we need a basic understanding of what they are.

Objects are structures that usually relate to some real-life entity. Examples of objects in a program could be a library book, a room in a hotel, or an airline reservation. Objects are created using classes. Thus, we could have classes such as the following:

1. A class, say, Book, that can be used to create instances of books.
2. A class called Room using which we can create all of the rooms in a certain hotel.
3. A class for representing the reservation held by a passenger in a certain flight.

Java has an extensive collection of constructs for defining classes. We cover most of those issues in the main part of the book.

The first line

```
public class HelloWorld {
```

declares a class called `HelloWorld`. Class names, like other identifiers, can begin with letters, the currency symbol, or the underscore. Succeeding characters can be any of these or digits.

The word `public` means that the class is accessible from anywhere in the file system. We will discuss this aspect elsewhere in the book. The left curly bracket essentially begins the description of the class.

Every Java program will contain at least one class. Typically, you will put the code for each class in a separate file. Java requires that the file be named `<class_name>.java`. If you put more than one class in the same file, at most one of these classes can be designated `public`, and the file must be named using that class. If no class is public, pick any one of the class names for naming your file.

Let us proceed to examine the other lines.

Consider the second line

```
public static void main(String[] args) {
```

This defines a method named `main`, which begins the execution of any Java application. Java requires that this method be preceded by the words `public`, `static`, and `void`. The word `void` indicates that the method returns nothing. `static` means that the method can be invoked without any objects.

Methods can accept parameters just as functions and procedures do. `main` accepts any number of `String` arguments when the program is invoked. These are collected into an array of `String` objects and passed to the program: `String` is a class supported by the Java language itself and one that we will use throughout the book.

In our example, the program does not expect any parameters.

The left-curly bracket begins the details of the method, which has just one statement:

```
System.out.println("Hello, World!");
```

Let us examine each part of this statement.

`System` is a class known to the Java language. Among other things, the `System` class captures and supplies an assorted set of features for performing standard input and standard output, and querying system properties and environment variables. `out` is an object that represents the standard output (console). `System.out` is the syntax for accessing the `out` object that is kept track of by the `System` class.

`println` is another example of a method. In object-oriented languages, methods are usually associated with objects. In this case, `println` is a method that can be executed by the object `System.out`.

The method println accepts one parameter, which should be a `String`: that is, something between double quotes. The method causes that string to be printed on the standard output.

Finally, the semi-colon terminates the statement.

The first right-curly bracket ends the method and the last right-curly bracket ends the class.

Comments There are three types of comments in Java programs. Two forward slashes (//) make everything till the end of line comments. /* begins a comment that ends with a */; such comments may span multiple lines. Multiple line comments may also begin with /** and end with */; Files containing such comments may be processed using the javadoc utility to produce HTML documentation.

A.3 Primitive Data Types

Java supports eight *primitive data types* using which we can define variables to denote numbers, characters, and logical values. These types are: int, long, float, double, char, boolean, short, and byte. Among these byte, short, int, and long are numeric types supporting negative and non-negative integers. Float and long are used for floating point numbers.

The length of the corresponding variables are given in the following table.

Type	Size
byte	1
short	2
int	4
long	8
float	4
double	8

Variables are defined by first specifying the type and then a list of variable names. The definition must be terminated by a semi-colon. Although more than one variable may be defined in single declaration, the usual style is to define only one.

Variable names may begin with the currency symbol, an alphabetic character, or the underscore. These and digits may appear in succeeding positions.

We now show examples of defining variables and assigning values.

```
int numberOfClasses;
numberOfClasses = 4;
System.out.println("I am taking " + numberOfClasses
                                  + " classes");
```

In the above, "+" concatenates the arguments after converting them to string objects.

Variables may be initialised as they are defined:

```
double balance = 750.00; double
deposit = 200.00;
double $cost = 8.5;
System.out.print("Initial balance " + balance + " Deposit "
                                    + deposit);
```

Character constants begin and end with single-quotes.

```
char stop = 's';
char _delimiter = ':';
```

Like many other languages, Java uses the operators +, -, *, and / with their usual meanings. The operator % is used for finding the remainder after division. As in most other languages, multiplication and division have precedence over addition and subtraction.

The mod operator has the same precedence as multiplication and division.

```
double balance = balance + deposit;
System.out.println(" New balance " + balance);


double income;
double taxRate;
double tax;
double netIncome;
```

```
income = 30000.00;
taxRate = 0.15;
tax = (income - 15000.0) * taxRate;
netIncome = income - tax;

int numberOfCookies = 36;
int numberOfChildren = 8;
int cookiesPerChild;
int cookiesLeftover;
cookiesPerChild = numberOfCookies / numberOfChildren;
cookiesLeftover = numberOfCookies % numberOfChildren;
```

Booleans are used for logical operations. These variables can take one of two values: true or false.

```
boolean succeeded = true;
```

A.4 Relational Operators

Java uses the following operators for comparing variables of primitive types. (Only equality and inequality testing is applicable to boolean variables.)

== equals
! = not equal to
> greater than
< less than
>= greater than or equal to
<= less than or equal to

Strings We create a String object by writing code like the following.

```
String errorMessage = "could not find the file";
```

In the above, errorMessage is a variable that refers to a String object, which contains the character sequence enclosed between double quotes.

Objects respond to methods, which are like functions and procedures in other languages. For example, the above String object can be used as below to print the number of characters stored in it.

```
System.out.println(errorMessage.length());
```

We are invoking the method length() on the object errorMessage. It should return 23.

In general, a method is invoked as below.

```
<object_reference>.method_name(parameters);
```

Incidentally, objects of type `String` respond to a large collection of methods including the following:

```
indexof(char c) - returns the first location of the character
c in a string

charAt(int index) - what is the character at the given
(0-relative) index?
```

A.5 A Note on Input and Output

Inputting numeric values through the keyboard has been a problem in Java. We need to read a string and extract a number from it. One way of inputting data is through a graphical user interface (GUI). A class called `JOptionPane` has a method named `showInputDialog`, which can be used for accepting a `String`. The `String` can then be parsed to retrieve the proper value.

```
String response;
response = JOptionPane.showInputDialog("Enter a number");
int num = Integer.parseInt(response);
```

The code opens up a dialog box for entering a string. After inputting the data, the user can click "O.K." The string is stored in response, which is parsed by the code

```
Integer.parseInt(response);
```

It returns the integer value stored in the string. (If the string does not have an integer in it, it would cause an "exception.")

Messages can also be displayed in a window using the method `showMessageDialog` in `JOptionPane`. The format is

```
JOptionPane.showMessageDialog(null, message-as-a-string);
```

A.6 Selection Statements

Java supports if else statements and switch statements. Both allow nesting. The syntax of the if else statement is

```
if <condition>
   <statement>
[else
    <statement>]
```

The else part is optional.

Here is a program that accepts the age of a person and prints out whether the person is eligible to vote.

```
import javax.swing.*;
public class VoteEligibility {
  public static void main(String[] s) {
    int age;
    age = Integer.parseInt(JOptionPane.showInputDialog(
                           "Please enter your age"));
    if (age >= 18) {
      JOptionPane.showMessageDialog(null, "you are eligible to
                  vote");
    } else {
      JOptionPane.showMessageDialog(null, "wait " + (18 - age)
                           + " years!");
    }
    System.exit(0);
  }
}
```

The next example selects people younger than 20 and all females over 30.

```
selected = false;
if (age < 20) {
    selected = true;
} else if (age > 30) {
 gender = JOptionPane.showInputDialog("Enter gender: ")
             .charAt(0);
  if (gender == 'f' || gender == 'F') {
    selected = true;
  }
}
```

Logical operators are

&&	logical and
||	logical or
!	logical not

The switch statement allows us to handle the situation when there are numerous cases. Here is an example.

```
int month = Integer.parseInt(JOptionPane.showInputDialog(null,
                           "Enter month 1-12"));
switch (month) {
    case 1:    JOptionPane.showMessageDialog(null, "January");
               break;
    case 2:    JOptionPane.showMessageDialog(null, "February");
               break;
    case 3:    JOptionPane.showMessageDialog(null, "March");
               break;
    case 4:    JOptionPane.showMessageDialog(null, "April");
               break;
    case 5:    JOptionPane.showMessageDialog(null, "May");
               break;
    case 6:    JOptionPane.showMessageDialog(null, "June");
               break;
```

```
case 7:      JOptionPane.showMessageDialog(null, "July");
             break;
case 8:      JOptionPane.showMessageDialog(null, "August");
             break;
case 9:      JOptionPane.showMessageDialog(null, "September");
             break;
case 10:     JOptionPane.showMessageDialog(null, "October");
             break;
case 11:     JOptionPane.showMessageDialog(null, "November");
             break;
case 12:     JOptionPane.showMessageDialog(null, "December");
             break;
}
```

A.7 Loops

Java, like C and C++, allows three types of loops: for, while, and do.

while The while loop has a simple syntax.

```
while (condition)
   statement;
```

The statement is executed as long as the condition is true. Before each iteration, the condition is checked. If it is true, the loop is executed once and the condition is checked once again and the process repeats until the condition is false.

Here are some examples of the use of while loop.

```
int number = 10;
while (number <= 25) {
   System.out.println(number);
   number++;
}
```

The second example is a program that reads in a string and counts the number of vowels in a String and prints each occurrence. The charAt method returns the character at the given position (zero-relative) in the string. The method indexOf checks whether a given character appears in a String.

```
import javax.swing.*;
public class CountVowelsWhile {
  public static void main(String[] s) {
    String vowels = "aeiou";
    String string = JOptionPane.showInputDialog("Enter a string");
    int counter = 0;
    int position = 0;
    while (position < string.length()) {
      if (vowels.indexOf(string.charAt(position)) >= 0) {
        counter++;
        System.out.println(string.charAt(position));
      }
```

```
            position++;
        }
        System.out.println("There are " + counter +
                    " occurrences of vowels in " + string);
        System.exit(0);
    }
}
}
```

for The for loop has the following syntax.

```
for (expression1; condition; expression2)
    statement;
```

The code works as follows:

1. Evaluate expression1.
2. Evaluate condition.
3. If the evaluation in (2) returns true, enter the loop and execute the statement, which can be a block. Otherwise, exit the loop.
4. Evaluate expression2.
5. Go to (2) above.

Here are examples of the use of for loops.

We solve the problems given for while using the for loop. The first example prints all integers from 10 to 25. The code first creates an int variable number and initializes it to 10. It then checks whether number is less than or equal to 25. Since it is not, it enters the loop and prints the current value of number, which is 10. It then increments number by 1 and checks again whether number is less than or equal to 25. The loop continues this way until number is 26 at which time the loop is exited.

```
for (int number = 10; number <= 25; number++) {
    System.out.println(number);
}
```

The program that reads in a string and counts the number of vowels in a String and prints each occurrence is given below using the for loop.

```
import javax.swing.*;
public class CountVowels {
    public static void main(String[] s) {
        String vowels = "aeiou";
        String string = JOptionPane.showInputDialog("Enter a string");
        int counter = 0;
        for (int position = 0; position < string.length(); position++) {
            if (vowels.indexOf(string.charAt(position)) >= 0) {
                counter++;
                System.out.println(string.charAt(position));
            }
        }
        System.out.println("There are " + counter +
                    " occurrences of vowels in " + string);
        System.exit(0);
    }
}
```

A program that uses both while and for loops to examine a sequence of strings to see if they are palindromes is given below.

```java
import javax.swing.*;
public·class Palindrome {
  public static void main(String[] s) {
    String input;
    boolean endOfInput = false;
    while (!endOfInput) {
      input = JOptionPane.showInputDialog(null, "Enter a string");
      if (input.length() == 0) {
        endOfInput = true;
      } else {
        boolean isAPalindrome = true;
        for (int left = 0, right = input.length() - 1; left < right;
                          left++, right--) {
          if (input.charAt(left) != input.charAt(right)) {
            isAPalindrome = false;
          }
        }
        if (isAPalindrome) {
          JOptionPane.showMessageDialog(null, input
                              + " is a palindrome");
        } else {
          JOptionPane.showMessageDialog(null, input
                              + " is not a palindrome");
        }
      }
    }
    System.exit(0);
  }
}
```

do The do loop executes at least once. At the end of the first and succeeding iterations, a condition is checked. If the condition is true, the next iteration is performed. The syntax is

```java
do
  statement
while (condition);
```

The following example makes the user enter "Yes", "No", or "cancel" (case-insensitive).

```java
String response;
do {
  response = JOptionPane.showInputDialog
                  ("Enter yes, no, or cancel");
} while (! response.equalsIgnoreCase("yes")
    && ! response.equalsIgnoreCase("no")
    && ! response.equalsIgnoreCase("cancel"));
```

A.8 Methods

Method are like functions in C. They are always enclosed within a class declaration. A method must return void or a known type. Methods may accept any number of parameters. Each formal argument must be written with the type name followed by the parameter name. Parameters must be separated by a comma.

Parameters are passed by value. Changes to the parameters in the callee do not affect the original. In the following example, although the values of c and d are swapped, the values in the actual parameters are unchanged.

```
void swap(int c, int d) {
   int temp = c;
   c = d;
   d = temp;
}
...
int a = 1;
int b = 2;
swap(a, b);
```

A.9 Arrays

Java supports the creation of arrays of any number of dimensions. The process of creating an array can be thought of as consisting of two steps:

1. Declare a variable that refers to the array. This is not the array itself, but eventually contains the address of the array, which has to be dynamically allocated.
2. Allocate the array itself and make the variable declared in (1) above to point to this array.

The following code creates a variable that can serve as a reference to an array of integers.

```
int[] a;
```

An array of five integers is created during execution by the following code.

```
new int[5];
```

The new operator returns the address of the array; this is termed the reference in Java. We make a hold the reference to the array by writing

```
a = new int[5];
```

The first cell of the array is indexed by 0. If the array has n elements, the last cell is indexed $n - 1$.

Array cells are referred by the notation a[index].

The following code stores 1 in a[0], 2 in a[1], etc. and then prints these values.

```
for (int index = 0; index < 5; index++) {
    a[index] = index + 1;
}
for (int index = 0; index < 5; index++) {
    System.out.println(a[index]);
}
```

The following program reads in a sequence of numbers and prints them in reverse. The number of numbers is the first number read in. An array large enough to hold the sequence is then allocated.

```
import javax.swing.*;
public class PrintInReverse {
  public static void main(String[] s) {
    int[] numbers;
    int numberOfNumbers = Integer.parseInt(
            JOptionPane.showInputDialog
                    ("Enter max. number of numbers"));
    numbers = new int[numberOfNumbers];
    boolean lookForAnotherNumber = true;
    int count = 0;
    while (lookForAnotherNumber) {
      if (count >= numbers.length) {
        lookForAnotherNumber = false;
      } else {
        String string = JOptionPane.showInputDialog
                            ("Enter a number");
        if (string.length() == 0) {
          lookForAnotherNumber = false;
        } else {
          int number = Integer.parseInt(string);
          numbers[count++] = number;
        }
      }
    }
    for (int index = count - 1; index >= 0; index--) {
      System.out.println(numbers[index]);
    }
    System.exit(0);
  }
}
```

Multi-dimensional Arrays

Let us look at an example of creating multi-dimensional arrays, which will suggest how to allocate arrays of higher dimension.

```
double [][] prices;
prices = new double[5][10];
prices[2][4] = 76.5;
```

Index

Printed in the United States
By Bookmasters